ALSO BY TOM SANTOPIETRO

The Importance of Being Barbra

Considering Doris Day

Tom Santopietro

THOMAS DUNNE BOOKS
St. Martin's Griffin *New York*

THOMAS DUNNE BOOKS.
An imprint of St. Martin's Press.

www.thomasdunnebooks.com
www.stmartins.com

Book design by rlf design

Library of Congress Cataloging-in-Publication Data

Santopietro, Tom
Considering Doris Day / Tom Santopietro.
p. cm.
ISBN-13: 978-0-312-38214-8
ISBN-10: 0-312-38214-6
1. Day, Doris, 1924–. 2. Motion picture actors and actresses—United States—Biography.
3. Singers—United States—Biography. I. Title
PN2287.D324 S26 2006
791.4302'8092—dc22
[B]

2006050361

First St. Martin's Griffin Edition: August 2008

10 9 8 7 6 5 4 3 2 1

For Parker, Chapin, and Pierce

And for my mother,

Nancy Edge Parker Santopietro,

who always liked Doris Day

Contents

Acknowledgments

Special thanks to Liz Smith for her support and appreciation; Mark Erickson; Jeanine Basinger, extraordinary film scholar/author and good friend; Ruth Mulhall and Rheba Flegelman, who are, respectively, my Connecticut and New York "agents" and great friends; Ron Mandelbaum at Photofest; Peter Joseph, Tommy Semosh, and Harriet Seltzer at St. Martin's Press; Henry Kaufman, Esq.; Jim Pierson for his help with *Doris Day's Best Friends*; Michael Wilkie and John Gaden, my Aussie pals who let me overstay my welcome in Melbourne and Sydney, respectively, and still gave me a great place to write; and my editor, Tom Dunne, who now knows more about Doris Day than he thought possible.

Introduction

I'm always looking for insights into the real
Doris Day because I'm stuck with this
infatuation and need to explain it to myself.

—John Updike

Doris Day's least-impressed fan
is Doris Day herself.

—Betty White

I think that Doris Day is the most
underrated, underappreciated actress that
has ever come out of Hollywood.

—Molly Haskell

HOLLYWOOD, 1947: DORIS DAY IS CRYING. SOBBING, actually. Here she is, living out every American girl's fantasy—screen testing to star in the Warner Bros. feature film musical *Romance on the High Seas.* And she's not testing with any Johnny-come-lately director, either: Her test is being directed by none other than Hollywood legend Michael Curtiz of *Casablanca* fame. There's just one problem: Singing "Embraceable You," Doris Day breaks down in hysterics. Mascara smeared, nose running, she stumbles out of the room. In his heavily accented Hungarian version of Americanese, a nonplussed Curtiz asks Day's agent Al Levy, "What's the matter with her—she sick?" Informed that she is having marital difficulties, Curtiz is relieved that the problem is not even more serious, a reaction that is short-lived when Day returns, begins singing, and breaks down in sobs once again. At which point Curtiz begins to ask Doris Day a series of questions, the responses to which startle this worldly A-list director.

Accustomed to hearing every fabrication under the sun designed to land a desperate aspiring actress a starring role in Hollywood, Michael Curtiz encounters something most unusual from Doris Day: the truth. Certainly never before has Curtiz asked a Hollywood aspirant about her acting experience, and instead of hearing exaggerations and half-truths about brilliant credits, he hears the neophyte actress state: "I've never acted. I don't know a thing about acting." It soon became even more unusual, because asked if she'd like to become an actress, Day half-heartedly responded, "Oh, I suppose. I guess it might be interesting."

She's being tested by a Hollywood giant and the best she can muster is, "Oh, I suppose"? It's a scene that no screenwriter could possibly invent. It's too impossible to believe, and yet the clichéd Hollywood film image of a movieland wannabe eagerly putting her best foot forward in order to impress the all-powerful director does in fact morph into this very real-life picture of Doris Day's sobs and tear-stained makeup. The image of this big-band singer who mutters "I suppose" is hilarious—and a bit frightening in its implications. This girl couldn't pretend. She was without guile, and it's a very big reason why she went on to become the biggest damn female star in post–World War II America. Well, that and her pretty freckled face, knockout figure, one-in-a-million singing voice, and knack for playing comedy, drama, musical, and farce, all with absolutely no sign of strain or effort.

But that's getting ahead of the story. At the time of the screen test, Doris Day felt compelled to tell Michael Curtiz that she was depressed over her newly failed marriage and just wanted to reunite with her mother and young son waiting back in Cincinnati. Well, Curtiz must have thought, this is interesting, a reaction that could only have been heightened when Day asked what part she would be playing. "The lead," Curtiz replied, whereupon Day's immediate response was an incredulous, "How can I possibly be the lead? I haven't had any experience—I don't know how to act. That seems pretty crazy to me." Agent Al Levy was, in Day's own words, having a heart attack, but Michael Curtiz simply stated, "You let me decide that," and a screen test was slated for the very next day. This Hollywood veteran knew he was dealing with someone most unusual, someone his intuition told him could be a very big star: a genuine, artifice-free woman whose personality would leap off the screen.

And what happened on that most nerve-racking of all days, the day a Hollywood screen test would decide Doris Day's future? Well, on a day when most young women would have been experiencing a heady mix of fear, adrenaline, and overwhelming excitement, Doris Day fell asleep under the hair dryer while the Warner Bros. makeup and hair department got her ready for the opportunity of her life. Already depressed about the state of her personal life, Day became even more upset when she awoke to view her finished hair and makeup. Heavily made-up, her natural blond hair virtually cemented into place, Doris Day thought she looked awful. This wasn't just three strikes and you're out. This was ten strikes and—you're still in the ball game, because Michael Curtiz was one smart Hollywood director and stated simply, "It was not like actress reading. This was something I was not used to. The little lady read like human being. . . ."

The screen test began, and remarkably enough—well, maybe it wasn't so much astonishing as it was kismet—Doris Day soared. She could find her marks without even looking for them—it was intuition. She found it all effortless, thoroughly enjoyable, and in her own words "felt a nice exhilaration at hearing the word 'Action!' and then responding to the pressure of the rolling camera." Doris Day was a natural—she loved filmmaking, the camera loved her, and so what did she do after this terrific screen test? She promptly booked a reservation for Cincinnati and called her mother to tell her when

Hair and makeup test for her very first film, *Romance on the High Seas* (note the original title). Doris hated the Warner Bros. lacquered look. *Photofest*

she'd arrive. This young woman—only twenty-four—was either clueless or the ultimate realist. Maybe she was a little of both, but the next day her phone rang and actor Jack Carson, the star of *Romance on the High Seas,* was on the phone to tell Doris Day that he believed the part was hers. At which point hometown Cincinnati went the way that hometown Allentown, Pennsylvania, did for ingenue-about-to-turn-star Peggy Sawyer in the ultimate backstage musical, *42nd Street*: It went the way of no way, no how, because in the space of that very short screen test a star was born, a star who evolved over the next three decades into nothing short of a worldwide icon who spelled AMERICA to audiences around the world: Doris Mary Anne von Kappelhoff was on her way to becoming not just the nation's biggest-selling female recording star for over a decade but also one of the biggest box office attractions in the history of Hollywood. This was not just stardom. This was superstardom—the province of genuine icons.

Just how big a star did Doris Day become? The answer is simple: Doris Day is the biggest female box office star in Hollywood history. That's right. In history. She spent ten years ranked as one of the top ten attractions in the country, including four years at number one—a record for any actress, ever. Her closest competitors in this category were not exactly slouches in terms of popular appeal: Betty Grable spent ten consecutive years in the top ten, and Elizabeth Taylor ranked in the top ten for a grand total of ten years, but neither of them matched Day's record of four years at number one. Further proof of Day's enormous appeal came in the form of the annual survey of film exhibitors and distributors, the Quigley Poll, which ranked her as the top female box office draw of the 1960s—only John Wayne ranked ahead of her. She was the only woman to appear in *Variety*'s 1980 list of the top ten all-time box office attractions (John Wayne held down the number one position). Even more significant, at the height of her popularity, no one ever cast a bigger shadow in the entertainment world, for the simple reason that she was also the number one female recording star in the nation from the mid-1950s through the early 1960s, garnering multiple gold albums. True, beginning in the early 1960s, Barbra Streisand sold more records, but in overall career terms, Streisand's clout at the box office never topped Day's.

How and why did all of this happen to a woman who has always viewed a happy personal life as more important than professional success? What talents did this former band singer possess that caused her to become the biggest star in the world—alternately idolized and reviled throughout the decades? How could someone who genuinely thought her personal life was more important than her career churn out thirty-nine feature films and more than six hundred recordings, some good, some terrible, and some so brilliant that even forty years later they remain a source of amazement? And just what did the success of this "freckle-faced three-million-dollar corporation" say about the United States of America, about its very identity at home and abroad—because it did in fact say a hell of a lot: Thirty years after her last professional activities, three decades after her CBS network television series ended, and forty years after the last recordings and feature films, Doris Day remains hugely popular around the globe, her popularity growing each year through the sales of videocassettes and DVDs of her films. As to her recordings, in the words of her late son, acclaimed record producer Terry Melcher, "Her music catalogue each year seems to sell a multiple of two or three times what it did the previous year." It's only when one reads Melcher's follow-up statement that one realizes how unique the phenomenon of Doris Day remains today, because all of this acclaim is a matter of little import to Day herself. She is grateful for her fans, but it all makes absolutely no difference in how she lives her life today. Said Melcher, "I think she's very surprised—almost amazed—that there would be a continuing interest, with absolutely no encouragement on her part. I think she gets about as much mail today as she got in 1960—two hundred letters a week." In other words, nearly ten thousand letters per year. A genuine superstar, Doris Day has no discernible interest in her legacy, and yet her legacy looms larger with each passing year.

Was Doris Day actually talented, or was her stardom, as her detractors would have it, a case of a naïve, uninformed American public reacting to bland, forced optimism relentlessly supplied by the Hollywood dream factory and this paragon of sunniness? In other words, just why did Doris Day succeed so enormously?

For starters, Doris Day could do it all. She could play comedy brilliantly—James Garner called her the Fred Astaire of comedy—she could dance beautifully, undertake the heaviest of dramas (*The Man Who Knew Too Much*), and sing in a variety of styles, ranging from belting to ballads, that few if any have ever matched. She did it all so naturally, in such an unintimidating package, that people didn't realize just how great she really was. The effort never showed; there were no heaving epics featuring the drunken scenes so beloved by the Academy, no attempts to make herself appear dowdy and thereby telegraph the fact that she was a serious actress. Rather, Day kept step with the times, advancing her career across the entertainment spectrum, until she stopped her television series in the mid-1970s and turned her back on show business, seemingly forever.

And yet. Having carved out one of the truly great careers in show business history, Doris Day received very little respect for her remarkable achievements. In fact, beginning in the late 1960s, she began to be derided for the very talent that had made her beloved in the first place. In that most American of fashions, the public turned its back on one of its own authentic heroines.

Why did this happen? Was it the roles Day played? That shouldn't have been the case; she was effortlessly natural—there was no artifice about this woman—and in the words of respected critic Molly Haskell, "She was both romantic and wild. . . . She suggests sexiness and warmth and appears to be above reproach." Especially in the late 1950s into the mid-1960s, women wanted to be Doris Day, and men wanted to marry her. She projected an utterly real, down-to-earth persona and was equally believable as a glamorous single career gal who determined her own destiny—while not so coincidentally outfitted in the latest high fashions—and as a mother struggling to negotiate her way through the jungle of suburbia.

In a way, Day, that most reluctant of superstars, hurt her own cause with her unstarlike behavior. She was not a partygoer and preferred stay-at-home dinners to raucous nights in nightclubs. She was not a part of the scene in those midcentury decades when a glamorous black-tie-and-formal-gown Hollywood nightlife still existed. In the late 1950s and into the 1960s, when drinking and smoking were considered the height of sophistication, she quit smoking and, in strict adherence to her Christian Science religion, swore off alcohol and installed a genuine soda fountain in her house. Long before it became fashionable to do so, she attended Los Angeles Lakers and Dodgers ball games instead of nightclub openings and eschewed chauffeured limousines in favor of riding her bicycle around Beverly Hills. Such exercise might be the norm in 2006, but in 1959 Hollywood, it was considered downright weird. The response to this wholesome lifestyle? She was ridiculed by the press, who were relentless in their sarcastic accounts of Day's Goody Two-shoes image. It was as if the press found her too good to be true. (Reading her autobiography closely, one realizes that this Hollywood superstar, who has endured such rough treatment at the hands of the press, is never judgmental or complaining of others.) Of course she wasn't too good to be true. She was a vibrant, flawed, genuinely nice person, who just happened to possess a once-in-a-generation talent for singing, dancing, and acting.

It was the baby boomer generation most of all that turned on Doris Day. Misreading the sex farce comedies that propelled her to the number one position at the box office, these post–World War II men and women seemed to decide that Doris Day represented the past and the confining roles into which women had been locked. She became the person most closely associated with the way it used to be for women. Having maintained a standard and stardom that reeked of the establishment, it was Day who took the rap for the winking nature of the sex comedies she popularized with costar Rock Hudson. People may have whispered about Hudson's sexuality offscreen, but he was never ridiculed for his roles in these comedies with the fervor that characterized the attacks on Day. It may be, as John Updike mused, that her "starriness has a challenging, irritating twinkle peculiar to her . . . there is nothing about Katharine Hepburn's 'goodness' that asks us to examine our own." (Which only goes to show how strong Doris Day's star persona truly is.) But with the advent of greater sexual freedom in the late 1960s, the movie sex farce became irrelevant, and the glossiness and optimism of the late 1950s and early 1960s were deemed not only passé but worthy of ridicule. And, the reasoning seemed to run, it was Doris Day who was most worthy of ridicule.

It was all wrong, of course, because Doris Day happened to be a very sexy woman whose films presented her as a successful, independent woman with a healthy sexual appetite. As two-time costar James Garner stated, "She exuded sex but made you smile about it." Part of the appeal of Doris Day in the sex comedies was that hers was in some ways a buttoned-down sexuality—she was always pulled together, even a little tense. As each film progressed, her clothes became sexier, featuring form-fitting gowns, a little cleavage, and an accent on her terrific shape and derriere (it was with good reason that Bob Hope referred to her as "JB"—Jutt Butt). As the film in question unspooled, Day inevitably loosened up and indeed appeared more than ready to go to bed with her male pursuer—be it Hudson, James Garner, or Rod Taylor. Inevitably, it was at just this point that she would pull back, not because of a fear of sex but because she had discovered the duplicity of these men; in an effort to bed her, they always lied to her and she couldn't abide that. It is only in 1962's *That Touch of Mink,* costarring Cary Grant, that she played a woman who appeared determined to hold on to her status as a perennial virgin, but that fact was lost in the noise and tumult of the sexual revolution.

Given the onset of the feminist revolution in the mid- to late 1960s, baby boomers may also have turned on Day because of her heavy dependence on husband Marty Melcher for career advice and strategy, not to mention her disastrous decision to place all financial power within his purview. In the prevailing view of the press, this was definitely not behavior worthy of a strong feminist heroine. In the A&E television biography of Day titled *It's Magic,* the theory is set forth that in order to compensate for her extraordinary success on the worldwide stage, she became subservient in these financial areas as a way to reinforce her femininity—to herself as well as to others. Only Day can accurately assess that assumption, but it does appear to be borne out not only by Terry Melcher's contention that his mother liked to rely on a father figure when it came to business, but also by a 1953 profile of Day in the *New York Herald Tribune.* In the words of journalist Louis Berg, "It was my pleasure to observe Miss Day at a business conference. She squirmed, she fidgeted, she stared out the window and eventually signed the documents before her with obvious relief. She was like a little girl waiting to be released from conversation with adult visitors."

It's almost as if Doris Day's career symbolizes the schism between the generations in the tumultuous 1960s. If the rock-music-loving baby boomers derided Day as passé—a living Hollywood anachronism—their parents, the "greatest generation," who had grown up with Day as the big-band singer who codified their youth and young adulthood with songs like "Sentimental Journey," never turned their back on her. She was their gal—the singing, acting embodiment of their journey from adolescence to parenthood. Which leaves the key question: Which generation had it right? Was Doris Day a major-league talent or merely a lucky second-tier talent who succeeded until the American moviegoing public grew up?

In reality, this question is moot; even someone with a tin ear should be able to hear what a beautiful singer Doris Day was—perfect pitch, flawless intonation, and an actress's ability to imbue lyrics with layers of shading and emotion. Yet so strong was the public's perception of Day's film persona that the reaction to her work often could not be separated from the reaction to her "image," the very expression Doris Day detested more than any other. No, the central question actually remains: Just how strong is Doris Day's legacy? Does her work as a singer and actress really constitute a body of work representative of a truly great twentieth-century popular artist?

The answer, as with all lasting popular culture, is complex, particularly so in the case of Doris Day, because the arc of her entire career reveals a mass of contradictions. A brilliant singer, Day was often forced to record novelty dreck that is wince-inducing when heard forty years after initial release. Making a mind-boggling seventeen feature films in the short span of her seven-year contract with Warner Bros., Day had to suffer through inane scripts that resulted in only three of the seventeen films truly registering as top-drawer vehicles. Yet, when freed to work as an independent agent upon the expiration of the Warners contract, she made three terrific films in a three-year span of time in the mid-'50s; she then soared to even greater heights of popularity with a series of sex farce comedies in the late '50s and early '60s, only to watch her feature film career dribble away to nothing when she was forced into fifth-rate "comedies" because of deals signed by her agent/husband Marty Melcher. At one time the highest-paid recording star in the world, Day's recording contract was let go in the late 1960s because she was deemed noncommercial—this after recording a series of stunning concept albums whose stature has only increased over the ensuing decades.

A genuinely sexy, beautiful woman who in fact was married, divorced, and a mother by the age of eighteen, Doris Day had to endure endless derision as "America's perennial virgin," a one-note symbol of American hypocrisy. Yet, far from being a cardboard cutout of an actress, the reality was, as Joe Pasternak, producer of *Love Me or Leave Me,* presciently noted, that "For all her effervescence and apparent joie de vivre, I sometimes have the feeling Doris is busting inside. Sure, Doris is a wonderful, wholesome girl, but she is complex and she does have uncertainties about herself. That's what makes her such a great performer. Simple girls can't act. If she were as uncomplicated as her publicity would lead you to believe, she wouldn't be the tremendous box office draw that she is." The most popular female film star in the world for an entire decade, Day received only one Academy Award nomination, and that was for her work in *Pillow Talk*—one of her lesser performances. The winner of numerous gold records and a singer of stunning interpretive abilities, she received a mere two Grammy nominations throughout her extraordinary decades-long singing career. While she has received a special Lifetime Achievement Golden Globe Award and a 1991 Lifetime Achievement Award from the American Comedy Awards, there has been no honorary Grammy, and most notably, no honorary Academy Award. Day has never received recognition in the form of the coveted Kennedy Center Honors, yet in 2004, she received the Presidential Medal of Freedom from President George W. Bush, the highest civilian honor bestowed in the United States. (In typical fashion, Day's response when informed of the award was a simple, "For what? I'm not being coy. . . . I have never thought about awards whatever I do.") Suffice it to say, it's not just Day herself who registers as a mass of contradictions—it's the very shape and scope of her career.

And just what did Doris Day's success say about America? Why did Americans—indeed, citizens worldwide—make her an international star of the highest rank? That answer is actually simple: Doris Day became the biggest star in the world because even with the terminally dopey scripts often foisted upon her, even with all of the silly songs of no discernible merit that she was forced to record, one overwhelming answer leaps out at even the most casual viewer or listener: When Doris Day was given the right movie script to act and the right song to sing, she was nothing short of terrific. She was an astonishingly talented woman who could do it all, and do it brilliantly. In her very complexity, in her tomboyish self-assertion combined with complete femininity, in the optimistic paeans to "Que Sera, Sera" combined with the extraordinarily intimate and heartfelt vocal declarations of lost love and future possibilities found in her recordings, Doris Day embodied the all-encompassing post–World War II American will to happiness. In short, Doris Day became nothing short of a mass-media symbol of twentieth-century America, the flesh-and-blood personification of what came to be known as "the American Century."

Beginnings

She lives in the belief that happiness has to
be made—and can be made—by the individual.
In her sunny exuberance, she seems to
be living proof of it.

—Louella Parsons, 1954

Nothing seems to daunt the persistent image
of me as the unsullied sunshine girl. . . . So there
must be something about me, about whatever
it is that I give off, that accounts for this disparity
between who I am and who I appear to be.

—Doris Day, 1976

How, exactly, did Doris Day, née Doris Mary Anne von Kappelhoff, from Cincinnati, Ohio, end up in Hollywood? Day's own answer in 1991, disarming in its simplicity and total lack of ego, does not exactly tell the entire story: "I'm still Doris Mary Anne Kappelhoff from Cincinnati, Ohio. All I ever wanted to do was to get married, have a nice husband, have two or three children, keep house and cook—a nice clean house—and live happily ever after—and I ended up in Hollywood. And if I can do it, you can do it. Anyone can do it." Uh, not quite, Doris Mary Anne Kappelhoff (the "von" was dropped shortly after her birth on April 3, 1924). Not everyone has a seductive, velvet-smooth voice, great dancing ability, a beautiful face and a sexy body, and the ability to play everything from comedy to drama to farce and back again. But then again, Doris Day really does believe these self-effacing words, because she never coveted a show business career. That ambition resided in her mother, Alma Sophia.

Alma Kappelhoff may have been a stage mother, but she never acted like the stereotypical frustrated parent living out her thwarted ambitions through her daughter. Alma would not have made a convincing Mama Rose in *Gypsy,* because mother Alma and daughter Doris remained close throughout Alma's life, indeed, living together throughout much of Doris's adulthood and generally enjoying each other's company. In fact, the only public mention of Alma's ambitions was Day's own statement that she thinks her outgoing, personable mother (so opposite in personality from her conservative father) would have liked to perform. "When I mentioned this to her, she'd say 'Oh, no. I didn't want you to do it for that reason.' And I'd say, 'Oh, I don't know about that. I think so.' But she never admitted to that." What did remain clear is that Alma Kappelhoff never pushed Doris against her will—it would have been impossible, anyway, with such a strong-willed daughter. Alma never attempted to pull the focus from her daughter onto herself. Doris was the star, Alma the solid backup. Nonetheless, Alma did love the glamour and excitement of show business—loved it, in fact, far more than her daughter did. So when the music-loving Alma—country-western music was her favorite—divorced Doris's choirmaster father Frederick after discovering his infidelity when Doris was twelve, all of that energy and passion had to be directed elsewhere, and the target happened to be daughter Doris. It was Alma who encouraged Doris to take dancing lessons: Starting at age five, Doris studied acrobatic, tap, toe, and ballet, even thinking that one day she might become a ballerina.

And how did Doris's public performing career begin? In her kindergarten minstrel show, where the long wait backstage caused her to wet her pants. An understandable childhood accident, but in the context of Day's extraordinary career, perhaps significant, as the first unhappy incident she would associate with performing live; even more significant to the shape of Day's career was the fact that any such live performance conflicted with her perfectionist instincts. However, this full-blown dislike of live performances lay well in the future, not surfacing completely until after she began making feature films in 1948. In her childhood, there was no avoiding performances before live audiences, and having teamed up with twelve-year-old tap dancer Jerry Dougherty, the team of Dougherty and Kappelhoff began entertaining in the Cincinnati area, eventually winning the top prize of $500 in a contest sponsored by a Cincinnati department store. The winning routine? A dance with comedy titled "The Funny Little Bird on Nellie's Hat." It's a laughable title, until one realizes that it's no worse than many of the novelty songs Doris would have to record for Columbia Records two decades later. In Hollywood parlance, it may have been the prequel to Day's recording of "The Purple Cow" . . .

Encouraged by this contest win, Alma and Jerry's parents agreed on a plan to send Doris and Jerry to Hollywood; chaperoned by the two mothers, the children would study tap dancing at the Fanchon and Marco dance school with Louis DePron. It was the summer of 1937; the Kappelhoffs and Doughertys shared one small apartment for a month, Doris and Jerry progressed nicely in their lessons with DePron, and it was decided that a permanent move to Hollywood was in order. It's not known how strongly Mrs. Dougherty (or Mr. Dougherty, who was left behind in Cincinnati with his dairy business) felt about the move, but Alma Kappelhoff strongly believed that her daughter could make it. And big. (In the mid-1950s Alma stated that a Paramount Pictures scout had seen Doris on this first trip and felt she had the potential to be in films; the studio was not, however, interested in Jerry Dougherty, and Doris refused to leave her partner behind. End of Paramount's interest. Whether or not the story is apocryphal, it does sound exactly like what Doris Day would say. On the other hand, one can't be so sure that Alma really would have let her thirteen-year-old daughter turn down a chance to work at Paramount Pictures.)

So it was that the Dougherty and Kappelhoff foursome returned to Cincinnati to prepare for a permanent move to Hollywood. At which point Doris Day's life changed forever. It's as if a Hollywood scriptwriter had arrived at the point in the story where he needed to produce a plot twist, because the ensuing turn of events seems right out of an overstuffed Hollywood melodrama. On the night of Friday the 13th, October 1937, Doris Day left a farewell party in her honor, only to have the car she was traveling in with three friends smashed by a train. With her leg shattered—a double compound fracture coupled with bone fragments lodged throughout her right leg—her dancing career seemed to be over. Instantly. After surgery and the placement of a large cast covering her entire right leg, Doris returned home to recuperate, only to slip on a rug, break her leg again, and spend another year recovering from her severe injuries.

The solution? That arrived in a roundabout way. This fifteen-year-old girl, immobilized in a cast, her dreams of becoming the next Ginger Rogers or Betty Grable shattered, began to pass her time listening to the radio. Singing along with her favorite vocalist, Ella Fitzgerald, Doris tried to model her voice on the smooth Fitzgerald style so memorably characterized by Lena Horne as that of "a golden typewriter." Doris's natural gift for singing quickly became apparent, and Alma, happy to see her daughter's interest in show business reignited, began to take in extra sewing in order to pay for Doris's voice lessons with vocal coach Grace Raine. It was Raine who imparted the lesson that would prove to be the key to Day's extraordinary success and artistic accomplishment as a singer: "Sing each song as if directly to one person, not a large audience. You're acting." In Day's own words, "Grace Raine couldn't sing a note but she was a great coach."

Raine quickly realized that Day possessed unusual talent and gave Doris three lessons a week for the price of one. Day soon landed a job singing at a Chinese restaurant, where she earned all of $5 per night; with the help of Grace Raine, she began appearing as a (nonpaid) vocalist on *Carlin's Carnival* on WLW radio. This was no small achievement; WLW-AM was at that time the most powerful station in the United States. Broadcasting on a half million watts, WLW could literally be heard around much of the nation and was nicknamed "The Nation's Station." It was at this point in the *A Star Is Born*–type rise that characterized Day's beginnings that bandleader Barney Rapp heard her sing on WLW, liked her sound, and had her audition—an audition she won over two hundred other singers. Even at this earliest stage of her professional career, the driving forces that characterized her approach to work throughout her professional life were already in place. She may have felt nervous about auditioning for Barney Rapp, but it wasn't nervousness about not measuring up. In Day's own words: "I have never had any doubts about my ability in anything I have ever undertaken. . . ."

Whew. No wonder she appeared so confident and self-sufficient throughout no fewer than thirty-nine feature films. This is an attitude for which most performers would give their eyeteeth. Doris Day simply didn't even think about it. The natural sense of security is there—end of story. No, the nervousness with Barney Rapp came about because of the mere fact of having to perform in public—to be judged in a live situation where there was only one chance to get it right. Given this perfectionist attitude, it should come as no surprise that Day, like Barbra Streisand after her, eventually eliminated nearly all live performances in favor of the controlled environs of the recording studio and film set.

Doris Day, still a young teenager, signed on to sing with Barney Rapp, and in the process she also signed up for nothing less than a new name. In another scene right out of a Hollywood movie, Rapp asked Day, "What's your name? Doris Kapps? That'll never work. I liked the way you sang 'Day After Day'—your name should be Doris Day." It's a name Doris Day has never particularly liked—to this day she states, "It sounds phony." But ever the agreeable girl, perhaps still searching for a father figure (all contact with her own father having virtually ceased at this point), she agreed. Good-bye Doris Mary Anne Kappelhoff. Hello Doris Day.

Day's first gigs with Rapp took place at his own nightclub, the Sign of the Drum; this Cincinnati-based location enabled Doris to live at home with her mother and commute to the club every night. Or rather, commute to the club with Rapp's trombonist Al Jorden. Nodding acquaintances at first, the daily commute deepened their friendship and they soon began dating. When Rapp's nightclub began to fail, the band went on the road for a series of grueling one-nighters, often as many as four per week. Traveling in crowded conditions on a bus, the only female among all the men, Doris accepted such discomfort as a necessity, but the grind seemed to plant the seeds for her lifelong aversion to travel.

Learning that the popular bandleader Bob Crosby was looking for a female vocalist, Day auditioned for him and landed the job at a salary of $75 per week—a threefold increase over her salary with Rapp. Bob Crosby was a much bigger name than Barney Rapp, a true star in the world of big bands, but that didn't faze the very young Doris Day. In her own words, "It never occurred to me that I wouldn't get the job." This consistent pattern of total self-belief coupled with little or no ambition puts the hilariously successful film audition for Michael Curtiz in even sharper relief: "I really had no ambition about my singing." Even though Doris Day shares many career similarities with Judy Garland and Barbra Streisand—the extraordinary singing voice, the very real acting ability, the larger-than-life star persona—here is one area in which she differs markedly from them. No one, including Streisand and Garland, would ever have said that they had no ambition about their singing. For Streisand in particular, the naked quality of her ambition was nearly overwhelming in the early stages of her career. She had to be a star—and she was. Big time. Doris Day didn't have to be a star, but she was. Her sort of talent couldn't stay hidden.

Day's tenure with Crosby proved to be quite short-lived, however, because after only three months, he announced that he could keep only one singer, and that would have to be previous vocalist Bonnie King, who was returning to the band. Day's solution? Out with Crosby—in with Fred Waring and his Pennsylvanians. Doris Day continually landed on her feet for one simple reason: She was already a very good singer and every musician on the circuit knew that. Couple this talent with Day's total self-confidence and it's no surprise that after only a few weeks, Day moved on from Fred Waring to Les Brown and his band, courtesy of Bob Crosby's recommendation. By 1940, Doris Day, exactly seventeen years old, was singing with one of the biggest-name bands in the entire country.

And how did Doris Day capitalize on this opportunity? By leaving Les Brown to marry Al Jorden (who was now playing with Jimmy Dorsey's band in New York). Les Brown, Alma, even Al's own mother (albeit for different reasons) all told Doris that marrying Jorden was a big mistake. Doris didn't listen. Always pliable in professional matters, this was one stubborn girl when it came to matters of the heart. Driving to New York with the ever-loyal Alma, she married Al Jorden at City Hall between shows. Settling down in New York City, due to the Dorsey band's lengthy gig there, Doris Day then made an unpleasant discovery: Her husband was obsessively jealous, accusing her of affairs when she merely said hello to a male acquaintance, heaping emotional abuse on her, even beating her. At which point Doris Day became pregnant.

Passionate reconciliations between Doris and Al were followed by horrifying incidents of abuse, with Al not only threatening Doris but also beating her while she was pregnant (an incident that found its way into Martin Scorcese's *New York, New York,* a film that appears to have utilized "The Doris Day

The young Doris Day in the days with Les Brown and His Orchestra. *Photofest*

Story" as the template for its screenplay: Nice-girl big-band singer marries big-band musician who is both physically and emotionally abusive; they divorce and the woman goes to Hollywood where she becomes the biggest musical film star in the land while raising her young son—sound familiar?). Faced with the reality of a husband who not only told Day that she should have an abortion but also tried to induce the abortion himself, Doris Day told her mother that she would leave Jorden when her baby was born. After giving birth to her son, Terry, on February 8, 1942, in New York City, Doris returned to Cincinnati, where further spousal abuse caused her literally to lock her husband out of the house and obtain a divorce. Looking back on this harrowing time from the vantage point of 1991, Day, in characteristic fashion, emphasized the one positive feature in the entire awful experience: "One beautiful thing came out of the marriage. If I hadn't married this bird I wouldn't have my terrific son Terry. So out of this awful experience came something wonderful."

Not quite eighteen, Doris Day was now a divorcée, the mother of an infant son, and possessed no visible means of support. Only one thing to do—go back to work. In this context, there are two salient factors to consider, and both revolve around Day's infinite capacity for hard work. For all of Day's genuine belief that *que sera, sera,* for all of her statements that she never pursued stardom, it must be noted that in some way she was driven to perform. She went right back to work singing after this breakup with Jorden, she screen-tested at Warners immediately upon the dissolution of her second marriage, to George Weidler, and she began filming her television series almost immediately upon the death of third husband, Marty Melcher. Work was Day's salvation in each case, but on some level, she not only needed to work but also wanted to work. (She herself relates that the psychiatrist she saw after her midfifties's breakdown termed her "self-demanding.")

It is also worth remembering that Doris Day, born in 1924, came of age in the Depression, a fact that fostered a mentality in her—and in other similarly hardworking Golden Age Hollywood female movie stars like Barbara Stanwyck, Susan Hayward, and Rita Hayworth—that it was crucial to work as hard as possible, earn money, and keep afloat. For a woman raised in a household without a great deal of money, during the depths of the Great Depression, this was the one and only solution. Like Bette Davis, Joan Crawford, and Betty Grable, and unlike many of the stars of today, Doris Day did not attend college. Higher education wasn't even discussed as an option. Doris Day had to earn a living, support her mother and son, and make her way in the world. It is no surprise then to hear Terry Melcher state that his mother "denies herself luxuries and pleasures—there's something almost religious about her self-denial."

Doris Day relied on no one. She'd make her own way, and it was this philosophy of self-reliance that was to inform so many of her screen portrayals. This girl didn't just preach the importance of fending for yourself—she lived that life for all of her adult years.

Self-sufficient in the extreme, refusing to lean on a man for emotional or financial support, but with an infant son to care for, Day refused to go back on the road with any of the bands. Instead, she once again accepted a job at

WLW, singing on the midnight show five times a week. As fate would have it, during one of her performances, Les Brown happened to be listening and, in Day's own words, "Les heard me and called; he said to my mother, 'You've got to get her to come back.' I did and all the good things happened."

Day once again left Terry with her mother. (She later commented that nursing Terry after his severe motorcycle accident in the 1970s was really the first time she'd ever "taken care of him.") Back on the road, Day still disliked the travel, but the money was good and she, Brown, and the musicians all genuinely liked one another: "All the boys in the band were like brothers to me." Les Brown's band was highly popular, and Day was certainly appreciated by the general public as a very good singer, but everything was to change—everything was to become bigger, faster, and more public—with the late 1944 arrival of the song "Sentimental Journey."

Day and the band members felt certain from the very first rehearsal that the song would be an enormous hit. What no one could have predicted, however, was exactly *how* big the song would become. In an odd way, the song's rise to number one on the charts for an astonishing nine weeks after its release in January 1945 was almost incidental. This song became iconic because of what it represented; it quickly turned into *the* song for war-weary servicemen and their loved ones, all desperate for the end of World War II. "Sentimental Journey" raised Doris Day's public profile in a way no mere best-selling record could have, because through this one song, Doris Day became an official voice—and a very beautiful face—of the World War II generation. Couple the iconic nature of "Sentimental Journey" with the follow-up single "My Dreams Are Getting Better All the Time," which also rose to number one, and Doris Day was becoming a valuable and very famous show business property.

And what did she do with this newfound prominence? Married Les Brown's saxophonist George Weidler on March 30, 1946. And when Weidler quit the band, Doris left the band as well. The couple moved to Los Angeles, where Weidler found band work and Doris began singing on CBS radio. Dropped by CBS because she was deemed to be without promise (what, one wonders, did those executives think just a few short years later when she became the biggest recording and movie star in the land?), Day signed a recording contract with Columbia Records. It was a propitious moment to sign; the very identity of the big bands was changing because the success of songs like "Sentimental Journey" had provided a new focus on the featured vocalists, and record companies were eager to capitalize on the new trend.

Beginning her solo recordings in February of 1947, Doris also now took on

Al Levy from Century Artists as her agent. Levy was a partner with Dick Dorso in Century Artists, and a third partner came on board in the person of Marty Melcher. It was Al Levy who landed Doris a job singing at the prestigious Billy Reed's Little Club in New York, an engagement that proved so successful—at a salary of $150 per week—that a four-week extension was offered. She did not accept the offer, because it was at this time that she received a letter from husband George Weidler announcing that he wanted a divorce. Weidler felt that she was going to become a very big star, and he did not want to be known as "Mr. Doris Day." With no warning at all, Doris found herself with a second marriage on the rocks. She returned to California to try and repair the marriage, but the couple separated in April 1947 (although Day did not file for divorce until June of 1948).

A thoroughly miserable Doris Day, realizing that her marriage had broken down irrevocably, planned to leave Los Angeles and return to Cincinnati for a permanent reunion with her mother and son. It was at this low point in Day's life that Al Levy asked her to go to a party at well-known composer Jule Styne's home. Levy had developed personal feelings for Doris that she did not return, and with a second failed marriage, she was in no mood for a party: Never a big partygoer to begin with, she particularly disliked the then prevalent Hollywood custom of entertainers having to perform at such gatherings. Nevertheless, she went to the party and sang the Gershwins' "Embraceable You" to the assembled crowd of industry bigwigs.

And that's when it all really did begin to resemble a scene out of *A Star Is Born.* Al Levy, of course, knew that Jule Styne and Sammy Cahn were desperate to find a leading lady for their upcoming Warner Bros. musical *Romance on the High Seas.* The deal for first-choice leading lady Judy Garland had fallen through, and when second choice Betty Hutton turned out to be pregnant, everyone concerned with the film was frantically searching for a new leading lady. Jule Styne, a particularly savvy connoisseur of female singers (Ethel Merman and Streisand lay in his future), was duly impressed by Day, as was Cahn. In fact, this A-list songwriting team was more than merely impressed: A meeting with the film's director, Michael Curtiz, was immediately scheduled. And while Al Levy was jubilant about this very big break, the vocalist in question, Doris Mary Anne Kappelhoff—make that Day—from Cincinnati, Ohio, just didn't care. She didn't care when she met with Sammy Cahn for rehearsal before meeting Michael Curtiz himself, and she did not care one way or the other what happened when she went into her meeting with Curtiz. All of Al Levy's wheeling and dealing on behalf of this client for whom he cared a great deal was about to come to nothing because this beautiful, sexy, extraordinarily talented young woman had only one thing on her mind: Cincinnati, Ohio. She wanted to get out of records, out of radio, and now she wanted out of the crazy world of Hollywood movie studios. She wanted to go home. Only one thing stood in the way of Doris Day's heart's desire: Michael Curtiz. He had other ideas. Big ones.

Film

She can sing, be sexy, has presence, has personality—it was almost too much to deal with; you had the sense that in a way she had to be narrowed down in some way to be more acceptable.

—*Molly Haskell*

Those eyes, the intelligence, the intensity—she didn't know how good she was. She just knew she could do it . . . It's like she genuinely felt if it's that easy; there couldn't be much to it. It *isn't* that easy for the rest of us. She was a natural.

—*Three-time costar Tony Randall*

Doris was everybody's darling and I wish I could have done fifty more pictures with her.

—*Two-time costar James Garner*

Michael Curtiz may have possessed total confidence in the singing and acting talents of his newly signed but as yet unknown discovery, but he also certainly knew that she wouldn't receive any help in her movie debut from the silly script for *Romance on the High Seas.* With its vibrant 1940s Technicolor wash, *Romance on the High Seas* looks great, but it is a genuine surprise to learn that the screenplay is by Julius and Philip Epstein (of *Casablanca* fame), with additional dialogue by I.A.L. Diamond (soon to achieve fame with writing partner Billy Wilder). Such notables are surprising simply because this screenplay contains little in the way of wit or flair. Instead, the viewer is presented with a jerry-rigged plot that tells the tale of socialite Elvira Kent (Janis Paige) who thinks husband Michael (Don DeFore) is having an affair. Elvira tells her husband that she is going on a cruise but stays in New York City to spy on him, hiring nightclub singer Georgia Garrett (Doris Day) to take her place on the cruise. For his part, Michael Kent hires private detective Peter Virgil (Jack Carson) to spy on Elvira. In the way of such farces, Peter naturally thinks Georgia is Elvira and falls in love with her, a fact complicated by the appearance of Georgia's friend Oscar Ferrier (Oscar Levant), who also loves Georgia. In the ensuing melee of confused identities, Elvira and Michael reconcile and Georgia and Peter realize their love for each other.

Since neither Day nor Curtiz could count on the script to provide any support for Day's screen debut, the issue of her viability as a screen personality would depend totally on her own skills and the sympathetic framework provided by Curtiz. Would it be enough? After all, Samuel Goldwyn had tried mightily to make a big star out of Anna Sten, but the American public said *nyet*—quickly and repeatedly—until even Goldwyn was forced to give up. So it was that when *Romance on the High Seas* opened in July of 1948, the same question was asked—quickly and repeatedly: Is she any good? She was, and then some, because in her very first film Doris Day was already a star. She just wasn't yet an actress.

While it would be nice to report that Day's first performance on film shows a relaxed mastery of film acting much like the initial film forays of Audrey Hepburn in *Roman Holiday* and Barbra Streisand in *Funny Girl,* such is not the case. Day's natural beauty shines through, even under the elaborate hairdos and pancake makeup she abhorred, but there is no scale to her performance. It starts out big and grows bigger. She does in fact look great; at five foot seven and 122 pounds, she appears graceful onscreen, filling the frame as all true stars do. In her first scene she is dressed in a nicely tailored gray suit and hat, accessorized with a bright red blouse and pocketbook, but the problems begin as soon as she speaks. Forced by the screenplay to spout archetypal '40s dialogue, coming on like a groovy hepcat, she chews gum, walks with her soon to be trademark jaunty bantam rooster strut (which at least showed right from the start what a great figure she possessed), and repeatedly tells other characters, "That fractures me." Calling people "chooch" and "schmoes," Georgia's idea of playful fun, "natch," is to spit liquid through a straw at Jack Carson. So relentless is the script's determined hipster quality that Doris even overemotes while singing the up-tempo Styne/Cahn numbers "Put 'Em in a Box, Tie It with a Ribbon" and "I'm in Love," repeatedly popping her eyes à la Betty Hutton.

Much of this overeagerness is the fault of the script, but Day's performance doesn't help matters. Playing a rube trying to act sophisticated, Day, complete with fake accent, flutters her eyelashes and comes across as nothing so much as an untrained actress. Her performance is all surface speed—like one of the Andrews Sisters on amphetamines. She swings and sways when walking and delivers her lines at one hundred miles per hour. She possesses a star's aura, but she's exhausting to watch as an actress. Her performance is best summed up by the review in the *New York Herald Tribune:* "Day has much to learn about acting, but she has personality enough to take her time about it."

And yet, Day in fact managed not only to survive the mediocre script but even triumphed in no small measure. It's a triumph centered around exactly two musical numbers out of an entire film, but the viewer does, in fact, allow these two moments to make up for the other ninety minutes of silliness. Why? Well, as that well-known musical comedy aficionado Gertrude Stein might have said, a star is a star is a star.

Exactly when and how does that star quality burst to the fore? Whenever the tempo slows and she has the chance to sing a ballad. Then, all bets are off. One forgets the silly plot, the sight and sound of Jack Carson trying desperately to sell the song "Run, Run, Run" complete with a fake Trinidadian accent, the surprisingly flat choreography by Busby Berkeley, the horrible clothes with which nominal lead Janis Paige is saddled—including what may well be the ugliest wedding dress in film history, a white gown that could easily double as a football player's uniform. One even forgets that Oscar Levant cannot seem to summon enough energy to play even himself convincingly, turning in a performance marred by flat line readings. (In a strange way Day and Levant, both here and throughout their careers, prove to be true polar opposites: If he is all morose cynicism, she is all can-do optimism and boundless energy—in fact, here possessed of too much energy by half.) Instead, when Day begins to sing a ballad, one only remembers a truly great singer sounding and looking so sensational that you'd think she has been acting all her life. In fact, she had been. It's just that there was never a camera, certainly no film, and the setting was always the same—front and center on a bandstand, standing in the spotlight, and buoyed by the support of twenty first-class musicians.

On the film's very first ballad, "It's You or No One," Doris sounds so great, delivering the song lyrics so subtly, that she gives the song a reading and resonance that instantly tell the listener that something special is going on. For the first time in the entire silly enterprise, the audience sits up and pays attention. Shot in loving close-up by Curtiz, this is, out of the blue, first-rate musical acting.

Even better is the rendition of her soon to be million-seller song "It's Magic." A beautiful, gentle ballad, the song is introduced in the film by a guitar-strumming duo who begin to sing the song in Spanish. Day is handed the English lyrics, and while sitting at a table, she begins to sing the song directly to Jack Carson in a soft yet totally controlled voice. In this, her very first film, she exhibits an instinctive understanding of how to act through song on film: how to phrase the lyric, how to tell the story directly, and even how to provide the emotional subtext required. In these ballads, she beautifully expresses her voice teacher Grace Raine's instruction to "not think of a big audience out there. Sing into someone's ear—a person." Day completely relaxes and as Curtiz slowly moves the camera in for a close-up, there are no excessive facial expressions, just a beautiful woman (and it was already clear at this early stage that Day photographed sensationally) singing a touching ballad in her slightly husky, wonderfully evocative voice. When the guitarists join back in for the final two lines—"When in my heart I know/Magic is my love for you"—the song has come full circle, a perfect little three-act play. Doris Day has arrived.

And what, exactly, did it mean to have arrived as the soon to be queen of the Warner Bros. musical? Working under contract at Warners (which had taken over Day's personal contract with Curtiz) proved to be a very mixed blessing in terms of her career. On the rather large negative side of the ledger, Warners, a studio noted for its gritty social melodramas (*I Was a Fugitive From*

"It's Magic," from *Romance on the High Seas*, 1948. *A Star Is Born* played out in real life. *Photofest*

a Chain Gang), prison pictures (*White Heat*), and women's films (*Mildred Pierce, Now, Voyager*) did not have the focus, salaried talent, or musical structure in place to turn out anything resembling first-rate musicals. By way of contrast, at MGM, the famed musical Freed unit headed by producer Arthur Freed had the studio interest and resources, as well as the financial backing, to explore and expand the style and content of the movie musical. Extraordinary dancers like Fred Astaire and Gene Kelly, as well as great singers like Judy Garland, were given the freedom and support to push the boundaries of the musical form. Directors like Vincente Minnelli, with his sophisticated use of color and design, and brilliant orchestrators and arrangers like David Rose and Roger Edens, worked with top-flight screenwriters to make movie musicals look and sound like the cutting-edge, distinctly American artistic statements they were. These artists also pushed to further integrate story, song, and dance into one cohesive whole. It was these MGM musicals that paved the way for the fully developed Broadway concept musicals of Stephen Sondheim (*Company*), Bob Fosse (*Chicago*), and Michael Bennett (*A Chorus Line, Dreamgirls*).

By way of contrast with MGM, Warner Bros. did not have a great deal of interest in the expensive, hard-to-produce movie musical form and, as a result, made musical films on the cheap, complete with process shots, phony soundstage locations, and mediocre direction and choreography. Day never had the chance to work on musicals with the masters of the genre like Vincente Minnelli and Gene Kelly, suffering instead with the likes of David Butler (who directed no fewer than six of her films), Roy Del Ruth (four films), and Jack Donohue. Even an accomplished director like Michael Curtiz, who directed four of her films, was not a true director of musicals; the form never feels natural in either his direction of the actors or in his use of the camera, and only rarely does it feel organic in his direction of the songs themselves. Moreover, in film after film, Day, a terrific dancer, was saddled with the at best pedestrian, and at worst second-rate choreography of LeRoy Prinz. So consistently underwhelming is Prinz's musical staging that his one inspired and witty number in a Day film, "I'm Gonna Ring the Bells Tonight," from *April in Paris,* comes as nothing less than a shock to the viewer. Aside from this one routine, the only outstanding numbers among the plentiful dance routines in Day's Warner Bros. musicals were choreographed by her frequent costar Gene Nelson.

Yet at the same time that one totes up all of the negatives associated with making musicals at Warners, one can't lose sight of the fact that the lack of attention to musicals there meant that Doris Day was very quickly built up as the studio's one indisputable musical star. There was no shared focus or splitting of attention. Contracts for Janis Paige and June Haver were not pursued further, and Day's initial movie appearances, combined with her hit recordings and starring role on Bob Hope's NBC radio program (1948–1950) meant that she received national attention from millions of viewers.

Given Day's disastrous state of mind on the day of her screen test, it's fascinating to note that she never exhibited the slightest qualms about acting on film. Freed from what she considered to be the straitjacketlike concerns of live radio and singing appearances—appearances that gave her only one shot to get it right and were thus at odds with her perfectionism—Doris Day felt liberated on the film set. She found that acting in movies came to her "with greater ease and naturalness than anything else I had ever done." Moviemaking appealed to Doris's self-sufficiency; this was a professional, punctual actress who brooked no nonsense. Remarkably uninterested in playing the role of diva, Day seemed to reserve her greatest scorn for those who exhibited less than independent behavior: "There is one actress I know who has eight people running to her aid as soon as she does a scene. It's really disgusting."

Preparing for an NBC Radio broadcast circa 1949. Doris strongly disliked the live performances. *Photofest*

Day's ease on film was heightened by her happiness at being settled in one place and working during the daytime. She felt liberated by living in her own home with her mother and son. The days of constant bus travel, of a nocturnal lifestyle, were over. Day's happiness at this change helped her project the confidence and ease on camera that she clearly felt.

Day may have instantly felt at ease on camera, but with Warners' less than first-rate attention to musicals, it is not surprising that with the notable exceptions of *Young Man with a Horn, My Dream Is Yours, I'll See You in My Dreams,* and, arguably, *Calamity Jane,* all of the musical films Doris Day made while under a seven-year contract (1948–1954) at Warner Bros. are best viewed as charming antiques. Silly scripts, wacky production numbers, and the occasional terrific moment when Doris sings a ballad proved the order of the day, and her second film, *My Dream Is Yours,* is a prime example of this formula at work.

In *My Dream Is Yours,* Doris was once again directed by Michael Curtiz. The plot, such as it is, concerns show business agent Doug Blake (top-billed Jack Carson) and his attempt to find a singing star to replace the popular but ungrateful Gary Mitchell (Lee Bowman) who has left Doug's agency in search of greener pastures. Doug travels to New York, discovers Martha Gibson (our gal Doris) singing with a selection-by-phone jukebox, and launches an all-stops-out campaign to make Martha a star. After complications that include Martha falling for heel Gary Mitchell, Doug succeeds in making Martha a star, and Martha comes to realize that Doug is her true love.

Along the route to happy-ending-ville, there are wacky production numbers aplenty: "The House of Beauty Musical Hour of Enchantment," presented on the radio by sponsor Felix Hofer (S. Z. Sakall), features an all-female orchestra decked out in fuchsia ruffled gowns. This all-debutante orchestra, however, pales in comparison to the crazy production number that Doris Day must endure near the end of the film. Having become both a singing star and a movie star in approximately twelve minutes' time (the screenwriters evidently not having looked much farther than Doris's own life for the plotline), Martha has been reunited with her young son Freddie (Duncan Richardson). And how does Martha celebrate this reunion and spend quality time with Freddie? By having Doug read him a Bugs Bunny bedtime story. The result is one of the strangest musical sequences in Hollywood history: a surreal spectacle in which Freddie dreams that Mom and Doug are both dancing rabbits. Beefy Jack Carson and a buck-toothed Doris in rabbit suits? This is not exactly material to give Fred Astaire and Ginger Rogers sleepless nights. Given that Bugs Bunny was a Warner Bros. figure, this sequence just goes to show that blatant product placement wasn't invented in the corporate Hollywood of the 1990s. The number itself, staged by the reliably pedestrian LeRoy Prinz, veers from silly to awful to unwatchable. It's a textbook example of the sort of number that would never have passed muster with the Freed unit at MGM but at Warner Bros. seemed to qualify as inspired creativity. It's not a phrase one often associates with Doris Day, but here the viewer's only possible reaction is, "Oy vey."

Typical bargain-basement Warner Bros. production number, from *My Dream Is Yours,* 1949. *Photofest*

At this stage of her career, Day had not yet learned how to act for the camera. She consistently oversells up-tempo musical numbers; on "You Must Have Been a Beautiful Baby," she literally bounces as she sings. When she auditions for corporate sponsor S. Z. Sakall, her legs twitch, her eyes pop, and both arms flap. Yes, this is all to make the point that Martha needs to tone it down, but it is still a case of too much, too often. Doris Day is overacting Martha Gibson's overacting. There is, however, genuine wit in the screenwriter's take on Day's boundless energy: When she finishes this high-octane number, Carson proudly asks Sakall, "Great little personality isn't she?" to which Sakall replies, "Yes—and so much of it." No wonder Sakall wants only waltzes on his show: Day's Martha Gibson is one chick who's way too "hep." She needs decaf—fast.

Faced with this nonsense, one waits for a Doris Day ballad to lift the film, but in the meantime, Eve Arden is on hand as agency owner Adolphe Menjou's faithful secretary Viv, to detonate a wisecrack and make one think, "Hey, there's actually a real person in the film." Arden cuts through the idiocy of the screenplay with each well-timed bon mot and in the process delivers a master class in comic timing. Cajoled by Doug into taking on both Martha and her son as roommates, Viv can still joke about being forced to sell her car in order to finance the "make-Martha-a-star" campaign. "We're on our way," cries Doug, once things begin to look up for Martha. Viv's quick retort? "Well, wherever we're going we could get there faster if I still had my car." Scrubbing away in a suds-filled tub, she croons, "You wouldn't put soap in Auntie Vi's face would you?" only to receive a face full of suds from the object of her scrubbing—Martha's dog. Viv bankrolls Jack Carson's operation to make Doris a star, and what seems to be her reward? In typical 1940s fashion, she goes back to being Adolphe Menjou's secretary.

Given these absurdities, why watch the film at all? Two reasons. First, even with as yet underdeveloped acting skills, Doris exhibits a likability, and at times a tenderness, that makes the audience reach out to her. She possesses a smile of such warmth and sincerity, a smile that radiates such inherent decency, that the audience is instantly drawn to her side. This is no small attribute—after all, Julia Roberts's smile is an oft-cited reason for her stardom—and it connected Day to the audience, forming a bond that was never really broken, no matter how weak the vehicle. Such likability and tenderness manifests itself when Martha seeks her big break in Hollywood and has to leave her young son behind with his uncle. Watching Day's anguished response to leaving her son, one genuinely believes that Martha is devastated. In the midst of this cartoon plot, real emotion is generated. Day was always great with children onscreen, from *My Dream Is Yours* to *The Thrill of It All,* right down to her CBS television series. Such rapport is a tribute to her native acting ability, because Day herself has confessed that she is not one to "gush" over children.

The second reason to watch the film is even more basic: When Doris Day sings a ballad, you are watching a genuine Hollywood star in peak form, even this early in her career. Music is in Doris Day's soul, and when she sings "I'll String Along With You" to her cute blond son, she sings it in such a tender and pathos-filled fashion that her entire body relaxes and her true persona shines through. Day has often spoken of her love for ballad singing, and here is the proof, visually and vocally. After hearing Martha/Doris sing this ballad to her son, agent Carson of course realizes that in order for Martha to succeed, she must audition with a ballad, not hep jive. So it is that when Day sings "My Dream Is Yours," she is in fact singing to one person, just as vocal coach Grace Raine always told her to do. Corporate sponsor S. Z. Sakall thinks she's singing to him and gives her the big break she has always wanted, but the reality is that everyone in the movie audience *knows* Doris Day is singing to him or her. Talent and star power, pure and simple.

Any doubts about this star power are dispelled in the closing sequence of the film. Nice guy Doug has arranged a comeback for Gary Mitchell, who has not only ditched Doug but also turned out to be an abusive drunk. When Gary (Lee Bowman) falters on the vocal of his comeback song, "My Dream Is Yours," Doris gets up from the audience and, winding her way through the tables (thank goodness for the perfect amplification that magically appears from absolutely nowhere), helps him complete the song. They may be singing the song together, and Lee Bowman does have a rich, deep voice, but it doesn't matter one bit—the movie audience can watch only Doris.

Day's character here is an interesting template for many of her future parts, roles that reflected Day's own nature. In film after film, she is an energetic show business wannabe who never lets failure get her down or self-pity interfere with the business at hand. This onscreen girl loves life. The combination of such driving ambition with genuine sincerity seems organic with Day. As a result, at their best, her performances seem natural while at the same time establishing a true star persona. Michael Curtiz, smart old pro that he was, intuitively understood the strength of Day's personality even at their semidisastrous first meeting. As to his advice that Day not study acting, she followed it throughout her career, with varying results—mostly good and only occasionally very bad. (In 1991, even Day herself mused, "Sometimes I think I should have studied.") Film critic Molly Haskell summed up this strong screen persona as emerging from Day's "dazzling personality. She had confidence, an intensity, a freshness, quite unlike anyone else."

By the time of Doris's third movie, 1949's *It's a Great Feeling,* she was already receiving second billing in the credits and was a major part of the standard Warner Bros. musical film team: musical direction by Ray Heindorf, dance staging by LeRoy Prinz, direction by David Butler. Butler was, for the most part, a competent but rarely inspired director, a fact all too obvious in *It's a Great Feeling,* one of the strangest films of Day's career. The story may have been written by I.A.L. Diamond, and the songs composed by songwriting royalty Jule Styne and Sammy Cahn, but the resulting film? A resounding thud.

Filmed and released in 1949, *It's a Great Feeling* feels like an antique from the early 1930s, when Hollywood was first learning to talk. The plot, such as it was, centered on Warner Bros. commissary waitress Judy Adams (Day), a small-town girl from Gerkin Corners, Wisconsin, who is desperate to make it big in Hollywood. Both Jack Carson and Dennis Morgan fall for Judy, realize that she's talented, and try to get producer Arthur Trent to notice and sign her up. For plot purposes, a who's who of Warner Bros. contract actors and directors, all playing themselves, are paraded onscreen to voice their refusal to work with star Jack Carson: The film quickly degenerates into "Look, there's Sydney Greenstreet," "Isn't that Jane Wyman?" and so on and on and on, through Patricia Neal, Danny Kaye, and Joan Crawford, as well as directors Michael Curtiz, King Vidor, and Raoul Walsh. This movie asks the burning question: If all of these actors and directors refuse to work with star Jack Carson, how will the picture get made? A better question is: Why should it be made? This is all nonsense, and unfunny at best. Ironically, the only funny sequence comes with the notoriously dramatic Joan Crawford sending up her own image, slapping both Carson and costar Dennis Morgan, and then blithely announcing, "I do that in all my pictures." It's funny because it's unexpected, which none of the rest of the film is.

It is a tribute to Doris Day's talent that she survives this picture intact, because rarely has she been called upon to clown so desperately. Day has spoken of liking comedy that arises from situations, not jokes. Which means she must really have disliked this film, because it is nothing so much as a series of extremely unfunny jokes. Doris is called upon to ham it up in a bad audition scene for Carson and then to pose as Mrs. Carson in order to secure Morgan's commitment to the film. These leaden sequences are followed by Doris's turn as French chanteuse Yvonne Amour; rigged up in a black wig and gold dress while singing with an amazingly fake French accent, Doris is forced to mug in song, perhaps the only time she did this in her entire film career. To add insult to injury, there is a second "French" episode, a dream sequence in which Doris, playing the most unbelievable French streetwalker in film history, dresses in a glittery striped blouse and skirt and has to sing "Nothing Rougher Than Love" in a dance sequence staged by LeRoy Prinz at his clumsiest. Worse yet, in one of the low points in Doris Day's twenty-year career in feature films, she must pose as an elevator operator in order to secure the attention of producer Arthur Trent. Reduced to making goofy faces, complete with fluttering eyelashes and grimacing mouth, she mugs desperately, all to a sound track of music that sounds like nothing so much as a Porky Pig cartoon. Pretty damn humiliating.

It's not just the fact that when a film like *It's a Great Feeling* is staged in such a wooden fashion, Hollywood's self-referential condescending delight in letting the "little people" in on the wacky "fascinating" world of motion pictures is of interest only to those working in the industry. It's the fact that Doris Day is out of place in such shenanigans. Aside from the unflattering black wig and outfits in the "French" sequences, Doris looks great; she is youthful, direct, and modern in her forthrightness, and one expects her to cut through all the malarkey and tell everyone else in the film, "Will you just buzz it out?"

There is, however, one shining sequence near the end of the film that almost makes up for all of the preceding nonsense. Fed up with all of the scheming and endless empty talk about people wanting to help her make it in Hollywood, Judy decides to go back to Wisconsin and marry fiancé Jeffrey Bushfinkle. After wreaking more havoc on her trainmate, producer Trent, Judy wanders into an empty compartment: As the nighttime American landscape slowly rolls by, Doris Day then proceeds to sing "Blame My Absent-Minded Heart" in such a warm, seductive, yearning voice, which tells you everything the song is trying to express and then some, that the audience is tempted to forgive everyone involved for the preceding eighty-five minutes of silliness. When Trent, after listening to the song, exclaims, "You really are talented," he's the last one in on the discovery. The audience knew it after the first four bars. As music critic Gary Giddins wrote in the *New York Sun,* Doris Day "was the coolest and sexiest female singer of slow ballads in film history."

The film ends with Carson and Morgan desperately chasing Judy all the way to Wisconsin, only to arrive just as she has finished exchanging her wedding vows. The bride and groom kiss, and Jeffrey Bushfinkle is revealed to be none other than—Errol Flynn. It is a funny, lighthearted sequence, infinitely better than those involving the ham-fisted cameos foisted on the audience during the rest of the film, but as with Doris's vocal on "Blame My Absent-Minded Heart," it is a case of too little, too late.

Given the wildly uneven quality of Day's initial Warner Bros. films, why then did she become a bona fide movie star? To begin with, there was her extraordinary singing voice, a perfectly pitched, slightly husky instrument with which she was able to convey meanings and shadings unavailable to the merely talented. Coupled with Day's innate acting ability, her voice ensured that viewers were hooked as soon as she began to sing. Equally important, Day's persona resonated with the changing self-definition of women in America, indeed, throughout the world. After holding highly skilled and well-paying jobs throughout the war, American women, the Rosie the Riveters of the world, looked at themselves differently. They possessed increased self-confidence, based upon the belief that they belonged in the workforce and had a contribution to make to society beyond the confines of the home. The free-swinging optimism and self-confidence of Doris Day fit their changing worldview; once you've welded America's bombers and realized that you've made a real difference, baking pies in the kitchen doesn't seem like the only means of self-fulfillment. Day could hold her own in any job or situation:

She could be a journalism teacher or a nightclub entertainer, a working girl or a stay-at-home mother, and as a result she resonated equally with both working women and stay-at-home mothers. With her sunny sexiness, she appealed to men as well as to women; men wanted to sleep with Day but also wanted to take her home to meet Mom. She seemed to be the idealized girl next door. Of course her appeal was just that—idealized—because lost in the hubbub surrounding this new golden girl was the fact that no girl next door looked this great, sang so beautifully, or danced up such a storm. Doris Day could do it all, the effort never showed, and above all else, she was damn good at all of it.

Day's next film, 1950's *Young Man with a Horn*, is so different from *It's a Great Feeling* that it's hard to reconcile the two as having been made only one year apart by the same studio. Loosely based upon the life of jazz musician Bix Beiderbecke, Edmund H. North and Carl Foreman's script is based on Dorothy Baker's novel of the same title. Atmospherically filmed in black and white by Michael Curtiz, *Young Man* presents the life story of Rick Martin (Kirk Douglas), from orphaned youngster with an indifferent older sister, to his adult years as a jazz-obsessed white trumpeter with a black mentor, Art Hazzard (Juano Hernandez). Brilliant real-life composer Hoagy Carmichael is along for the ride as the film's narrator, Smoke, and with his lived-in face and a cigarette perpetually dangling from the corner of his mouth, he lends an authentic musical aura to this highly music-centric film.

Doris, as big-band vocalist Jo Jordan, is really playing a version of herself, right down to the alliterative name. This is not just a case of a movie star's persona shining through every role she plays. This is a case of Doris Day reliving events from her own life, a youth spent touring the country on hundreds of one-night band gigs. Jo's first vocal, "The Very Thought of You," is sung with such knowing intimacy that the fact that this woman knows her way around the music world is instantly established. Watch Doris Day's body language in the film when she is either singing in front of the band or recording in the studio—she is thoroughly relaxed and at ease. She is home. Music is in this woman's soul. If, for instance, the heart and soul of Barbra Streisand, another terrific singing actress, lies in the world of Broadway musical theater, that of Doris Day is in the big-band era. She is in her natural element, and the tenseness she sometimes radiates onscreen completely evaporates. Day helps to establish the all-important musical milieu so well that when Curtiz at one point nicely cuts between the band's rehearsal and its actual performance before an audience, the viewer is swept up into this world of jazz and dance bands, and accepts the film's depiction of that world as totally authentic.

The atmospheric, moody *Young Man with a Horn,* with Kirk Douglas, 1950. *Photofest*

In this, her fourth film, it is apparent that no matter what the role, Day is a star without irony. She is the perfect embodiment of post–World War II America, when problems were deemed solvable with a little determination and a lot of straightforward positive thinking. The reflexive, and usually self-protective, irony of the baby boomer generation is absolutely foreign to Doris Day. It is this direct quality that made her such a big star and also made her a target for derision from the baby boomers as they came of age.

Although Doris Day's Jo Jordan is presented as a "nice" girl, she is no shy flower. She expresses interest in Rick before he does in her, and she is willing to lend him money when he is fired. As a result of Rick being fired, he and Jo are separated, and when, sometime later, a flat-broke Rick lands in New York, he discovers that Jo has already become a star. The audience could have told Rick this fact as soon as they heard her begin to sing "Too Marvelous for Words" because what's often lost in the talk of Doris Day's singing on film is how damn sexy she was. This song, often taken at a finger-snapping up-tempo, is here slowed down considerably, and one realizes that this woman feels the man is so damn "marvelous" that the bedroom is just around the corner.

The screenplay for *Young Man with a Horn* repeatedly echoes Doris Day's own life; just as Day's star increased when she sang at Billy Reed's Little Club in New York City, so too does Jo Jordan grow ever more successful at this small club in New York. In fact, in her autobiography, Day speaks of *Young Man with a Horn* as being a depressing picture to film, because it brought back such unpleasant memories of her big-band days with abusive first husband, musician Al Jorden. However, although parallels between Day and the character of Jo Jordan abound, *Young Man* takes a decided twist of its own with the introduction of Lauren Bacall as "bad" girl Amy North. Amy's slinky character is presented as the antithesis of Jo Jordan, just as Bacall's onscreen persona is nearly the opposite of Doris Day's. In fact, Jo and Amy are, for all intents and purposes, presented as black/white 1950s depictions of the two faces of women: good/bad, innocent/knowing, mother/whore. (Ironically, physically speaking, curvy good girl Doris/Jo is much more traditionally sexy than is whippet-slim Amy.) Both of these two sides of 1950s womanhood hold appeal to tormented genius Rick Martin, and in the scenes between Amy and Rick, the film often veers far off track, but never without at least maintaining the viewer's interest, no matter how bemused such interest may be.

Bad girl Amy, who is studying to be a psychiatrist, is given to declarations that jazz is a "cheap mass-produced art" as well as self-analytic pronouncements that she is an "intellectual mountain goat leaping from crag to crag, doing a lot of things well, but not well enough." Amy's withering declaration that Jo is "so simple and uncomplicated—she's so terribly normal" is a direct reflection of the audience's perception of Doris Day, a woman who almost always radiated Midwestern American decency, or at least an idealized version thereof. It's no accident that at the time of the film's release, U.S. servicemen in Korea voted Doris the "girl we would like to take a slow boat back to the States with."

Amy North, in the form of Lauren Bacall, is a woman with the persona of someone who had seen it all by age five. She is actually a much better match for Rick Martin than is Jo; after initially turning Rick down because she doesn't respect herself enough, saying that she can't love freely, Amy throws him a lifeline:

Amy: Call me sometime.
Rick: Call you what?

Whatever he's calling her, it's a pretty tempestuous matchup. She's jealous of his commitment to music, and her studied indifference drives him to drink, causing him to ignore and abuse his musical mentor Art Hazzard. By the end of the film, Bacall has also seemingly dabbled with lesbianism, having found, in 1950s parlance, a female "friend," Miss Martin (played by Mary Beth Hughes). There are a lot of heaving dramatics and Bacall smashes Rick's beloved record collection, but around about this point in the film, the viewer finds himself or herself asking one question: "Where the hell is Doris/Jo?"

For very long stretches of this film, Doris Day simply disappears, reappearing near the end for a recording session of "With a Song in My Heart," one of the two musical motifs consistently heard in the film, along with Ray Heindorf's moody "Melancholy Rhapsody." It's at this recording session that Rick develops a much dreaded "roll"—an inability to hit the high notes—and Jo, who seems to function as a combination of mother, sister, and girlfriend to Rick, counsels him that "you're trying for something that doesn't exist—that note." Nearing the end of the film, the viewer is still unclear as to the exact nature of Jo's relationship with Rick; a little ambiguity may be good, but after nearly two hours, why does she flash in and out of the movie without any real rhyme or reason? When Rick lands in an alcoholic sanitarium, quick as a flash good girl Jo reappears to visit him. There is a second recording session of "With a Song in My Heart," and then wise old Smoke wraps things up by stating, "Rick became a success as a human being first, then as an artist—and what an artist." Nice statement, but the viewer is still left wondering, "Exactly who the heck are these people?" It's an oddly upbeat ending for what is essentially a downer of a film; for long stretches, *Young Man with a Horn* plays like a film noir musical, yet the film ends on a strangely optimistic note, presenting a much happier outcome than Beiderbecke's real-life death at age twenty-six.

There are in fact many pluses to *Young Man with a Horn*. The lead characters are recognizable human beings grappling with real-life problems. Musically the film is first rate, featuring both big-band great Harry James's trumpet playing and Day's remarkably smooth jazz-inflected vocals. Beautiful black-and-white cinematography by Ted McCord effortlessly sets up mood and atmosphere, summoning up the smoke-tinged ambience of late-night jazz clubs. Best of all, Michael Curtiz is much more at home with this noirish world than he was with the Technicolor happiness of *Romance on the High Seas*. If his handling of the material in *My Dream Is Yours* proved to be more sympathetic than it was with *Romance on the High Seas,* he is clearly that much more at home with *Young Man with a Horn* than with either of those two films. The director of *Casablanca* and *Mildred Pierce* has a feel for people in desperate circumstances and elicits strong performances not only from all three leads but also from supporting players Hoagy Carmichael and Juano Hernandez. This foreign-born director seems to identify more strongly with outsiders and the nighttime than with sunshiny Technicolor musicals, and as a result, *Young Man with a Horn* reeks not only of atmosphere but also of authenticity.

The only problem, and it is a somewhat large one, is that in many ways Lauren Bacall seems a much better match with Kirk Douglas than does Doris Day. Day may lend the film its musical authenticity, but her sunny disposition is less suited to Douglas's angst than is Bacall's knowing, urbane persona. Day and Douglas inhabit two different film worlds, and it makes a curious kind of sense that they exchanged jabs in Day's autobiography, with Douglas calling Doris "about the remotest person I know," and Day referring to the making of *Young Man with a Horn* as an "utterly joyless experience." Joyless in execution it may have been, but *Young Man with a Horn* served the important function of alerting viewers to the fact that Doris Day was an actress of surprising depth and was capable of playing much more than the simple girl next door. This increased stature makes it all the more unfortunate that she was right back where she started, silly plots and all, with her second release of 1950, *Tea for Two.*

Loosely—very loosely—based on the 1925 smash hit musical *No, No, Nanette, Tea for Two* in many ways is the quintessential Warner Bros. musical. The story, thin to begin with, here makes little sense and the musical numbers range from the inspired to the hackneyed. The standard Warner Bros. musical team, director David Butler in conjunction with musical sequences director LeRoy Prinz, does its usual workmanlike, somewhat plodding best. The film does, however, possess one shining asset: Doris Day.

Structured as a flashback from what seem to be the 1940s to the roaring '20s (there is no attention to period detail and the '20s costumes look more like clothes from 1950), *Tea for Two* concerns Uncle Max (S. Z. Sakall) and his beloved niece Nanette (Doris Day), her ambitions to be a star, and his loss of her money in the stock market crash. When money to produce the show falls through, Nanette sees no problem at all—she'll just put up the remaining $25,000, and of course she'll star in the show. (Good thing she took those tap lessons . . .) Even though Uncle Max has not told Nanette that all of her money is gone, somehow a bet is made that if Nanette says no to every question put to her for twenty-four hours, Uncle Max will pay her $25,000, and the show will go on. Never mind that he supposedly has no money to pay her with. Never mind that after the money for the show falls through, the only solution is, of course, for the forty cast members to spend the weekend at Nanette's Westchester mansion, rehearsing in the foyer and swimming in the pool. (If only Jerome Robbins had known that this was the way to keep a cast intact—just think of what he could have accomplished.) And especially never mind that when Nanette loses the lead in the show to the original star of the production, she is so upset that there is only one solution—she of course changes into a new ball gown.

There is absolutely no semblance of a coherent plot, and all of the shortcomings of the Warner Bros. approach are here writ large; in fact, the only relief in sight is supplied by the ever-reliable Eve Arden as Nanette's secretary, Pauline. When Nanette, after kissing composer Jimmy Smith (Gordon MacRae), sees Pauline eyeing them, she asks Pauline, "What do you want?" Pauline's retort is a very crisp "everything you have left over." It's as if Eve Arden can cut through all of the nonsense and restore a sense of fun to the proceedings. Unfortunately, in a microcosm of what could go so wrong with the Warners studio system, contract players are assigned completely inappropriate roles and the film suffers. In the Hollywood of 1950, it was simply a matter of economics and keeping the contract players working; as a result, the funny but effeminate Billy DeWolfe plays director Larry Blair, a character presented as a renowned Casanova. Believability quotient? Right up there with Nanette solving her emotional crises by changing her ball gown. As soon as Larry's supposed sexual appeal to both Nanette and original star Beatrice Darcy (Patrice Wymore) is pushed to the

Production number from *Tea for Two,* 1950. Costar Gene Nelson's choreography for their numbers was first-rate—and difficult. *Photofest*

fore, any possibility of caring about the characters as real people is out the window. What woman in her right mind would believe his romantic interest for even one second? Even more striking, in the film's ultimate absurdity, Gordon MacRae, as the show's composer Jimmy Smith, is shown onstage as the singing star of the Broadway musical in question (*No, No, Nanette*), but in the very next shot he has reappeared in the orchestra pit to conduct and play the piano. That's some busy opening night, and a laughable interpretation of Broadway procedures equaled only by the unintentionally hilarious John Travolta/Sylvester Stallone *Staying Alive.*

The script is so out of balance that both Billy DeWolfe and S. Z. Sakall seem to have more actual screen time than Doris Day; this is a musical, but their comic shenanigans are weighted more heavily than the star's singing and dancing. Since director David Butler does not have the visual style to overcome this large miscalculation, it is left to Doris Day to haul the musical back to life with her musical numbers. Which is exactly what she proceeds to do, beginning with her first number "I Know That You Know" (written by *No, No, Nanette*'s composer Vincent Youmans). Day is here paired with Gene Nelson, an appealing personality and terrific dancer, who would have been a very big star if he had come on the scene ten years earlier and not been stranded by the decline of big musicals. Gene Nelson is a first-rate dancer, and in this big tap number, Doris Day keeps up with him every step of the way. It's a fast-paced number, complete with intricate patterns, staged in a mirror-laden rehearsal hall. The ambience is genuine, the number works, and right away the film takes off.

Unfortunately it clunks right back down to earth when, after Gordon MacRae sings "I Only Have Eyes for You" in his beautiful tenor voice, his vocal is followed by a clumsy dance that could charitably be called interpretive. A woman whirling through two dozen pinwheel turns in a circle around the stage does not exactly constitute movement organic to this romantic ballad. The "Crazy Rhythm" number that follows is an embarrassing jungle-motif production number that features calisthenics more than actual dancing. It's numbers like this one that make the viewer realize just how stylish, inventive, and talent laden the Freed unit at MGM really was. By way of contrast, the leaden musical style exhibited here is light-years away from not only MGM but even from the "I Know That You Know" number at the start of this film. It is no surprise that these few first-class numbers were in fact choreographed by Gene Nelson himself—with assistance, from his choreographer/wife Miriam.

In addition to "I Know That You Know," there is one other first-rate production number in the film, the tap number "Oh Me, Oh My." Here, Day blends beautifully with Nelson, no easy task when Nelson taps up and down a staircase and literally jumps from a standing position onto the newel of the banister. This man can dance, and so too can his female costar. The indefatigable Day referred to her film dancing here, and in *Lullaby of Broadway,* as the hardest work she ever undertook, but absolutely none of the effort shows. She exhibits no signs of the career-shattering broken legs she suffered as a teenager and dances with an ease and fluidity that translate effortlessly on camera. In the history of Hollywood musicals, the only other female star who combined singing and dancing at such a high level was Judy Garland.

It is not that Doris Day is perfect musically. At this early stage of her career, although flawless in the ballads, she is still too bright—grinning, not smiling—in the up-tempo numbers "Do, Do, Do," and "I Want to Be Happy" (both sung with Gordon MacRae). But the overly eager demeanor completely disappears when she is singing a ballad. Standing at the piano, she sings "Tea for Two" in a beautiful warm voice, subtly putting across the well-worn lyric with something miraculously approaching freshness, in the process giving a lesson in what talent and star power are all about.

Whatever its silliness, and there is plenty of it, *Tea for Two* plays like an experimental Stephen Sondheim concept musical compared to *The West Point Story,* Doris's third release of 1950. Representing Day's first teaming with James Cagney, the nonsensical screenplay that they are forced to endure here certainly gives no hint of the terrific team they would make in 1955's *Love Me or Leave Me.*

With a script by John Monks Jr., Charles Hoffman, and future novelist Irving Wallace, *The West Point Story* tells the tale of tough Broadway choreographer Elwin Bixby (Cagney) accepting the offer of Broadway producer Harry Eberhart (Roland Winters) to stage the annual cadet show at West Point. This job is accepted once Cagney has punched the producer in the face and stated, "Okay—I'll take the job." Interesting interpretation of standard job-application procedure on Broadway . . . In another cuckoo Hollywood screenwriter plot twist, it turns out the producer's nephew Tom Fletcher (Gordon MacRae) has written the show but won't allow it to be brought to Broadway by his uncle—well, not until Cagney calls in reinforcement in the person of his movie star protégée Jan Wilson (Doris Day). Tom and Jan fall in love, Tom goes AWOL to follow Jan, and as a result the cadet show is canceled. Conveniently, and most preposterous of all, Elwin—himself a former plebe at West Point—has been forced to reenlist at the academy after hitting a cadet; faster than any audience member can spell "ludicrous," Elwin happens to remember that the visiting French premier can grant amnesty for all cadets who have been punished. All is forgiven, the show goes on, Tom and Jan are reunited, and of course Tom gives the rights to the show to Elwin.

Faced with the utter lunacy of such plots jerry-rigged by the Warner Bros. scenarists, it's a tribute to Day that her talent enabled her to spend the time in these films honing her craft. Always singing and dancing well, she slowly learned to tone down the exuberant acting as well as the excessive gesticulations present in the up-tempo numbers. Anyone less gifted would have been done in by even one of these ramshackle films, let alone seven years' worth of them.

After a fairly good start, with its pungent backstage atmosphere in New York City, all credibility is lost as soon as the story relocates to West Point. For starters, any thinking adult might just wonder if a forty-year-old choreographer really would take the unusual career path of becoming a plebe again in order to stage a show—a show that is playing not on the glittering White Way of Broadway but at that well-known musical theater institute, West Point. Then again, what's a Broadway show when you can become a plebe all over again. As to the musical numbers themselves, it may be fun to watch Cagney's distinctive on-his-toes dance style, but that's about as far as the musical pleasures in this film extend; well, to be fair, one does idly wonder whether Cagney and girlfriend Eve Dillon (Virginia Mayo) wore tap shoes on the trip to West Point and while walking across campus, because as soon as they arrive at rehearsal, they instantly launch into "By the Kissing Rock" without stopping to change shoes. In order to pump desperately needed energy into the film, even Cagney resorts to overacting, literally jumping up and down in order to convey anger.

When Bixby's protégée Jan then arrives on the scene in the person of Doris Day, turning up a full—and endless—fifty minutes into the film, the screenplay gives us hints of Day's own personal life; Jan announces to the other characters that "at fifteen I was singing with big bands on [a series of] one night stands," but that's the only note of verisimilitude in the entire screenplay. As it is, when Day arrives on campus she brings some much-needed energy with her—in fact, too much energy, as it turns out. Eyes a-blazin', Doris sings "Ten Thousand Four Hundred Thirty-Two Sheep," and while she sounds great, the grin she wears while selling the song is still too broad. Then again, who can blame her—she has to force her way through the film's bizarre production numbers like the "Military Polka" (once again the insipid "dance direction" is courtesy of LeRoy Prinz). Suffice it to say, bobbing her head from side to side, she's at her very bounciest here.

In true upside-down Warner Bros. musical film fashion, the screenplay has film star Jan nervously ask Cagney, "Do you think I can swing it?" Evidently in the Warner Bros. version of Broadway and Hollywood, it's logical for a star of Jan's stature not only to have canceled all other obligations in order to appear in an amateur military show, but also to be nervous about appearing with totally untrained soldiers (who mysteriously execute the choreography flawlessly after one day's rehearsal with Jan). Of course, that's no stranger than the fact that when Jan arrives, it's winter, but Doris is comfortably clad in a sleeveless gown, while crickets chirp musically in the background. This take on nature makes as much sense as anything else in the film.

Exactly two moments of musical interest exist here. The first occurs when Gene Nelson (in the thankless role of cadet Hal Courtland) whirls through a fast tap in his limber, loose style. The second is when Doris Day tap dances—unfortunately briefly—with Cagney and matches him step for step every inch of the way. This brief minute shows what the film could have and should have been—two great stars bringing out the best in each other. That pleasure, alas, would lie a full five years in the future with *Love Me or Leave Me.*

Finally, after poor Gordon MacRae is saddled with an endless recitation of West Point's history in a production number complete with humming cadets, and after the appearance of a chorus of tap-dancing cadets who look like nothing so much as the Rockettes in the Radio City Music Hall Christmas Show, the gibberish mercifully ends. Doris and Gordon MacRae are reunited in the Warner Bros. version of true love; Doris will give up her film star career, but that's no problem. Why be a Hollywood star when she can now spend her life as an army wife in Brooklyn? Faced with this final absurdity, the sensible viewer can have only one reaction to the entire film: file and forget.

After this succession of innocuous musicals, Doris Day was due for a change, and she found it in a big way when producer Jerry Wald brought her the script for his next film, 1951's *Storm Warning.* A tight, efficient little thriller, *Storm Warning* is a moody, hard-hitting indictment of the Ku Klux Klan and an early indication of how effective Doris Day could be as a dramatic actress.

Third billed after Ginger Rogers and Ronald Reagan, Doris Day plays small-town waitress Lucy Rice, whose husband Hank (Steve Cochran) is, unbeknownst to her, a member of the Klan. When Lucy's fashion model older sister Marsha (Ginger Rogers) comes to town for a visit, she witnesses the Klan murdering a newspaper reporter, a vicious assault led by Hank. The film then spends the remainder of its time unraveling the question of whether Marsha will supply evidence of Hank's involvement, or lie under oath in order to prevent sister Lucy from losing her husband.

Director Stuart Heisler, working closely with director of photography Carl Guthrie, effectively limns the claustrophobic small-town Southern atmosphere that gave rise to the Klan. Hank Rice is stuck in a dead-end job at the local mill, and wife Lucy works as a waitress at a bowling alley. From the opening shots of a rattletrap bus barreling down the darkened highway to enter the town of Rock Point, an atmosphere of foreboding is established. (In case anyone misses the point, the ominous music by Daniele Amfitheatrof underscores the point repeatedly—and loudly.) The entire first half of the movie takes place on the night of Marsha's arrival in town, and the viewer is presented with what is, literally, a dark world—overwhelming shadows only occasionally pierced by jagged sections of light. Interior and exterior settings alike possess the smoky late-night atmosphere of film noir, and the loud "jungle music" playing at the bowling alley further heightens the jittery mood.

This tense atmosphere is intensified by Daniel Fuchs and Richard Brooks's cynical screenplay. This is a town of hidden passions and identities—no one is who he or she seems to be, and the harshness of the setting is matched by the grimness of the characters' lives. There is, in fact, not one single laugh in this entire film. It's a world of so little hope and charity that when two men from the coroner's office arrive to take away the body of the murdered reporter, they barely glance at the body they are roughly carting away, instead talking all the while about their upcoming trip to the racetrack. These are men and women living lives of quiet desperation; the noisy bowling alley where Lucy Rice works is run by a henpecked husband who kowtows to his wife, just as the baggage handler who knows how the murder occurred is afraid to speak up for fear of retaliation against his family. Even townspeople who theoretically don't like the Klan are exposed in all their weakness: "We don't like the Klan but this prosecution is bad for the town—bad for business." In other words, what's a little murder as long as business isn't disturbed? Not a bad way for the screenwriters, especially in the fervent anticommunist days of the early 1950s, to present the hypocrisy running rampant in this small-town conformist atmosphere. In a few broad strokes, the screenwriters give the viewer flesh-and-blood three-dimensional characters whose frailties are all too recognizable.

The cowardice of Klan members is similarly presented in swift fashion—"They're no heroes without the hoods"—but it's not a point beaten into the ground. There's no need to do so, because the visual images of Klan members capable of mustering courage only when hooded and in a group take care of that. The self-delusion that leads one character to state, "You have to think about all the good the Klan does," is completely unraveled by the Klan leader's snarled threat that he will reveal Hank Rice as the reporter's killer if Marsha does not quickly develop amnesia on the witness stand. Rock Point is presented as being so rife with cowardice that the news of the Klan's acquittal turns into a townwide celebration.

Interestingly, the forbidding atmosphere is so successfully created that it is fractured only in those moments when real-life knowledge inevitably colors one's reaction to the screenplay. Specifically, crusading county prosecutor Burt Rainey, the only man seemingly willing to stand up to the Klan, is played by none other than Ronald Reagan; it is an unavoidable jolt nowadays to have Reagan's first close-up accompanied by another character saying to him, "Everything would be okay if nobody interfered with us from Washington." Even more startling is the townsman who wants Burt Rainey to adopt a hands-off attitude toward prosecuting the Klan, snarling at him: "If you go on like this, you won't get one vote for dog catcher next year." Reagan actually turns in a solid job here, faltering only at the moment of his big "I have to do what's right" speech; he simply doesn't have the gravitas as an actor to pull off this bit of sermonizing. (It's also interesting to note that county prosecutor Reagan seems to accept the rules of a very relaxed courtroom. While presenting his case, Burt Rainey is yelled at by the assembled spectators, and no one objects in the slightest.)

The single most noticeable aspect of the screenplay, however, is how closely both the characters and the very structure of the piece resemble Tennessee Williams's *A Streetcar Named Desire*. To wit: When fashion model Marsha Mitchell arrives in town with her "highfallutin ways," she interrupts the blissfully ignorant blue-collar marriage of younger sister Lucy and Hank Rice, just as in *Streetcar*, Blanche DuBois's arrival intrudes upon her younger sister Stella's marriage to Stanley Kowalski. Hank Rice is, like Stanley Kowalski, presented as a crude, bigoted roughneck, and Steve Cochrane is here outfitted like Marlon Brando's Kowalski, right down to the tight-fitting T-shirt. Most striking of all, however, is the fact that the long-simmering sexual tension between Stanley and Blanche is here mirrored in the quick-to-boil sexual attraction Hank feels for Marsha, an attraction that ends in an explosion of violence and death.

Doris Day is here slotted in to play the role that Stella occupies in *Streetcar*. She is the younger sister of the "glamorous" female protagonist, a faithful, constant wife whose slavish devotion to her husband is shattered by her older sister's arrival. The character of Lucy Rice echoes Stella Kowalski, right down to Lucy's maternal comforting of husband Hank, just as Stella soothes the crying Stanley. Faced with this markedly different role, Day acquits her-

The surprisingly tough *Storm Warning,* 1951, with Doris's childhood idol Ginger Rogers. The only time Doris died on film. *Photofest*

self admirably in *Storm Warning.* If it is not a great performance, it is certainly a solid one, and in Day's performance, the viewer can understand why this scared, not terribly self-aware young mother-to-be defends her husband against her older sister's warnings; says Day to Rogers: "He isn't bad. I don't care what he's done. I'm not going to leave him." Day effectively subdues her effervescent personality throughout, faltering only when she twice skips to the door to greet her husband, an over-the-top action that rings false even from such a clinging vine of a wife. That misplaced action aside, Day turns in a performance that makes one understand why, after the film's release, Alfred Hitchcock spoke to her at a Hollywood party and said, "You are Doris Day, are you not? . . . You can act." The payoff for that recognition would come exactly five years later with *The Man Who Knew Too Much.*

Granted, this screenplay nowhere near approaches the genius of *Streetcar,* but then again, what does? Fuchs and Brooks managed, however, to fashion a screenplay containing actual complexity. Marsha Mitchell agonizes over whether to tell the truth or lie in order to preserve her sister's happiness. It's a hesitation that Rogers conveys very nicely in her scene of courtroom testimony; speaking with a halting cadence, and clearly still conflicted, it is only on the stand that she makes up her mind to protect her sister. Family loyalty trumps all, and she lies under oath to say that she couldn't even tell if the Klan were involved in the murder, let alone be able to identify any individuals.

It is at this point in the film that events turn from dark to pitch-black. Marsha's lies have saved Hank, but his way of thanking her is to corner her at the bowling alley, sex heavy in the air between them. He then turns voyeur, peering at the slip-clad Marsha through the glass of his own front door. When he comes into the house, his body blocking the bedroom door in order to prevent her escape, the only thing missing from this parallel version of *Streetcar* is Stanley Kowalski's snarled statement, "We've had this date from the very beginning." When Marsha calls Hank "a stupid, vicious ape" he attacks her sexually and shoves horrified onlooker Lucy across the room and into the door. He then punches Marsha and throws his pregnant wife across the room. (In her autobiography, Day does not comment on this unfortunate parallel to her own real-life treatment at the hands of Al Jorden.) Marsha is then forcibly brought to the Klan rally being held in the woods, and after refusing to state that she will obey the Klan, is whipped for her disobedience. It's a disturbing scene on many levels and one that Heisler underscores by his casual panning of the women and children present in the surrounding crowd of Klan members.

County prosecutor Rainey and sister Lucy arrive at the eerie nighttime rally in order to try and save Marsha. With a giant cross burning in the wooded area and criss-crossing shadows highlighting the fractured small-town atmosphere, Doris Day rushes to her sister's side and is then shot dead—by her own husband. For the first and only time in her feature film career, Doris Day dies onscreen. The camera pulls back, and the screen fills with a meticulously prepared wide shot of the empty robes scattered by the fleeing Klan members, the dead body of Lucy Rice, and in the film's final frames, the burning cross crashing to the ground and splintering into pieces. Fade-out. Needless to say, this is all a very long way from *Romance on the High Seas.* Regardless of the occasional heavy-handedness, it's an interesting, thought-provoking film, dark and bitter material by the standards of any day, and a welcome anomaly in the early screen career of Doris Day.

After the grim dramatics of *Storm Warning,* Day was back in familiar territory with her starring role in 1951's *Lullaby of Broadway.* It's nearly a mirror image of 1950's *Tea for Two,* right down to the identical personnel involved: Gene Nelson, Billy DeWolfe, S. Z. Sakall, Ray Heindorf, and David Butler. All of the Warner Bros. contract players are present and accounted for, and all are pressed into service to put across another terminally silly musical that is redeemed only by a few gleaming musical numbers.

The plot, such as it is, concerns young Melinda Howard (Day) who is returning to New York from London in order to visit her mother, Jessica (Gladys George). Still under the illusion that her mother is a big Broadway star and not the down-on-her-luck alcoholic honky-tonk singer she really is, Melinda ends up living in the basement of her mother's "home," having been told that the house is being rented by the wealthy Adolph Hubbell (S. Z. Sakall). Viewers today—and truth be told, probably in 1951—can only scratch their heads and laugh out loud at this inanity, as Melinda starts living in the basement with great equanimity and nary a question. Well, why not—it's the same universe where Melinda can not only fall in love with dancing star Tom Farnham (Gene Nelson) but also become his costar on Broadway as soon as the wealthy Hubbell sees her talent for singing and dancing. In the wacky world of Warner Bros. musicals, all ends happily when Melinda hears the truth from her mother, decides to stay in New York, and becomes—what else—a Broadway star.

With a story this stale even in 1951, it's once again left to the musical numbers to carry the day, and they do—barely—thanks to Doris Day, and to Gene Nelson's self-choreographed numbers. When Doris Day makes her entrance in this film, decked out in top hat and tails, singing "Just One of Those Things," the viewer may think, "Ah, yes—just like the girl next door," but she's a girl next door who performs like a real Broadway star. Doris still does grin a bit too much, endlessly flashing a great many white teeth, especially in the up-tempo numbers, but put her within reach of a ballad—here it's "You're Getting to Be a Habit With Me"—and she hits nothing but home runs. That silky, seductive voice, so intimate and full of feeling, can make even a mediocre song work, and given a great song such as this one, Doris triumphs.

In the musical numbers, she is matched with the ever personable Nelson, and his very athletic solo to "Zing! Went the Strings of My Heart" makes one wonder just how big a star he could have become if he had been under contract to MGM and utilized by the Freed unit. Nelson's talent would grow through the years, not diminish, and by the time he starred in Stephen Sondheim's legendary 1971 Broadway musical *Follies,* his acting had grown to the point where he could not only sing and dance with ease but also create a fully realized, recognizable human being—no easy task in a musical.

Lullaby of Broadway does contain a first-rate mirrored tap number for Day and Nelson set to "Somebody Loves Me." These two stars work well together—their blond good looks complement each other nicely, as do their musical talents: She a singer who dances, he a dancer who sings. They are charming together and once again she keeps right up with him throughout the entire number. Doesn't matter that in the never-never land of Warners musicals, Melinda's talent is discovered when she dances in perfect unison with Tom even though they have had no rehearsal and she doesn't know which song they will be performing. This kind of talent makes its own rules.

After several grade-Z musical numbers—a pointless mechanical doll number that is visually uninteresting and stops the movie dead in its tracks, as well as the clumsily staged "I Like the Way You Say Goodnight"—Melinda and Tom have a fight; in a sign of Doris Day's growth as an actress, even in the midst of this silliness, she actually manages to inject some believability into their verbal altercation. That believability is immediately undercut when Melinda then turns her back on stardom, deciding to sail back to England on the day the show opens. Problems all sorted out, the film then ends—and peaks—with the title number. Tapping, leaping, and whirling up and down a stage-filling staircase, Doris Day, in partnership with Nelson, finishes the number with full spinning turns that take the two dancers down, up, and then down the stairs again. She, like all good dancers, makes it all look effortless.

Although Day has spoken often of disliking her artificial and stylized look in these early Warner Bros. films, her appearance (which is certainly better

Keeping up with Gene Nelson every step of the way. *Lullaby of Broadway,* 1951. *Photofest*

than she thinks) is beside the point. What matters is how terrific her dancing proves to be in this very difficult number. Once again working with Gene and Miriam Nelson, Doris had conquered her fears—and the mountainous staircase. It was only after filming that Miriam admitted to Doris that she could not manage what Doris had done, that unlike Doris, she was unable to turn up and down stairs while dancing at full speed. It was, in Doris's estimation, the hardest number she ever performed on film. Yet no matter how hard the filming, the result appeared effortless, and audiences responded in increasing numbers. Doris Day was on her way to the top of the box office rankings.

It is interesting to note that in a not so coincidental piece of cross-marketing synergy, shortly after recording the title song for the film, Doris rerecorded her vocal in a joyous, driving arrangement propelled by Harry James's trumpet. This interpretation proved to be so popular that it reappeared eleven years later on 1962's *Doris Day's Greatest Hits*. She may prefer to sing ballads, but on this trumpet-driven all-stops-out belter, she delivers what is unquestionably the best-ever recording of this up-tempo pile-driving number that spells "SHOW BIZ" in capital letters. In a recording rivaled only by the swinging Tony Bennett/Count Basie interpretation, Doris here fully reveals the kid with the vocal chords who personified swinging, confident, eyes-on-the-horizon post–World War II America.

The July 1951 release of *On Moonlight Bay* represented Doris Day's third film of the year, an extraordinary output for any year. This was also the year she married her agent, Marty Melcher, who was to impact Day's career—and life—more than anyone else ever would. Although Marty's relationship with Doris began as that of agent and client, with time they became close friends, and as Melcher's marriage to Patti Andrews (of the Andrews Sisters) unwound, they began to spend more time together, especially when Marty bonded with Doris's son Terry. In Day's own words, her involvement with Marty evolved over time and "kind of snuck up on me." When lapsed Catholic Doris introduced nonpracticing Orthodox Jew Marty to Christian Science, and Marty wholeheartedly embraced the religion, the last piece seemed to fall into place (Marty's fervent adherence to Christian Science, with his attendant refusal to see doctors, ultimately helped lead to his premature death). On Doris's twenty-seventh birthday, April 3, 1951, she and Marty were married. In retrospect, even with all of the horrific financial entanglements with Jerome Rosenthal that would ruin Day financially, it is clear that Marty Melcher loved Doris—he simply began to be obsessed with making a success on his own, and not as "Mr. Doris Day." Marty became the father-figure protector, which Doris at first embraced and later rejected. Melcher understood

April 3, 1951: marriage to Marty Melcher on her twenty-seventh birthday. Tumult lay ahead after Marty's death in April 1968. *Photofest*

Doris Day in a way that few if any others did, and although Day wrote extensively about their relationship in her autobiography, very few interviews exist where Marty spoke extensively about his wife in a personal, not professional, sense. It's why Marty's interview with the *New York Mirror* on September 12, 1957, is all the more interesting for the eerily accurate analysis of Doris that he offered six years into their marriage: "[She's] a girl who tried to grow up but never quite made it. But she's smart because she can be objective about herself." This clear-eyed view of his wife doesn't read like any sort of grand passion, but it does make it clear that Doris Day and Marty Melcher each received something from the other that they needed. Doris found a partner with whom she was comfortable, someone who seemed to love her son and would theoretically look out for her best interests careerwise and financially. Marty Melcher gained access to one of the biggest stars in all of Hollywood, access to the money that figured so prominently in his worldview, and yes, a marriage to a woman he seemed to love. As many of the Day/Melcher friends pointed out in Doris's autobiography, a number of interesting parallels can be found between the Melcher/Day marriage and the Ruth Etting/Marty Snyder relationship depicted in *Love Me or Leave Me.*

That film lay four years in the future, however. For now, Doris filmed yet another nostalgic Warner Bros. musical, but one of a higher caliber than the usual silly pastiche churned out by the studio. Based on the Penrod stories of Booth Tarkington, *On Moonlight Bay*'s script, by Jack Rose and Melville Shavelson, paints an idealized "misty water-colored memory" musical portrait of pre–World War I America. The fact that it depicts an America that never could have existed did not deter moviegoers, and the film proved to be a turning point in solidifying Doris Day's star appeal. If *On Moonlight Bay* showed an idealized America, well then, with the release of this movie, Doris Day seemed to officially seal her status as the idealized girl next door.

Set in 1917, *On Moonlight Bay* begins with the prosperous Winfield family moving into a new and larger home. Father George (Leon Ames) is a banker and mother Alice (Rosemary DeCamp) functions as the steady anchor at home who looks after tomboy daughter Marjorie (Doris Day) and young son Wesley (Billy Gray). Opening with still photo slides of early twentieth-century America superimposed over the credits, the first forty-five minutes of *On Moonlight Bay* are terrific fun, right up until the moment when the focus of the story switches from Marjorie to Wesley. In fact, these first forty-five minutes are enough fun to land the film in the same county, if not the same ballpark, as the MGM masterpiece it so clearly wants to emulate, *Meet Me in St. Louis.*

In many ways, *On Moonlight Bay* crystallized the Doris Day film persona that existed for the first half of her feature film career (the second half began with 1959's *Pillow Talk*): forthright all-American tomboy exterior and vulnerable feminine interior. Marjorie Winfield is first glimpsed clad in a baseball uniform, carrying a big chair into the family's new house. She beats a rug on the clothesline, then plays baseball—the one girl on the boys' team—whacking a triple and stealing home. In fact, soon to be sweetheart William Sherman (Gordon MacRae) even spanks Marjorie for trouble he thinks she caused before he realizes she's a girl. Marjorie's assertive tomboylike behavior reads very nicely in Day's hands—her natural athleticism lends great credibility to the character's self-sufficient exterior.

When William apologizes and comes courting with flowers, Marjorie and he spar in witty fashion and the courtship is great fun. They take a canoe onto Moonlight Bay, and when Bill begins to serenade Marjorie (undercutting the heavy-handed nostalgia by making fun of the lyrics he secretly believes in), the oblivious Marjorie contentedly munches popcorn. When they first dance together, Marjorie steps on William's toes and actually loses one of her falsies. She compounds her faux pas by outpitching William at the carnival game of knocking over milk bottles with a baseball, and this nicely unexpected role reversal is further built upon when pompous William intones, "What's love when all of Europe is bathed in blood?" Marjorie's riposte, delivered in perfect deadpan fashion by Day: "Won't you come in and have a nice glass of buttermilk?" Doris Day's Marjorie is not a simpering young girl eagerly looking for a man to protect her. She actually agrees with William about postponing, or even ignoring, marriage, telling her pro-marriage father, "Papa, you're so old-fashioned."

In these opening sections, the courtship of Marjorie and Bill is so enjoyable that the viewer roots for both of them. In fact, in this fun-filled first half, even the musical numbers are well staged. When William serenades Marjorie by singing "Cuddle Up a Little Closer," brother Wesley, who is hiding beneath the porch, makes fun of them with moans and groans that completely, and very humorously, undercut any hint of sentimentality.

This musical fun even extends to the "Love Ya" duet Marjorie sings with her unwanted suitor, milquetoast piano teacher Hubert. It's a particularly funny number because Marjorie does not especially care for Hubert, so she deflates the too-sweet lyrics by chomping vigorously on an apple while singing. Munching popcorn in the boat, chomping on an apple while being courted—Marjorie Winfield had one healthy appetite. (In fact, someday a doctoral dissertation may be written analyzing the hidden meaning of Doris Day's unendingly vigorous appetite on film. This girl let *nothing* interfere with her meals.)

All-American tomboy Marjorie Winfield in *On Moonlight Bay,* 1951. *Photofest*

Unfortunately, the fun ends when the film switches focus to brother Wesley. Even though Wesley is played by the appealing child actor Billy Gray, the story line declines into endless depictions of his mischief: He reads Marjorie's letter to Bill out loud in his class, suffers through dancing school, falls asleep in class, and then attempts to talk his way out of trouble by stating that his father is both a carouser and a violent man. Each of these vignettes is so attenuated in the storytelling that it falls flat, and the viewer is left to wonder: What kind of child tells such horrible stories about his own father? And why aren't Wesley's parents a little more perturbed over his lies, since word that father George is a drunk has spread all over town?

Director Roy Del Ruth has very little idea how to overcome this unfortunate shift of focus, and instead of the hints of real characterization presented in the first half of the film—character-defining traits such as Marjorie's healthy appetite, athletic ability, and awkward young womanhood—he settles for merely photographing Wesley's silly antics. As a result, the characters cease to be real and become cardboard cutouts with little or no humanity. After an initial forty-five minutes of honest sentiment, not sentimentality, the characters unfortunately become dewy-eyed stick figures from a sentimentalized early twentieth-century America that no longer feels real; it's all a far cry from the flesh-and-blood characters presented in Vincente Minnelli's *Meet Me in St. Louis.* In that brilliant film, Judy Garland and her entire family agonized over moving from St. Louis to New York, a dilemma to which all viewers could relate. Those characters were actually defined by their connection to home and hearth, something only hinted at in *On Moonlight Bay.*

Fortunately, Mary Wickes is on hand to liven things up as acerbic family maid Stella (the forerunner of the Thelma Ritter roles in Doris's early '60s sex comedies). Wickes is great fun as she cuts through all of the waxworks with her muttered comments; after Wesley runs into her and causes her to drop a platter of food, she deadpans, "I wonder what you get for manslaughter in this state." Wickes's presence helps a lot, but the problem remains that in the second half of the film there is too little Stella and Marjorie and too much Wesley.

There is, however, one lovely, totally redeeming moment in the second half of the film, a moment which naturally occurs when Doris Day sings. As Doris sings "Christmas Story" outside in the snow to Wesley's choir, Gordon McRae joins in, and as parents George and Alice watch from the snow-covered living room windows, one of the reasons why the film proved so popular becomes clear. The Winfields are the idealized family everyone wanted but in reality never existed, just as Doris represented the daughter/sister/girlfriend of whom everyone always dreamed. For once in a Warner Bros. musical, script, art direction, acting, and song all blend into one cohesive whole, and the resulting number lingers on in the memory long after the film has ended.

This beautiful song is soon followed, however, by a classic "only-in-Hollywood La-La Land" moment that shows just how out to lunch some of these Warner Bros. musicals could be. When, at Bill's graduation, everyone in his class reveals a doughboy uniform under his cap and gown because they've all enlisted in the army, their families leap to their feet in a standing ovation. That's right. These parents have just paid for four years of college only to have their sons blithely enlist to be shipped off to the inferno of trench warfare. Who cares that these boys stand a good chance of being killed? In the never-never land of Hollywood musicals, all of the assembled moms and dads are overjoyed at the news of the mass enlistment.

Immediately thereafter, the film ends with a fade-out on Marjorie and Bill embracing, as a chorus sings the title song. Marjorie and Bill are clearly headed for a life of eternal bliss together—just as long as that pesky world war can be dealt with. . . .

Day's role in *On Moonlight Bay* won her the *Photoplay* Gold Medal award for favorite female star performance, and combined with her other two films released in 1951, resulted in her first appearance in the Quigley Top 10 box office rankings. There are many reasons for her vault to the top strata of Hollywood stardom, but chief among them is the fact that as this film demonstrates, unlike any other female star of the time, Doris Day was able to convincingly depict the transition from tomboy to "proper" young lady and retain her appeal in both roles. In *On Moonlight Bay,* she trades her baseball uniform for hair ribbons and soft pastel-colored dresses, underlining her transformation by discreetly knocking her baseball cap to the floor when MacRae first kisses her. At the same time, Doris's Marjorie Winfield is still awkward enough to step on William's toes when they are dancing. Girls across America—and, judging by the growing international box office receipts, girls around the world—could relate to this awkward display of burgeoning womanhood, and Doris Day made it all seem natural. This convincing delineation of the universal transition from girl to woman connected Doris Day with her fans in a way unavailable to any other star. Girls might envy Elizabeth Taylor's voluptuous beauty, Audrey Hepburn's sylphlike elegance, or Marilyn Monroe's sexual magnetism, but Doris—well, Doris they could not only envy but also identify with and emulate.

Starlift, the 1951 black-and-white all-star Warner Bros. extravaganza that followed close on the heels of *On Moonlight Bay,* hands down wins the award as the wackiest and strangest of Doris Day's thirty-nine feature films. Beginning with opening credits that unfurl to the martial strains of the Air Force hymn, *Starlift* plays like nothing so much as an unrealistic armed forces recruiting poster of a film. Chockablock with Warner Bros. contract players appearing as themselves, *Starlift* features a clunky story in which lonely soldier Rick Williams (Ron Hagerthy) crafts a plan to meet his old school friend from Youngstown, Ohio, Nell Wayne (Janice Rule), who now just happens to be a movie star. Along with his friend Mike Nolan (Dick Wesson), Rick pretends to be leaving for the Korean front, whereas in reality he flies only between Honolulu and mainland United States. Gossip columnist Louella Parsons (playing herself, and not very well at that) publicizes Mike and Nell's romance, but Nell discovers Mike's subterfuge and pretends to still like him only for the sake of the public. When Rick finally receives an actual assignment to overseas duty, all ends happily with Nell.

Along the way to yet another ending featuring characters who are happy because they are voluntarily marching off to be shot at in the front lines of an international war, stars such as Gary Cooper, Phil Harris, and Randolph Scott appear as themselves. Also playing himself is James Cagney, which makes *Starlift* the second—and definitely the least—of Day's three screen pairings with him. And where does Doris Day herself fit into such fatuous goings-on? In a wild stretch, Doris plays . . . herself. She may be playing herself, but even a brief recitation of the plot cannot begin to do justice to the lunacy contained herein and to the craziness Doris must endure. For starters, when Doris agrees on the spur of the moment to entertain soldiers, she arrives at the staging area from which the soldiers will depart, and lo and behold there's a piano right there, complete with a soldier noodling around with his own composition. Doris dances to the song, a roomful of soldiers are revealed behind her, a microphone magically appears, and lickety-split Doris sings to a jukebox recording of "'S Wonderful." She sounds great, but in her best Betty Hutton eyes-a-poppin' tradition, oversells herself as herself. Roy Del Ruth is such an uninspired director that he can't even help Doris Day to play herself properly (and the task is not helped by the once again second-rate work of choreographer LeRoy Prinz).

The lunacy soon rises to even greater heights and exerts its own peculiar, wacky fascination. Doris, who according to this film appears to have blithely decided to spend her time entertaining the troops as they await shipment overseas, drives soldiers back to Travis Air Force Base along with Ruth Roman (appearing as herself). Ruth drives their convertible car to the base, with Doris wearing, what else, a mink stole. Arriving at the base, Doris sings "You Oughta Be in Pictures" to injured soldiers in the hospital, wearing the always-suitable-for-hospital-visiting outfit of an evening gown and black gloves as she warbles while strolling among the patients. She then visits a soldier whose brother, on the other end of the telephone, won't believe it's really Doris Day at the hospital. One-two-three, Doris comes up with a crafty solution—she simply belts out a chorus of "Lullaby of Broadway" over the phone. What else can a gal do?

The standout moment of lunacy? That would have to be Doris singing "You Do Something to Me" and cheering up a soldier by lighting his cigarette for him. Doris Day then disappears from the entire movie after only thirty minutes. Where'd she go? If she had any sense, and Doris always did, she probably left in order to light up another cigarette—this one for herself.

Of course Doris's hilariously unrealistic moments are more than equaled by the sight of Ruth Roman shaving a soldier while in her evening gown, and Jane Wyman (!) singing "I May Be Wrong" while wearing a formal hat. Nor are the male stars left out of the melee. After a long-winded and abrasive stand-up routine, Phil Harris then appears in a Western-style production number with Gary Cooper. Forget the fact that the number is unfunny and terribly staged. It's the sight of a terminally uncomfortable Gary Cooper in a production number that lingers in the memory. So uneasy is Cooper that he appears in an even worse light than Virginia Mayo, who dances—and the word is here used loosely—a wacked-out tropical production number called "Noche Carib," written by that well-known Latino musician Percy Faith . . .

So stupefying is the plot that one simply has to wonder: Did no one at Warners actually sit down and say, "Hey, maybe we should have a coherent story line." Didn't it occur to production heads that it was totally unrealistic to have Gordon MacRae, backed by the Air Force Choir, turn his rendition of "Good Green Acres of Home" into a sing-along with hundreds of unrealistically happy soldiers? Somehow, one doubts that these singing soldiers were really all that ecstatic about being shipped off to fight in the Korean War.

Questions such as these are actually what make *Starlift* worth even a brief analysis. The film is of no import in terms of Doris Day's oeuvre and persona, but it reveals a great deal about America or, more specifically, Hollywood's soon-to-crumble romanticized view of America, in 1951.

America was not united about fighting the Korean War, as it had been in World War II, but you wouldn't know it from this film. In typical rose-colored-glasses Hollywood fashion, audiences are asked to accept a hospital ward full of men who may be bandaged but are also clean, cheerful, and suffer from absolutely no discernible serious injuries. Evidently in the studio heads' view, audiences were supposed to be happy just to see stars playing themselves onscreen, but in the newly reshaped world of postwar America, film noir spoke much more coherently to audiences than did such white-washed studio fare as *Starlift.* The whole misbegotten enterprise was best summed up by the *Time* magazine review, which bluntly stated, "When *Starlift* exploits a wardful of wounded veterans to raise a lump in the throat, it raises only a gorge."

Doris Day's next film, *I'll See You in My Dreams,* the first of her two 1952 releases, is in many ways the undiscovered gem of her Warner Bros. contract years. Directed by Michael Curtiz, it is not only the best of the four Day/Curtiz collaborations but also a surprisingly affecting biopic of lyricist Gus Kahn (Danny Thomas). Along with *Young Man with a Horn,* it is the best of the seventeen films Day made while under contract to Warner Bros.

I'll See You in My Dreams works extremely well because not only is there genuine chemistry between the leads, but also because all of the songs occur as natural outgrowths of the show-business settings that dominate the film. The songs feel organic to the story being told. Crucially, this believability is established in Doris Day's very first scene. Day's character, Grace LeBoy, is an early twentieth-century working woman, a piano-playing song plugger working at Rossiter's Music Publishing Company. In the atmospheric opener, Doris plays "Shine on Harvest Moon" for prospective customers, and when unknown lyricist Gus Kahn (Danny Thomas) relentlessly pursues her to take a look at his lyrics, she is every bit his equal. It is Grace who instructs the neophyte Gus: "You've got to say 'I love you' for boys and girls who don't know how to say it. You've got thirty-two bars—no more, no less." This is not love at first sight; Gus is rough around the edges, refuses to wear a tie, and has an ever-present cigar clamped in the corner of his mouth. Grace is the business dynamo in this relationship: She puts music to his lyric "Gee I Wish I Had a Girl" and encourages him—nearly forces him—to quit his job and promote the song. He is oblivious to her interest in him until she once again almost forces the recognition upon him.

Curtiz is here working with a great deal more confidence in the musical genre than he exhibited in Day's first two films, utilizing atmospheric, fluid camera movements that mesh beautifully with the musical world so central to the film. After Gus and Grace are married, it is at a late-night jazz club jam session that she tells him of her pregnancy. She sleepily tells him they will have a "pretty baby," thereby giving Gus the song title he has desperately been seeking. When Day then falls asleep in her chair, Gus slowly walks down the stairs, picks her up, and carries her out of the club. Curtiz films this sequence in one continuous take, and with the smoky lighting, late-night bar-closing atmosphere, and faintly dying music, the sequence is not only affecting but also downright beautiful.

In a forerunner to Doris's ambitious career woman roles of the early 1960s, Grace is here presented as unceasingly ambitious on behalf of her husband. Forty minutes into the film, we finally arrive at a Doris Day solo: She sings "The One I Love" for producer Sam Harris (Jim Backus) in order that he might buy this song of her husband's. Of course, given how terrific Day sounds on the solo, if Harris had any brains at all, he'd buy the song *and* put Grace in the show instantly (just in case anyone doubted Grace's importance, the swelling strings on the soundtrack underscore the point).

In quick succession, Doris sings a series of superb songs: She starts at a World War I Liberty Bond rally, then sings "My Buddy," and follows up with "Toot Toot Tootsie Goodbye." She sounds marvelous on both songs; Day is equally at ease with ballads and up-tempo numbers, but there's one enormous problem with the latter song—Doris sings "Tootsie" in blackface and in a tux, complete with a Jolsonesque entreaty on her knees. Not only is the moment wildly inappropriate—it's also embarrassing.

With acerbic Mary Wickes on hand as housekeeper Anna, there is also genuine wit in the screenplay. When Grace is in the hospital giving birth to their second child, Gus is nowhere to be seen—he has stayed out all night writing the lyric for "It Had to Be You." When he finally shows up at the hospital, Wickes takes one sidelong glance at him and barks, "Well, what did you come up for? A bow?" The audience laughs—it's a funny line, especially because the audience has been wondering the very same thing.

Even better, however, is the sequence that immediately follows. Gus shows Grace the lyrics to the song, and as Grace begins to recite—not sing—the lyrics, the beautiful Isham Jones melody is heard as accompaniment. Grace, and by extension the audience, is being shown how very much Gus loves her, and now Curtiz beautifully and subtly heightens the emotion: Gus silently takes back the lyric and tenderly sings it to his wife. Watching Doris Day's silent but very detailed response to this declaration of love, one realizes how far she has come as an actress and how genuinely moving she can be, given first-rate material.

It's a sign of the surprising depth to this anything-but-standard biopic that even after achieving enormous success, Gus and Grace continue to hit bumps along the way; they are fully rounded, recognizable human beings. When Grace interferes by overriding Gus's objections and telling the powers that be that her husband would love to write the Ziegfeld Follies with Walter Donaldson, he hits her in the eye with the phone. It's an accident, of course, but he still tells her that she is too bossy. In fact, Gus does team up with Donaldson, who is presented as a gambler and heavy drinker. In this musical's unusually detailed screenplay, even the supporting characters like Donaldson are given some genuinely witty lines; when Donaldson, still wide awake and very drunk from a party the previous night, meets the disapproving Gus for their first (morning) meeting, he quickly tells Gus, "My grandfather started every day with a bottle of beer and he lived to the ripe old age of . . . twenty-eight." In addition, there are even some more-than-subtle hints of extramarital dalliances, with Ziegfeld star Gloria Knight (Patrice Wymore) making a rather concerted play for Gus. When Gloria sings Gus's new song over the phone to Grace, Day's silent reaction to Gloria's boldness speaks volumes not only about Grace but about Gloria as well. With post-1952 hindsight, what lends the scene additional resonance is the fact that the song in question is "Love Me or Leave Me." This is three years before the filming of *Love Me or Leave Me* began, but the kicker to the scene is that when Gloria sings the song on stage, the setting, her dress, and the tuxedo-clad male chorus eerily mimic the "Shaking the Blues Away" production number in *Love Me or Leave Me.*

In fact, there is really only one musical misstep in the film, the staging of Kahn's famously sardonic "Makin' Whoopee." Gus and Grace sing the song to each other while unpacking on their train trip west, and because it is the first song in the film that does not arise out of a backstage show-business setting—they even sing the final line to the train porter—it is startling and essentially violates the heretofore flawless musical vocabulary of the film.

So good is the film, as are both Curtiz's direction and Danny Thomas's career-best performance, that it's a notable disappointment when the film slackens toward the end. In order to depict Gus's downfall, the otherwise excellent screenplay by Melville Shavelson and Jack Rose (significantly, Grace Kahn is one of two people credited for the story) takes no more than sixty seconds to show Gus not only fighting with Donaldson about Grace's bossiness but also enduring the stock market crash of 1929, the decline of the sheet music market due to the advent of radio, and the eventual loss of all of his money. It's just too much territory covered in too short a period of time.

Even in this late stage of the film, Gus and Grace squabble like a real married couple and not just like the stick figures found in the typical musical biography. When Gus is reduced to writing parodies of his own work, Grace is not supportive in the I-understand-and-support-whatever-you-do-honey tradition of composers' wives. She is upset that he is cannibalizing his own work and lets her husband know it. When Grace calls Gus's music publisher in Hollywood to ask for his help, Kahn's pride is hurt and in great frustration he yells at her; "There's such a thing as too much help." He walks out on her and heads to Hollywood. Sinking into depression, Gus collapses and suffers a heart attack. This is all a long way from the sanitized world of the Cole Porter biography *Night and Day*.

In the end, Walter Donaldson comes to the rescue by pretending that he needs Gus for a new show, and when Donaldson's call is followed by those from Isham Jones and Jerome Kern, the Gus Kahn hits begin to flow again: "Liza," "I'm Through With Love," "I'll See You in My Dreams"—Gus is back on top. All ends triumphantly at a surprise dinner for Gus where he makes a speech paying tribute to Grace. Day's performance is so fully realized that she actually pulls off the not so easy feat of appearing to be both surprised and moved by his speech; you believe in Doris Day—you're not aware that she is acting—and that is why she became a star of the first rank. What really sets her apart is her ability to blend the disparate elements of her persona; in *I'll See You in My Dreams,* she presents an ambitious, determined, but completely feminine woman, and by now, movie audiences across America had begun to realize just how good this particular star could be.

After the triumph of *I'll See You in My Dreams,* Day next filmed *The Winning Team,* the second dramatic role of her career (*Storm Warning* being the first). It was to remain her last nonmusical role until 1956's classic *The Man Who Knew Too Much,* but *The Winning Team* is not a classic by any stretch of the imagination. In fact, such a long wait between straight dramatic roles may have been the result of her role in *The Winning Team;* the character of Aimee, Grover Cleveland Alexander's wife, is so bland and nondescript that even Doris Day fails to make much of an impression. It's a nonevent of a role—and film—and because it vanishes from the viewer's mind without a trace, it's very likely that Day's dramatic abilities may have similarly, and undeservedly, vanished from people's minds.

The Winning Team stars Ronald Reagan as early twentieth-century baseball pitcher Grover Cleveland Alexander, depicting his rise from telephone line repairman to baseball star, while detailing his battle to overcome both double vision and epilepsy along the way. The structure of the film's screenplay, by Ted Sherdeman, Seeleg Lester, and Merwin Gerard, dictates that Ronald Reagan carry the entire movie on his shoulders, and therein lies the problem. His wooden performance herein glaringly points up why his A-list film career halted soon after the release of the film.

Indifferently directed by Lewis Seiler, *The Winning Team* begins with the young Alexander overcoming opposition from girlfriend Aimee (Doris Day) to his career in baseball. Doris feels baseball "should just be a hobby—like my father playing checkers," while her father opines, "He'll be nothing but a baseball player." (Needless to say, both Aimee and her father would be singing a different tune today, given that even mediocre ball players now routinely land multi-million dollar contracts.) After an injury causes Grover to suffer double vision, his baseball career comes to an end, much to the relief of Aimee, who doesn't want to share her fiancé with the game he loves. Grover and Aimee are married, and in the midst of this plodding, predictable unfolding of the plot, the viewer at least receives the scant consolation of Doris singing "Ol' Saint Nicholas" while decorating the Christmas tree (the song resurfaced as an additional track on the CD release of her 1964 *Doris Day Christmas Album*).

Realizing that only baseball can ever make Grover completely happy, Aimee is glad to see him return to baseball once his normal vision reappears (a segment accompanied by swelling music complete with crescendos worthy of the arrival of the three wise men). After returning to the Chicago Cubs, Alexander begins to suffer from the recurring blackouts that began during his service in World War I; drinking to blot out the pain, Grover disappears across the country playing bush-league ball, only to receive a second chance from fellow all-star Rogers Hornsby. Grover begins to win games once again, and the movie climaxes with Grover pitching the winning seventh game of the World Series.

Unfortunately, the problems with *The Winning Team* all center around Ronald Reagan, beginning with the very fact of his physical appearance. Reagan was forty-two years old at the time of filming, and while Grover is called the "old man of baseball" at the movie's climactic 1926 World Series, Ronald Reagan himself looks too old to be a ballplayer, especially at the film's start when he's supposedly still a "young man" repairing phone lines. Unfortunately, Reagan is not anybody's idea of a professional ballplayer; while he looks passable on the pitching mound, he appears to be nothing so much as ill at ease at bat. An even greater hindrance is the fact that Reagan was thirteen years older than Doris Day, and the age discrepancy in their scenes together shows.

The most significant problem, however, is that Reagan did not have the emotional depth or acting chops to bring off the complex characterization required. He is simply not a very interesting actor and is not up to the task of appearing in every scene. His lack of technique and resulting inability to access the required emotional complexities are evident in nearly every scene requiring a display of emotion. The viewer can almost hear Reagan saying to himself, "Okay, now I act upset. Then I act scared." The action is never organic because no true depth of characterization is possible. (Reagan actually gave one performance filled with genuine emotion, in the 1942 Sam Wood film *King's Row,* but that proved to be the exception to the rule.)

Doris Day is here reduced to the status of secondary helpmate and at one point even appears at one of Grover's games as a nearly angelic figure, dressed all in white, and ready to calm him down with her mere appearance. (The look and scene seem to predate the famous backlit shot of Glenn Close as inspiration for baseball player Robert Redford in *The Natural.*) *The Winning Team* presents Doris's Aimee as a woman whose inner strength and belief in Grover prove key to his success. Struggling in the seventh game of the World Series, Grover looks in vain for Aimee's arrival. When she finally appears, courtesy of an only-in-Hollywood version of a New York City cabdriver who expresses excitement about the ball game by exclaiming, "Hot diggetty," Doris's effect is immediate. She enables Grover to stave off both epilepsy and double vision, and he proceeds to strike out batters one-two-three. This is asking a bit much, even of Doris.

It's not that Doris is bad in the film; she in fact received generally positive reviews, *The Hollywood Reporter* stating, "Miss Day gives her finest dramatic performance to date, playing Aimee with sensitiveness and understanding." The problem is that she is not required to do anything but appear helpful and supportive. She has nothing to do but show up, and a passive Doris Day is not the Doris Day of viewer interest.

After the excellent script Shavelson and Rose wrote for *I'll See You in My Dreams,* it is disappointing to see them return to nonsensical shenanigans for Day's next film, 1953's *April in Paris.* A top-billed Day stars with Ray Bolger in a tale of chorus girl Ethel "Dynamite" Jackson (Day) mistakenly being sent Ethel Barrymore's invitation to represent the United States at an international arts festival in Paris. It is then up to diplomat S. Winthrop Putnam (Bolger) to tell Day that it has all been a mistake and she will not be going to Paris. So tired is the script, so prevalent are the clichés, that within the first minute of the film, the viewer knows exactly where it is heading as well as all of the stops that will be made along the way. As the film unfolds, it comes to represent a contest between the often first-rate Vernon Duke/Sammy Cahn songs and the dopey script. The songs win the day, but barely.

The endless complications keeping Ethel and Winthrop apart are just that—complications—and have nothing to do with character development that would make an audience care. These characters never evolve; they are simply shoehorned into the silly events required by the plot. Winthrop has traveled to New York to tell Ethel that she isn't the representative to the festival, but the press has now heard about her supposed appointment and likes the idea of a chorus girl being the U.S. envoy. As a result, Dynamite now boards the ship as the U.S. representative to the conference. This is about as likely as the film's depiction of a Washington press corps eagerly awaiting Bolger's character, an "assistant secretary to the assistant to the undersecretary of state," outside of his office. This would never happen in real life, but it sure does in the world of bad musical comedy. Turns out that Winthrop, a bureaucratic toady if ever there was one, is engaged to Marcia (Eve Miller), the daughter of his boss; Winthrop of course falls in love with Ethel, and as a result they are "married" on board. Turns out the "ship's captain" who performed the ceremony is a fake, and therefore so is the marriage. So is the movie.

Complicating the picture, Winthrop and Dynamite are also traveling with Philippe Fouquet (Claude Dauphin), a rich and famous French entertainer, whose money has been frozen because of tax problems, thereby forcing him to work his way across the Atlantic as a waiter. Of course. Just what Maurice Chevalier would have done. Doesn't it occur to anyone that it might be easier to pick up a phone or send a cable? There are a lot of long, drawn-out quarrels among Winthrop, fiancée Marcia, and Ethel, which are resolved when Winthrop finally tells Marcia that he loves Ethel.

Sacré bleu—that is a lot of silliness to sit through in order to get to the sometimes excellent musical numbers. Day is once again playing a New York City–based show business aspirant—shades of *Romance on the High Seas*—hell, shades of every single one of her twelve previous films except for *Storm Warning, The Winning Team,* and *On Moonlight Bay.* Those Warner Bros. screenwriters did not exactly expend a lot of energy thinking up fresh scenarios. Day is first glimpsed fifteen minutes into the film, dancing and singing in a chorus girl routine. Without a top-notch director to guide her, Day still tends to smile too broadly, but in a welcome sign of her development as an actress, when she speaks softly of her disappointment at the trip being called off, one totally believes her. Sincerity and vulnerability truly do lie at her core, and five minutes later, her silken rendition of the beautiful title song lifts the film to an entirely different level, if only briefly. The emotional directness of her singing, which only the very best vocalists ever achieve, is what matters here and what the audience responds to. This is true artistry and why even a trifle like *April in Paris* is worth examining.

Ray Bolger, who did not get along with director David Butler during the filming, turns in a variable performance here. He is a vocalist of no great distinction, but when he starts to dance, well, then he becomes the proverbial horse of a different color. His rubber-limbed dancing style brings fresh energy to the stale plot proceedings, and when, in his first number, he dances with full-length portraits of himself costumed as George Washington and Abraham Lincoln, *April in Paris* becomes a bona fide first-rate screen musical. This fun immediately dissipates, unfortunately, whenever Claude Dauphin's Philippe disconcertingly addresses the camera directly, thereby undercutting any belief that we are watching a story about real people. (The fact that Dauphin also launches into the second-rate song "Give Me Your Lips" in a third-rate voice compounds the problems.)

The indefatigable Day comes to the rescue, however, at the onboard dinner where she is taken to task for not acting with proper decorum. She still bounces too much when she walks, but she is genuinely funny chomping on her celery and expressing bafflement as to which utensil to use. Doris calls the assembled politicos who are her tablemates exactly what we think they are—representatives of "an undertaker's convention"—and she heads to the kitchen with Philippe for some fun. The ensuing number, "I'm Gonna Ring the Bell Tonight," is not only the first musical number in history to start off with the conjugating of French verbs to the accompaniment of celery stalks but also an absolutely terrific number. As George Morris wrote in his *Films of Doris Day,* "It may well be the best number LeRoy Prinz ever staged."

This routine is a textbook example of what an upbeat production number should be. The infectious Vernon Duke melody starts, and Day begins high kicking on top of a kitchen table. As she possesses enough energy to propel the boat herself, one can even overlook her still-disconcerting habit of fluttering her eyelashes at top speed in order to convey irony; in fact, her singing and dancing are so exhilarating that it is possible to forget every silly plot development that has come before. Ray Bolger's Winthrop gets drunk on champagne, begins to dance himself and, in the song's reprise, joins Day in banging pans while dancing on tables. The two stars dance an exuberant polka—for once in a Warner Bros. musical two first-rate dancers are paired. This polka segues into Bolger's own tap dance on the kitchen tabletop, and it ends with Doris and Ray kissing. In and of itself, this number represents their real courtship—attraction, wooing, mating. It makes perfect sense that the only logical follow-up is for Doris and Ray to get married onboard ship. Unfortunately, the manner in which the ensuing ersatz marriage is presented is where the real problems with the film begin.

For starters, it is ridiculous, even by the elastic standards of plausibility inherent in the movie musical format, that after Doris and Ray are supposedly married, Doris has only one overwhelming desire. Nope, it's not sex: why, she's so happy at being married that she just has to sing a song—"The Place You Hold in My Heart." But that's not even the real problem. Doris and Ray's fake marriage means that the audience must now sit through endless farcical entrances and exits through adjoining cabin doors, in order that this nonmarried "married" couple may be kept apart. One wants to yell out, "Just tell her the marriage is a sham and stop slamming doors." None of this is funny—it's simply exhausting.

Things are a little better when Doris ends up spending her "honeymoon" night in the tub with the sprinklers going off, and there is a genuinely amusing catfight between Ethel and Marcia in which Doris actually—there's no other phrase for it—bitch slaps Marcia; it's funny because Marcia is a loser, a whiny, imperious daddy's girl, and worth neither Ethel's time nor Winthrop's attention. There is even real wit in the funny reprise of the title song sung by Philippe to Ethel: Now that the characters are actually in Paris, far from it being the beautiful city of "chestnuts in blossom, holiday tables under the trees" described in Day's wistful reading of the lyric early in the film, April in Paris turns out to be, in fact, freezing cold, with garbage flying in the wind and poodles yapping in the background.

And speaking of poodles: The film's last production number, "That's What Makes Paris Paree," featuring chorus girls holding poodles dyed different pastel colors, must win the award for the strangest production number in any Doris Day feature film (given Day's real-life status as an animal activist, one can't help but wonder what she must think when she views it today). Her outfit for this number is every bit as bizarre as the multicolored poodles, featuring a two-piece ensemble, complete with a bare midriff and topped by a hat sprouting two enormous feathers. The resulting routine is very poorly staged, but even more striking is the fact that evidently Ethel must be a quick study, because she's flawless in the number, and it's being performed on the very same day she joined the company. Not only that, but she has already landed a palatial dressing room beautifully decorated with dozens of bouquets. Pretty good for a chorus girl hired that afternoon . . .

The film's final sequence finds Day and Bolger fighting, so the only way to solve their dilemma, of course, is for them to sing. It may be April in Paris, but Doris Day is so foursquare American in demeanor and appearance that at film's end she is the proverbial fish out of water in the sophisticated City of Light. No sly winks and knowing glances for our gal. She's too up-front for all of that, and that's exactly why the romance with Bolger irritates when they are not singing or dancing together. This guy is not worthy of Ethel. It takes him forever to level with her and tell her about his engagement to Marcia. The constant telling of lies by Doris's suitors is a motif repeated in the endless subterfuge that pervades *Pillow Talk* and *Lover Come Back* with Rock Hudson, and even *Teacher's Pet* with Clark Gable. Gable and Hudson are so charming that one roots for them to end up with Doris, even though her behavior and moral honesty are far superior to theirs. In *April in Paris,* Bolger's endless prevarication simply becomes wearing. Ethel and Winthrop may end up together at the end, but one isn't exactly sure why Doris wastes her time on this guy when he's not dancing.

Given the success of *On Moonlight Bay,* it was inevitable that Warner Bros. would look into the Booth Tarkington stories once again in an attempt to continue the story of the Winfield family. This search resulted in Doris Day's next film, *By the Light of the Silvery Moon,* an innocuous piece of fluff that, unlike most sequels, is in some ways actually superior to its predecessor, *On Moonlight Bay.*

Narrated directly to the camera by Mary Wickes in her continuing role as Stella, the no-nonsense Winfield maid, *By the Light of the Silvery Moon* is a pleasant nostalgic bath in a Warner Bros. fantasy version of early twentieth-century America—no crime, no evidence of minorities, no real family tensions. Women happily tend house all day, the men all seem to work at banking jobs that are never actually glimpsed, and there is nary a trace of poverty. In fact, "nostalgia" is the very word Day herself used to describe her reaction to viewing the films forty years after making them: "Both films bring back such nostalgia for me. We made the films back to back and became a real family." But even more than this fairy tale version of America, what stands out in the viewer's mind is how direct and self-sufficient Doris Day's character, Marjorie Winfield, really is.

When Marjorie first appears on camera, she is glimpsed prone beneath the car, dressed in overalls and fixing the body of the auto. She is eighteen years old and covered with grease; with boyfriend William (Gordon MacRae) away at war, Marjorie has clearly reverted to her tomboy ways. When William returns home he declares his desire to postpone the wedding Marjorie and her family expect, until he is more firmly established at Mr. Winfield's bank. Bill's idea of breaking the news to Marjorie? He announces the postponement to everyone in town at a dance he and Marjorie attend. Nothing like an intimate heart-to-heart in front of the entire town to gently break off an engagement. Yet even such amusing plot points take second place to Doris's extraordinary self-sufficiency, the like of which rarely reared its head in early 1950s movies. As John Updike has mused, "She's a symbol of female energy, trying to tell us what we can do. Don't get downhearted. Bounce on." Even in these light-hearted Warner Bros. musicals, Doris Day resisted any tendency toward feminine passivity.

When William and Marjorie go out on a date and the car stalls, it's Marjorie who fixes the engine. Without missing a beat, Marjorie, dressed in her ball gown, gets right under the car and blithely states, "I have a hunch the valve under the gas tank is jammed." Bill, who doesn't appear even to know where the engine is, allows Marjorie to do all of the work and when all is fixed opines, "Good thing I got it going." Day's double take and deadpan exclamation of "Uh-huh" upon hearing this self-deluded rationalization provide genuine comic merriment. We laugh because it's clear Marjorie is far more practical and grounded than is the college-educated Bill. Bill also does not help his own cause by declaring that women have a "sacred duty" to stay home and bypass the business world, a statement that's particularly ridiculous given Marjorie's talents; this girl could probably run her father's bank and fix all the cars in town at the same time, and it's a kick to see such a resourceful and attractive heroine—in a musical, no less.

Once again, there is a great deal of gibberish to slog through in order to arrive at the musical numbers. Too much time is spent on the subplot of younger brother Wesley trying to save his pet turkey from becoming Thanksgiving dinner. Even worse, there is an endless digression in which father George (Leon Ames), who is on the board of trustees for a theater that will showcase actress Miss LaRue (Maria Palmer), rewrites a "questionable speech" in the play before the show can be deemed suitable for presentation in town. When Marjorie and Wesley find a copy of the "questionable" speech, about a married man wanting to be with his girlfriend, they think it is a letter their father has written to Miss LaRue. Not only is the sequence attenuated to the point of inducing sleep, but even a five-year-old would have known that stuffed-shirt father George would never enter into such an affair.

What makes all of this silliness palatable is the fact that several of the musical numbers are downright enjoyable, probably due to the fact that they were staged by Broadway stalwart Donald Saddler and not by LeRoy Prinz. "Ain't We Got Fun" becomes a vocal accompaniment to housecleaning undertaken by Wickes, MacRae, and Day, while "If You Were the Only Girl in the World" is a lovely duet between MacRae and Day in a sled; having made five films together, the two truly knew how to blend their voices together effectively—or rather, vocal arranger Norman Luboff knew exactly how to arrange the song. Whatever the reason, MacRae gives a more relaxed than usual performance here, and the film is all the better as a result. The romance between William and Marjorie actually lets off a few sparks; William is a stuffed shirt who just doesn't know how much of a stiff he really is, so it's a good thing Marjorie is around to loosen him up a bit.

The title song is the occasion for another duet at the player piano, but best of all are two solo numbers. The first is MacRae's joy-filled singing of an undiscovered gem of a song "Just One Girl." Propelled by a gently surging melody line that fits his voice perfectly, "Just One Girl" finds MacRae singing and sliding in the snow as he arrives at the Winfield house to pick up his "one girl"—Marjorie—for a date. (This is a truly charming number, marred only by the fact that at one point MacRae is singing to a black lawn jockey.) You believe that Bill loves Marjorie, and the terrific staging by Saddler puts a perfect cap on the number by having Bill hop up the front porch stairs, ring the doorbell, and as the number ends in a musical exclamation point, find Marjorie cheerfully awaiting him. If it's all a fantasyland version of small-town America, then this is the sort of number that makes the viewer want to live in that very town.

Equally terrific is Day's solo "I'll Forget You," which she sings while lying on her bed. Like all first-rate movie musical moments, the song pushes the film forward, revealing the depth of Marjorie's feelings for Bill; so superb are Day's vocal abilities that you believe she actually is singing about a real man, not the stock figure presented in the screenplay. Once again, it is Grace Raine's lesson to Doris writ large: Sing the lyric to one person, and it will connect with everyone. Doris does, and the song does.

The last production number in the film, "King Chanticleer," finds a barefoot Doris, dressed in lavender overalls accessorized with a red handkerchief and red hair ribbons, strutting around a barnyard and singing to various animals. It is not a particularly good song and seems to exist simply to allow Doris the chance to dance vigorously. The number does nothing to advance the movie or tell us about any of the characters. More important, the large scope of the number feels out of place in this smaller-scale movie musical in which all of the other numbers are more intimate. No matter. The concluding scene finds all complications worked out, with Doris and family arriving at the town skating pond in a sleigh in order to celebrate Mr. and Mrs. Winfield's anniversary. After realizing that the cameo role of the bandleader at the rink is played by none other than soon-to-be-famous television host Merv Griffin, what one notes is that Doris Day really can ice-skate, gliding around the rink as she sings the title tune with Gordon MacRae. Happy fade-out on one self-sufficient, athletic young woman.

Day's next film, 1953's *Calamity Jane,* the fifteenth of the seventeen movies

Day made while under contract to Warners, is certainly one of the five best of the bunch, which is not exactly a recommendation for the Hall of Fame. Its reputation as a great Doris Day vehicle remains intact to this day, and the film is always cited by Day as her own favorite. In fact, she pinpointed the similarity between Calamity Jane and herself: "Calamity Jane is the real me. When I was a little girl I was a tomboy; I liked to do what the boys did—climb trees, go skating. Yet at the same time I loved dolls . . . I loved playing house. I pretended I was married and I would cook and had babies." It's this mixture of the tomboy and traditionally feminine that underlies so much of Day's appeal. Yet putting aside the synchronicity of actress and role, a cold, hard look at the film reveals that it's not a particularly good musical—it's just great compared to the usual Warner Bros. fare.

Calamity Jane is best viewed as Warner Bros.' answer to the success of Irving Berlin's *Annie Get Your Gun.* Day herself was very eager to film *Annie Get Your Gun,* but Warners wouldn't let her out of her contract to work at MGM. *Calamity Jane* was, in effect, a consolation prize, as it shared many qualities with *Annie Get Your Gun.* Both films featured rambunctious, masculine-acting women who survived, indeed thrived, in the Wild West, fighting with and eventually succumbing to famous male marksmen, and along the way handling rifles and ballads with equal ease. Indeed, both films shared the same leading man—Howard Keel—a terrific musical actor who possessed a film persona with real heft, a relaxed acting style, and a rich baritone voice. It's just that *Annie Get Your Gun* is the far superior vehicle, in terms of both score and script.

Calamity Jane is directed by WB stalwart David Butler, but perhaps inspired by a script by James O'Hanlon that actually made sense, he directs with something approaching flair, resulting in what is surely the most inspired of the six films he made with Day. In a similar fashion, the musical direction from Ray Heindorf is top-notch (Heindorf's work was almost always first class, but he was consistently saddled with second-rate material). Best of all is Jack Donohue's staging of the musical numbers, which flow logically from the demands of the script. For once a Warner Bros., musical script had characters who actually bore some relation to real people and situations, yet preserved the heightened reality that allows characters to break into song.

The script revolves around Calamity's efforts to help the rowdy men of Deadwood City by bringing famous actress Adelaide Adams (Gale Robbins) to town in order to entertain them; a mix-up in Chicago results in Calamity mistakenly bringing back Adelaide's maid Katie Brown (Allyn McLerie). Both Wild Bill Hickok (Howard Keel) and Lieutenant Gilmartin (Philip

Carey) fall in love with Katie, but complications ensue because of Calamity's own love for the lieutenant; this is a love Calamity manifests in rather atypical feminine fashion, by rescuing him from attacking Indians. Calamity helps Katie by moving her into Calamity's own cabin; in return, Katie helps to make Calamity more feminine, actually getting her into a dress. Eventually, Hickok and Calamity realize that they do really love each other, and a double wedding with Katie and the lieutenant ensues.

Even with all of this plot to be dispensed, the songs do rise organically out of the script. Doris's first entrance, in head-to-toe buckskin, finds her astride a stagecoach, belting out the very catchy Sammy Fain/Paul Francis Webster song "The Deadwood Stage (Whip Crack Away)." The rollicking tune and exuberant Day vocal match the physical staging of the song, and character is revealed. Similarly, later in the film there is a lovely quiet moment when Calamity, Bill, the lieutenant, and Katie all ride together in a wagon (with Calamity driving, naturally) to the regiment dance, softly singing the lilting "Black Hills of Dakota." These are such first-rate musical moments that one is bound to ask, "So what's the problem?" The answer lies in Day's performance itself.

Although Calamity Jane represents one of Day's most fondly remembered performances, it is all too much by half. Using a low, gravelly voice and overly exuberant gestures, Day, her body perpetually bent forward, gives a performance like Ethel Merman on film: She is performing to the nonexistent second balcony. This is very strange, because Day is a singer par excellence who understood from her very first film, at least in terms of ballads, that less is more on film. Her understated gestures and keen reading of lyrics made every ballad resonate with audiences, beginning with "It's Magic" in *Romance on the High Seas.* Yet here she is, fourteen films later, eyes endlessly whirling, gesturing wildly, and spending most of her time yelling both at Wild Bill Hickok and at the citizens of Deadwood City. As *The New York Times* review of the film held, in what was admittedly a minority opinion, "As for Miss Day's performance, it is tempestuous to the point of becoming just a bit frightening—a bit terrifying—at times. . . . David Butler, who directed, has wound her up tight and let her go. She does everything but hit the ceiling in lashing all over the screen."

She is butch in a very cartoonlike manner, although as always, the tomboyish Day never loses her essential femininity (the fact that her manicured nails are always evident helps . . .). Her clothing and speech mannerisms may be masculine, but Day herself never is; it is one of the key reasons why audiences embraced her straightforward assertive personality. In the words of John

The exuberant "The Deadwood Stage (Whip-Crack-Away)" from *Calamity Jane,* 1953. *Photofest*

Updike, "There's a kind of crisp androgynous something that is nice—she has backbone and spunk that I think give her a kind of stiffness in the mind."

It is impossible to view *Calamity Jane* today without responding to the gay subtext; hell, it's not even subtext—the lesbian aspects of the film are all right out there. Dressed in buckskins, with a cap on her head and a red bandana around her neck, dirt streaking her face, Calamity says to Katie, "You're the purtiest thing I've ever seen. I didn't know a woman could look like that." Hugging Katie, she invites her to move in with her to "chaperone" each other. Helping Katie out of the horse and wagon, Calam tells Katie, "We'll batch it here as cozy as two bugs in a blanket." And after Katie cleans the entire cabin, the finishing touch is a front-door stencil that reads "Calam and Katie." It's not exactly difficult to guess which woman is the butch one in this relationship; similarly, it is no accident that *The Celluloid Closet,* the documentary examination of Hollywood's depiction of gay men and women on film, contains footage of Doris Day in buckskin singing "Secret Love," the very title itself a code in 1950s America. In *The Celluloid Closet,* this clip is supplemented by Day's vocal of the song playing on the soundtrack as homoerotic footage from *Gilda, In a Lonely Place,* and *Young Man with a Horn* flashes by onscreen.

Gay subtext aside, the relationship between Calamity Jane and Wild Bill Hickok also makes sense, and at the end of the film there is a feeling that each has found the right partner. Bill laughs right through her tall tales of how many Indians she managed to hold at bay while rescuing a stagecoach, but he's at ease with her, enjoying her challenge in a way he never would with the beribboned Katie. Calamity may have donned a dress to impress the lieutenant, but it's Bill who understands her best, demanding of her, "Who are you to tell people who to love?" (Again the gay subtext.) Continues Wild Bill, "You can't do that to Katie." It's after this dressing-down that Calamity realizes Bill understands her better than anyone else ever will; he really is her "secret love," a discovery audiences are glad she has finally made.

In fact, it is this last song that provides *Calamity Jane* with its one indisputably great musical moment, a moment so rich that during this one sequence the film is lifted into the pantheon of great musicals. Outfitted with a lovely understated orchestration that suggests rippling water perfectly in keeping with the outdoor staging of the song, "Secret Love" features a near-perfect marriage of music (Sammy Fain) and lyrics (Paul Francis Webster). With its gentle rhythm matched to the relaxed gait of the horse Calamity is riding sidesaddle, the song expresses Calamity's true nature in both music and lyric. Singing to the "friendly stars" above, she realizes

At last my heart's an open door
And my secret love's no secret anymore.

Calamity Jane is experiencing the freedom of true love, and it therefore makes perfect sense that the ballad is sung in the expansive outdoor beauty of the West. She may be dressed in a man's outfit and riding a horse, but she is riding sidesaddle and appears to be utterly feminine without compromising her essential self. Finding true love has allowed her to do the one thing she has not done for the preceding ninety-five minutes—relax. There is no more need to bellow, no more need to beat the audience into submission. Instead, a great singer is singing a terrific song, and the audience witnesses a star at her peak. It is no accident that "Secret Love" hit number one on the pop record charts, garnered Day a gold record single, won the 1954 Academy Award for Best Song, and in 1999 was inducted into the Grammy Hall of Fame. Like any great piece of popular art, its appeal has lasted through the years, and five decades later, when people speak of *Calamity Jane,* this is the sequence imprinted upon their memories.

1954's *Lucky Me,* Day's second-to-last Warner Bros. film while under contract, is one of the least appealing of the seventeen. In fact, this is exactly the sort of subpar script that Day must have had in mind when she mused in the 1991 PBS documentary *Doris Day: A Sentimental Journey,* "There were times when I didn't like scripts that I had, but a deal's a deal. I felt it was wrong to go on suspension. . . . My being good depends on someone much higher than Jack Warner. I know nothing will hurt me. I'll give 100 percent." This is rock-solid faith—in a higher power and in herself, and at this time in her life Doris needed both, because right before making *Lucky Me* she fell extremely ill due to a combination of nerves, depression, fear, and an overwhelming sensation of exhaustion.

It was at this point in Day's career that her strict adherence to all of the principles of the Christian Science religion began to fully impact not only her personal life, but her professional career as well. In fact, the evolution of Day's conversion to Christian Science, which began shortly after her divorce from George Weidler, bore full flower here. It is both noteworthy and ironic that Weidler's greatest impact on his wife came about after they were no longer married. Even though Day and Weidler's divorce became final in 1949, they still saw each other on occasion, and it was at one of these postdivorce meetings that George introduced Day to Christian Science with the book *Science and Health with Key to the Scriptures* by Mary Baker Eddy. Day now found Weidler a changed man: more communicative, no longer smoking or drinking, more at peace with himself. That very night, while George played with the Stan Kenton band, she first read his copy of Eddy's book. Day was instantly struck by the first line of the text: "To those leaning on the sustaining infinite, to-day is big with blessings." Finding this a refreshing change from her Latin-laden Catholic upbringing, Day was hooked: ". . . it brought spirituality into my life, spirituality that would sustain me through some very dark times . . ." (Day discusses the attractions of Christian Science in a less guarded fashion in her 1976 *Ms.* Magazine interview with Molly Haskell, where she bluntly states that she was receptive to Christian Science principles "because I'd been thinking that I should be happier than I am. . . . One ought to be able to control one's thinking instead of having depressions. . . . I didn't want that kind of life, but I didn't know how to change it.")

This conversion—and that really is the word—to Christian Science was to have far-reaching implications for Day's professional life. The sense of peace Doris found with Christian Science informed her life with a sense of purpose, a certainty in her existence. This clearly affected her work, enabling her not just to project self-reliance and contentment—after all, she was an actress—but also to feel that self-assurance deep down. Such self-assurance contributed to the buoyant personality that seemed to fairly leap off the screen. In short, her faith informed Day's star persona.

Shortly after finishing *Calamity Jane,* however, Day was experiencing heart palpitations and difficulty breathing. Her heart pounding at an increased rate, and overwhelmed by feelings of desperation, Day felt she could confide in only one person—her Christian Science practitioner, Martin Broones. Broones, the husband of English actress Charlotte Greenwood, felt that Day could overcome her physical problems by concentrating on one of the fundamental building blocks in Science and Health: "The cause of all disease is mental." Slowly Day's symptoms subsided but did not disappear. Relying on the CS prayer "Thou hast heard my prayer and I am blest," Day came to believe that one doesn't really have to "pray to anything but just go inside yourself, for that is where God is." It was this philosophy that led Day to a rock-ribbed belief that one can't take credit for any of one's own achievements. In her view, God the Creator put us on Earth to fulfill a function—everything is predestined. One performs as ordained.

As Day recuperated, tentatively feeling more able to return to work, she was handed the script to *Lucky Me,* a script she found so dismal that she wanted to back out of making the film. Broones pointed out that she had a contract with Warner Bros. and that she must uphold her principles by honoring her word and commitment. It's advice Day took to heart, not just in making the third-rate *Lucky Me* but also in honoring the commitments to which Marty Melcher obligated her in later years, as exemplified by the abysmal final scripts of her feature film career: *Do Not Disturb, Caprice,* and *Where Were You When the Lights Went Out?* Doris Day knew that these last feature films possessed grade-Z scripts. She had a strong instinct about what would work and what wouldn't, but she made each of those films because in her worldview, "A deal is a deal."

This advice from Martin Broones affected Day's career enormously, well beyond the fact that she recorded several songs he had written (featuring them on her 1962 album of hymns, *You'll Never Walk Alone*). Much more striking, Broones's advice informed a work ethic that caused Day to honor the contract for a television series to which Marty Melcher had seemingly committed her without her knowledge, a contract she discovered only upon Melcher's death in 1968. And yet, in keeping with Day's belief in Shakespeare's words that "there is nothing either good or bad but thinking makes it so," she found, as always, the good arising out of the bad: She may have known nothing about the television series, but by honoring her commitment, she not only paid off the debts that Melcher and Jerome Rosenthal's horrible financial mismanagement caused, but also gained financial security that would last the rest of her life.

In later years, Day would turn away from the more formal precepts of Christian Science, but always felt that it had led to a "very personal, gratifying" faith so central to her life. In Day's view, "I don't have to seek God. I don't pray. I just realize God." Doris Day may not have had certainty in her marriages—in fact, she had anything but; her faith, however, gave her a sense of certainty about her place in the universe. This certainty never permanently deserted her, even in the darkest moments after Melcher died and round-the-clock bodyguards became necessary during the trial of mass murderer Charles Manson because of concern that Terry had been Manson's real target. It was her certainty about her place in the larger scheme of life that fed Day's extraordinary, nearly unconscious belief in her professional abilities. Doris Day was never assailed by self-doubt as either an actress or a singer because of her faith that when she needed to call upon her abilities, they would simply surface, and that they did, time after time, in film after film. The sense of security brought about by belief in protection by a higher power seemed to release a great sense of freedom in Day, a loose openness that she could particularly enjoy in the totally controlled environment of a recording studio or soundstage. With no fear of the unknown in such strictly structured environs, Day was free simply to let loose according to her instincts. In this regard, her faith became one of the keys to her astonishing run of professional success.

Such unfettered belief in herself is key to Day's persona; it's as if she marches through these films wearing an invisible coat of armor. In that regard she is, in fact, very much like the America of the mid-1950s—convinced that it was doing the right thing and on the side of might and virtue.

Doris Day had not really recovered sufficiently from her stress-related breakdown to undergo the rigors of filming a movie, let alone an energetic musical. (And it should be remembered that Day's exhausting schedule had included not just feature films and countless recordings but her own CBS Radio *Doris Day Show* from 1952 to 1953 as well. Unlike Day's earlier radio performances with the big bands, which were broadcast from onsite locations, this weekly show originated from the actual network studio and featured Doris singing and performing skits with film costars such as Danny Thomas and Kirk Douglas.) Even without knowing about Day's personal travails, however, viewers of her onscreen performance can perceive the strain she felt. *Lucky Me* showcases a Doris Day who is full of energy but without any real joy, and joy in singing and dancing was always a key component of the Day persona and appeal.

Directed by Jack Donohue, who had successfully staged the musical numbers in *Calamity Jane, Lucky Me,* Warner Bros. first CinemaScope musical, centers around a traveling vaudeville troupe composed of Hap (Phil Silvers), Duke (Eddie Foy Jr.), Flo (Nancy Walker), and the superstitious Candy (Day). The troupe is staying at the same hotel as Broadway songwriter Dick Carson (Robert Cummings). In true oddball Hollywood fashion, this third-rate troupe has no money, but Doris wears white gloves throughout the day—the better to wash dishes with? In the hope that his new show will be financed by rich oilman Thayer (Bill Goodwin), Dick courts Thayer's daughter Lorraine (Martha Hyer). At the same time, Dick hears Candy sing and—no fool he—immediately wants her to star in his show (with parts for her three friends as well). Dick and Candy fall for each other, a romance laden with arguments (and reconciliations) when she discovers that Dick lied to her about being a garage mechanic! (One wonders in passing, and not so idly, that lie or not, doesn't life with a rich, successful Broadway songwriter sound better to a singer/actress than life with a mechanic?) Jealous Lorraine is unable to stop her father from investing in the show and at final fade-out Candy and Dick are on their way to Broadway.

The one word to describe Doris Day's performance in this nonsense is "exhausting." From the very first shot of Candy bouncily walking down the street, arms swinging and petticoats swirling, she is in constant motion. In her opening scene, a musical number titled "Superstition Song," where Candy sings about avoiding black cats and stepping on cracks, the routine is cute at first but ultimately just tiring. The strain is somehow evident—Day is all taut, coiled energy, with a neurotic core that's ready to burst. The gestures are too broad and the white teeth flash too much (in the group number "High Hopes" one doesn't even really see Silvers, Walker, or Foy—and all three are practiced scene stealers). Instead of enjoying Day's musical prowess, the audience becomes more tired than she—exactly the opposite of the sense of release a great musical number should provide. In the majority of Doris Day's films, her own persona shines through, whatever the role, and her essential optimism is contagious. Such does not prove to be the case in *Lucky Me.* It may be the confluence of Day's illness with the second-rate script, but this film features a fairly angry Doris Day; she pops her eyes, yells at people, slaps faces, and smashes mirrors.

There are no inspired musical numbers to relieve the tired plot machinations.

Doris must sing "The Bluebells of Broadway" with a Scottish accent, duet with Phil Silvers on "Men" while wearing a ridiculous black wig, and worst of all, don a lace mantilla, cat's-eye spectacles, and another black wig in order to impersonate royalty at Mr. Thayer's formal dinner party. This disguise wouldn't fool a toddler, let alone supposedly wise adults.

None of these shenanigans is aided by the equally exhausting performance of Phil Silvers, both as entertainer Hap Schneider and when posing as a rich Texas oilman. This is a scenery-chewing performance that would read "too broad" from the second balcony in a Broadway theater let alone in close-up on a large motion picture screen. One suffers through all of these third-rate contrivances in the hope of hearing Day sing by herself, but even though she sounds lovely on "I Speak to the Stars," effortlessly negotiating the melody's harmonic shifts, the song's effectiveness is marred both by setting (Doris singing underneath a see-through crystal tree!) and by background vocals that feature a chorus sounding eerily like the munchkins in *The Wizard of Oz*. Dramatically and musically, this is a Doris Day film best, and easily, forgotten.

By the time of her last Warner Bros. contract film, the January 1954 release *Young at Heart,* Doris had become a very big star indeed; both financially and in terms of popularity, she sat at the top of the Hollywood A-list. Her yearly income approached a half million dollars, and her record sales were approaching a cool $5 million a year. With her contract about to expire, agent/husband Marty Melcher felt it was time for Doris to spread her wings and fly solo without the protection, good and bad, of an ironclad major studio contract. First, though, this last contractual film had to be undertaken, and nice as it would be to report that Day departed Warner Bros. in a blaze of glory, the truth is that *Young at Heart* is one of the most disjointed films she ever made. Interesting to view because it represents the one screen teaming of Day and Frank Sinatra, the film never really catches fire and at times is downright peculiar.

Young at Heart, a semimusical remake of the nonmusical 1938 John Garfield film *Four Daughters,* revolves around the Tuttle family of Connecticut. Sisters Fran (Dorothy Malone), Amy (Elizabeth Fraser), and Laurie (Doris Day) live with their music professor father (Robert Keith) and Aunt Jessie (Ethel Barrymore, no less). When composer Alex Burke (Gig Young) comes to town, he quickly moves in with the family, falls in love with Laurie, and brings along his self-pitying musician friend Barney Sloan (Frank Sinatra) who is to orchestrate the score Alex is writing for an upcoming Broadway musical. In a plotline worthy of any daytime television soap opera, Barney also falls in love with Laurie, but on the day Laurie is to marry Alex, she discovers that sister Amy loves Alex; Laurie's solution is to ditch Alex at the altar and elope with Barney. After a difficult first year of marriage, Laurie and Barney return to her family, but the still morose Barney attempts suicide by giving up control of a car that he is driving during a blizzard. Laurie visits him in the hospital, tells him she is pregnant, and that fact seems to cause Barney to snap out of his depression, leading to a family reunion around the piano at the final fade-out.

It's not just these plot absurdities that undercut the film's effectiveness, though they go a long way to doing so. For starters: Alex (Gig Young) invites himself to live in the Tuttle family house, and everyone agrees without a moment's hesitation. Musical colleague or not, it just wouldn't work that way in real life. When Alex bossily begins to take over everyday family life in the Tuttle household, no one says to him, "Get the hell out of here," as normal people would. When Laurie visits Barney in the hospital, at a time when it's not even clear that he will live, how does she help her husband? Of course—she lights a cigarette for him to smoke. Scenes of family life are presented in such an idyllic fashion that Barney's scowling cynicism is almost a relief: Laurie plays the piano, father plays the flute, Amy plays the violin, and Fran plays the harp, all harmonizing musically to the soothing clicking of Aunt Jessie's knitting needles in the background. This nearly surreal depiction of a perfect family does nothing so much as irritate the viewer until Barney arrives on the scene.

Barney, in fact, is the peg on which the entire film hangs; all of the characters' life-altering decisions stem from the central relationship between Laurie and Barney, i.e., Day and Sinatra. This peg doesn't hold for the simple reason that there is not one shred of rapport between the two. So different are their styles that at times it seems as if there is a line bisecting the screen, with each star's footage having been filmed separately and then pasted onto the screen.

Laurie falls for Barney because she senses his vulnerability, just as Sinatra's own vulnerability existed beneath his tough-guy exterior. The problem is that Day and Sinatra, who do share the common background of being big-band singers whose artistic souls lie in their musical roots, approach every scene together in totally different ways. She never sheds her hands-on-hips, head-on approach to life's problems, an approach that feels light-years away from Sinatra's moody methods. It's hard to believe that these two ever would connect. The only time they truly click onscreen is when he yells at her; Doris Day's persona informs Laurie's resulting reaction, because she really is hurt that someone would yell at her in this manner. It's this quality of believability that constitutes a major reason why Doris Day became such a big star. As

Fascinating, mismatched pairing with Sinatra in *Young at Heart,* 1954. *Photofest*

James Cagney said of Day regarding a fight scene in *Love Me or Leave Me,* "When I actually slapped her, tears welled in her eyes and the surprise was 100 percent genuine. And so is Doris."

Sinatra, for his part, conveys his hurt through his singing, but it's never clear why his character is so self-pitying. One only has to hear Barney bemoan his fate as a poorly educated, orphaned, Depression-era baby, or hear his cry that "the fates won't let me succeed," to know that Laurie/Doris Mary Anne Kappelhoff wouldn't give him the time of day. Similarly, he would be turned off by her relentless optimism. In many ways Day and Sinatra represent the optimistic and dark sides of postwar 1950s America; both worldviews held genuine appeal, both had adherents, and they never really mixed until the social upheaval of the 1960s.

Day's acting may still be too broad upon occasion, laughing too loudly and too much in the film's high-spirited moments, but musically she is impeccable. To hear her sing "Ready, Willing, and Able" in this film is to understand exactly what Rosemary Clooney meant when she said, "I hear an entire rhythm section when I listen to Doris sing." A quiet scene on the beach where Laurie sings "Hold Me in Your Arms" features a vocal so totally relaxed and filled with emotion that one actually sees the movie that could have been.

In point of fact, Sinatra's acting is quite good here; he even has a few humorous encounters with seen-it-all Aunt Jessie:

Barney/Sinatra: What kind of aunt are you?
Jessie/Barrymore: I'll let you know what I think about you later.

The attempted suicide scene in the car is first rate, and Barney's frustration is conveyed solely through Sinatra's facial expression—there is no dialogue, and none is needed. It's interesting to note that while John Garfield was killed in *Four Daughters,* Sinatra refused to be killed in this remake. On the one hand, the silly happy ending is completely unexpected given all that has happened before. On the other hand, it's also true that audiences would, in theory, want their two stars to live happily ever after together. Damned if you do, damned if you don't.

The real problem here is that Sinatra's style is so different from Day's that he fully scores only in his musical solos, where one can react solely to his musical genius. Fortunately, there are several solos, and each one is a gem, beginning with Barney playing piano in a saloon and singing "Someone to Watch Over Me"; it's a great song, the right setting, and the best male saloon singer of all time here lets loose with a brilliant vocal. Another slam dunk follows when he sings "Just One of Those Things," a moment so good that the movie comes fully alive for the first time. Best of all, there is Sinatra in a throwaway version of signature song "One for My Baby" before an inattentive crowd. (The crowds sure as hell weren't inattentive when he sang the song in his real-life concerts; accompanied by just a single piano, a glass, a cigarette, and a pin spot, he would turn this ultimate saloon song into a complete three-act play.) His singing is so damn good in this portion of the film, so moving in delivering this paean to loneliness before a heedless crowd, that you want the rest of the film to go away. Then again, one has the same reaction to Day's solo vocals.

In an odd way, the clash of styles that so hurts the picture is best summed up by conjuring up an image of these two larger-than-life stars actually singing in the saloons that figure so prominently in *Young at Heart:* Frank Sinatra invented the modern-day notion of singing in Las Vegas saloons, helping to define an entire entertainment era in the process. He was totally at home in those smoke-filled, boozy rooms, working and staying up all night, going to bed with the dawn. Doris Day, on the other hand, turned down every offer she received to sing in Vegas, stating that she would do it under the following conditions: one performance only—in the afternoon. In the context of *Young at Heart,* it's obvious that Laurie/Doris comes alive in the morning sunshine, while Barney/Frank does so at night in a smoky bar. Why these two were ever attracted to each other remains a total mystery even at the end of the film, and as the camera pulls back during the final shot of an unnaturally clean suburban street, Sinatra singing the title song over the closing credits, one can only think, "Those two won't last one week together—especially with that damn harp in the living room."

Having fulfilled her seven-year contract with Warner Bros., Doris Day, freedom in hand, began to search for properties that would take her far away from the fairy-tale-like nostalgic musicals that had so dominated her life at Warners. When it was announced that her first independent film would be at MGM, starring as singer Ruth Etting in the biographical musical drama *Love Me or Leave Me,* brows were raised: Could Doris Day pull off such a demanding role? After all, Ruth Etting had led a very tough life opposite gangster husband Marty "The Gimp" Snyder. Could Day hold her own against costar James Cagney? Upon the film's release the answers were immediately apparent: Doris Day had delivered on every possible level and in the process gave the single best musical performance of her film career. Drawing on all of her skills as singer, dancer, and actress, Doris Day in *Love Me or Leave Me* actually gives one of the greatest musical film performances of all time. It is proof of legendary singer Rosemary Clooney's comment that "The same thing applies to Doris's acting as to her singing—it was seamless." Anyone wondering why Doris Day became such a big star for such a long period of time need look no farther.

The opening credits of *Love Me or Leave Me* immediately announce that the lush MGM treatment has been accorded this property: Filmed in Cinemascope, the titles are laid out against a background of plush curtains, announcing the fact that Doris Day's music is arranged and conducted by no less a personage than chart-topper Percy Faith. Directed by Charles Vidor, the film features a screenplay by Daniel Fuchs and Isobel Lennart (who subsequently wrote *Funny Girl*) that perfectly captures the backstage show-business milieu.

The film opens in 1920s Chicago at a dance hall; hoodlum Marty Snyder is shaking down the owner for the club's laundry business, and dance "hostess" Ruth Etting, clad in a red fringed dress, is kicking an overzealous customer and getting fired in the process. Right off the bat it's clear that these two are tough customers and that we are a long way from the never-never land of the Warner Bros. musicals. One look at Ruth Etting's defiant stance and body language, and you know that she is indeed "going places." This is a new Doris Day: sullen, tough, ambitiously clawing her way to the top. It is also immediately apparent that Day has matured enormously as an actress, or maybe it's simply that, finally given first-rate material, she responds with a great performance. She not only sings in her customary mellow tones, but speaks in an entirely appropriate intimate manner as well. There is no comedy here, and there is no mugging. What does exist is a thoroughly fleshed out, three-dimensional and recognizable human being, one whose warts-and-all characterization makes her all the more compelling.

Snyder, instantly attracted to Etting (or as he mistakenly calls her, "Etling"), arranges a job for her at a nightclub, and it is there that she first meets true love Johnny Alderman (Cameron Mitchell) who works as a pianist/arranger. (In real life Alderman's first name was Myrl.) When Etting sings her first solo, "It All Depends on You," with Johnny's piano serving as the only accompaniment, the camera closing in on her as she continues her silken reading of the ballad, it is obvious that a full-fledged musical star is at her peak. In a darkened, empty rehearsal hall, her face resting at the level of the piano keys, she sings, in James Harvey's apt phrase, "with meditative intensity." It's a startling moment. It's not just that she sounds great; it's that Day makes Ruth Etting's ambition and toughness palatable, bringing texture and layers to scenes featuring often unpleasant people behaving horribly—in a musical, yet. One understands Etting's drive, her need to become somebody and escape her ordinary existence. Her deliberate naïveté with Snyder—"I need a manager"— establishes that they will be partners in her career and that she is also partially to blame for his ensuing rough treatment of her. The expression on Doris Day's face when Ruth hears of a possible chance to work at a first-class club across the street completely reveals Etting's naked ambition. This character has dimension. Willing to lead Snyder on in order to further her career, she is one tough customer.

Etting's rise to the top is conveyed via perfectly chosen period songs, which also give the audience a chance to revel in Day's excellent vocals. Suggesting Ruth Etting but never slavishly imitating her, Day delivers the goods across a wide range of song styles; her first nightclub solo, "You Made Me Love You," delivered as a ballad, is followed by the driving "Stay on the Right Side, Sister," lyric advice Etting does not heed. In a sexy spangled dress, she delivers the bright-tempoed "Everybody Loves My Baby," followed by the sultry "Mean to Me," whose lyric reflects Marty's increasingly rough treatment of Etting (as well as containing unfortunate parallels to Day's own real-life husbands). The audience is not just hearing a variety of first-class Doris Day vocals—they are also learning about Ruth Etting through the songs.

Although radio, with Johnny Alderman conducting, proves to be the next stop on the road to fame and fortune, Ruth refuses to leave Marty for Johnny.

She loves Johnny, but her ambition overrules everything. In an absolutely terrific scene set in a radio station, Ruth and a male backup quartet sing "Sam, the Old Accordion Man." Day looks the part in great 1920s clothes—beret, pearls, and period dress—and seeing Johnny's sullen face, she registers an expression of such sadness that she almost misses her vocal entrance cue. In this one short musical sequence, gesture, vocal, and body language all combine to speak volumes about Ruth Etting.

Marty's pushing and maneuvering, combined with Ruth's genuine talent, get her to the Ziegfeld Follies in New York. The film's big production number, Irving Berlin's "Shakin' the Blues Away," takes place onstage at the Ziegfeld Follies, and the number gets off to a terrific start with horns blaring a bluesy melody, backlit dancers in silhouette, and a thunderous storm breaking; as the music mounts in tempo, the storm clears, revealing top-hatted men awaiting a sexily clad Ruth Etting downstage. After this buildup, the viewer expects the movie to soar. Instead, the number virtually stops dead.

There may still be a great belting vocal from Day, but the choreography by Alex Romero is downright awful. Doris Day is a star who can really dance, but instead she is called on only to pose and stand on a circular settee while the chorus boys carry her around the stage, as they did Marilyn Monroe in the "Diamonds Are a Girl's Best Friend" number from *Gentlemen Prefer Blondes.* Here the star is a bona fide trained dancer who can really deliver the goods, but she is never allowed to do so. What should be the crowning musical moment in the film is further undercut by Vidor's inexplicable decision to shoot the number in long-distance setups, thereby negating any sense of audience involvement or impact. It is ill-advised decisions like these that keep the film from being classified as an all-time great musical.

Fortunately, it is at this point that James Cagney comes to the fore and delivers one of the great performances of his legendary career. Marty, a man Johnny calls a "cheap crook pushing people around," argues with the director and choreographer, and like Mama Rose in *Gypsy,* vents his frustration at being marginalized. The look on Cagney's face as Marty realizes "Ruthie" doesn't need him, that she has outstripped him, lays bare both his ruthlessness and his vulnerability. The fight between Etting and Snyder on opening night of the Ziegfeld Follies contains an almost frenzied quality; it's a fight that can end only with Marty in effect raping Ruth. Marty Snyder and Ruth Etting go at it toe to toe, and when the next shot after this brutal fight is a cut to a newspaper headline of their marriage, the viewer knows that Ruth Etting is paying the price for her ambition. This is one hell of an adult musical, with often fierce dialogue that can still disturb fifty years later: As Marty tries to tell Ruth

The full, expensive MGM treatment. "Shakin' the Blues Away," from *Love Me or Leave Me. Photofest*

about how he is getting jobs for her, how big he'll make her, she replies with an ego-crushing, "You don't have to sell me. I'm already sold." The hurt that Cagney registers at this verbal knife thrust simultaneously repels and invites sympathy; this is screen acting of the highest order.

Director Charles Vidor nicely propels the film forward with montage shots of trains, nightclubs, sheet music, and newspaper clippings, while the viewer hears snippets of standards such as "I Cried for You" and "My Blue Heaven." This is all excellent movie musical filmmaking, but the staging of the full musical numbers continues to frustrate. When Ruthie sings the Rodgers and Hart

The great, explosive pairing with James Cagney in *Love Me or Leave Me. Photofest*

standard "Ten Cents a Dance," a first-rate song that also serves to remind the viewer of Etting's dance hall origins in Chicago, Day looks sensational in a black fringed dress, complete with a feather in her hair and a hands-on-hips c'mon-big-boy tough stance. The viewer knows that this woman has been around the block—a few dozen times. But the effectiveness of what should be a great number (and one excerpted in the MGM compilation *That's Entertainment, Two*) is undone by continual cuts away from close-ups to full-body shots. Volumes of information and feeling are lost in the process.

Doris Day had never previously behaved like such a tough, driven woman onscreen, but so assured is her acting that one believes her every step of her often drunken, sarcastic, jaded way. Marty expects Ruth to be excited at the news of her upcoming film debut in Hollywood, but instead he is greeted with an indifferent, world-weary "It'll be a change, anyway," a line delivered with such a perfectly calibrated inflection by Day that it borders on the nihilistic. Any form of gratitude from Ruthie would please Marty by this stage of their relationship, but all he hears is a sarcastic "What d'ya want—a thank-you note?" Ruth finally expresses happiness when Johnny calls her—they will be reunited professionally on the upcoming movie—but for all of her toughness, she is afraid to continue speaking on the phone when Marty comes back into the room. In lines worthy of an explosive drama, Ruth and Marty go at it hammer and tongs:

Ruth (with loathing): Who are you, Marty?
Marty: Whoever I am, I'm what makes you tick.

Happy to be reunited with Johnny, Ruth still won't let him into her life: "I'll make a deal with you, Johnny—I won't tell you my sad stories and you won't tell me yours." Day is right on the money with her delivery here; there is no melodrama, no crying in her drink, just a clear-eyed acknowledgment of the bargains she has made with the devil. Has a musical biography ever contained so many literate adult lines? Very few, if any, have achieved this sustained level of excellence, and certainly no others have featured two Hollywood legends at the very peak of their form.

As the film spins forward to its climax, it becomes apparent that the scenes set in Hollywood lack the grit and texture of the atmospheric Chicago and New York scenes that opened the film. Just when the tension should be peaking because of the reintroduction of Johnny—the third part of the love triangle—it lessens. The film doesn't turn bad, in fact far from it, but in dramatic terms it loses steam. Fortunately, musically speaking the movie remains first rate, and the songs beautifully reflect Ruthie's torment—witness "I'll Never Stop Loving You," which Ruth sings in rehearsal with Johnny, delivering the song as a release of her true feelings. It's a great song, but the viewer once again experiences a sense of frustration as Day's vocal is undercut by the camera pulling away for long shots. Day is better served by "Never Look Back," a recording-session torch song that finds Ruth confessing, "If you look around, you may see my broken heart." This character-defining song contains a vocal so compelling that the resulting single spent nineteen weeks on the U.S. charts.

All of these ballads are fully developed songs that not only please the audience but simultaneously propel the story forward. It is also of note that seventeen years before Bob Fosse's landmark film *Cabaret, Love Me or Leave Me* registers as a full-scale musical in which every single number arises out of a backstage performance setting, a concept that was groundbreaking at the time. It is one reason why audiences fifty years later can still respond so strongly to the film—these are not characters breaking into song for no discernible reason. Each song arises out of a realistic show-business setting, a stylistic demand that film audiences in the twenty-first century demand in order to accept the artificially heightened reality of the musical genre.

The final portion of *Love Me or Leave Me* finds Marty Snyder buying a nightclub in order to make a success on his own and prove his worth. After Marty tries to get Johnny fired, he hits Ruth, an action which finally pushes her to the breaking point—she wants a divorce. At long last, is it happily-ever-after time? Not in this musical, not by a long shot. Telling Johnny that she loves him, Ruth kisses him, which prompts Marty to shoot him. Marty is eventually let out of jail on bail, but he can't open the club—he has run out of money. Ruth agrees to sing at the club's opening in order to give Marty back his pride and self-respect, and in a ruefully self-aware acknowledgment states, "I didn't want him to help me, but I took it." Realizing she owes Marty a great deal, Ruth sings "Love Me or Leave Me" as the film concludes.

It's a terrific song, a true standard, but once again Vidor elects to shoot the entire number at a distance, a decision that not only lessens the effect of what should be a first-rate musical and dramatic finale but is also emblematic of the film as a whole: numerous moments of greatness mixed with frustration at what could have been. What there was no doubt about, however, was that Doris Day had arrived as a first-rate dramatic actress. As the *Hollywood Reporter*'s review of her performance stated so memorably, "Miss Day comes through as a subtle and sure emotional actress . . . she makes every sullen glance, every cautious smile and every murmured commonplace phrase speak volumes. A great popular star has become a great actress." Indeed.

Day followed up this triumph with the single best performance she ever gave on film, in Alfred Hitchcock's *The Man Who Knew Too Much,* a 1956 remake of his 1934 film of the same name. With a taut screenplay by John Michael Hayes, cinematography by Robert Burks, a first-rate score by the great Bernard Hermann, and the master himself directing one of his certifiable masterpieces, *The Man Who Knew Too Much* represents a triumph on every level, a fact borne out by its successful 1984 theatrical reissue.

The plot of *The Man Who Knew Too Much* revolves around American Dr. Ben McKenna (James Stewart), his wife Jo, a former Broadway singing star (Day), and their son Hank (Christopher Olsen). Vacationing in French Morocco, they meet a Frenchman, Louis Bernard (Daniel Gelin), and a friendly-seeming English couple, the Draytons (Brenda de Banzie and Bernard Miles). Bernard, an intelligence agent, is stabbed in the market the next day, and as he dies he tells Ben that a political figure will be assassinated in London. Concurrently, the Draytons kidnap Hank before Ben is able to tell the police about the assassination plot. Following the kidnappers back to London, Ben and Jo thwart the assassination attempt and ultimately rescue their son.

Such an abbreviated recitation of the plot elements cannot begin to suggest the layers of terror and psychological depth that Hitchcock and his stars bring to this material. This is filmmaking at its finest. For starters, Hitchcock turns audience expectations regarding his stars upside down. Doris Day and James Stewart—those two icons of middle American normalcy, stalwarts of can-do optimism—who could make a better married couple? Plenty of people, it turns out, because right from their first scene together, the McKennas bicker. Isn't this the all-American girl who loves her man unquestionably? Not here she isn't. Turns out that Jo McKenna is miffed that her Broadway career was cut short when Ben refused to practice medicine in New York. This may be the very reason why Jo seems unnaturally attached to son Hank. Her maternal devotion verges on the smothering, and if the child is the compensation for giving up her career, it is no accident that while walking in the market she pointedly asks her husband, "When are we going to have another child?" Day and Stewart are so in sync as performers that their speech patterns blend right in with each other. Their verbal jousting sounds like that of a real married couple—an incipient squabble leads Jo to bluntly ask her husband, "Are we about to have our monthly fight?"

Hitchcock also proves highly adept at utilizing the tightly wound quality inherent in many of Day's performances. Up until this point in her career, this quality manifested itself most prominently in the nearly manic "up" behavior she exhibited in her brightest musical moments. Although Day never faltered in performing ballads on film, she did exhibit a marked tendency to oversell some of the production numbers, smiling too brightly as if telling herself and the audience, "We're having good wholesome fun, *right?*" Here, Hitchcock uses this quality to suggest the unhappiness in her marriage and to point out the inadequacies of her behavior: Jo McKenna, that overly devoted mother, is so horrified by the murder of Louis Bernard that she freezes in shock, allowing the Draytons to kidnap her son beneath her very own eyes.

There are many famous Hitchcock set pieces in the film: the murder of Louis Bernard in the bazaar, Ben's frenzied—and mistaken—belief that the Ambrose Chappell taxidermy shop is where his son is being held, and most important of all, two sequences featuring Doris Day: the first a scene in which James Stewart forces her to take medication, and the second an extraordinary twelve-minute climactic episode at Royal Albert Hall that culminates in the assassination attempt.

The sequence where Ben forces wife Jo to take sedatives because their son has been kidnapped stands out as the single best piece of acting Doris Day ever performed. Period. It is also as good a depiction of complicated maternal anguish as has ever been committed to film. The sequence begins when, before telling Jo the news that Hank has been kidnapped, Ben asks Jo to take some pills in order to relax. Jo replies, "You used to tell me I took too many pills—now you tell me to take them." (Yet again, the hints that all is not blissful in the McKenna marriage.) As the sedatives start to take effect, Ben breaks the news to Jo that Hank has been kidnapped. Horror rising within her, Jo cannot fully express her anguish because the pills have begun their work. Crying over the loss of her son, angry at her husband for his duplicity and his infantilizing treatment of her, Jo wants to rush out and find her child. Her husband restraining her, Jo collapses into a tear-filled stupor as the full strength of the medication takes hold. In running the gamut of emotions, Doris Day does not hit one false note—with her entirely believable line readings, her body language changing from brisk and forthright to defenseless terror, she is superb. It is no wonder that when Doris Day complained to Alfred Hitchcock that she was frustrated by his utter lack of direction, he simply replied, "You have been doing what I felt was right for the film and that's why I haven't told you anything."

Speaking of this sequence years later, Day offered a fascinating glimpse into both her actual preparation for this harrowing scene and her extraordinary self-confidence (it's never bragging with her; in fact she seems to assume—oh so wrongly—that the ability to access these deep wellsprings of natural talent is something that everyone possesses). Day's technique entailed rehearsing the entire scene—dialogue and action—"in my head, which is the only place I like to rehearse." The necessary blocking rehearsal for the camera then found Day walking through the set-up with Stewart while "covering our action with a running monologue" as to action, position, and emotion. As to the extraordinary emotional demands placed upon her as an actress portraying a mother whose son has been kidnapped: ". . . whatever I really need—not want but need—will be there . . . that scene seemed very real to me. I actually experienced losing my little son to a kidnapper." Whether speaking of such specific acting demands or of her career in general, Day genuinely seems to believe, in her own words, "If I can do it, you can do it. Anyone can do it." To which the only possible retort is, "It ain't that easy." Only a talent of the highest caliber could access such complex, powerful emotions for one of the world's best and most famously demanding directors, but in Doris Day's worldview, she isn't doing anything unusual. Fascinating. And wrong.

The second extraordinary scene takes place at the film's climax in Royal Albert Hall. Hitchcock here constructs a twelve-minute sequence without dialogue that culminates in the assassination attempt. Just as in the sequence where Ben forces Jo to take drugs, Hitchcock here ratchets up the tension by

The Man Who Knew Too Much. Conferring with director Alfred Hitchcock. She thought his lack of direction meant he wasn't pleased. *Photofest*

use of camera angles and constant crosscutting between the actors; the tension increases because in both sequences the audience is anxiously anticipating Jo's reaction. Without any spoken words, Doris Day must communicate Jo McKenna's mounting hysteria: a mother's overwhelming primal need to save her child conflicting with her knowledge that a politician may be assassinated, the knowledge that disaster is imminent and that she is near and yet so far from helping—she communicates every last one of these necessary components without one word of dialogue. Her face registering utter terror as she spots the assassin and realizes who his target is, Jo's abject fear finally explodes into a piercing scream that startles the assembled throng and causes the assassin to miss his target. This sequence alone should have guaranteed Day an Academy Award for Best Actress; she wasn't even nominated.

The Albert Hall assassination attempt sequence provides the climax of the film, but *The Man Who Knew Too Much* actually concludes with the rescue of

The harrowing concert hall sequence at the end of *The Man Who Knew Too Much*. *Photofest*

son Hank at the foreign embassy. The use of the song "Que Sera, Sera" to bring about Hank's rescue proves to be a particularly effective tool. Hitchcock has set up the use of the song by an earlier sequence in the movie where smothering mother Jo teaches Hank the song and has him dance with her. This catchy novelty tune lodges in the listener's brain immediately, so the audience is instantly able to recall the tune when Jo, playing the piano and singing the song very loudly, thereby transmits the fact of her presence in the building to her son Hank, who is being held captive upstairs. In another dig at the McKennas' marriage, Hitchcock makes sure that it is Jo's talent for the career she had to give up that ultimately saves her child. When viewing this sequence today, audiences can't help but react with the knowledge that the song ultimately became Doris Day's theme song, a gold-record Academy Award–winning tune that espoused her personal philosophy in life: whatever will be, will be. In 1956, however, what audiences realized was that Jo McKenna's reaction to her son's abduction was the exact opposite of the philosophy espoused in the song. Jo McKenna is a woman terrorized into forceful action, and one realizes that this is a return to the assertive personality she surely must have displayed as a Broadway star.

Shortly after the career high point of *The Man Who Knew Too Much,* Day filmed the 1956 black-and-white MGM release *Julie.* In the Day canon, the movie is notable for three reasons. First, the film marked the solo producing debut of husband Marty Melcher, a role he would assume with increasing frequency on her future films, with very mixed results. Most noteworthy in this regard, it was at this point that Melcher began his business relationship with Jerome Rosenthal in earnest, working closely with Rosenthal on contracts and tax shelters. It was a relationship that would prove disastrous for Melcher, seemingly causing him to lose his health when the extent of Rosenthal's duplicity became clear. The Melcher-Rosenthal relationship also was catastrophic for Doris herself, in both personal and professional terms. On a personal level, Day lost all of her money, millions of dollars, because of Rosenthal's investments. Professionally speaking, in order to fund Rosenthal's business "ventures," Melcher, in his role as husband and agent, began signing Doris to second-rate vehicles without obtaining her consent. When this practice became rampant in the mid- to late 1960s, it completely derailed Day's feature film career. Of Melcher's role as both husband and agent, Day has said, "I wanted to be with other agencies. They had so many good writers, producers and directors and I wanted to be a part of one of those great projects. I'd say 'I want to be with so and so' and Marty would say 'No, you're with me and that's it . . .' I really felt I should have had another agent—not my husband. It really is not good for a relationship. The romance goes out the window when you suddenly feel you're married to your father."

Second, the filming of *Julie* proved extremely upsetting to Day because the character of abusive husband Lyle Benton (played by Louis Jourdan) reminded her of her abusive first husband, Al Jorden (not to mention the "bizarre jealousy" of former agent Al Levy, and second husband George Weidler's jealousy of her career). As a result of the terror Day often experienced while filming *Julie,* only one other movie in her career, *Midnight Lace,* would ever be structured around a similarly dark theme.

Third, Day felt ill throughout much of the filming and began to hemorrhage quite badly. With her Christian Science beliefs, Day vacillated about consulting a doctor, especially because Marty, who by now was an even more ardent Christian Scientist than Day herself, insisted that she follow Christian Science precepts and in effect cure herself by a strict interpretation of mind over matter. It was only after filming was completed that she returned to her doctor in Beverly Hills and was immediately admitted to the hospital for the removal of a large tumor. A hysterectomy ensued, leaving Day upset that she could never bear another child.

Any one of these factors would have been enough to leave a sour taste in Day's mouth, let alone all three. That sour taste can only be heightened by a full consideration of the finished film, because regrettably, the movie looks and plays like a B movie that just happens to have been shot with an A-list star front and center. A-list star notwithstanding, the result is a grade-Z film.

The true auteur of *Julie* was writer-director Andrew L. Stone, who, with his editor wife Virginia, turned out a series of small-budget films shot on location in the 1950s. (In this case, filming took place on the Monterey coast, a fact of interest because the location shooting introduced Doris to the area where she would ultimately settle in 1981 for the rest of her life.) Stone's B-movie origins are evident from the very first scene: The film bolts out of the gate with Day's character, Julie Benton, striding out to the parking lot of a country club while chastising husband Lyle (Louis Jourdan) for his obsessive jealousy. They hop into their car, and as Julie drives the auto down a winding cliffside road, Lyle slams his foot onto the accelerator, nearly killing them both in the process. In the classic pattern of abusive spouses, he then apologizes profusely and the film is off and running—often literally. The audience knows right away that Lyle may be a concert pianist, but he's also a wacko. Julie's in trouble. Big trouble.

Starting on this note of hysteria, in true B-movie fashion the film only accelerates. No meandering character exploration here, no attempt to explain Lyle's motivations, and certainly no attempt at setting up a mystery about who is terrorizing Julie. It's crazy husband Lyle, end of story, and the audience knows this from the very first scene. Julie narrates the movie in voice-over flashback, explaining that her first husband committed suicide, a suicide that new husband Lyle does not want her to investigate any further. And, it turns out, with good reason: He's the one who secretly shot Julie's husband and, with the playing field clear, then married her himself. Confessing the crime to Julie at night when they're in bed (!), he warns her, "Don't ever try to leave me." Every time Julie takes off at a run to escape Lyle—and it happens so often that one begins to wonder if Doris is in training for the marathon running she'll undertake in *It Happened to Jane*—overwrought music comprised of thundering piano scales is heard. Just to complete the picture, in true 1950s fashion, Julie appears to be accessorized for each of these runs with both handbag and high heels. She first runs to the police, who don't believe her, and then collapses in the arms of family friend Cliff Henderson (Barry Sullivan). Escaping to San Francisco, Julie is once again found by Lyle, who calls to tell her that she will die, leaving her a tape-recorded message of his "love" for her and a message composed of—what else—thundering piano music.

The plot twists exert their own peculiar B-movie fascination as Julie now tries to escape Lyle by returning to her job as a flight attendant. Her reentry into the job world proves to be no problem at all—make one phone call and presto, you get your old job back the very same day. Good thing too, because Cliff has been shot by Lyle so Julie's now completely on her own. It is at this point in the movie that logic appears to completely fly out the window; by now everyone knows that Lyle is a killer but he encounters absolutely no problem sneaking onboard Julie's flight in order to murder her. At the airport, no one asks Lyle, "Hey, who are you?" or "Where did you come from?" or even the old tried-and-true, "Where's your ticket?" Lyle just plops into an empty seat, and soon enough he shoots the pilot *and* the copilot and then collapses from the gunshot wound he himself receives. The captain's dead, a psychopath is onboard, the passengers are terrorized, and the copilot keeps losing consciousness from his gunshot wound; in other words, there's only one solution—Julie has to fly the plane herself (and everyone thought *Airport 1975* wrote the book on flight attendants who pinch-hit as pilots . . .).

It's up to the copilot to coach Julie on how to land a plane, but first they engage in dialogue that is right out of *42nd Street,* when young chorus girl Peggy Sawyer takes over for the star. Just substitute a ten-ton jet airplane for a tricky tap routine and a new star is about to be born:

Julie: I can't do it.
Copilot: But you must.

Lickety-split Julie's behind the wheel like it's opening night on Broadway. At times the dialogue proves downright, if unintentionally, hilarious: when the copilot coaches Julie on how to fly the plane with cries of "That's right, Julie!" or "That's too much!" it sounds like nothing so much as him barking out orders while they're having sex.

The film ends with genuinely exciting footage of Julie landing the plane, but it's a case of too little, too late. The footage, shot from the pilot's perspective, is visually stunning, hooking the viewer with a verisimilitude lacking in so many other parts of the script, namely the beginning, the middle, and the end. To wit: The plane has landed, Julie has saved hundreds of lives, and how does the film depict the aftermath of this action-packed finale? The police detective in the control tower intones, "I wouldn't go through that again." Huh? What do you suppose Julie's thinking? *She's* the one who just landed the plane. There's a close-up of Julie looking relieved, and that's it. In true B-movie fashion, there's no wrap-up. The movie just ends. "Gee," an audience member wonders, "maybe, just maybe, Julie's thinking, 'I just landed a plane even though I'm not a pilot. The captain's dead, my husband tried to kill me and he's dead on the floor right behind me.'" But no—evidently everything's hunky-dory now that Julie's an ersatz pilot.

Once again, Day's versatility provides the note of interest here. Her winning brand of no-nonsense practicality, combined with more than a touch of vulnerability, makes one almost believe Julie is really flying the plane. It is hard to picture any other screen queen of the time, with the exceptions of Katharine Hepburn and Barbara Stanwyck, proving to be this competent. Piloting airplanes is not the province of a Marilyn Monroe or Audrey Hepburn. (Of course this being the '50s, the flight controllers coaching Julie on how to fly the plane call her "honey" and "girl.")

It is also significant that Day undertook flying lessons to prepare for the role; having developed a fear of flying during the extensive and often hazardous air travel she suffered through on her barnstorming radio tour with Bob Hope in the late 1940s, these lessons solidified her fear of flying. It's a fear that had numerous career ramifications, influencing everything from choice of roles (she almost pulled out of *The Man Who Knew Too Much* and turned down other roles that would have required travel) to declining honors that would require her to fly to the ceremony. The fear Julie exhibits onscreen is palpable not only because Day is an excellent actress but also because for Doris Day the fear of flying is genuine.

Aside from a surfeit of hysterics, Day's performance is assured and believable, but the fear of flying and memories of her own abusive first husband appeared to take their toll: Looking grim throughout, the normally sunshiny Doris Day does not smile once during the entire movie. Yes, the character of Julie fears for her life, but Day's performance is unrelentingly tense throughout. The movie gave further solid evidence of her versatility as an actress, but it is probably best remembered by aficionados for the hit title song that spent ten weeks on the *Billboard* charts (and was nominated for an Academy Award along with, amazingly enough, the *Julie* screenplay). One trek through such

Ludicrous and overblown. *Julie,* 1956. *Photofest*

grim material proved to be more than enough for Day, and she happily and triumphantly reestablished herself on more congenial ground with her next film, 1957's *The Pajama Game.*

After playing a former Broadway singing star in *The Man Who Knew Too Much,* Day starred in the film adaptation of an actual Broadway musical, the smash hit *The Pajama Game.* For the first and only time in her career, Doris Day had the chance to star in a classic musical comedy, and she triumphed. A great musical star finally had musical material worthy of her talents, and the resulting film gives the viewer a good sense of how great she would have been in the role she was born to play, Nellie Forbush in *South Pacific.* If the basic material of *The Pajama Game* is not quite in *South Pacific*'s class—and few musicals are—it is still top notch and represents one of the peaks in Day's film career.

Transferring the smash hit to screen, Warner Bros. retained most of the original Broadway cast: John Raitt, Carol Haney, and Eddie Foy Jr. all made the trip to Hollywood. But perhaps with an eye on the box office, original female lead Janis Paige was replaced by Doris Day, a move which for once reaped multiple dividends. Paige, a talented performer on all counts, is a fine comic presence on film (e.g. *Please Don't Eat the Daisies*), but it is also clear why it's Day who became the film superstar: Her unique and winning combination of self-confidence and feminine vulnerability leaps off the screen. Combine that with one of the great singing voices of the twentieth century, and it's apparent why the choice of Doris to play Babe Williams involved a great deal more than mere box office considerations.

The Pajama Game, surely the only musical comedy in history to be centered on a union strike at a pajama factory, epitomized the brassy self-confident tone of Broadway and the United States in the 1950s. The first-rate Adler/Ross score yielded no fewer than three standards—"Hey There," "Steam Heat," and "Hernando's Hideaway"—and was woven into a story that concerned superintendent Sid Sorokin (John Raitt) clashing with labor union grievance committee head Babe Williams (Day). The instant mutual attraction between Babe and Sid at first manifests itself in verbal jousting, but

Doris as Broadway Baby belting out "I'm Not at All in Love,"
from *The Pajama Game,* 1957. *Photofest*

by the time of the annual company picnic, they have fallen in love. The union wants a seven-and-a-half-cent hourly raise, but when the factory owner refuses to grant it, an employee slowdown ensues. Babe makes her sewing machine short-circuit, causing an electrical blowout, and Sid fires her. Sid then discovers that factory boss Mr. Hassler really has set aside enough money to cover the raise, and when the raise is granted, Babe and Sid are happily reunited.

This was one musical Warner Bros. did not produce on the cheap, and the tech credits, top-notch all the way down the line, result in a downright exhilarating musical: directed and produced by George Abbott and Stanley Donen, screenplay by Abbott and Richard Bissell, cinematography by Harry Stradling, orchestrations by Nelson Riddle and Buddy Bregman, choreography by Bob Fosse—it didn't get better than this in the Hollywood of the 1950s.

Doris Day not only rises to the level of the veteran Broadway cast, who knew this material intimately, but actually pulls them along for the ride on her coattails—that's how assured and musical her performance is. Her very first song, "I'm Not at All in Love," in which she denies her obvious attraction to Sid Sorokin, is delivered in her best Broadway belt voice; beautifully staged by Fosse and Donen, the song not only establishes Babe's no-nonsense business persona, but through her characterization the viewer also realizes the vulnerability underneath the forthright exterior. The number is choreographed with a genuine sense of movement, and as she moves through the factory, stepping onto a hand cart and gliding in perfect synchronicity with the upswing of the music, the film takes off as well, remaining a free-floating delight all the way and faltering only in the last twenty minutes.

This opening solo number of Day's is equaled by her reprise of "Hey There," where her interior monologue turns into a vocal so gently and dramatically sung that the viewer is made totally cognizant of just who Babe Williams is and why she is indeed a character worth caring about. Knowing that she had to cry during the song, and feeling that this song constituted more of a dramatic scene than a song, Doris insisted on recording the vocal live, an unusual occurrence in a Hollywood musical. The gamble paid off. As with Barbra Streisand and her live recording of the "My Man" finale to *Funny Girl,* the ensuing scene and reprise of "Hey There" gain in richness as a result. Day sounds terrific, and her vocal is every bit as good as the hit Rosemary Clooney recording of the same song.

The character of Babe Williams is a three-dimensional woman. She is no pushover, and that's what audiences love about Doris Day—her spunk, sass, and grit. She volunteers to be the target for Hinesy's (Eddie Foy Jr.) knife-throwing act at the company picnic, and when Sid tells her "absolutely not," she defiantly steps up to be the target again. Babe has fallen in love with Sid, but she'll neither give up her union activities nor acquiesce in regard to the strike. Indeed, after Sid confesses his love to Babe, her response is to talk about the seven-and-one-half-cent raise: "Don't treat me like a baby—the union is important to me." Her principles take precedence over her love life, and in this regard the character of Babe Williams presages the independent career woman roles that vaulted Day to the peak of her popularity in the early 1960s.

Babe falls in love with Sid at the company picnic, a sequence complete with the big "Once-a-Year Day" polka production number staged by Fosse, but their love really blossoms with their "Small Talk" duet. In the tight pants and midriff blouse she sports in the film showing off her great figure to full advantage, Doris Day is one very sexy woman. She wants to kiss Sid, just won't kiss him until after her father leaves the room. She is no coy virgin, and their "Small Talk" counterpoint duet is melodic and erotic at the same time.

Babe and Sid's love is fully unleashed with the exuberant "There Once Was a Man" duet, in which they loudly proclaim their love for each other to the skies above (and to anyone within a fifty-mile radius). As the two stars belt it out side by side, it is interesting to note the differences between Day and John Raitt, and why Raitt, for all of his talents, never became a film star. Raitt is handsome and masculine, and has a great voice, but he is very stiff on camera, hunching his shoulders and acting vaguely ill at ease, as if he's always looking for the camera in order to make sure he'll hit his marks. Day, by contrast, has all of the necessary physical attributes, and one further not so incidental asset—she is totally at ease in front of the camera, her body fluid and relaxed. Doris Day enjoys singing and acting for the camera, and that comes through on screen—the audience responds instinctively to her enjoyment. The exhilaration that Day felt on camera shows up in one form or another in virtually all of her films but is especially apparent here in *The Pajama Game.*

With such a brilliant first two-thirds of the film, where music, acting, choreography, cinematography, and art direction all blend together to tell a coherent, tuneful story, it is a decided disappointment when the final one-third eases off considerably. Carol Haney spends too much screen time screaming at her jealous boyfriend Hinesy about his knife throwing, indeed screeching at seemingly anyone in her path. Additionally, in structural terms, tuneful as both "Steam Heat" and "Hernando's Hideaway" are, they serve no actual story purpose. "Steam Heat," especially, features terrific, quintessential Bob

Fosse choreography—all hunched shoulders and knocked knees—but neither number advances the plot or arises organically from the script.

These are small quibbles, however, because thanks to Doris Day and company, *The Pajama Game* fully registers as an exuberant, fun-filled movie, ranking just below the top echelon of the very best musicals. Although a success, the film was only a minor hit, and Day and husband Marty Melcher now faced a big problem: With musicals falling out of favor, how was Doris going to maintain her stardom? How could she equal, let alone top, the fact that three of her last four movies had been excellent, featuring Day at the very top of her form? The answer to these questions was to come two years later from a very surprising direction, but in the meantime, Day signed on to make what turned out to be one of the best films of her entire career: 1958's black-and-white Paramount release *Teacher's Pet.* This film proved to be an out-and-out winner, from the catchy title song (which rode high on the charts) to the witty screenplay by Fay and Michael Kanin. Best of all, Doris Day and top-billed Clark Gable made a terrific team: the all-American girl next door and the King of Hollywood—who'd a thunk it?

Right from the start, the film sets up a nice clash of opposites, with journalism professor E. R. (Erica) Stone (Doris Day) and city editor James Gannon (Gable) verbally and physically jousting over the relative values of classroom knowledge versus real-life experience in the newspaper world. Gannon, enrolling in Professor Stone's class under a false name (James Gallagher), pretends to be a neophyte journalism student. Quickly knocking out professional-quality stories, Gannon impresses Professor Stone as a student of unusual promise. Despite, or maybe because of, their diametrically opposed views of journalism, Gannon and Stone are attracted to each other. This attraction is complicated by Gannon's lie about his identity, and by both Erica's involvement with know-it-all psychiatrist Dr. Hugo Pine (Gig Young), and Gannon's girlfriend, bombshell nightclub "entertainer" Miss Peggy DeFore (Mamie Van Doren). Crushed to find out that Gannon has deceived her, Erica cannot discount their strong mutual attraction, and at film's end, both Erica and James acknowledge that each has much to learn from the other.

What makes *Teacher's Pet* so much fun to view nearly fifty years after its initial release is that this battle of the sexes takes place between two equally successful professionals and in realistic workplace settings. Gable, sporting a battered fedora, presents the very picture of the hard-drinking, seen-it-all city newspaperman. Cigarette perpetually dangling from his mouth, this self-made man is proud of never having attended high school, let alone any "cockamamie university." Day, outfitted in a tight 1950s-style skirt (which shows off her terrific body) and a short no-nonsense hairstyle, is coolly authoritative as a journalism professor, and here continues the string of first-rate understated performances that began with *Love Me or Leave Me.* Day's work here is light-years beyond the broad stylings found in her Warner Bros. contract efforts, proof that she had evolved into the most versatile A-list female actress in Hollywood.

The enjoyably hostile relationship between Day and Gable is made clear in their very first exchange regarding the correct attribution of a quotation—was it Kipling or Emerson? This literate dialogue is quietly charged, and the attraction between the two is obvious, but the antagonism is even more overt. What makes it fun for the viewer is that Day matches Gable every step of the way. When Gannon point-blank asks her, "How do you feel about sex?" far from flinching, she instantly retorts, "Well, I'm all for it." The perpetual virgin? Not here, not by a long shot. Just before Gannon stalks out of Erica's office in anger and disgust, he plants a long, lingering kiss on her, a kiss that

Terrific pairing with Clark Gable in *Teacher's Pet. Photofest*

results in a classic bit of comic acting from Day. Gable strides out of the room, and Day gathers up her papers; it is only at this point that her delayed reaction to the kiss sets in: She trips, stumbles, clutches her stomach, blows the hair off her face, and in the end has to resort to fanning herself. This woman has been kissed—and how.

This battle of the sexes is also a battle of ideas. Along the way there are telling observations about the role of newspapers, Gannon emphasizing that the public must be told *why* something happened: "The man on the street is a lot more curious than people think." Line after line contains not only comic zingers but truly thoughtful analysis about newspapers and the obligation to inform the public.

Director George Seaton keeps things moving along at an appropriately fast-paced clip, a pace that aids the viewer's pleasure when the film's two key supporting characters are introduced: Erica's boyfriend, Dr. Hugo Pine, and Gannon's girlfriend, Miss Peggy DeFore. The shallow attractions of Hugo and Peggy are obvious, but since the viewer is miles ahead and knows how wrong these two are for Day and Gable, the fun comes in discovering exactly how their unsuitability will be revealed. In the nightclub sequence where all four characters interact—and then some—Hugo, a handsome renowned author, war hero, and doctor who speaks seven languages, is revealed as being simply too good to be true. The viewer is happy that Gannon, in his escalating attempts to secure Erica's favor and show up the seemingly perfect Hugo, has bribed the waiter to make Hugo's drinks triple strength. It's even better that Hugo's drunken reaction to the mind-boggling succession of triples is delayed until the very end of the sequence. (The viewer may also be doubly glad just to have Hugo vanish. Young may have been Oscar nominated for his performance, but his mugging antics contrast unfavorably with the crisp style of the two leads.)

Similarly, the hilariously inept and obvious Miss DeFore serves only to make any red-blooded male—or discerning female—realize how much more alluring the more subtle Erica actually is. Gannon refers to Peggy DeFore as "very talented—talented and unassuming," and Peggy herself, not exactly a candidate for Mensa, further opines, "Where would I be if I just read books?" Good question, Miss DeFore. As Gannon drinks to hide his embarrassment at having Erica and Hugo discover just how "talented and unassuming" his pal Miss DeFore really is, the stakes escalate. Gannon and Pine continue their game of one-upsmanship to impress Erica, but it's a game Hugo wins every time. Gable can't mambo to the nightclub band's rhythm, but Hugo can—expertly. Hugo didn't just serve in the war—he was a decorated war hero. Anything Gannon can do, Hugo can do better—much better. Erica, for her part, hopes to make Gannon jealous, and in order to ensure that he sees her dancing with Hugo, mambos her wiggling rear end surprisingly close to Gannon's face. To up the ante even more, this mambo is, well, nothing compared to Miss DeFore's bump-and-grind performance of "The Girl Who Invented Rock and Roll." In this deliberately tacky—and very funny—musical sequence, there is some stellar comic acting from Doris as she reacts to Peggy DeFore. Eyeballing Miss DeFore in disbelief, Day never topples into the land of triple takes that would mar some of her '60s sex-comedy work; her incredulous reactions to the burlesque-sounding rim shots that underscore Miss DeFore's undulations cause the audience to laugh, and Gable/Gannon to sweat. A lot.

Following this dance lesson, as Erica and James ride in a cab back to Erica's apartment—Hugo having passed out and Miss DeFore undoubtedly on her way to the library for some late-night studying—they share their first mutually desired kiss; murmuring about the necessity of maintaining the all-important teacher/student relationship, they kiss again at Erica's apartment. There are real sparks here and the atmosphere is heady with the promise of sex. In fact, it is no surprise to read in Day's autobiography how thoroughly she responded to Gable's no-nonsense masculinity; that real-life reaction definitely translated onto film.

Best of all, when Erica and James return to the apartment, Erica playfully launches into a hilarious parody of "The Girl Who Invented Rock and Roll." Of course the real punchline here is that Doris Day, with her seductive singing voice, natural dance ability, and sensational figure, is far sexier than blatant sexpot Mamie Van Doren ever could be. It takes only the twenty-five seconds of this parody for every last man and woman to realize who the real sexy dame is here. Back to the library, Miss DeFore.

Day equals this inspired comic business with the genuine hurt she displays upon learning that Gannon is an imposter. There are no hysterics as she confronts him, just a quiet to-the-core wound at having been deceived: "I'm not angry—just hurt, like I've been kicked. . . . You're ignorant and proud of it, and that makes you stupid." This is terrific, true-to-life adult dialogue, as true today as it was fifty years ago. When Erica and James make up, it is with a sense that they are true equals; she acknowledges having been in a rut, giving the same tired lectures over and over, and he recognizes the need for a newspaper to run the interpretative think pieces she so favors. Together they come to agree that "Experience is the jockey and education is the horse." This truly coequal partnership is one an audience member really thinks will last, and the viewer is left wishing that the Day-Gable partnership had as well.

Unfortunately, Day's next film, 1958's *The Tunnel of Love,* is a different sort of winner—it wins the award as the worst film of Day's entire career. It may have some stiff competition from *Where Were You When the Lights Went Out?* but the puerile, juvenile tone in *Tunnel of Love* ensures that it takes home the booby prize.

The truly offensive plot of the film, written by Joseph Fields and based on the play he wrote with Peter De Vries, finds Isolde and Augie Poole (Day and Richard Widmark) desperately trying to conceive a child. When their efforts prove futile, they turn to adoption and are paid a home visit by the adoption agency's caseworker, Estelle Novick (Gia Scala). Augie creates a bad impression, so he makes up for it by taking Ms. Novick out to dinner (evidently the fact that he's married doesn't present a problem . . .). Waking up alone in a motel the next day, Augie subsequently comes to believe that his one-night dalliance resulted in his fathering a child with Ms. Novick, the very child he has adopted with wife Isolde. When Isolde ultimately learns that Augie did not cheat on her, the Pooles reconcile and Isolde soon becomes pregnant herself.

Right from the start, the film exudes all the energy of a deflated balloon. In fact, the only pep in the entire proceedings is provided by the bouncy title song, which Doris Day sings over the credits. The song doesn't have much to do with what follows, and while it may be enjoyable as long as one doesn't listen too closely to the lyrics, it's actually symptomatic of the mess that is to follow—nothing in the film really makes any sense. Right off the bat, it's clear that any thinking audience will find lead character Augie Poole to be an offensive dolt. He is a struggling artist who is able to move from Greenwich Village to tony Westport, Connecticut, only by living off of Isolde's inheritance from her grandmother. This sponging off of his wife is not exactly a recipe for sympathy or audience identification; when, at the film's end, we're supposed to accept that it was Augie's inability either to sell his drawings or have a child that caused him to drink, pop pills, and ask the adoption agency social worker out for a date, the audience response is not one of understanding, but rather, "Get lost, you creep."

In fact, it is hard to choose the most offensive aspect of the film, so numerous are the candidates. For starters, it is assumed that a couple trying desperately to have a child is a source of hilarity. Never mind the heartache all such couples endure; here the problem is dealt with by calling up the Rockabye Agency where the Rockwells "got theirs." In other words, a baby is discussed in the exact same terms as buying a television set. Similarly, when agency worker Ms. MacCracken (who has replaced the pregnant Ms. Novick) tells

Augie that he and Isolde have been approved as parents, she laughs hysterically and brightly trills, "There's a tremendous demand for our little ones and a very small supply." This statement manages to be offensive to adoptive parents as well as to the adoptees themselves and makes Ms. MacCracken sound like she's selling cosmetics, not caring for a human being.

When Ms. Novick checks on the Pooles, it's not just that Doris Day is clad in a Brownie troop leader uniform and Richard Widmark is dressed only in his underwear. It's that best friend Gig Young's (Dick Pepper) idea of turning around Augie's disastrous interview with Ms. Novick is to make a pass at her. Subsequently, when Ms. Novick comes back to the Pooles' to apologize for her part in the unpleasant tone of the previous visit, she wears, what else, a low-cut evening gown—evidently standard garb for all social workers—and asks for a drink even though it's still the afternoon. For his part, married man Augie asks her for a date and she of course says yes. It's a wonder that the National Association of Social Workers didn't sue MGM for slander. Such boorishness is topped when Augie and Ms. Novick go out for their "date" and Augie pops two tranquilizers during their car ride; even a nincompoop wouldn't behave in this fashion while out with the adoption agency social worker. Then again, even a nincompoop wouldn't have asked the social worker out on a date to begin with. This isn't humorous, it's just plain stupid. After Augie wakes up alone in the motel and finds his way home, there isn't a scene of wife Isolde's outraged reaction. Doesn't it seem likely that Doris may have said something to her husband, something along the lines of, "Where the hell were you last night?" But nope—Augie thinks the baby Ms. Novick will have is his, gives her a check to help her out financially, and accepts the fact that she's off to the Australian archipelago. Of course.

The entire movie appears to have been shot on a budget of $12.95 and its stage origins are glaringly apparent in the very talky screenplay. For all intents and purposes, there is only one set, an amazingly artificial-looking rendering of suburban Westport, Connecticut. Come to think of it, the Westport Chamber of Commerce should have joined the National Association of Social Workers in a joint lawsuit; according to this film, the town appears to be populated by drunken leches whose idea of parenting is exemplified by Gig Young's screaming at his own children, "Shut up, or I'll send you to reform school." (It's no surprise that Gig Young's character, who is a walking mass of inappropriate behavior, launches into a diatribe against that tried-and-true Hollywood bogeyman, the psychiatrist. Dick Pepper needs some heavy-duty analysis, but in the filmmakers' view, he's a charming fellow, and it's the psychiatrists who need help.)

For the first time in her film career, Doris Day registers as nothing more than a cipher. The action is propelled forward by Widmark and Young, and Day is given nothing to do. Her straight-ahead style of acting is ill matched with that of the usually terrific Widmark, or rather is ill matched given the juvenile level of the situations exploited herein. Isolde Poole may claim "I'm dead tired," but the bounce in Doris Day's walk proclaims otherwise, and the contrast with Widmark, who is called upon to mope and whine from sexual tiredness, makes their pairing even more inappropriate.

Isolde Poole is a passive character, and Doris Day without her drive and energy is not a particularly compelling screen figure. Maybe if Day had been willing to explore the darker side of Isolde's character—the pain of not having children in a land where such inability means you aren't considered "normal," the stifling conformity of social expectations in the '50s, well, that might have made for an interesting character study. Then again, that would have been an entirely different film, very possibly one whose dark roots Day would not have been comfortable exploring.

As it is, the filmmakers clearly find the basic premise of a woman's inability to conceive to be funny. In reality, as even a young adult would know, the overwhelming desire to start a family can be heartbreaking. It certainly shouldn't rate as the source of smarmy humor. This "humor" is leeringly underlined by the fecund nature of Dick and Alice Pepper's marriage—five children and counting. In real life, Augie and Isolde Poole probably would have found their proximity to the Peppers a painful reminder of what they lacked, but in *The Tunnel of Love,* the Peppers' proximity is presented as a source of amusement.

Yes, there are laughs in the movie, but they are all inadvertent. Augie and Isolde constantly call their doctor and are able to get him on the phone instantly. Evidently gynecologists in Westport spend all of their time anxiously waiting by the phone for their patients to call. Augie and Isolde must make love constantly in their quest to have a child, but according to the MGM set decorators, they sleep in twin beds. Silliest of all is the sequence in which the Peppers throw a party for Isolde and Augie, a party celebrating a child they haven't even been told they will definitely be able to adopt. During this sequence, Doris literally skips next door to the party wearing a mink wrap, and when it's clear that a neighborhood sexpot has her eye on Augie, how do the screenwriters have Doris deal with the dilemma? She sings "Run Away, Skidaddle, Skidoo" to her husband as they dance at the party. The mind boggles.

There is exactly one moment of interest in the film and it is the darkest; the Pooles have adopted their baby boy, but Isolde, fed up with Augie's prevaricating, and suspecting that their son is really Augie's child by Ms. Novick, explodes at her husband, "I'm sick of you, Westport, and everybody in it." There is genuine anger in her delivery, and it is a sentiment undoubtedly echoed by anyone who has been forced to sit through the film.

The movie then ends on perhaps the most offensive note of all: Now that the Pooles have reconciled and have their baby boy, Isolde actually becomes pregnant. It's not the utter predictability of this plot twist that grates as much as the unspoken message it sends: Now the Pooles can have a "real" child. Awful.

One key question remains at the end of the film: Why did anyone involved want to make this movie? Doris Day, Richard Widmark, and Gene Kelly were all at the height of their powers in 1958 and surely had their pick of dozens of possible properties. Kelly, who could be a terrific director of musicals, has here made a film that forms an unbecoming bookend with his 1967 *A Guide for the Married Man:* Both films share the unfortunate underpinning of finding a husband's infidelity an occasion for hijinks and all-around good fun. For her part, Day's involvement stemmed from husband Marty Melcher's status as the film's coproducer. Perhaps the only charitable assessment is to point out that husband and wife would make better choices in the future.

Fortunately, the leering *Tunnel of Love* was followed by the charming 1959 comedy *It Happened to Jane,* costarring Jack Lemmon. Directed and produced by Richard Quine, with a screenplay by Norman Katkow, and beautifully photographed by Charles Lawton Jr., *It Happened to Jane* presents a Capraesque vision of small-town America. In this idealized America, one individual—here it is Day, in the role Jimmy Stewart would essay in a Capra film—can bring an entire corporation to its knees, raise two sons, find love, and remain true to herself. Such is an audience's sense of Day's individuality that the viewer never doubts that Doris is up to the task. And, needless to say, with energy to spare.

It Happened to Jane centers on young widow Jane Boyd Osgood (Day) and the mail-order lobster business she runs in her small home town of Cape Ann, Maine (Chester, Connecticut, doubled as Maine for the purposes of filming). When the Eastern and Portland railroad delays a delivery, her lobsters perish, and Jane sues the giant railroad concern (presided over by a cigar-chomping Ernie Kovacs, in the role of Harry Foster Malone). When Jane levies execution on one of the E&P trains, the ensuing nationwide publicity is a bonanza for her—not to mention garnering her a new beau, newspaperman Larry Hall (Steve Forrest). Temporarily sidelined by the Cape Ann citizens, who feel that she has placed her own interests above those of the town, Jane is saved by boyfriend George (Jack Lemmon), the Democratic candidate for first selectman. Impassionedly defending Jane at a town meeting, George wins the townspeople over, helps Jane overcome Malone's nefarious train rerouting plan, is elected for the very first time, and proposes marriage to Jane. Faced with this beehive of activity, the viewer is left with only one reaction: Who knew these small New England towns were busier than Times Square at rush hour?

This movie may start with the obligatory—and here rather insipid—title tune sung by Doris, but after that, it takes off at a run and never stops. Or, more precisely, Doris Day takes off at a run. Day spends the first half hour of the movie running—and truth to tell, she looks pretty damn fast. She chases after cars, children, costars, you name it. It is hard to imagine any other 1950s movie queen being this athletic. Elizabeth Taylor? Ava Gardner? Susan Hayward? Literally impossible to picture. Even Katharine Hepburn at her free-striding best never ran this much, or at least did so only on the tennis court, not all over town. What makes it all work is that Day appears entirely natural in these actions. Just as her corporate career girl roles in the 1960s—all featuring crisp, innuendo-laden dialogue in upscale urban settings—fit her like a glove, this outdoorsy, small-town mom role suits her as well. Doris Day made it all look easy.

The witty, underrated *It Happened to Jane,* 1959. *Photofest*

Sporting a softer, more relaxed hairdo, Doris Day here (as opposed to in *The Tunnel of* Love) really does make sense playing a den mother. Wearing shorts and kneesocks, leading her son's scout troop in the song "Be Prepared," Doris Day registers as a true-to-life small-town mother of two. One small but telling example: After winning the first round of her court case against E&P, Jane takes off her high heels as she continues walking on the grass; this is exactly what any constantly-on-her-feet mother would do in real life. It's a small gesture that rings absolutely true, grounding her character in reality. Perhaps Debbie Reynolds could also have played this spunky mom, but Reynolds goes for the hard sell more than Day. Reynolds mugs because, an audience senses, she *needs* the spotlight. Day doesn't.

Similarly, it makes perfect sense to see Jack Lemmon as George in a red jacket and scout master outfit leading the Boy Scout troop to which Day's sons belong. Day and Lemmon have an inherent rapport with each other, and of all her costars, only James Garner and Rock Hudson matched the easy naturalism Lemmon here achieved with Day. Early in the film, when Jane and George share coffee at her house and reminisce about their childhood together in Cape Ann, George's love for Jane is obvious, but Jane is not ready to commit. He is proposing marriage, but as she hands him coffee, simply by quietly saying, "sugar?" she manages effortlessly and gently to deflect the topic at hand. Doris Day is a terrific film actress because the rhythms of such line readings are instinctive for her. Superb musician that she is, it is as if she hears these lines internally in musical terms and is able to convey volumes of information with merely an inflection. George is not quite worthy of Jane yet—she knows it, he knows it, and so does the audience. Thus, when at last he tells off the townspeople for disparaging Jane, he finally gets himself elected; emboldened by this success, he actually barks an order at the self-doubting Jane: "Don't give up!" He goads her back into action and is now worthy of her love.

Of course, it is actually Doris/Jane who, shouting over the din of the locomotive, proposes to George; as with Gable in *Teacher's Pet,* Lemmon and Day are here presented as equals. George may be an attorney and a newly elected town official, but Doris has overcome an entire corporation, regained a thriving business, and continued to raise two children. In roles like these, Doris Day really did personify the can-do, take-charge attitude of post–World War II America—one never doubts that Doris Day could achieve any and all of her goals. When, at the end of the film, Doris leads the entire town in running after evil mogul Malone, everyone knows she'll catch up to him and haul him back to justice one-two-three. At this point in her career, it's all part of Doris Day's appeal. She's charming and so is the picture, and its box office failure is hard to fathom. The soggy, generic title couldn't have helped (nor could its alternative title in the United Kingdom, *Twinkle and Shine*), or it may be that audiences simply found the stakes too low (all this over some lobsters?). Whatever the reason, the lack of box office success was no fault of Day's or Lemmon's, and it's a pity that they never teamed up again.

Coupled with the middling returns on *The Pajama Game,* the lackluster box office reception accorded *It Happened to Jane* caused Day and Marty Melcher to search for a new career direction. Where to turn? Musicals were seemingly passé, wholesome comedy had not played well in either New York or Peoria, and with Day turning thirty-five, the girl-next-door image was at the breaking point of believability. The unexpected answer to this career dilemma came from producer Ross Hunter: Make a sophisticated sex comedy. His reasoning to Day: Let everyone see that "under that dirndl lurked one of the wildest asses in Hollywood." In Hunter's reasoning, men would want to see that body, and women would want to be like her.

Ross Hunter had hit the nail on the head. Teaming Day with Rock Hudson, Hunter produced *Pillow Talk,* a smash-hit 1959 release that stands as the archetypal film of the second half of Day's career. To this day, it remains the film most closely associated with Doris Day in the public's eye. Forget the fact that it gave Doris Day her only Academy Award nomination. This is the film that, for good and bad, solidified Doris Day's image in the public's mind, seemingly forever.

In *Pillow Talk,* Doris plays interior decorator Jan Morrow, a career girl who has temporarily been forced to share a telephone party line with lothario songwriter Brad Allen (Rock Hudson). Jan and Brad have never met, but his use of the telephone to romance numerous girlfriends not only prevents Jan from using her phone, it also infuriates her. When Brad and Jan finally do meet in a nightclub, Brad introduces himself as Texan "Rex Stetson," a shy Southern boy. Brad/Rex's carefully displayed reticence, which causes Jan to doubt his masculinity, is calculated ultimately to seduce her on a planned weekend getaway in Connecticut. Jan tumbles to Brad's deception and, as revenge, takes him up on his request that she decorate his apartment. Unbeknownst to Brad, she decorates his apartment in the gaudiest fashion she can manage. Enraged upon seeing the result, Brad storms into her apartment and fighting and true love ensue, as does a fade-out on the happy couple.

Pillow Talk is a true mixed blessing as a film, but Ross Hunter was right: The public was ready to see Doris Day in form-fitting, glamorous Jean Louis gowns, cavorting in beautifully decorated New York City apartments. (As in *Teacher's Pet,* here the leading man is totally hooked, and understandably so, upon watching her wiggle her caboose in a sexy cha-cha.) There is a sense of lightness and fun about the proceedings—no one is taking himself or herself too seriously here. This relaxed, leisurely style begins with the opening credits: Letters are arranged by use of pillows flipped in the air, the letters then dissolving on a split screen, all in sync to the catchy title tune sung by Doris. Later in the film, this is cleverly echoed in the well-remembered bathtub scene in which "Rex" and Jan, both lounging in their own tubs, in their own apartments, appear to sexily touch feet courtesy of the split screen. There is a nice dose of healthy sexuality being injected here; in fact, beginning with director Michael Gordon's first shot of Jan, clad only in a slip and sensually smoothing stockings onto her shapely legs, the public is made aware that they are seeing a new Doris Day. *On Moonlight Bay* this ain't.

Supporting characters are quickly introduced in the screenplay by Stanley Shapiro and Maurice Richlin, and it's a first-rate gathering of character actors: Thelma Ritter is on hand as Jan's acerbic housekeeper, Alma, who arrives every day with a "peach of a hangover," ice bag conveniently resting directly underneath her hat. Tony Randall, who was to serve as second banana in all three Day/Hudson film comedies, is here playing Jonathan Forbes, the neurotic financial backer of Brad's Broadway show, a man who is helplessly dependent on his psychiatrist and hopelessly in love with Jan.

Best of all, however, is the depiction of Jan herself as a high-powered, successful interior decorator. Doris Day's own natural energy and bouncy determination fit perfectly with Jan's drive to succeed; audiences in 1959, particularly female audience members, were ready to see a successful woman in charge onscreen. Americans were poised on the cusp of a revolution in terms of sexuality and the role of women: It would be a few years before the feminist revolution hit its stride, but it was only one year before FDA approval of the birth control pill was to revolutionize contraception and the manner in which women expressed their sexuality, and only four years until Betty Friedan published her groundbreaking *The Feminine Mystique*. The currents of change that were to burst forth over the next few years were already in place.

In this regard, Doris Day's career-girl film oeuvre, of which *Pillow Talk* was the first and prime example, fit the zeitgeist. Jan didn't cook, she didn't raise the kids or wait for hubby to come home, and she didn't depend on any man for her happiness. She was working because she loved it and was good at her job, not because she wanted to snare a man. Women in particular loved this screen paragon: Here was a big-screen glossy Hollywood comedy that showed the possibility of women creating successful careers for themselves,

First shot of Doris in *Pillow Talk*, 1959—no more Warner Bros. barnyard production numbers. *Photofest*

and in glamorous New York City, yet. It provided an entirely new image, not just of Doris Day, but of women in general, and in the words of Molly Haskell, "Doris Day really in a sense led the way." How ready were women for such a screen image? The answer lies in the fact that the release of *Pillow Talk* propelled Doris Day to the position of number one box office attraction in the world, a position she was to hold for a record-setting total of four years.

It wasn't just Day's persona that intrigued women, however; the Jean Louis gowns also made a fashion statement that interested scores of women. *Pillow Talk* marked the beginning of Doris Day sporting fashions that women could actually picture themselves wearing; with the meticulous attention to detail that attended both Jean Louis's work and Day's perfectionist approach to fittings, Doris Day had evolved into a fashion icon, a quantum leap from the frilly and often frumpy clothes she donned in the Warner Bros. contract films. Ross Hunter had read the times properly, and Day in fact continued to set trends throughout the early 1960s. The key to this new role was that both Doris and her clothes appeared, to the average viewer, to represent what one saw on Main Street, America. It wasn't true, of course, but Doris Day and her style were infinitely more approachable and imitable than those other 1960s fashion icons, Jackie Kennedy and Elizabeth Taylor. (In one of the hilarious and right-on-the-money early scenes of the popular film *Dirty Dancing,* women at the early '60s Catskills vacation resort are given the choice of dressing up in either the Jackie Kennedy bouffant wig or the Liz Taylor Cleopatra hairdo.) Jackie Kennedy, with her aloof aristocratic air, and Elizabeth Taylor, with her voluptuous beauty, existed on another planet. Doris Day seemed like the woman next door.

It's not just the Doris Day show here, however, and Rock Hudson turns in an assured, confident performance as both Rex and Brad. It was Hudson's first comedy, but the newness of the genre to him never shows. Hudson is a smoothly masculine presence here, a Cary Grant for a new era, and through the years he continually gave credit to Day for teaching him how to properly play film comedy. Doris Day and Rock Hudson genuinely liked each other, and that easy rapport created an instant chemistry that shines through in all three of their films.

It is impossible to watch *Pillow Talk* today without responding to the gay subtext of the film. Playboy Brad Allen knowingly impersonates a shy Texas man who likes to talk about recipes and drinks with his pinkie lifted. In the words of the screenplay, "Some men are very devoted to their mothers. They like to exchange cooking recipes." Straight Brad is purposely playing gay, all

One of the screen's legendary teams: Day and Rock Hudson in *Pillow Talk*. *Photofest*

but saying, "I, Brad Allen, am so butch and have so many girlfriends that I'm the last person who would ever be gay—so that's why I'll portray Rex as gay." The actor undertaking this impersonation just happens to be Rock Hudson, a rugged he-man Hollywood icon who just happened to be gay in his offscreen life. In other words, a gay actor plays a straight character impersonating a gay character in order to bed a virginal woman. Except, crucially, Jan Morrow is not presented as a virgin—the audience just remembers it that way. The unmarried Jan Morrow is perfectly content to go to Connecticut with Brad Allen, and she knows they're not driving all that way to discuss the weather. She says to herself, and about Rex, "[Jan], you've gone out with a lot of men in your time . . . if he only knew what I was thinking." It's clear to every member of the audience that what she's thinking about is sex. If any doubts remained, they are dispelled by Jan/Doris's singing in voice-over as she prepares for her time alone with Rex: "My darling—possess me . . ."

Why then the subsequent fifty-year-long lingering image as America's eternal virgin, not to mention Oscar Levant's endlessly repeated quip, "I knew Doris Day before she was a virgin"? Why is *Pillow Talk*'s sexual innuendo remembered as only being about Doris Day's character protecting her virginity? Most important of all, why is the "perennial virgin" tag remembered at the expense of Day's extraordinarily varied and successful film career, one in which she often portrayed self-sufficient, successful, independent career women? After all, in *Pillow Talk* and almost all of the following Doris Day sex farces (the puerile *That Touch of Mink* being the notable exception), Doris Day was not so much protecting her virginity—if the character even possessed it to begin with—as testing the man in question to see if he was worthy of her. She said no to men who were trying to manipulate her into the bedroom, and that is not at all the same thing as endlessly protecting her virginity. After all, Jan herself talks of "knowing many men." Years later, Day herself mused on this endlessly discussed aspect of her film persona: "The audience—*you* thought I was a virgin. *You* thought when I went off with him, 'Oh, she'll think of some way to wiggle out.' "

In point of fact, the answer to the questions about Day's virginal image appears to lie in the fact that Doris Day was a victim of timing. By the late 1960s, the feminist and sexual revolutions were in full foment and, casting about for objects of scorn, baby boomers seemed to settle on Doris Day as the iconic representation of the backward way in which women were depicted on film. To the younger generation, Doris Day epitomized a standard and stardom that screamed establishment. Never mind that Day did not write the films in question, and that women in the Hollywood of 1959 rarely possessed the power to produce or direct the films themselves. Day was the star and therefore became the object of derision. The fact that she refused the role of Mrs. Robinson in *The Graduate,* refused to appear in films that emphasized overt sexuality, no matter how worthy the film, only added to her image as a hopelessly behind the times Goody Two-shoes. In fact, Day's successor as the out-of-it virginal good girl, Julie Andrews, was able only to partially banish that image by baring her breasts in 1981's *SOB.* It is therefore all the more noteworthy that even in the new millennium, Andrews is still most strongly identified with her roles as *Mary Poppins* and Maria von Trapp in *The Sound of Music,* just as Day is remembered for *Pillow Talk* and the sweet Warner Bros. musicals. It's almost as if a three-stage cycle must evolve: mass popularity, widespread derision and, years later, a nostalgic embrace of fondly recalled cultural touchstones that evolves into a cultural reassessment. The problem lies in the second stage of the cycle, that of cynical rejection, because it finds audiences ultimately rejecting the very role models they first embraced, often in defensive reaction to the criticism of others. It's a reaction that inevitably gives short shrift to the very real reasons behind the initial mass popularity, in effect throwing out the baby with the bathwater.

Day and Hudson mesh smoothly throughout the film, and in truth the film remains great fun, even viewed nearly fifty years later. Nonetheless, there are several aspects to the film which do jar by the standards of the twenty-first century. Jan has a remarkably extensive wardrobe, but her true glamour is epitomized by the now controversial wearing of lavish furs: Animal lover Day herself admits to "cringing" when she views scenes from her films in which she wears furs. Similarly, housekeeper Alma's perpetual drunkenness is depicted as the height of hilarity, and at one point Jonathan (Randall) hits Jan (Doris) and it's presented without comment as being for her own good. Yesterday's dose of good common sense is today's physical abuse.

But that is getting ahead of the film's initial reception in 1959 as a smart, funny, up-to-date sex comedy filled with sparkling performances. Rock Hudson underplays throughout, making the plot machinations actually approach believability, and Tony Randall, with his idiosyncratic delayed line readings, admirably complements Hudson. Truth to tell, Day's performance, Oscar nomination notwithstanding, is the weakest of the three leads, and her much stronger work in *Love Me or Leave Me* and *The Man Who Knew Too Much* was actually far more deserving of nomination.

Doris's performance in *Pillow Talk* is hit or miss throughout. On the plus side, her drive and movement propel the film forward and contrast nicely with Hudson's more deliberate style. On the negative side of the ledger, she indulges in double and triple takes that telegraph the character's reactions in such an exaggerated fashion that the audience can't discover anything for itself. Watch Day's expression as Rex/Brad says, "What with television, there's just not much time for families"—Day nearly crosses her eyes in furious disbelief at his deception. The subtlety of touch she displayed from *Love Me or Leave Me* right through *It Happened to Jane* is mostly lacking here, but it didn't matter to critics or audiences. Doris Day was now more than the girl next door—she had become the sexy independent career girl women wanted to emulate and men wanted to bed (as well as take home to mother). And if getting married was the only way to make that possible, well then, so be it. That's how strong Doris Day's appeal was in 1959.

America's girl next door had now become a number one star with a difference. On the one hand, she was reserved, a bit of self-protection necessary due to her worldwide iconic status; in the words of actress Betty White, "The guard is up but she keeps such a lovely lace guard on the cuff I don't even know that she's aware of it." Yet on the other hand, as the cowriter of her autobiography, A. E. Hotchner, stated, "It never occurred to Doris to say 'I'm a movie star—I'll do that when I bloody well feel like it.' She came to the set on time and was the last to leave." Audiences instinctively understood the niceness inherent in Doris Day. There were never press reports of temper tantrums on the sets of her films, and audiences knew there wouldn't be.

If, at various stages of her career, Doris Day represented the idealized career woman, the perfect mother, and the longed-for girl next door, she thereby came to personify the very woman Americans wished they knew, or were. Such a primal response on the audience's part solidified Day's specific bond with the American public. It is this special type of personal bond that allows an actor to register with the public not just as a star but as one of the rare breed to make the leap to genuine icon. As longtime Doris Day aficionado John Updike stated, "What do stars mean to us, after all? They're kind of an indication of what people can be. . . . There are people up there onscreen who are enacting humanity in their dazzling ways and she was one of them. Even for me she was a kind of directive image . . . I'd like to be that good."

After the dazzling success of *Pillow Talk,* Day's next film, the 1960 release *Please Don't Eat the Daisies,* proved a very effective change of pace. Based on Jean Kerr's best-selling book of the same title, the film featured a solid screenplay by Isobel Lennart (co-screenwriter of *Love Me or Leave Me*) and sympathetic direction by Charles Walters. Day, in her role of Kate MacKay, is utterly relaxed and charming onscreen, turning in a beautifully modulated performance.

The story of *Please Don't Eat the Daisies* revolves around the harried and loving family life of Kate, her drama critic husband Laurence (David Niven), and their four rambunctious sons. The ever-expanding brood having outgrown their cramped New York City apartment, Kate longs to move to a house in the country. Laurence, enamored of his growing eminence as a major drama critic, is less sanguine about such a move but bows to Kate's wishes. The result? Larry feels neglected as Kate immerses herself in repairing and redecorating the big ramshackle house, losing his temper completely when he realizes that the local dramatic society is presenting a performance of the one and only (bad) play that he wrote. In the end, Kate may realize that she has been somewhat distracted, but it is Larry who realizes that he has been, well, a jerk, and their loving marriage is back in place, a marriage of equals.

In *Please Don't Eat the Daisies,* Doris Day gives a nearly pitch-perfect comic performance. The film's opening, where she gets ready for a night at the theater with Laurence, is not only a terrific depiction of modern-day motherhood circa 1960 but also a lesson in comic acting for any aspiring film actress: This sequence is as good as it gets. In this hilarious start to the movie, youngest son Adam, egged on by his brothers, is dropping water balloons on unsuspecting passersby below. Trying to organize the four boys, who are wreaking havoc with both the phone and the lamps, giving instructions to deadpan maid Maggie (Patsy Kelly), attempting to slip into a new form-fitting black dress ("I even lost five pounds"), Kate MacKay is a mother with too much to do and too little time. As she puts on her dress, the four boys drop everything to stare at their mother. Sighs Doris/Kate in exasperation, "Just once I'd like to get dressed without an audience." Day's inflections are so perfectly calibrated that she manages to convey layers of meaning with just this one sentence: She is frazzled, overextended in her multitasking, and yet completely accepting of the fact that nothing will change for the next eighteen years. . . . Asking her son for help zipping up the dress, Kate is forthrightly told by him, "Maybe you should have lost ten pounds, not five." Kate is harried and loving, exasperated with her boys, but seemingly quite proud that eighteen-month-old Adam can pick locks. (It's a measure of how much film comedy has changed that in *Please Don't Eat the Daisies,* much is made of eighteen-month-old Adam's one-word vocabulary, "Cokey-Cola," while in 2004's *Meet the Fockers,* Robert De Niro and Blythe Danner's infant grandson's one-word vocabulary consists of his endless repetition of the word "asshole.")

Doris Day, the world's number one movie star, had evolved into an expert and successful comedian, and in the process registered as one of the few film actresses of her generation whose very presence conveyed intelligence. She is believable in all of the roles required of Kate MacKay: wife, mother, and lov-

Super suburban mom—the raucously enjoyable family comedy
Please Don't Eat the Daisies, 1960. *Photofest*

ing daughter. When extended to the mother-daughter relationship, this realism is at times hilarious; disagreeing with daughter Kate, her mother Suzie (Spring Byington) tells her, with natural exasperation, "You were one of the dumbest children I ever met." Similarly, confronted with the self-satisfied theatrical "in" crowd at a lavish party, Doris Day's Kate acts as would any stay-at-home mom with four sons: She wants to look her best and tries to ingratiate herself with fellow partygoers, but she is nothing so much as bemused at the endless posturing of the New York City glitterati set.

David Niven's Britishness—his stuffiness—is a perfect complement to Day's all-American verve. His occasional smugness also provides a nice target for vampy Broadway sexpot Deborah Vaughn's (Janis Paige) comic face-slapping attack on him at Sardi's restaurant. (Paige is very funny throughout, toying with Larry MacKay as she tries to unsettle his staid demeanor with increasingly overt passes. Janis Paige may not have Day's star power, but here she is very funny indeed.) Kay and Laurence have a real marriage—loving but not lovey-dovey. They disagree over moving to the suburbs, yell at their kids to "stop jumping on those beds," and have a normal ten-year-old son who picks his nose at a school interview.

Because Doris Day is adept at so many genres—comedy, drama, and musicals—the audience accepts the versatility she displays here; she makes it look so easy that audiences are charmed, not threatened. When she's called into the principal's office because her son has a chair stuck on his head (?!) Kate simply marches into the office and saws the chair off her son's head without a second thought. The audience doesn't for one minute worry that Kate might hurt her own son with a saw. Doris incompetent with a saw? Don't be ridiculous. This is one wife and mother who can decorate a house and saw chairs with equal aplomb, and then turn right around and wear a glamorous designer gown to a fancy New York City cocktail party.

In many ways, Doris Day here exemplifies a perfect wife by the standards of 1960 America. She is sexy in a wholesome way, loving and attentive to her husband, a great down-to-earth mom, and oh, yeah—when rehearsing the community play she sings, too. Of course, when the audience is treated to her musical rehearsal from the local amateur dramatic club's performance of her husband's terrible play, it takes exactly four bars of music and two dance steps for everyone to realize that the lady in the makeshift costume belting out "Any Way the Wind Blows" should be starring on Broadway—and fast. The notion that this huge talent would be hidden in the suburbs is laughable in a very pleasant fashion.

Day hits all the right acting notes here; when husband Larry interrupts this musical rehearsal, outraged at learning they are performing his bad play, Kate's hurt over her husband's small-mindedness registers as the real thing. Similarly, so does the look of disbelief on her face when he sanctimoniously delivers a "speech" to the school principal outlining why he won't volunteer for any activities. Kate's mother may give Larry the ridiculous-sounding advice that he should "keep Kate under your thumb—where she belongs," but Larry knows the real score; he has been foolish and wants to reunite with his wife as equal partners in marriage.

Please Don't Eat the Daisies certainly isn't flawless. The opening city scenes establishing the necessity of moving to the country have more bite and verve than do the sequences at home in the suburbs. A sequence in which Kate leads a group of well-scrubbed playground children in a sing-along version of "Please Don't Eat the Daisies" as she strums the ukulele strikes one as a playground not to be found on this planet. These are small problems, however, alongside the warm, family-centered comic antics. In addition, at times the film displays a wit that is surprisingly subversive; when the welcoming committee comes to the new MacKay household in the suburbs, the committee consists of the local minister, a suburban matron, and a rather butch veterinarian.

The MacKay son's response? Looking at the vet, the MacKays' son asks, "Are you a man or a woman?" Her riposte? "I'm a vet—that's somewhere in the middle."

This rather subversive note may have been the work of director Charles Walters, a gay man noted for his smooth and understanding direction of women: Leslie Caron in *Lili,* Grace Kelly in *High Society,* Debbie Reynolds in *The Unsinkable Molly Brown,* and Joan Crawford in *Torch Song.* Here, Walters found a substantial supporting role for lesbian actress Patsy Kelly (Maggie the maid), but more to the point, his direction is undoubtedly a big reason why Day turns in such a beautifully modulated performance, one infinitely more accomplished than her Oscar-nominated turn under Michael Gordon's direction in *Pillow Talk.* When working with top-notch directors—Walters in *Billy Rose's Jumbo,* Norman Jewison in *The Thrill of It All,* Stanley Donen in *The Pajama Game,* and especially Alfred Hitchcock in *The Man Who Knew Too Much*—Day triumphs. Faced with the pedestrian (her six Warner Bros. films with David Butler), she marks time—no one could do any more—truly scoring only with her expert delivery of ballads. Here it's smooth sailing all the way and a true delight for audiences.

After the successful one-two punch of *Pillow Talk* and *Please Don't Eat the Daisies,* it was more than a little disconcerting to see Day returning to the *Julie*-like damsel-in-distress mode of *Midnight Lace.* Coproduced by Marty Melcher and Ross Hunter, the glossy 1960 Universal Technicolor release looked far superior to *Julie,* thanks to the trademark lush Ross Hunter production values, but the story presented is every bit as ludicrous as that found in *Julie.*

This time out, Doris plays wealthy American Kit Preston, who lives in London with her new husband of three months, Tony (Rex Harrison). Kit receives numerous threats on her life but the police don't believe Kit's tale about a stalker, and neither do husband Tony or Kit's Aunt Bea (Myrna Loy). Only sympathetic building contractor Brian Younger (John Gavin) stands by Kit. At the film's climax, it is revealed that Tony and his mistress Peggy have been the people tormenting Kit. Fleeing Tony, Kit escapes onto the scaffolding of the house being built next door and eventually is rescued by Scotland Yard and Brian.

Midnight Lace starts off well enough, with director David Miller establishing the aura of Kit's terror with an atmospheric oppressive London street scene. Employing little dialogue, Miller instead smartly relies on a primal fear of the unknown, injecting a genuine note of mystery into the proceedings. (One idly notes that Doris can still run fast, even in the fog and in high heels. Clad in a fur-trimmed suit and matching muff, Doris looks the part of the wealthy American she is supposed to be; this being a Ross Hunter film, there are, after all, separate single title credits for Doris Day's wardrobe and jewels.)

Unfortunately, it is all downhill from here, because the plot stretches the willing suspension of disbelief right up to, and then beyond, the breaking point. There are plenty of red herrings strewn along the way: Doris has to listen to samples of obscene phone calls, Roddy McDowell shows up as the ne'er-do-well son of the Prestons' housekeeper, even John Gavin as stolid building contractor Brian Younger briefly comes under suspicion, but none of this is terribly convincing. Doris is being terrorized, yet she rather easily agrees to stay alone in her town house until Aunt Bea arrives—not exactly believable behavior from someone who has been screaming hysterically about her stalker. It's also at this point that any suspense as to the identity of Kit's stalker flies out the window; as soon as it's clear that husband Tony is too busy to take Kit on a trip to Venice, plying her with jewelry instead, you know he's a no-goodnik. Rex Harrison's Tony is too smooth an operator by half, and even a London street urchin would have quickly been able to tell Kit, "Hey, lady—your husband's a whackjob. He's after your money."

There is no subtlety in the plot development, and as a result, Doris Day's performance suffers markedly. Continually menaced by phone calls claiming that she will be killed within the month, surviving an attack in her apartment building elevator, and even being pushed in front of a bus, Kit Preston is presented as a passive victim; as a result, Day is reduced to a one-note performance of sustained hysteria. She is not helped by director Miller who, in a scene where Tony grapples with a mysterious stranger, in fact allows her to convey terror by literally biting her knuckles. She is far too skilled an actress for this kind of cartoonlike performance.

One senses genuine terror building in Day, but it is of a disturbing variety and not the cathartic terror the audience experienced when she was in the hands of a master such as Alfred Hitchcock. It's as if the neurotic underpinnings of Doris Day's cheerful persona, the persona that can in fact become too cheerful, have been exposed. The pressure of always being up and happy seems to have gotten to her, and when she collapses in hysterics, one has the slightly discomfiting reaction that Doris Day's believable but overwrought performance stems from some deep-seated but suppressed hysteria within herself. As she wrote in her autobiography, Day is here remembering the terror of her life with Al Jorden: "I wasn't *acting* hysterical, I *was* hysterical."

Yes, the audience feels Kit is in definite danger, but what is more terrifying is the notion that Doris Day is becoming unhinged onscreen. This is not a case of an excellent actress giving a finely calibrated performance, as in *The*

The shrill, over-the-top *Midnight Lace,* 1960. *Photofest*

Man Who Knew Too Much, but rather, the audience uneasily begins to feel that Doris Day is one raw mass of emotion. It all cuts too close to the bone, and the audience never feels a genuine sense of relief when she is rescued.

The character of Kit Preston is not a working woman and she's not a busy mother raising children. Instead, she's presented as a businessman's wife who shops, and as a passive victim of terror she is an object of pity but not of genuine interest. At the same time, a curious dichotomy takes hold in the viewer, because although one is watching Doris Day collapse in disturbing ways, at the same time, so strong is Day's take-no-prisoners persona that she often seems too inherently spunky for the role of damsel in distress. Far from being terrorized, Doris Day would probably just walk away and briskly tell the murderer, "Don't be ridiculous."

The effectiveness of Kit's dilemma is not helped by the film's presentation of the secondary characters. John Gavin, as building contractor Brian Younger, sports a bad British accent and in the often rough-and-tumble world of construction surely must rank as the first-ever contractor who makes a point of always wearing a trench coat and keeping a pipe tucked in the corner of his mouth. Screen legend Myrna Loy, playing Kit's Aunt Bea, looks great, but with pronouncements such as, "Men must work and women must weep," Loy seems to have wandered in from a totally different movie. In fact, the one genuine note of interest here lies in analyzing how Myrna Loy and Doris Day represent two very different all-American ideals of womanhood. Loy, all sophisticated sass and class, and a woman who depended upon the well-timed barb for her power, exudes an entirely different persona from the late '50s/early '60s Doris Day, who embodied the post–World War II American ethos of meeting the world head-on.

At the climactic moment of the film, when Kit escapes from Tony and his accomplice/lover Peggy, she flings herself onto the construction site next door. One hundred minutes into the film, director Miller finally manages to once again work up some genuine suspense, shooting the sequence with strikingly atmospheric camera angles that convey the physical danger Kit is in as she negotiates the narrow beams and girders, uneasily glancing down and nearly plummeting to her death. The imminent danger of falling is convincingly conveyed, but at what is supposed to be the most terror-filled moment of the film, the viewer is once again reminded of the striking lack of authenticity, simply because Doris, our woman in terror, is clad for her derring-do in her midnight lace outfit and high heels—always a good bet for climbing girders in order to escape with your life. And what do villain Tony and accomplice Peggy do during Doris's frenzied escape? Do they cut and run? No way. They just stand by idly and watch Doris on the girders. There is no attempt to hide or escape. It's as if Tony and Peggy are saying to the police, "Hey, just come on in and arrest us." How can an audience be expected to take such behavior seriously? It can't—and doesn't.

The film ends with Doris walking off into the distance side by side with contractor Gavin and understanding Aunt Bea, head held high, tears streaking her face. At which point the audience wonders exactly one thing: Why did Doris Day make this film? Kit is vulnerable, but she has no drive or ambition, and one doesn't become caught up in her travails. Why did Rex Harrison think it would be a good idea to star with Doris Day, when their styles are completely opposite? Did Doris Day make this film only to help out husband Marty Melcher? Why interrupt a string of hit comedies for this misbegotten hysterical pseudosuspense? At the height of her career and box office power, why did Doris Day take a passive role in which she has no drive, no ambition, and simply screams a great deal in the bargain? Day has written of her willingness to let others take charge of her career, and *Midnight Lace* is a prime example of the dangers of doing so. On her own, she is far too intelligent to have chosen such nonsense, but her seemingly passive acceptance of such fare has hurt her screen legacy. Doris Day is here doing nothing but marking time. It's a loss for everyone, including Doris, but things began to look up with the news that Day and Rock Hudson would team up once again for a comedy titled *Lover Come Back.* Could lightning strike a second time? The answer came back a resounding yes.

Given the success of *Pillow Talk,* it was not surprising that Day and Hudson were quickly reteamed, and they returned to the screen with the 1961 release of *Lover Come Back.* With Tony Randall again on board as second banana, the Stanley Shapiro and Paul Henning screenplay rang enough changes on the *Pillow Talk* formula to ensure audience favor. In point of fact, the script for *Lover Come Back* is actually better than that for *Pillow Talk*—it's just that the second teaming doesn't have the element of happy surprise that marked *Pillow Talk.* No matter—*Lover Come Back* remains a fun picture that proved the felicitous pairing of Day and Hudson was no accident.

Playing Carol Templeton, a highly successful Madison Avenue advertising executive, Day once again portrays a hard-charging single New York City career woman. Carol, she of high business standards, spends hours on market research and new design products only to be defeated by archrival Jerry Webster (Rock Hudson), who enlists the help of sexy nightclub singer Rebel Davis (Edie Adams) to help land a big account. As thanks for not testifying against him at the Ad Council ethics meeting, Jerry designates Rebel the television spokesperson for VIP; to this end, Jerry films a set of bogus television commercials with Rebel, commercials he intends never to air since the product doesn't exist. When Webster's ineffectual agency head Peter Ramsey (Tony Randall, once again slavishly tied to the apron strings of his psychiatrist) decides actually to get involved with his own business instead of leaving the operations to Webster, he takes over the VIP account and puts the ads on the air—unaware that the product doesn't exist. Jerry and Peter quickly hire Nobel Prize–winning chemist Linus Taylor to invent VIP, and Carol, in her desire for revenge, visits Linus's laboratory herself. Carol mistakes Jerry for Linus, and Webster strings her along, not only to exact business revenge but also in order to sleep with her. Discovering the truth of Webster's deception, Carol visits the Ad Council again, but Jerry, smooth as ever, has obtained an actual VIP product from Dr. Taylor—liquor-laced candy wafers. Everyone eats the wafer, all concerned become drunk, and Carol and Jerry wake up the next morning in a motel room—married. Carol has the marriage annulled, but having become pregnant, she and Jerry remarry just as she is about to deliver the baby. Fade-out on the near exhausting shenanigans.

No simpering virgin—successful advertising executive Carol Templeton at work in *Lover Come Back,* 1961. *Photofest*

The best parts of *Lover Come Back* are actually the ideas underlying the film. Madison Avenue's obsession with using sex to sell products was ripe for satire by this time, and in many ways the Shapiro-Henning script delivers on this score; Rebel's faux VIP ads, which feature Edie Adams in increasingly skimpy outfits, are witty and winning. The idea that archrivals Carol and Jerry are furiously competing to sell a nonexistent product is indeed a funny one. (There are, to be sure, some anachronistic notes in the script, and modern-day audiences are likely to groan when hearing Doris's Carol Templeton refuse Rock's offer of help with the dishes with a crisp "No, that's a woman's job!") In fact, the film grows progressively funnier as it unwinds, but its success once again rests upon the Day-Hudson chemistry, and for the most part, they deliver in spades. Or, to be more specific, they deliver what the audience of the day wanted.

Hudson is even more relaxed than he was in *Pillow Talk* and seems to be enjoying himself thoroughly as he delivers the lines with detached bemusement. His line readings have grown in assurance, and when an outraged Carol demands to know how he, sweet Linus Taylor (the man Webster is impersonating), got into the horrible Jerry Webster's apartment, she implores, "Try to think, Linus!" He, with an eye out for any possible alibi, desperately replies, "I am, I am . . ." with a nice understatement that makes the audience all the more readily accept the frenetic farce elements. Day, for her part, looks great, and the now standard credits for a Doris Day film list "Miss Day's gowns by Irene" and "Miss Day's jewels by Laykin." The years of Doris wearing overalls for production numbers set in the barnyard are light-years behind her. This is the Doris Day audiences wanted to see—has any other major star so reinvented her persona to such stunningly successful effect? Day is still extremely trim and glamorous, although the soft-focus close-ups first noticeable in *Pillow Talk* are much more obvious here.

It's the reception to Day's performance, however, that must be a bit more guarded. It may once more be a function of working with a less than top-notch director—here Delbert Mann—but Day again indulges in triple takes in order to register her disbelief; why would such a skilled comedian stoop to pointless overkill like this? Was she guided by Mann to underscore any bit of comic business? Are these over-the-top reactions Day's own invention? Whatever the reason, her performance registers as overly bright—almost exhausting. Carol, who is here the sexual aggressor with supposed scientist Linus Taylor, takes Linus/Rock to a strip club so that he can be reassured of his essential masculinity. When the stripper onstage (never glimpsed) displays her "remarkable muscle control," Day's eyes almost literally pop out of her head.

Occasionally, Day's overexuberance actually works for the character, as when a phone call from her agency head alerts her, right before she is going to bed with Webster, to the fact that she is alone with Webster, not Linus Taylor. In order to exact revenge (which she does by leaving him stranded naked on a remote beach), Carol must pretend to still believe Webster; the dichotomy between her purposely sweet speaking voice and her infuriated facial expressions (which he can't see) is quite humorous. Similarly, when, near the film's end, after consuming the alcoholic VIP wafers she wakes up drunk and in bed with Webster, her scream at seeing him is humorous; when this scream is followed by an even louder one upon learning that they are married, the effect is truly funny. The problem is that even here the reactions nearly topple over into caricature. Less would have been more.

Interestingly, two somewhat disconcerting elements present in *Pillow Talk* become even more pronounced here: the deceit in which the Rock Hudson character(s) engages, and the multiple levels on which homosexuality is presented. For starters, once again the Rock Hudson character is presented as an irresistible lothario who casts aspersions on the Doris Day character's femi-

The strip club sequence in *Lover Come Back*. Doris and Rock = box office magic. *Photofest*

ninity because she is a working woman. He says that she is undersexed, while she retorts that he is oversexed. In order to bed Day's Carol Templeton, Jerry Webster impersonates Linus Taylor, inventing a wildly naïve rube complete with hayseed wardrobe and an inability to dance. These comedies are not about Doris Day desperately protecting her virginity—they are about deceit. Carol Templeton is going to sleep with Linus Taylor, and knowing that even one drink makes her inebriated, she purposely has a cocktail. She is well aware of the course of action on which she is embarking, debating her actions through the voice-over song "Should I Surrender?" Day's vocal prowess, of course, is a big asset here; her ability to shade so many different meanings with her singing provides a variety of inflections and thoughts that no mere line reading could ever deliver, and goes a long way to making the silly situation believable. The lyric blatantly refutes the perennial virgin charge: "I'd much rather surrender, surrender, surrender, surrender." As it turns out, Carol doesn't sleep with "Linus," not because she wants to hold on to a virginity that she may not even possess but because he has lied to her about his work, his character, and his very identity. No sap she, Carol exacts revenge by stringing Jerry Webster along, pretending to still believe him, and then deserts him in the middle of the night, stark naked, on a deserted beach far away from the city.

Of further note, just as in *Pillow Talk,* the idea of rugged Rock Hudson posing as a man unsure of his masculinity is played for laughs, as if it is the most ridiculous notion in the world. Says Carol to the supposed Linus, "Do you think you'd enjoy watching a girl undress?" Well, hmmm . . . In order to land Carol in his bed, Webster, as the faux Linus, worries aloud that he'll "be a failure," to which Carol insistently tells him, *"You're* the real man, not Jerry Webster." Even Tony Randall's character, the overly neurotic Peter Ramsey, half enviously sighs to Jerry, "What's this obsession with girls?" Jerry Webster is presented as being casually capable of landing any woman he desires, a questionable attribute since he apparently possesses no genuine feelings for any of these women, until guilt sets in at having deceived Carol Templeton. Once again, in light of real-life events and Rock Hudson's death as the first top Hollywood star to die from AIDS, the multiple levels of deception, both on film and in the closeted existence Hudson had to lead in the Hollywood of the 1950s and 1960s, can't help but inform a viewer's response to the film.

All of this subtext aside, however, the film really does entertain and often charm, at times scoring genuinely funny satirical jabs at Madison Avenue and the world of high-stakes advertising. Unfortunately, such wit did not prove to be the case with Day's next film, 1962's *That Touch of Mink,* costarring Cary Grant.

That Touch of Mink, yet another vehicle scripted by Stanley Shapiro and directed by Delbert Mann, is the one Doris Day comedy that really does concern itself exclusively with the issue of her virginity. The plot, such as it is, concerns wealthy business tycoon Philip Shayne (Cary Grant) and his attempts to bed Cathy Timberlake (Doris Day). Philip and Cathy meet "cute" when his limousine splashes water on her; Philip is instantly attracted to Cathy and invites her on a trip to Bermuda. First refusing and then changing her mind, she flies to Bermuda, but when the time comes actually to sleep with Philip, she develops a rash—ergo, no sex. Arriving back in New York, the couple split up, but when Cathy expresses a desire for a return trip to Bermuda, back they head. This time, Cathy becomes drunk and falls off a balcony—ergo, no sex. Once more returning to New York, Cathy, advised by best friend Connie (Audrey Meadows), plots to make Shayne jealous by pretending to elope with sleazy unemployment office clerk Beasley (John Astin). Philip chases after Cathy and Beasley, and upon reunion, Philip and Cathy marry; on their honeymoon, this time it's Philip who develops a rash—ergo, no sex. In the final frames, a baby has appeared—somehow the rashes have cleared up and the couple theoretically lives happily ever after.

Which is exactly what the audience does not do. *That Touch of Mink* fails on virtually every level, even though the comic template for a Doris Day sex farce is in place. Doris is once again a working girl in New York City; the central question is when and how she will succumb to the charms of the leading man; male and female second bananas are on hand for comic relief (Gig Young in the Tony Randall role, Audrey Meadows in the Thelma Ritter role); and the script is by veteran sex farce scenarist Stanley Shapiro (here sharing credit with Nate Monaster). And that's exactly where the trouble starts—with the script.

Here, Cathy Timberlake may be a working girl in New York, but she is unemployed. No taking on the male-dominated working world in this scenario, because Cathy Timberlake has no job, and aside from the occasional visit to the unemployment office, she seems to spend all of her time in her apartment—which appears to be five times the size that an unemployed single woman with an Automat waitress roommate (Meadows) would be able to afford. Cathy seems to spend all of her time waiting around for Philip Shayne's call about a trip to Bermuda. Even when, near the end of the film, Cathy lands a job courtesy of Shayne, she ruins the company's computerized billing system, destroying all records in the process.

In fact, it's not just Cathy who's out of synch; all of the characters are out of balance, and so is the film. In order to outfit Cathy for her trip to Bermuda, there is a nutty fashion show sequence at Bergdorf Goodman that plays like an outtake from the fashion shows featured in 1930s films such as *The Women.* Just like a sugar daddy, Philip Shayne is buying clothes to keep Cathy Timberlake happy—she is another one of this rich man's possessions. Doris Day isn't even modeling the clothes here—she passively sits by and watches others parade about in them. The only thing missing from this off-putting scenario is Day breaking into a chorus of Cole Porter's "My Heart Belongs to Daddy." This isn't the Doris Day audiences wanted to see, and more to the point, the film has no energy as a result. It is inert—dead on arrival.

Second, and extremely damaging, there is scant evidence of any rapport between Grant and Day. Grant, a terrific stylized comic actor, fares best with equally stylized female costars—Katharine Hepburn in *Bringing up Baby* and Audrey Hepburn in *Charade.* Doris Day's straightforward, foursquare approach combined with Grant's urbanity makes for a chalk and cheese combination. They do not make sense as a couple, a fact not helped by the fact that she calls him "Mr. Shayne" throughout the entire movie. He wants to bed a

The spots meant no sex. The leering, overly coy *That Touch of Mink*, 1962. *Photofest*

woman who calls him "Mr."? Cary Grant's Philip Shayne has every right to be frustrated with Cathy Timberlake, but in Grant's performance, he is actually downright brusque with her; it is not a persona likely to seduce audiences, let alone the woman in question. He is more grumpy than charming.

It is also a major hindrance that both stars appear to be too old for this kind of nonsense. Even though the ever charming Cary Grant is playing Shayne, he simply appears far too advanced in age for Cathy, a fact not helped by his habit of wearing grandpa-style cardigan sweaters throughout. Doris Day, nearing forty, is here spending her time, talent, and energy on a film concerning her virginity. This is the one film in her career that really could justifiably inspire all of the wisecracks made at her expense.

Far more than in the Day-Hudson sex comedies, the dated social attitudes present in *That Touch of Mink* grate when viewed today. Once again, but in a much more distasteful manner, the two biggest subjects for disdainful laughter are those oh-so-hilarious standbys, homosexuality and psychiatry. Roger (Gig Young) constantly visits his psychiatrist, who, misunderstanding what Roger is saying, thinks that Roger wants to settle down with another man. What could be more hilarious than that? Both homosexuality and psychiatry are presented as guaranteed laugh-getters, subjects worthy of audience mockery. "Those people," the screenplay seems to say, aren't real Americans. Those aren't people worthy of being treated as actual human beings because they're not, according to the two-dimensional screenplay. It's all played for laughs, but strikes the viewer as smarmy.

Equally offensive is the early '60s casual condoning of violence toward women. When Shayne, sitting poolside in Bermuda, commiserates with a bookie from Detroit about women, the bookie states matter-of-factly that when his wife caused him trouble, "I belted her." The audience is asked to approve of this behavior. Even worse, when Gig Young's Roger sadly says to Cathy, "We sold out for that touch of mink," her reply is, "If only he got mad or hit me." This from forthright Doris Day? This, an attitude espoused onscreen by the number one female star in the world? What the heck is going on here? The answer—nothing good.

In a film nearly devoid of wit or humor, there are a few—very few—bright spots. Day still looks great, especially in a form-fitting evening gown, and the movie looks lush—the money spent shows up onscreen. Audrey Meadows manages a few fairly funny wisecracks as waitress Carrie: "My raven hair wasn't too bad. I got whistled at by a bird." Even Grant's Philip Shayne has one humorous line: "She's direct, sincere, uncomplicated; those qualities bring out the worst part of a man—his conscience." After spotting a wedding party complete with rice and minister, Cathy begins to visualize a bed everywhere she looks: in the middle of the pool, as a vehicle for a horse-drawn carriage ride, even in the elevator. It's a humorous visual joke but also underscores the fact that Cathy Timberlake appears to be terrified of sex. Nearing age forty, this isn't funny, it's just dumb.

It is only when Cathy finally musters up some energy that the movie shows signs of life. Totally drunk in Bermuda, she falls out of the window onto a canopy, and for the first time in the film, Doris Day is allowed to display some zip. Similarly, skilled comedian that she is, Day actually succeeds in making Cathy's nausea at having to date Beasley funny. Disgusted by riding with him in a poultry market truck, horrified by his talk of eating haddock TV dinners and drinking muscatel in paper cups, she at last displays backbone. But such energy is all in service of trapping Philip Shayne by making him jealous; it is all too emblematic of everything wrong with the film that after Shayne rescues Cathy from having to stay at a motel with Beasley, she is tossed into the rear of the chicken truck. Displaying no gumption and still a virgin, her one and only accomplishment is a successfully concluded campaign that has trapped a man. Awful.

Fortunately, Day's next film, 1962's *Billy Rose's Jumbo,* proved to be everything *That Touch of Mink* was not: beautiful, stylish, and filled with genuine emotion. *Jumbo* not only represented Day's first musical since *The Pajama Game* in 1957 but also proved to be the last musical of her feature film career. It was a lovely swan song, because along with *Love Me or Leave Me* and *The Pajama Game, Jumbo* captured Doris Day at her very best, further proof that she had evolved into the premiere movie musical actress of the day. The movie may not have succeed at the box office, but it's a beauty of a film nonetheless.

Jumbo features a screenplay by soon to be famous novelist Sidney Sheldon based on the original musical stage book by Ben Hecht and Charles MacArthur. Sheldon has here constructed a libretto that provides an excellent setting for the classic Rodgers and Hart score. The story line focuses on Kitty Wonder (Day), co-owner of the Wonder Circus with her father Pop (Jimmy Durante), and her attempts to hold the circus together in the face of the charming but ne'er-do-well pop's continual gambling losses. With little money in the till, Kitty comes to gratefully accept the sudden appearance of Sam Rawlins (Stephen Boyd), whose multiple talents allow him to fill in as both repairman and high-wire performer. If his sudden arrival seems too good to be true, that's because it is—Sam turns out to be the son of rival circus owner John Noble, and he has been sent to take over the Wonder Circus and specifically its chief asset, Jumbo the elephant. Kitty and Sam fall in love, but when Sam's true role is revealed, and the Noble Circus acquires the Wonder Circus, the couple breaks up. Feeling guilty over deceiving Kitty, Sam fights with his father and subsequently returns to help Kitty, Pop, and Pop's "fiancée" Lulu (Martha Raye) start a new circus—with Jumbo. Kitty forgives Sam and, reconciliation complete, all four of them begin to build a new circus.

It's no accident that *Jumbo* was filmed at MGM, because this lavish, expansive musical, so foreign to the budget-minded executives at Warner Bros., represented one of the last musicals from the famed Freed unit at MGM. Just as she had in *Please Don't Eat the Daisies,* Day thrived under the direction of Charles Walters, never sounding better on film than when here singing the classic Rodgers and Hart songs, beautifully arranged by Roger Edens (the man responsible for so many of the classic Judy Garland musical moments captured on film). Walters deserves a great deal of credit for his first-rate direction here; working well with second-unit director Busby Berkeley, coordinating music, dialogue, and camera work into one joyous and seamless musical expression, Walters displays the skills that made him such an effective director of first-class musicals such as *Good News, The Barkleys of Broadway,* and the classic *Easter Parade.*

Doris as Kitty Wonder in the first-class and elegiac *Jumbo,* 1962. *Photofest*

The film begins with a lengthy overture from the acclaimed Richard Rodgers/Lorenz Hart score, and surprisingly gets off to a rather slow start. The opening band solo and circus tent raising are taken at extremely slow tempos, and it is not until a good ten minutes into the film that the first number, "Over and Over Again," is heard. It's as if the musical takes as much time to get cranked up as does the circus tent itself. This number is followed by "The Circus Is on Parade," but even this song, a natural for a film musical if ever there was one, receives a rather stately treatment instead of the full-fledged bright musical attack required. However, this all changes when Doris Day's Kitty Wonder charges to the fore, because when she does, the film lifts off into the stratospheric heights reserved for only the very best musical films.

Kitty is first glimpsed swinging into action as defender of the circus animals, talking to Jumbo and firing the circus roustabout who she feels has been abusing the elephant. This woman is no shy flower; she is an acrobat, clearly runs the circus far more effectively than does Pop, and in fact cleans up the problems caused by his gambling. It's no surprise that the film picks up a full head of steam when Kitty rides into town to stop Pop's gambling losses, because she does more than put an end to the losses; she herself steps up and gambles. She beats the men at their own game—"While other little girls were playing dolls, I was rolling four the hard way"—yet she remains utterly feminine even while besting them at the gambling table. Doris Day makes all of this behavior believable; whether gambling or citing the state statutes in order to evade the circus's creditors, she allows Kitty to register with the audience as one self-sufficient, tough, yet vulnerable young woman. Any audience worth its salt can't help but cheer her on.

Kitty is attracted to Sam Rawlins, but this is not a woman who turns coy and simpering at the sight of an attractive man. She doesn't melt right away, and her willingness to take her time makes the inevitable romance with Sam all the more appealing. Kitty doesn't rush head-on into Sam's arms because after all, as in any good musical, first there is a song to sing! And it's a terrific song, "Why Can't I," a beautifully staged duet with a pleasantly subdued Martha Raye. Kitty and the long-suffering Lulu (engaged to Pop for fourteen years and counting) are riding in an open coach, rocking in their chairs, the music perfectly meshed with the gently swaying movements of the coach as it rolls across the countryside. It's a plaintive song of yearning, and even though Raye is not Day's match vocally, she still sounds very good here. As the coach fades down the country path, one realizes that this terrifically staged number can actually be read as symbolic of the end of the Freed unit and of the musical film as audiences have known it: Tastes are changing, but these extraordinary professionals are going out with great style. They know how to make an exit.

Since Sam is in reality a traitor to Kitty and her father, the musical gains another level of interest: When will Kitty find out? Will Sam really betray her? The fact that Sam comes to dislike his own behavior grants Kitty's pursuit of Sam additional texture; the audience wants to see them together, but he is not yet worthy of her. In the meantime, while she remains ignorant of Sam's true intentions, it's great fun to watch her follow her prey, and "prey" is indeed the operative word. In Kitty's phrase, "I'm not hunting him—I'm just dogging him a little," and dog him she does, following him onto the trapeze and swinging from platform to platform in pursuit of their ongoing conversation. The camera angles chosen by Walters stress not only the height of the platforms but also the isolation the characters feel as they try to connect. When Kitty slips and Sam catches her, their mute hesitant touching hints at their true feelings for each other, but each is reluctant to state them. In fact, this sequence actually achieves some of the depth found in the justly famed "If I Loved You" sequence from Rodgers and Hammerstein's *Carousel.* Just as that musical's lead characters, Julie Jordan and Billy Bigelow, could express their love for each other only by a blend of song and speech all couched in the conditional—*if* I loved you—here Kitty and Sam similarly reveal themselves slowly, layer by layer. It's a conversation that started in their carriage ride home after Kitty's successful gambling venture and here continues in the air, platform to platform, the characters catching and holding each other, their mutual attraction increasing.

When first Sam, and then Kitty, somersaults into the trapeze net, with Kitty literally rebounding forward into the immediately ensuing song "This Can't Be Love," it all makes perfect sense. Music, lyrics, dialogue, setting, and action have all merged together in order to further the story in a nigh onto perfect blend. "This Can't Be Love," propelled by the terrific, buoyant orchestrations by Conrad Salinger, lifts the viewer right along with Kitty, as she happily discovers that, title of the song to the contrary, she really is in love. Kitty, performing acrobatics on the horse as she gleefully rides bareback around the circus tent, bursts into song because it is the only form of expression that can convey her tumultuous, joy-filled emotions. It's all perfectly choreographed, literally and figuratively, right down to the pink hooves on the horses that match Kitty's costume. That the audience accepts the progression of Sam and Kitty's mutual attraction from a sparring, tentative expression into a full-blown declaration of love is due to the now fully developed musical acting skills of Doris Day.

There is a second beautifully staged musical sequence later in the film, set to the famous Richard Rodgers waltz "The Most Beautiful Girl in the World." This number is actually a three-act play complete unto itself, forming a perfect circle from beginning to end. The number begins in humorous fashion with Kitty attempting to fix the broken carousel music box, an attempt that succeeds only in covering her face with dirt. When Sam happens by, he starts to fix the music box, humorously whistling "The Most Beautiful Girl in the World" to himself—Kitty still has no idea she has dirt all over her face. When Kitty discovers her disheveled state, she rushes off to change, reappearing in a beautiful pink skirt and jacket. As the newly fixed carousel plays "The Most Beautiful Girl in the World," she looks longingly at Sam, who returns her adoring gaze by barking, "Hand me that screwdriver." Dismayed, Kitty joins him on the whirling carousel, and as he first whistles the melody, then sings it, the carousel smoothly spins in circles perfectly synchronized with the waltz tempo of the song. Kitty continues to pursue Sam, the carousel abruptly stops, and when Sam gets it going again he sings the song directly to Kitty. They begin to dance, and as the orchestra glides into the beautiful melody, the audience is swept up right along with Sam and Kitty. Kitty gracefully steps into the waiting carriage, motioning for Sam to join her; instead he slaps the horse with a command to trot forward, an axle breaks, and Kitty lands in the mud, ending just as she started—the most beautiful girl in the world, indeed. By wisely playing against the expected action at crucial moments, and thereby undercutting any excessive sentimentality, Walters succeeds in allowing the audience to enjoy the song all the more.

Similarly, Doris Day's character also undercuts expectations, always marching to the beat of her own drummer. After a hurricane has destroyed the circus tent, and Sam declares his love for the first time—"I thought I was going to lose you"—it is actually Kitty who proposes to Sam with the words "I wouldn't mind being a sunshiner's wife." It is only after hearing Kitty's proposal that Sam asks Kitty to marry him. Doris Day sings "My Romance" at this point in the film precisely because the setting for this proposal is anything but romantic: There has just been a hurricane, the circus tent has been destroyed, and there are roustabouts screaming in the background. It's why the Lorenz Hart lyrics are all the more effective in Day's silken rendition:

My romance doesn't need a moon in the sky
My romance doesn't need a blue lagoon standing by . . .

In this, her last film musical, Day displays an acting ability every bit the equal of her extraordinary singing. When John Noble forecloses on the Wonder Circus at the exact moment that Pop is finally going to marry Lulu, and

The terrific "The Most Beautiful Girl in the World" sequence from *Jumbo. Photofest*

Kitty realizes that Sam is the son of her archenemy, the look on her face—the sense of betrayal—speaks volumes. Through a combination of acting skill and her own inherent persona, Doris Day makes an audience care for her, just as they did for Judy Garland. This acting ability is further evidenced in the "Little Girl Blue" number, another Rodgers and Hart classic. Wandering the deserted grounds of the circus, Doris sings "Little Girl Blue" in voice-over, lit, at first, only on her face; dejectedly walking in the empty big top, Kitty is singing because she has lost both her love and the family business. Only song could now express such heightened emotion, and the pensive ballad beautifully conveys Kitty's sense of betrayal and despair. Walters cannily stages the song so that the actual sight of Doris Day singing is visible on screen only when she sits down on the circus ring and reaches the climactic words

No use old girl—
You may as well surrender—
Your hope is getting slender—

The viewer really does feel genuine emotion for Kitty and her sense of loss. This is no small feat in any musical, let alone one where the titular star is an elephant who steals scenes merely by appearing. (Jimmy Durante, who gives Day terrific support throughout simply by being his lovable self, is perhaps the one performer in history who could ever upstage Jumbo; when Noble's men find him stealing away with Jumbo, and demand of him, "Where are you going with that elephant?" Durante stands in front of the elephant and innocently asks, "What elephant?" Perfection.)

In fact, the film stumbles only in the last number "Sawdust, Spangles, and Dreams." What should be a rock 'em, sock 'em ending instead registers as an overlong soggy production number that dissipates the energy and skill that have preceded it. By now, Sam has renounced his father and returned to join forces with Kitty, Pop, and Lulu, who have been plying their trade before pathetically small crowds in tiny backwater towns. Catching Kitty backstage, he explains all that has happened: In the curiously distorted logic common to even the best Hollywood musicals, Sam may have interrupted the circus midperformance, but strangely enough, there isn't even a murmur of protest from the crowd assembled on the other side of the stage. Evidently the savvy crowd meekly acquiesces to this unexpected interval because, after all, the lovers have to make up and the leading man has to begin his song.

Unfortunately, although Sam has brought back Jumbo, that's the only interesting thing about the endless number—it goes on for far too long, complete with a good five minutes of all four principals in clown suit and makeup belting each other and indulging in slapstick shenanigans. None of it matches the near-elegant tone of the previous numbers and would seem much more at home in one of Day's early bargain basement Warner Bros. musicals. Ah, well, it has been a terrific show up until now and the flat final number doesn't nullify the preceding two hours of fun. Raye, Durante, and a surprisingly relaxed and effective Stephen Boyd are all first rate, but this is really Doris Day's show. She here bears no resemblance to the overly eager-to-please performer of *It's a Great Feeling* and *The West Point Story.* Day has matured into a skilled actress who can accomplish what she needs by a searching glance, not just a silky vocal. Not only is she calmer than in the sometimes shrill early films, she also looks softer and more appealing than ever before. Sporting a long, soft blond wig and both long skirts and circus clothes that show off her hourglass figure, she is relaxed, determined, and totally natural—the quintessence of her star persona fully revealed. Suffice it to say, if Doris Day ever allowed an evening's film tribute to her career, there are at least a half dozen moments in *Jumbo* that could make the highlights reel.

Jumbo may not have been a hit, but the next film *The Thrill of It All,* was a box office bonanza for Universal, and deservedly so, because the first two-thirds of this comedy is absolutely terrific, with Doris giving the best comic performance of her career. It doesn't get better than this, which is why the third act of the film is so disappointing. But until then . . .

The Thrill of It All is immeasurably aided not only by the smooth and assured direction of then newcomer Norman Jewison but particularly by Carl Reiner's script, from a story concocted by Reiner and Larry Gelbart (of *M*A*S*H* fame). This is, for the most part, a genuinely first-rate screenplay, which weaves a very funny satire of the advertising business into the story of the marriage between Dr. Gerald Boyer (James Garner) and his wife Beverly (Day).

The film begins with wealthy tycoon Gardiner Fraleigh (Edward Andrews) and his wife (Arlene Francis) ecstatic at the news that she is at long last pregnant. So happy are the Fraleighs that they insist on inviting obstetrician Boyer and his wife to their celebratory family dinner. At the dinner, Beverly charms Fraleigh's octogenarian father Tom (Reginald Owen), the power behind their family Happy Soap fortune; relating how using Happy Soap allowed her finally to shampoo her daughter's hair, Beverly is hired by Tom on the spot to be his new Happy Soap television spokesperson.

Beverly's disastrous yet utterly natural first attempt at a commercial captivates both Fraleigh and the viewing public, and Beverly is hired for a full year as the spokesperson. Husband Gerald does not like his wife being a celebrity and earning so much money, and after a fight, Gerald resolves to give Beverly a dose of her own medicine; he suddenly becomes too busy to spend time with

Housewife-turned-star. The hilarious *The Thrill of It All,* 1963. *Photofest*

her and pretends to have an affair with his secretary. Still at odds, the couple work together to deliver Mrs. Fraleigh's baby in a stalled taxicab in the middle of New York City; quicker than you can say "wrap it all up," Gerald and Beverly embrace, Beverly realizes that what she's always really wanted is to be a doctor's wife, and with a wink toward the couple having another child themselves, all ends happily.

Putting aside the rushed and unfortunate ending, this film operates at a consistently high comic level, right from the opening scene. Thanks to Doris Day—and James Garner—this is a real comedy about real people. And the reason it works is that Doris is here every bit as believable a stay-at-home mom as she has been in her Manhattan career girl roles.

The first glimpse the viewer has of Beverly Boyer is as she gives a bath and shampoo to her daughter Maggie (Kym Karath, who went to play Gretl, the youngest von Trapp in *The Sound of Music*). Dealing with her daughter's refusal to let her use the regular brand of shampoo ("Mommy, it smells like the cracks in the playground"), trying unsuccessfully to instruct her son Andy (Brian Nash) how to answer the phone and take a message from his father, Day is 100 percent believable—funny, exasperated, overburdened with chores—she is a real woman with real children (credit, too, to Nash and Karath, both of whom are utterly winning). When Day and Garner interact for the first time onscreen, they sound like a happily married fun couple, but she is no sappily adoring doctor's wife.

Gerald: Did you know I'm a great doctor?
Beverly (with smiling irony): I've always suspected it. How did you find out?

On their way to the dinner party at the Fraleighs', Beverly and Gerald kiss passionately in the backseat of the Fraleighs' limo (which makes the later glimpses of the twin beds seem all the more ludicrous; he's a doctor, they like sex—where the hell did those kids come from, anyway?). Garner and Day are great together—both of them sexy in an utterly believable manner—and it's no surprise to read Garner's description of Doris as having "this sexy whirlpool frothing around underneath her All-American-girl exterior." On screen and off, these two first-rate comic actors genuinely like each other and it shows.

At the dinner party where Beverly recounts how Happy Soap saved her life, she relates that the soap was necessary because Andy and Maggie, her not so perfect children, threw mudballs at each other. Beverly's naturalness charms elderly tycoon Tom Fraleigh and he instantly decides to sign her as Happy Soap's national spokesperson. Beverly Boyer likes the idea of earning her own money—$332—for appearing in the commercial and says yes. Which is how and when the fun really begins.

In a charming and very funny sequence, Andy and Maggie see Beverly, in front of her mirror, trying out different ways of performing her upcoming commercial. Each of her attempts at delivering the commercial is funny in its own way; adopting poses and deliveries that range from sophisticated to perky to gracious, Day manages to indeed fit all of those adjectives. At the same time, she is able to make the viewer realize that none of these personae will work because they aren't natural. And both Doris Day and Beverly Boyer are naturals.

Sporting a blond semibouffant hairdo à la Jackie Kennedy, Beverly then proceeds to make a fool of herself on national television. She becomes so caught up in watching the live World War II dramatic presentation that precedes her spot, that when that segment ends with a woman calling a Nazi officer "a pig," and the camera immediately switches focus to Beverly, she begins her Happy Soap debut on nationwide television by stating, "Hello. I'm Beverly Boyer and I'm a pig." Forgetting her lines, lacing her commercial with *umms*, *ahhs*, and erroneous words, Day is so charming and affectless that the viewer completely forgets that this is a meticulously thought out comic performance. Day has calibrated her line delivery within an inch of its life, yet absolutely none of the effort shows. Just as in the opening segment of *Please Don't Eat the Daisies,* Day here delivers a pitch-perfect performance.

Embarrassed by her television appearance, Beverly, busy in her basement making her own ketchup out of fresh tomatoes, does not even listen to ad exec Mike Palmer (Elliott Reid) pitch her to sign on as permanent spokesperson. Doesn't listen, that is, until she is told she will make $1,500 per week for fifty-two weeks. Husband Gerald doesn't want Beverly to make the commercials. (In a welcome sign of how natural and realistic the film is, Gerald's objections are first voiced in the basement while son Andy squishes tomatoes between his fingers, making a further mess—again, these are believable children with believable parents.) In what could be viewed as an opening salvo in the soon-to-arrive feminist revolution, Beverly calls her husband to account on his very own rhetoric:

Gerald: There is no reason for you to work.
Beverly: Dr. Boyer, you're a fraud. Right here in this magazine article—your own words—"Household duties may not be sufficient for a woman to express her ambitions."
Gerald: You've got the PTA and make your own ketchup.
Beverly: The PTA and home-bottled ketchup—it's not very fulfilling.

Beverly wants her own career, wants to earn her own money, and she succeeds. The audience cheers her on all the way because Day's performance here exhibits all of the attributes that made her the biggest star in the world at this time: She is sympathetic, beautiful, believable, ambitious, blessed with enormous drive—and never threatening.

Beverly is soon swept up into the "glamorous" world of television advertising and becomes nationally famous, but at heart she hasn't changed, and that's why the audience roots for her all the more. Beverly still rattles off reminders about the children to household maid Olivia (Zasu Pitts in the Thelma Ritter/Audrey Meadows role); she yells upstairs to the children, "I need a good-bye kiss," and generally behaves as any harried working mother would. Beverly needs to express her own ambitions, but her children still rate as her top priority.

Along the way, besides positing all sorts of interesting questions about the roles of women, specifically suburban mothers, the film also takes hilarious pokes at Madison Avenue advertising (zingers that are even funnier, and more pointed, than those in *Lover Come Back*). The *Happy Soap Playtime* basically shows the same drama every week— only the accents and costumes are changed. The advertising executives think no one in the audience is sophisticated enough to catch on but Beverly's two very young children figure out the duplication instantly, proclaiming "It's the same story every week" in hilariously bored tones.

As Beverly's celebrity grows, Gerald becomes increasingly frustrated over playing second fiddle to her; it is she who receives the celebrity treatment in the fancy restaurant they go to for dinner, Beverly who receives the bowing and scraping treatment accorded to the rich and famous. When the Happy Soap Company builds a pool in the Boyer backyard in order to shoot a Happy Dishwashing Soap commercial, Beverly neglects to tell Gerald that they now have a swimming pool, and he drives his car right into the water. Garner's slow burn as he sinks underwater gripping the steering wheel is every bit the comic equal of Day's hilariously inept first Happy Soap commercial. The visual of Gerald Boyer in the driver's seat slowly sinking in the pool is even funnier than the sight of mountains of soapsuds appearing in the Boyer backyard after overnight rain mixes with the boxes of Happy Soap detergent that Gerald has angrily kicked into the pool. Once again, even the soapsuds scene is beautifully set up; not content with the surefire visual gag of the voluminous soapsuds themselves, director Jewison and scriptwriter Reiner make Beverly's shock at the resulting suds even more pronounced by playing up the early morning stupor in which she finds herself. Urged by Maggie and Andrew to come see the acres of suds, Beverly is awakened by both children speaking loudly in her ear, at the same time poking her eyes open with their fingers—a sight and sound familiar in one form or another to any real-life parent.

Doris Day's films really did point the way for a generation of discontented suburban women, or rather, accurately reflected their frustrations and ambitions; witness Beverly and Gerald's increasingly angry argument about money:

Gerald: Our money is what I've earned as a doctor.
Beverly: And what I've earned?
Gerald: That's *your* money.
Beverly: And what about my rights as a woman?
Gerald: They suffocated my rights as a man. It's time you give up your career and go back to being a wife.

(So outrageous is this statement by modern-day standards that one is willing to overlook Day's foot-stomping, body-gyrating reaction to Gerald's idiocy; it's the only time in the film that she exhibits the comic exaggeration in which she sometimes indulges when faced with lesser material.) With chauvinistic attitudes like this still prevalent, no wonder the times they were a-changin'. Which makes it all the more unfortunate that as the years went by, all of the jokes about Doris Day's perpetual virginity made people forget what these films were really all about. It certainly wasn't about her refusal to have sex: It was about demanding truth and respect from the men in her life.

So good is *The Thrill of It All* up to this point that it comes as a real shock that the last third of the film plays like a 1930s take on a woman's "proper" station in life. Husband Gerald's way of making Beverly behave like a "real" (and "reel") wife again is to take a page out of her book and act too busy to spend any time with her. Taking the ruse one step farther, he pretends to have an affair with his secretary Miss Thompson (Anne Newman) by putting lipstick on his collar, having his photograph taken with her, and faking a drunken state in which he calls Beverly by another woman's name. There is something distasteful in all of this. It's not just that Beverly's rise to fame provided the audience with a real rooting interest and is so much funnier than such heavy-handed shtick; it's that Gerald is acting condescendingly to Beverly and has concocted all of these schemes out of his childish jealousy of her success.

Beverly's last appearance on the air is preceded by her saying to adman Mike Palmer, "My husband is a doctor and I'm a doctor's wife." In other words, I'm giving up money, glamour, stardom, and true partnership with my husband in order to make ketchup in the cellar. Just in case the audience doesn't get the message, the film concludes by repeating very similar lines after an unnecessarily long slapstick sequence featuring traffic jams and Mr. Fraleigh's inability to help deliver his own baby (Beverly, of course, has no problem taking over). Beverly and Gerald work together to deliver Mrs. Fraleigh's baby in traffic (with Arlene Francis wearing a maternity outfit, complete with black veil that makes her look like she is about to have an audience with the pope). Says Beverly at the conclusion of helping to deliver a baby, "I want to be a doctor's wife again." What?! Lickety-split, Beverly doesn't care about the great career she has carved out for herself? It no longer matters that she is fulfilled, famous, and recognized as a person in her own right? No one is going to buy this nonsense.

Of course, this script is still light-years ahead of the Stanley Shapiro confections for the Day-Hudson pictures, but the problem is that after a great first ninety minutes featuring a funny, feisty, and forthrightly appealing heroine, even Carl Reiner and Larry Gelbart undercut their own premise in order to reflect the supposed mores of the day. (At least here, however, unlike in the

Shapiro scripts, psychiatry is not held up to ridicule. When Gerald absent-mindedly wanders into a psychiatrist's office at the hospital, the psychiatrist may look goofy, but Gerald genuinely wants the doctor's opinion about what is happening in his life.)

In many ways, *The Thrill of It All* perfectly fits the construct of the "woman's film" posited by film scholar Jeanine Basinger in *A Woman's View.* In language that directly applies to 1963's *The Thrill of It All,* Basinger discusses the 1939 comedy *Honeymoon in Bali:* "It is interesting how a light romantic comedy maintains the basic point of the woman's film—a woman must make a choice, and her best choice is for love." As Basinger also notes, "The woman's film was successful because it worked out of a paradox. It both held women in social bondage and released them into a dream of potency and freedom. . . . To convince women that marriage and motherhood were the right path, movies had to show women making the mistake of doing something else. . . . Stereotypes are presented, then undermined, and then reinforced. . . . These movies were a way of recognizing the problems of women, of addressing their desire to have things be other than the way they were off-screen. . . . These are films that tell the truth, but only because they are about the unhappiness of women. They'll tell all the lies in the world to make that one point clear." Until the final third of *The Thrill of It All,* Day's skill and drive make one actually believe that this time the ending will be different. The time hadn't come yet for that statement to be made consistently, but for the America of 1963, it is not too far-fetched to say that Doris Day pointed the way. The simpering virgin next door? No way.

Day's follow-up film, 1963's *Move Over Darling,* reteamed her with James Garner. Directed by Michael Gordon (*Pillow Talk*), *Move Over Darling* is the last of Day's A-list pictures, a film, whatever its merits, whose production values are at least worthy of the biggest star in town. After this film, cheap production values and second-rate scripts unfortunately became the order of the day. It's as if all of the verve in Day's film career left with the last frame of *Move Over Darling.*

The production history of *Move Over Darling* is one of the more interesting in Hollywood history. Originally intended as a starring vehicle for Marilyn Monroe titled *Something's Gotta Give,* production on the film was scrapped when Monroe's emotional fragility caused her to be fired from that George Cukor film. Months later, the script reemerged as *Move Over Darling,* starring Doris Day. (When Monroe's existing footage from *Something's Gotta Give* was pieced together in 2005 in order to give a glimpse of what might have been, the resulting one hour of footage proved both fascinating and a bit heartbreaking. Monroe no longer had the fortitude to withstand a grueling production schedule and the remaining footage shows an ethereally beautiful, vulnerable, and nearly broken star.)

The *Move Over Darling* screenplay by Hal Kanter and Jack Sher is a reworking of the Enoch Arden character from the Tennyson poem, wherein a man returns to his family years after everyone has assumed he died. Several films have been made with this basic premise, the most notable being the 1940 Irene Dunne/Cary Grant film *My Favorite Wife; Move Over Darling* is, in fact, a close copy of that very film. Here the story concerns the return of Ellen Wagstaff Arden (Doris Day), a wife and mother who, having vanished five years ago in an airplane crash at sea, had been declared legally dead. As the film opens, she has been rescued by the navy and returns home, very much alive, on the same day that her attorney husband Nicholas (James Garner) has married Bianca Steele (Polly Bergen). Nicholas can't figure out how to tell Bianca that his first wife is alive, Ellen's two children don't recognize her, and myriad complications ensue before Ellen, Nicholas, and their two daughters are happily reunited at final fade-out.

The film gets off to a terrific start with what is for once, a first-rate title song, written and produced by Day's son Terry Melcher. A sexy, catchy pop tune, the song provided Day with the last hit single of her recording career. Were that the rest of the film lived up to the title tune.

With Doris front and center throughout all of *Move Over Darling,* the movie, needless to say, ended up very different than Monroe's *Something's Gotta Give* would have been. The only similarity between the two lies in Day's Monroe-like bouffant hairdo. Instead of Marilyn's palpable vulnerability, Day's Ellen Arden proves to be another version of her iconic American wife and mother, circa 1963. She is resourceful and energetic, and she certainly drives the comedy. Her chemistry with Garner intact, she has an easy natural rapport with her two screen children and the audience immediately wants this woman to win back her family, even while wondering exactly how Ellen maintained such luxurious false eyelashes and platinum blond hair while stranded on a desert island. Even though Day has a forthright female presence, her vulnerability is genuine; when Nicky's mother Grace (Thelma Ritter, once again hitting the sauce) tells Ellen that Nicky has remarried, Day's Ellen looks hurt and in genuine pain. When Ellen sees Nicky for the first time—at the Monterey Hotel, where he is celebrating his honeymoon, no less—it is clear from just one glance that Ellen genuinely loves her husband.

It is, unfortunately, to the film's detriment that the love triangle depicted has "no contest" written all over it. Ellen, the "real" wife, is still alive, and her competition, second wife Bianca, comes across as a total drip, even though played by the talented Polly Bergen. Bianca literally kicks and screams to get her way and is presented as worthy of ridicule from start to finish. Her shrillness begins with her very first appearance, when she arrives complete with a loud charm bracelet and wearing a hat that resembles half a grapefruit on her head. Her cartoonlike unpleasantness continues unabated until the final fade-out, and if husband Nicky had any sense at all, he'd find his own desert island in order to escape Bianca.

Move Over Darling presents a very physical Doris Day. She tracks Nicky and Bianca to their honeymoon suite, climbs on tables, and falls over while spying on them. When Nicky pretends his back is hurt so that he can avoid having sex with Bianca (note—it's not Doris Day who won't have sex), Day impersonates Swedish nurse Greta Svenson in order to take care of him. In this guise she also gives a very rough-and-tumble massage to Bianca (shades of Streisand and De Niro in *Meet the Fockers*) while cleverly reciting the plot of *My Favorite Wife*. Day does nothing short of beating up on Polly Bergen—whacking her back, walking on it while wearing shoes, and even chasing her around the bed.

This is all funny stuff, but the film as an entity is entirely hit-and-miss. For every funny massage scene, there is a sequence where Day mugs, stamps her feet, and shrieks in order to convey her displeasure at her husband's remarriage. Just as happened in *Pillow Talk*. Director Michael Gordon must share in the blame, because he here lets Day fall back on these easy scenery-chewing modes of expression instead of encouraging a more subtle and realistic characterization.

The movie is back on firmer ground when Day's Ellen is back at home with her two girls and mother-in-law Grace. When Day sings "Twinkle Lullabye" to the girls at bedtime, it is touching in the extreme and says everything about her maternal warmth. Four bars of song and it is clear that Bianca has absolutely no chance of remaining Mrs. Arden.

But—and it's a big but—the entire movie is attenuated to the point of completely losing its audience. Nicky avoids telling Bianca that Ellen is alive no fewer than six times, and these complications ultimately prove to be artificial and tiresome. The audience simply wants to shout out, "Why don't you just tell her already?" In addition, nearly all of the secondary characters are stock figures recycled from previous Day outings. John Astin is a smarmy insurance agent just as he was a smarmy unemployment office worker in *That Touch of Mink*. Bianca deals with her confusion by flirting with, who else, her psychiatrist, Dr. Schlink. Unethical behavior, anyone? Mainstream America sure was petrified of psychiatry in the early 1960s—or at least the creators of Doris Day films were.

It is all too indicative of the film's schizophrenic approach to comedy that even the final bit of inspiration undercuts itself. When James Garner realizes that wife Ellen has been stranded on the island with muscleman Chuck Connors, and not with milquetoast shoe salesman Don Knotts as she had claimed, it subsequently dawns on him that this muscle-bound "Adam" lived with wife Ellen as his own private "Eve" for five long years. Uneasily visualizing exactly what island life was like for "Adam" and "Eve," Nicky's resulting jealousy-tinged imaginings are downright funny. Presented as a silent film fantasy sequence, Garner's imagination leads him to picture Day lounging by an island lagoon, scantily clad and sexily offering an apple to he-man Adam. (Nicky could have saved himself a lot of worry by realizing that Ellen could have taken care of herself at all times. When, at movie's end, Ellen decks "Adam" with one punch, it's no surprise. This girl is self-sufficient in the extreme.) This is witty visual filmmaking, but the problem is that Nicky's jealousy is then manifested in a very silly speeded-up car chase, complete with Ellen maniacally driving a car while Nicky desperately chases her in a cab.

The entire sequence looks and plays like a cartoon, with no believability whatsoever. The asinine car chase isn't enough to ruin the entire sequence, however, because when Doris drives into a car wash in order to avoid Nicky, her car windows remain open, and in a genuinely funny slapstick scene, she gets washed right along with the car. Gargantuan flippers washing and drying both the car and Doris herself, this sequence once again makes clear that no other female star of the time could have undergone such physical exertion and made it so believable and yet so funny. It is a display of physical clowning that would have made Lucille Ball herself proud. Like the movie itself, Doris Day herein is simultaneously funny and exhausting.

At the end of the film, after Ellen is reunited with her daughters, what lingers in the viewer's mind is the realization that while Doris Day's appeal has remained intact, the strenuous efforts involved have begun to take their toll. The filmmakers don't trust their own script enough to allow her time to relax and charm the audience. Instead, hoisting the entire film onto her own shoulders, she must work harder and harder in order to score ever-diminishing returns. What Doris Day needed were first-rate scripts along the lines of *Teacher's Pet* and *The Man Who Knew Too Much*. Unfortunately, what followed proved to be exactly the opposite.

Whatever the failings of *Move Over Darling,* it at least contained a bona fide story. Day's next film, *Send Me No Flowers,* her third and final teaming with

Rock Hudson and Tony Randall, was a one-joke affair—and a decidedly unfunny one, at that.

In *Send Me No Flowers,* Hudson plays hypochondriac George Kimball, who overhears his doctor (Edward Andrews from *The Thrill of It All*) discussing a terminally ill patient and immediately jumps to the conclusion that he, George, is dying. After discussing his imminent demise with best friend Arnold (Tony Randall), George decides to find wife Judy (Doris Day) a husband she can marry after his death, ultimately deciding that Judy's college friend, the wealthy and handsome Bert (Clint Walker) will prove to be just the right man. Judy, in the meantime, jumps to the erroneous conclusion that George is having an affair when she sees him embracing their pretty and newly separated neighbor Linda (Patricia Berry). One hundred minutes later, complications all sorted out, Judy and George reconcile to theoretically live happily and healthily ever after.

By any objective standard, even a simple recitation of the plot reveals that this movie is a mess, the blame for which must be laid at the feet of the screenplay by Julius Epstein (*Romance on the High Seas*) It's a one-joke movie based on a second-rate Broadway play, just as are *The Tunnel of Love* and *Do Not Disturb.* Right from the opening salvos, the movie does not play like a fanciful farce but rather reeks of contrivance. Who is going to believe that Rock Hudson, the picture of health, would endlessly whine like his loser of a character does? Taking his temperature in the hot shower and popping pills with abandon from his seemingly endless supply, this man is not interested in anything but his own health, which makes him a very dull leading character indeed. It's one full hour into the movie before the audience even learns that he actually has a job at Cornell Electronics. He is defined solely by his hypochondria and does not change one iota from start to finish. If the character in question never grows or changes, then there is no reason to care about him, and not one single reason exists for the audience to spend two hours of its time in his company.

It's not that the Day/Hudson chemistry has disappeared. They're still effortless together, but there's nothing for them to play. As the movie begins, they are already married—there is no chase and therefore no energy. George Kimball whines so incessantly that the audience is only left wondering, "Why would Judy even stay with such a sad sack of a man?"

The single biggest flaw in the screenplay is that Day's character of Judy is given nothing to do. Day's other feature films that transplanted her persona of independent urban career girl to middle-class suburban mother worked as long as she still remained the dynamo of energy and self-sufficiency she was in *Please Don't Eat the Daisies* and *The Thrill of It All.* Conversely, her screen persona disintegrates when, as in *Do Not Disturb* and *Send Me No Flowers,* she is reduced to passive helpmate. Here, Judy's chief occupations seem to be replacing George's pills with sugar-filled placebos and playing golf (Doris is still dressed by Jean Louis, but designer golf clothes don't help the star—or the audience's interest).

Worse yet, Judy Kimball is presented as something of a dumbbell, and playing dumb doesn't sit will on Doris Day. The viewer instantly retreats from such dialogue:

George: What is the amortization of a mortgage?'
Judy: I don't care.

After a further discussion, Judy returns to the subject: "What *does* amortization mean?" The funny, feisty Jan Gordon of *Pillow Talk* could have answered this question with her eyes closed. Here, when Rock discusses his plight with neighbor Arnold (fittingly the discussion takes place near a sandbox), he simply tells Arnold, "Judy will never make it alone."

Day's performance is a mixed bag here. There are moments of inspired slapstick at the beginning of the movie, moments which Day herself devised. Waking up to make breakfast for her husband, Judy manages to lock herself out of the house, catch her robe in the door, drop eggs on the front porch, and step in the ensuing gooey mess. She is a harried housewife trying to get her day started and it is genuinely funny, just as she is when rolling her eyes in disgust at George's melodramatic assertion that he is at the "ebb tide of his life." However, once Judy goes back inside the house, she has nothing to do except react to George's hypochondria. As a result, the viewer's only real interest is to note that Doris's hairstyle seems to change midbreakfast.

More damaging is the fact that when dealing with such weak material, Day seemingly is unsure of how to elevate the nonsense—but then again, who would know? Faced with what she assumes is the doctor's callousness in the face of her husband's imminent death, Day falls back on her standard bag of tricks. Eyes popping, voice shrieking, mouth agape, she is a cartoon figure. This is a very long way from the subtleties she displayed in *Love Me or Leave Me* and *The Thrill of It All,* and Jewison, who guided her so beautifully in the latter film, must here share in the blame due to his resolutely heavy-handed direction.

A second note of blame for the film's many shortcomings must also go to the musical score composed by Frank DeVol. DeVol had arranged and conducted Day's brilliant uptempo *Cuttin' Capers* LP, but here his work is third rate and actually harms the movie. This is sledgehammer heavy "Do you get it" type of scoring. When prospective husband Clint Walker's cowboy boots are glimpsed, DeVol's score all but plays "Home on the Range." Similarly, when George punches out the slimy playboy Winston Burr, a boxing bell is heard. What were DeVol and director Norman Jewison thinking? Moviegoers were not this dense, and the film would have been immeasurably improved if the filmmakers had allowed audiences to discover the action for themselves.

For his part, Randall, who plays the second banana with his customary ease, gets the single funniest line in the movie. Informed by George that he has bad news to share, Randall's quickly horrified response is, "Bad news? Nothing that's going to affect property values, is it?" It's a very funny line and, because it is based on character, one that rings true forty years later.

Every time a funny line causes the movie to sputter to life, however, the flame is quickly doused again. When George, who is scouting a potential new husband for Judy, is at first jealous of the strapping Bert (Clint Walker) but then realizes that in fact Bert is the perfect new husband for Judy, the viewer is actually interested—here is a real plot development. Unfortunately, any such interest is immediately undercut by a cheap-looking rear-projection sequence in which Judy careens wildly out of control while trying to drive a runaway golf cart (never mind the fact that the top speed attained by a golf cart is roughly that of a senior citizen with a walker). More striking is the fact that once again the idea of Judy's helplessness is underscored. This, forced on an actress who fixed cars with ease in *On Moonlight Bay* . . .

The over-the-top sexist dialogue isn't much help, either, as when Bert stops the speeding golf cart and gravely intones, "It's okay, little lady. You're safe." Similarly unhelpful is the self-referential cuteness that informs so many of these later comedies (e.g., the movie theater scene in *Caprice*). Witness Bert's reaction to seeing college girlfriend Judy again after years of separation: "I just figured she'd marry Cary Grant." Evidently, when there's no real wit at hand, the solution is to resort to in-jokes about the star's other movies.

Even more than in the other Day/Hudson movies, the gay subtext is very prevalent in *Send Me No Flowers,* and it is the most interesting element of the entire film. Just how many viewers truly realized what they were watching in 1964 is an interesting question to ponder. It's not only that the two disparate personae of gay male America are here present in the handsome, masculine Rock Hudson and the fey, camp Paul Lynde (who plays Mr. Akins, the cemetery plot salesman). No, what registers most strongly is the relationship between Arnold and George that is like nothing seen since, well, Calamity Jane and Miss Adelaide in *Calamity Jane.* Witness George and Arnold discussing Bert as a prospective husband for Judy:

George: He's good looking—in good form.
Arnold: His form is not as good as yours.

And when dressing for the country club dance:

Arnold: I need to powder my nose. *You* need to powder *your* nose.

This is topped only by George's command to Arnold, while putting on his cummerbund: "Do me." Hell, this isn't even subtext—it's right out there. What the viewer really wants to know is, Where the hell is the supposedly married Arnold's wife? It is Arnold who gently pushes George in his wheelchair, just as if he were George's nurse. Arnold spends more time caring for George than does wife Judy. And where does Rock go for solace after he fights with Judy? To Arnold's house, where Arnold helps George into a sweater and they slip into bed together. Turns out Arnold's wife is conveniently enough, away, and the kids are at camp. Right.

Finally, one hour and ten minutes into the movie, the Day/Hudson magic returns. George and Judy reminisce about their first meeting, and all of a sudden the viewer begins to understand why they fell in love. Even better, when Judy suspects George of carrying on an affair and of faking his illness, Doris Day swings into action and the key ingredient in their onscreen courtship and coupling happily zings to life—Judy gets revenge. Pretending that she thinks George is having a nightmare, she boldly slaps him awake. It's a singularly funny moment both because her outrage makes sense and because it's unexpected.

Judy gets George all excited about the possibility of sex, and even though the employment of a soft-focus lens on Day's close-up is distractingly noticeable, it's still a very funny moment when Judy pushes him out of the house in his wheelchair and locks the door behind him. Standing by the second-story window, she throws all of the pills out the window and onto the top of his head. At long last, this is the gal of action for whom we've been waiting.

Yet even this fun is destroyed by a truly smarmy finale. Arnold, in a particularly demented piece of logic, has advised George to make a false confession of adultery. When Judy learns that there was no such affair, what does she do with this knowledge? She decides to "forgive" George for (his false report of) having strayed. She doesn't tell George that she knows he lied to her about the affair, so the movie ends with George's false confession of adultery. The mind boggles. Was this really what Hollywood thought marriage was like in America, or was it just particularly lazy screenwriting? Even by Hollywood standards, a happily ever after marriage based on a double deceit is cuckoo.

When the movie finally ends, the viewer's reaction is akin to the reaction at the conclusion of *The Tunnel of Love:* Why was this movie ever made? Of course one knows that it was made so that viewers could see Day and Hudson in action together once again, but they deserved much better. Sadly, *Send Me No Flowers* remained their last big screen pairing, and their only other joint appearances occurred on Day's 1971 television special and when the noticeably ill Hudson joined the healthy, youthful-looking Day for an episode of her 1985 cable television series, *Doris Day and Friends.* That show represented Hudson's last public appearance before his death from AIDS. Even on that sad occasion, however, their mutual love and respect rang out loud and clear as they bantered about their appearances together in *Pillow Talk* and *Lover Come Back.* Better to forget *Send Me No Flowers* and instead remember them from those first two hugely popular films, which properly showcased a truly legendary screen team.

It's not just that the script for Day's next movie, *Do Not Disturb,* is bad, although it certainly is. What's most disturbing about the entire misbegotten film is that it feels cheap and tired. Right up through Day's 1963 release, *Move Over Darling,* production values on her films reflected her status as the Queen of Hollywood. Money was spent on clothes, settings, hair—the works. Occasionally, money was even spent on hiring a first-class writer to deliver a crisp, literate script, as happened with *Teacher's Pet* and *The Thrill of It All.* In *Do Not Disturb,* however, a noticeably phony and cheap-looking English landscape appears to be as worn as is the script. It's as if Doris Day's film career slid from A to Z in one fell swoop, with no stop in between. From here on out, it was, for the most part, all downhill into the land of scripts that reeked of sitcom mediocrity. In effect, this film, which feels so tired and predictable in both situation and character, seemed to flick the switch that made people say that all Doris Day films were interchangeable: *That Touch of Mink* becomes *Send Me No Flowers,* which morphs into *Do Not Disturb,* until the plot contrivances and stale lines all blur together, and all that one remembers is her boundless energy. It's not an exaggeration to say that as a result, Doris Day's feature film career never recovered.

The juvenile plot of *Do Not Disturb* finds wool executive Mike Harper (Rod Taylor) moving to England with wife Janet (Day). Wool is not selling as it should, and since one man, German businessman Langsdorf (Leon Askin), is the buyer who matters to the market, Mike must curry Langsdorf's favor. Janet begins to think that Mike is cheating on her after realtor Vanessa

Courtwright (Hermione Baddeley) sees him dining with his attractive young secretary Claire Hackett (Maura McGiveney), while Mike thinks Janet is having an affair with suave interior decorator Paul Bellasi (Sergio Fantoni). Janet flies to Paris with Bellasi in order to purchase an anniversary present for Mike, becomes drunk, and spends the night in the window (!) of Paul's shop. Janet learns that Mike is not having an affair, is herself pursued by Langsdorf, and after Mike and Janet reconcile, Mike receives Langsdorf's business and all ends happily.

Happily for everyone, that is, except the viewer who sits through this drivel. Just as was the case with *Tunnel of Love, Do Not Disturb* is based on a second-rate Broadway play (by William Fairchild). Adapted for the screen by Milt Rosen and Richard Breen and directed with little wit or imagination by Ralph Levy, *Do Not Disturb* feels, looks, and sounds like the third-rate sitcom it really is. About the only things the film has going for it are a better than usual title song (which manages to provide a little pep to the opening credits) and a series of over-the-top outfits sported by Hermione Baddeley. This is one unusually dressed realtor, and her purple feathered dress would definitely be the talk of Ascot. That's it for fun, though—one song and some crazy dresses. Not a lot to write home about.

Instead, we are treated to a Doris Day character who has no job, no children, and spends her time bothering her husband at work with inane phone calls. Because Doris Day usually projects such a capable, intelligent persona, it is dispiriting to realize that the film's idea of humor is to depict Janet Harper (in very sexist terms, to boot) as a hapless American living overseas who spends her time very slowly learning the ins and outs of English currency, getting into trouble driving on the "wrong" side of the road, and saving a fox from the hounds during a hunt. These onscreen shenanigans are of so little interest that one begins to spend time noting that real-life animal lover Doris Day can herself be glimpsed in the character of Janet Harper; Janet, who unlike her husband loves the Kent countryside, thinks nothing of keeping chickens and roosters in the house, with a pet goat who eats the expensive shrubbery taking up residence right on the front lawn. Perhaps Day received some pleasure from "talking to the animals," because it is impossible to believe that she received the slightest bit of happiness from speaking the screenplay's flaccid lines.

When Janet's trip to Paris finds her becoming drunk due to the French children (!) supplying her with endless glasses of wine and champagne, Day is reduced to spending endless minutes of screen time in supposedly hilarious drunken carousing; at one point she must play a street musician's seven-in-one instrument, pounding and blowing loudly on the cymbal, drum, and horn. A brief interlude of such hijinks might be funny, but when stretched out for minutes on end, the resulting sequence reeks of desperation. So tedious is this ear-piercing carrying on, and so annoying are Janet's shrill yelps to express a drunken playfulness, that the only character one begins to feel any empathy with is the telephone operator she endlessly pesters to place a call to Mike in London. In the entire Paris section of the film, the only note of interest is struck when Doris kicks and heads a soccer ball while decked out in a designer frock, high heels, and a matching chapeau. Doesn't matter what country she's in, Doris is still athletic. The Paris section of the film ends with an extended sequence set in the fog, which is an apt metaphor for how the viewer feels while watching the film drag its way through an endless running time of one hundred two minutes.

There are no jokes here, no humorous situations arising out of characterization and setting. Instead, the best the screenwriters can come up with is another series of self-congratulatory witticisms, as when the French children ask Janet if she knows Rock Hudson. The succession of tired one-liners elicits in the viewer only a feeling of "Who cares?" Who cares that Mike punches out the antiques dealer? Janet's a fool for getting drunk and Mike's a fool for flying off the handle and then rushing off to the sales conference. Who cares if Mike loses Langsdorf's business? The reason it's impossible to care is that the premise underlying Langsdorf's importance is inherently distasteful, just as was the basic premise of *The Tunnel of Love.* Specifically, when Janet arrives at the conference, it is made clear that if Langsdorf learns that Janet is Mike's wife, Mike won't receive Langsdorf's all-important business. Langsdorf is a lech, and although married, he surrounds himself and his fellow executives with young women who appear to be high-class prostitutes. As a result, Janet masquerades as Mike's personal assistant, calling herself "Claire Hackett," the name of his secretary. In other words, the movie seems to tell us that getting business is more important than being honest about one's own marriage, and therefore it's okay to lie. Pretend to be your husband's secretary, and the money may come through. This is, in a word, awful, and the limp plot contrivances are a waste of Doris Day's extraordinary talents.

Day is not called upon to here tap into any of her resources as an actress and has to resort to broad overacting in the Paris sequences in order to inject even a little energy into the stale proceedings. At Langsdorf's climactic convention party, the only moment of interest is when Doris takes off her coat and reveals a form-fitting, backless orange spangled dress. She is far sexier than any of the twentysomethings who appear to have been hired as escorts for the businessmen. When Langsdorf gets an eyeful of Doris, he instantly wants to dance with her—the only reaction in the movie that rings true. Right on the spot he gives Mike the account and then asks Janet to come to Vienna to be his assistant. It's vulgar, but who can blame him? At age forty-one, Doris Day still has a near-perfect figure, and the lingering shots of her derriere while dancing prove that she is far sexier than the twenty-years-younger Claire Hackett. It's no contest: game, set, and match for Doris. This is scant consolation for the viewer who has been held captive for close to one hundred minutes at this point, and by the time the film climaxes with an endless slapstick scene in which Langsdorf chases Janet around multiple bedrooms in the hotel, one just wants the film to end. Janet ends up in Mike's bed, which collapses, and all of a sudden the Harpers are once again a happily married couple. It is all contrived, all totally unbelievable, and all unrelentingly vapid.

Day's 1966 release *The Glass Bottom Boat* reunited her with *Do Not Disturb* costar Rod Taylor, and while it's a mess of a movie, it's an enjoyable mess. Quite popular at the time of its initial release, *The Glass Bottom Boat* helped Doris land in the annual list of top ten box office attractions, the last time she ever attained that rarified rank. Even though the movie never holds together as a cohesive whole, it does have moments of genuine hilarity and afforded Day the opportunity to work with a first-class director, Frank Tashlin. Involving her in outright slapstick for the entire running time of the film, Tashlin rings many interesting changes on the Day persona. They're not all successful, but they do hold the viewer's attention.

The Everett Freeman screenplay finds widow Jennifer Nelson (Day) meeting Bruce Templeton (Rod Taylor) when his fishing reel becomes caught on the mermaid outfit she wears while working for her father's (Arthur Godfrey) glass-bottom boat sea tours. Bruce, an inventor at the space laboratory where Jennifer works as a tour guide and writer, is attracted to Jennifer, and in order to spend time with her he makes up an excuse to have her assist him in the writing of his autobiography. Because Jennifer is overheard telephoning instructions to "Vladimir" (who it turns out is her dog), the security operatives at the space laboratory suspect that she is a spy, setting the stage for a host of mistaken identity crises and patented Tashlin slapstick shenanigans.

The film gets off to a sluggish start with a terrible title song (by the usually reliable Joe Lubin) heard over the credits; this tune is unfortunately heard again, and at much greater length, in the middle of the film, when Arthur Godfrey plays it on his ukulele and a group sing-along ensues, complete with multiple choruses about the different kinds of fish in the sea. It's a silly song that stops the film dead in its tracks.

With the title credits out of the way, the film takes off an a series of set pieces that are not terribly coherent but serve to reinforce Tashlin's goal of satirizing modern-day life circa 1966. Tashlin here turns his gimlet-eyed gaze on everything from spying in the cold war to the overwhelming presence of mechanical "labor-saving" devices. Gadgets such as eggbeaters that come out of the counter and a vacuum-cleaning robot are presented as ingenious inventions that ultimately malfunction in disastrous ways. Instead of the gadgets helping to make life simpler, they run amok and cause chaos. Far from helping to clean the kitchen, the vacuum cleaner at Bruce's house attacks Janet/Doris, sucking on her toes and shoes, and, with its phallic-shaped snout, blatantly attacking under her skirt. In Tashlin's view, technology is out of control and is taking over modern life.

Tashlin is here aiming for satire, not reality. These self-contained episodes are amusing in and of themselves, but Tashlin, who began his career as a director of "Looney Tunes" cartoons, is taking on more than even he can handle here. The film is part satire, part romance, part cartoon, part caper film, part musical, and for all of its wit, more than slightly unfocused in its expression.

For the first time onscreen, the Doris Day presented in *The Glass Bottom Boat* looks her age—forty-three at the time of filming. She looks like the character she is supposed to be: a widow without children, basically youthful in appearance, but seasoned by life. Presented as a focused, hardworking career woman, she marches through the film with a determined gait, a train barreling along its predetermined course; indeed, at various points the score by Frank DeVol actually synchronizes Doris's actions with music that blatantly suggests trains (the wildly overblown brass-heavy score moves well beyond just satirizing the then very popular John Barry James Bond film scores and instead registers as an annoying, heavy-handed attempt to comment on the action). Doris is certainly not presented as a coy virgin here. She is a fortyish widow who clearly enjoys sex; after turning down Bruce Templeton, she changes her mind, making herself comfortable in his house and putting on soft seductive music. When the darkened living room leads Janet to mistakenly think that Bruce's friend Zach (Dick Martin) is actually Bruce himself, Day exchanges a long passionate kiss with him, leaving no doubt as to the state of her libido. When Day and Taylor rendezvous in the guest cottage on his estate (Huh? What's wrong with Bruce's actual bedroom?), it is Doris who turns off the light and first utters the words "I love you."

For all of the satire of modern-day life present in the film, there are still moments of genuine emotion, courtesy of Day and a director who occasionally knows when to let things alone. The title tune may not be very good, but

Technology run amok. Frank Tashlin's intermittently hilarious
The Glass Bottom Boat, 1966. *Photofest*

when Doris sings "Que Sera, Sera" accompanied only by her father on the ukulele, real emotion is generated, and flesh-and-blood characters actually seem to exist for a few minutes. Similarly, when Bruce Templeton kisses Jenny for the first time, she is simultaneously attracted to him, unsure of herself, and more than a bit confused. This is the way bona fide adults react in real life, and Day conveys such conflicting emotions beautifully.

Most interesting of all, there is a fascinating sequence set on an outdoor patio when a pensive Jennifer sings the lovely ballad "Soft as the Starlight" (a song first heard on Day's classic 1957 album *Day by Night*). While singing this song, Jenny comes to realizes that she truly does love Bruce. Rather than present the musical number in a straightforward fashion, Tashlin here cuts against the grain by showcasing it as if it were in a musical film and at the same time commenting on the essential artifice of the screen musical. It's an interesting idea, but just as happened with Martin Scorcese's deliberately artificial styling of certain musical numbers in *New York, New York,* Tashlin's desire to present and analyze at the same time ultimately proves self-defeating. In order to comment on the musical genre, the vocabulary of the musical film would have to have been established earlier on; if Tashlin had first embraced the genre and then commented on it, the commentary might have worked. The number might even have worked in voice-over, but Tashlin's choice to show Doris Day actually singing undoes the sequence. Here, Tashlin is all surface satire and ignores the genuine underpinning of emotion. Then again, that may have been the entire point.

Once it is shown that the government thinks that Jennifer is a spy, Bruce Templeton takes their misguided belief very seriously. Trying to defend Jenny against charges that she is a Russian spy, Taylor springs to her defense and cries, "This girl doesn't have the brains to be a spy." Putting aside the outrageously sexist choice of words (and Tashlin is unfortunately not satirizing here; the dialogue is a genuine reflection of the times), what registers with the viewer is that Bruce is trying to protect Jennifer, an attempt that results in her complete misunderstanding of his efforts. It's a particularly interesting sequence, because even in her early forties, Doris Day is here still able to provoke a genuine feeling of protectiveness in the audience. It's not a feeling that Day is hopelessly vulnerable. Rather, it's a feeling that anyone this nice, this much of a straight shooter, should be dealt with fairly. Even in this latter stage of her film career, it remains a key element in her persona and appeal.

Because Tashlin careens wildly between straightforward presentation and outright farce, the audience becomes confused. How is one supposed to take any of these plot developments seriously after sitting through numerous sequences of slapstick antics? How can an audience respond with any degree of seriousness when Paul Lynde portrays a security officer and Dom De Luise is presented as a spy? These two wildly idiosyncratic actors here present extraordinarily over-the-top characterizations: Lynde all but announces that he is a graduate of the Very Gay Police Academy, and De Luise fumbles endlessly as a hapless spy who inadvertently destroys any gadget within his reach (while pretending to fix the stereo system he smashes a cake and gets it all over Day). Lynde and De Luise are acquired tastes; with their overly stylized comic personae, both are simultaneously genuinely funny yet also laughable. De Luise's performance in particular is exhausting to watch; he is all grunts, groans, and mangled syllables. It is all ridiculous surface illusion, but that is Tashlin's point, right down to the pseudo–John Barry spy music blaring on the soundtrack.

Ultimately, even with all of these comic set pieces, the brash and not entirely coherent attitude ultimately does Doris in, but not until the final sections of the film. Nearing the climax, and after an unusually athletic performance even by her own strenuous standards, Day falls back on her standard bag of tricks for the first time. It's an easy but unfortunate solution to the problems at hand, and Tashlin must share part of the blame. Close to the end of the film, all of a sudden Doris Day begins to stamp her feet and pop her eyes at both Taylor and Dom De Luise. Taylor bodily picks her up, and just as always happened in the comedies with Rock Hudson, Day shrieks, "Put me down!"—which of course he doesn't. The film then degenerates into a silly slapstick chase through a neighbor's bedroom, which leads to multiple car crashes. The movie has by now lost all sense of coherence, just as, at film's end, Day loses mastery of the remote-control speedboat in which she is attempting to escape—Tashlin's final comment on modern gadgetry controlling, not helping, us. By the end of the film, one realizes that yes, Doris is the focus here, but she doesn't propel all of the action: De Luise's clumsiness and Paul Lynde's drag routine also shape the proceedings. Day's the star but not the auteur of the film. That title belongs to Tashlin and his satirical view of modern life.

Day's next film, the 1967 release *Caprice,* found her reteaming with Tashlin. The resulting movie is oddly dispiriting to watch; Tashlin continues his assault on modern technology and the artificiality of life today, but one of his prime targets appears to be Doris Day herself. No matter to what extent Day and husband/producer Marty Melcher were in on the joke, the result is disturbing to watch.

Viewers of *Caprice* might want to take along a study guide to the film's plot, because all of the twists and turns border on the incomprehensible. Day here plays industrial designer and undercover agent Patricia Foster, who is at the center of a war between two rival cosmetics companies. Both companies are interested in obtaining the formula for the water-repellent hairspray developed by research scientist Stuart Clancy (Ray Walston). While pursuing the formula, Patricia travels to a Swiss Alpine village in order to also investigate the shooting death of her Interpol agent father; nearly killed by enemy assassins, Patricia is saved by suave double agent Christopher White (Richard Harris). There is much carrying on about narcotics rings, a kidnapping or two, mountainside ski chases, and ultimately a helicopter rescue. Yet all of the heaving action is for naught because long before the end, any sensible viewer ceases to care. It doesn't matter what Tashlin was trying to satirize because almost none of it works, and the audience is once again left with an all-too-familiar reaction: Why did Doris Day waste her talent on such a third-rate vehicle? (And as becomes clear in reading Day's autobiography, the answer is because Marty Melcher signed her to the film.)

Using the labyrinth of a plot as the background, Tashlin is here upping the stakes he set in *The Glass Bottom Boat.* He is now not only taking on the increasingly synthetic nature of modern society, as evidenced by technological toys and plastic surgery, but also making fun of advertising, television commercials, and the entire computer age. (There's even a passing jab at psychiatry, always a sure target in a Doris Day film. When it is revealed that Clancy killed Patricia's father, Doris instantly turns amateur shrink and says, "Clancy really didn't like women; he just wanted to dress up as one." Guess Patricia received her MD along with her industrial design degree . . .) To point up the absurdity of the modern plasticized age, Tashlin (the cowriter of the screenplay along with Jay Johnson) makes the object of all the espionage something as seemingly trivial as a water-repellent hairspray. In Tashlin's view, nothing could be more artificial than the entire cosmetics industry, yet multiple murders are being committed by those lusting after such a trivial formula. Similarly, when Day is arrested at the beginning of the film, it is for passing a secret formula for . . . underarm deodorant, or as the screenplay puts it, she is arrested for "sabotaging the national armpit." What, Tashlin seems to be asking, really matters today? The desperate pursuit of money and power are all aimed at artificial products that bear no relation to the former building blocks of life—family, love, and country.

All of Tashlin's targets are indeed ripe for satire, but the problem is that he beats the audience over the head just to make sure that nobody misses his point. It is a heavy-handed approach that begins with Day's very first appearance. When she lowers the newspaper she is reading and we see her face for the first time, she is nearly unrecognizable. She wears a very synthetic-looking blond wig and sports oversized dark glasses that she doffs only to reveal thick false lashes and heavy eyeliner. She is dressed in a black-and-white-checked vinyl coat, a garish gold dress, mesh stockings, and knee-high gold boots. This Doris Day of *Caprice* bears no relation to the fresh-faced ingenue of the late '40s and early '50s (the wardrobe here was designed by Bob Mackie's partner Ray Aghayan). If America, the supposed fresh new world of opportunity, has become a brittle shell of its former self, then, Tashlin seems to say, so too has America's favorite girl next door. Time marches on, but Day's thick pancake makeup purposely makes her look robotic—she is ready for Madame Tussaud's wax museum. Yes, it may be Tashlin's point that Day's image is itself becoming artificial and due to crack open, but it's a cruel jab. This is the first movie in which her persona has gone from fresh faced, ambitious, and self-sufficient to tough, aggressive, and waxlike. Contrary to what George Morris posits in the *Pyramid Illustrated History of the Movies: Doris Day,* this is not really a logical extension of Doris Day's persona from the early 1960s—

determined, independent, and irrevocably true to herself. Rather, it is a perversion of that image. Even when she doesn't have to act upset, Day looks unhappy. It is the first time that she has ever looked genuinely dispirited on film. Given the fact that just as happened with *Do Not Disturb,* she has to carry this drivel all by herself, it's no wonder that the effort shows.

Once one gets over the shock of Day's appearance, however, her first extended sequence in the film is quite humorous, actually raising hopes for a clever satire. In a nearly silent montage, Patricia is followed all around Paris and the viewer becomes curious: What's happening? Is Doris a villain? Can't be. Not Doris. Or is she? Finally arriving at her destination, she rendezvouses with her contact in the restaurant situated at the top of the Eiffel Tower. In order to make sure that this buyer of the secret formula can't follow her, she makes him take off his pants—in the middle of the fancy restaurant. It's a clever gambit, one that is certainly unexpected from Doris Day, and it sets up the expectation of a clever tongue-in-cheek tone for the film.

Unfortunately, the tone instantly falters, and this clever opening is followed by so many story line twists and turns that the plot becomes incomprehensible. On the one hand, Tashlin is being satirical with his jabs at the cloak-and-dagger world of industrial spying, but at the same time he is asking the audience to take the mountainside chase sequences seriously. When Patricia is chased through the Alps on skis, the segment is so attenuated that instead of being excited, the viewer starts to mull over the obvious use of a double for Day; similarly, when Richard Harris lowers himself out of a helicopter, hanging onto a rope ladder and then pulling Doris to safety just as she goes over a cliff, it is beyond ludicrous. It's a takeoff on the James Bond films, but whereas the early Bond films featured recognizable villains, *Caprice* presents cartoon characters. When Patricia and Christopher effect this escape, the purposely cartoonlike music (by Frank DeVol) undercuts any viewer interest or ability to take the plot seriously. Tashlin is trying to eat his cake and have it too, but he ends up with neither.

Granted, Tashlin does send himself up as well, but it's a little too self-congratulatory a send-up to register as truly funny. Patricia, hot on the trail of the water-repellent hairspray, tracks Clancy's secretary, Su Ling (Irene Tsu) to the movies in hopes of cutting off a lock of her water-resistent hair. And just what movie is Clancy's secretary viewing? You've got it—*Caprice* starring Doris Day and Richard Harris. We even glimpse the 20th Century–Fox fanfare and hear a bit of Day singing the title song. A similar "inside" joke occurs when the viewer finally sees a picture of Patricia's father Robert, the Interpol agent killed in the film's opening ski chase; when the photograph is revealed, her father turns out to be Arthur Godfrey, who played Day's father in her previous Tashlin film, *The Glass Bottom Boat.* This is all funny but a little too much from the look-how-clever-I-am school of filmmaking. It's a form of parody very similar to that displayed in the Broadway musicals of the twenty-first century that comment on the musical form at the same time that they embrace it. It's all clever, if a bit arch, but more important, it all displays a profound distrust of genuine emotion. It's the ultimate artistic expression in the age of irony, and in this regard, Tashlin was well ahead of his fellow arbiters of pop culture.

There is, however, one genuinely hilarious sequence in the film, which shows the actual tone Tashlin was seeking and here achieves brilliantly. In a clandestine café meeting with Christopher, Patricia realizes that everything she says is being overheard thanks to a transmitter hidden in a tabletop sugar cube. Her solution? She proceeds to chomp down loudly on her potato chips, bangs her spoon vehemently on the dish of sugar cubes, and makes sure that a loudly bubbling glass of Alka-Seltzer is brought to the table. The eavesdropping agents are rendered temporarily deaf in hilarious fashion. It is a sequence that proves simultaneously funny, satirical (the preponderance of listening/camera devices that invade every corner of our lives), and pointed (nothing is private in modern life). If only the rest of the film had lived up to the wit of this sequence.

Caprice pushed Day through what was probably the most physical role of her career. Even performing only some of the stunts herself, this still comes across as an exhausting turn, and as she was forty-three at the time, her exertions register as a very impressive physical feat. She climbs hills, hangs from balconies, runs, skis, and generally acts as if in training for an Iron Man Triathlon. Day is still willing to make fun of herself and of this excessive physical energy, even satirizing her own appearance when she appears on-screen covered in dirt. It is, needless to say, an appearance light-years removed from that displayed in films featuring glamorous Jean Louis gowns. Significantly, this is a far kinder spoofing of her own image than that indulged in by Tashlin in the film's opening scenes.

In a movie chockablock with chase sequences set on and in everything from highway and mountaintop to cliffside and helicopter, the final chase is the most surreal of all. Doris Day ends up alone in a helicopter screaming, "Help me, help me!" Maybe it's a cry of help to the audience, because she appears to be as powerless to escape this mess as are the viewers. Doris is then called upon to land the helicopter on top of the Eiffel Tower, a sequence unfortunately reminiscent of flight attendant Julie Benton landing the plane at the climax of *Julie.* Yes, unlike Andrew Stone's direction of *Julie,* Tashlin is being purposefully satirical, but it's not funny—just stupid. Well, at least the viewer gets to hear Doris Day recite Shakespeare for the first time on film, as she intones, " 'Tis a consummation devoutly to be wished." It's certainly the classiest line in the screenplay and is uttered right before she injects Richard Harris with a hypodermic needle, whereupon he winks directly at the camera, and the movie ends. That's it? If these two are sauntering off into the sunset together, why the skullduggery? Ninety-eight very long minutes after the film began, the audience still has absolutely no clue as to who these people are.

It's as if Tashlin's background as a director of Warner Bros. "Looney Tunes" has come full circle. *Caprice* attempts to display the same demented logic that those often hilarious animated films displayed, but it's all for naught; lacking the wit and consistently absurd tone displayed in those cartoons, *Caprice* stands as a waste of the time and genuine talents of nearly everyone involved. The whole sorry affair was unfortunately best summed up by Judith Crist's review on NBC's *Today* show: "Miss Day, of course, has been many things; this time, thanks to a variety of wigs, soft lenses, and mod costumes, she looks like an aging transvestite. . . . Miss Day is not as young as she used to be for this sort of caper but she does have the energy, and I guess energy is about the one distinction of *Caprice.*" It's all true, just as is the fact that Doris Day deserved better—much better.

Day has spoken disparagingly of her next film, *The Ballad of Josie,* but in fact there are many interesting elements in a film that is surprisingly good in spots. The most overtly feminist film of Day's entire career, it plays like a 1967 nonmusical version of 1953's *Calamity Jane.* Written by Harold Swanton and directed by Andrew V. McLaglen, the movie, set in the beautiful countryside of the nineteenth-century Wyoming Territory, centers on the struggle for financial and emotional independence by Josie Minick (Doris Day).

As happened so often in late Doris Day movies, the film gets off to a bad start, with a horrible title song, courtesy of the usually brilliant Frank Sinatra arranger Don Costa. The tune, which is sung by frequent Barry Manilow collaborator Ron Dante, comes complete with simpering lyrics that extol Josie's spunk. All of this is accompanied by some very strange stop-action title credits, but with this silliness out of the way, *The Ballad of Josie* settles in and makes an often fascinating overtly feminist statement.

Doris Day sports a very strange mix of styles in the movie. She is first seen sewing a sampler, and evidently her eyesight must be very good indeed, because this is one Western lady who has access to exceedingly thick false eyelashes that would block any normal woman's vision. She also wears form-fitting designer gowns designed by Jean Louis—an interesting wardrobe for an independent rancher woman. Wardrobe aside, the movie really begins to take hold when Josie's drunk and abusive husband comes home after a night's carousing, chases her around the house and, in his drunken state, falls over the banister and dies. Josie is tried for his murder, and subsequently acquitted, but her father-in-law Alpheus (Paul Fix), who holds the mortgage on her house, takes Josie's son Luther to go live with him. Although Alpheus also offers Josie the chance to live with him, it is made clear that in order to do so she would have to function as a live-in maid for her own family. In answer to her father-in-law's offer, Josie firmly replies, "I have two hands. I can take care of myself." This is not your standard-issue Western woman, and in Day's hands, it's a believable statement that piques the viewer's interest.

Josie wants to use the Winslow Creek ranch for the grazing of cows, but Arch Ogden (George Kennedy), whose land surrounds Josie's on three sides, wants to complete his own holdings by taking over her land as well. Even love interest Jason Meredith (Peter Graves), who in fact sympathizes with Josie in many ways, laughs at the very idea of a woman raising cows. Telling Josie that such behavior just isn't proper, Jace is instantly rebuked by her quick retort: "I

The surprisingly feminist *The Ballad of Josie,* 1967. *Photofest*

don't want to be taken care of. I am strong, able to do anything. Don't 'tut-tut' me." This is more of an overtly feminist statement than what is found in many of the supposedly more radical films of the late 1960s, and Josie in some ways plays like a late-nineteenth-century precursor of the independent career women Day essayed on film in the late '50s and early '60s.

Desperate for an income, Josie takes the only job she can get, working as a waitress at the Trail's End Restaurant. There is quite a bit of the by now standard Doris Day physical clowning here: She is a bad waitress, mixes up orders, and gets a fly strip caught in her hair, but all of it goes to make a point. Josie wants to ranch, not rattle pots and pans. She quits the restaurant and strikes off on her own, taking on tough physical labors without batting an eye. This frontier woman knows how to prime the pump and put new glass in the windows. She is helped by Jace, but in a sign that some actual thought was put into the screenplay, theirs is a real give-and-take relationship. They squabble, but then make up; both stubbornly independent, they make sense as a couple.

Yet for all of their mutual affection, even Jace condescends to Josie, stating, "No woman can ranch alone." Josie's fiery retort: "To you a woman is a species of idiot to be kept in a back closet and fed three times a day." This gal brooks no nonsense. She's determined to farm her four hundred eighty acres and buys herself a pair of Levi's and some serious boots. It's great fun to see Day hit stride here, both literally and figuratively; when she makes up her mind to be an independent sheep farmer, her very walk changes, and she struts forward. The townspeople have never before seen a woman in pants and shirt, and the sight causes traffic to stop dead in the middle of town. She drinks brandy with the men who want her to quit grazing sheep, and in a remarkable speech, tells them, "Forget I'm a woman. I'm a human being, and I can take care of myself and my son without anyone's charity. . . . I can work. I don't want or need a man. I've got myself—and my sheep—and nobody, *nobody,* not a damn one of you, is gonna get in my way." After the drivel of *Do Not Disturb* and *Send Me No Flowers,* it is remarkably cheering to see the real Doris Day in action again.

Unfortunately, however, the final third of the movie seems to contradict everything that has come before, and as a result, in those last thirty minutes the movie falls apart completely. The cattlemen lay siege to Josie's sheep ranch, and Josie, who won't join in the seemingly inevitable gunfight between the farmers and the cowboys, queries, "What can I do, Jace?" Good question, but what's the solution? According to this screenplay, it's to have Josie and Jace kiss, with Josie riding her horse to town in order to get out of harm's way. As a result of such anomalous actions, any viewer with half a brain will then wonder, "What's going on here?" Josie does not back down from ranching four hundred eighty acres, but she gets scared of a possible fight, kisses her man, and leaves for town. It makes no sense.

So according to this screenplay, what exactly is the solution to the seemingly inevitable full-scale range war? Arch will pay Josie good money for her sheep and wool, and she can then get into the cattle business like the rest of the ranchers in the area. It's nice to see villainous Arch come around—"I aint tellin' you, Josie, I'm askin' you"—but this sense of equality is completely undercut when Josie weeps with joy at this good news. Worse yet, Peter Graves speaks on Josie's behalf, declaring, "She'll take your position, Arch." This is insulting and also nonsensical in the context of the film; after ninety minutes of self-assertiveness, are we now to believe that Josie can't speak for herself? But the absolute nadir fully arrives when Josie burns her men's clothes in the fireplace and tells her skunk house pet (that's right, it's a skunk), "It's not good to get too independent." Talk about the air being let out of a balloon. Doris Day is great at playing strong women who are still completely feminine, but here, in the third and final act of the film, Josie is reduced to a marshmallow. The one good thing about the outcome is that Josie will at last be reunited with son Luther, but when, at film's end, it is announced that Jace will run for the U.S. Senate, one can only hope that Doris's Josie will not turn into an adoring, simpering political wife.

In looking at the totality of *The Ballad of Josie,* one is confronted with a textbook example of what Jeanine Basinger posited in *A Woman's View:* Women struggle against the bonds society imposes on them, they actually do break free by asserting their independence and creating successful careers, but then these by now successful women must pay for the folly of their independence and renounce such unsuitable behavior. By following this construct all too closely, *The Ballad of Josie* is telling the viewer, "Don't take any of the preceding ninety minutes too seriously. Just enjoy the fact that Josie returns to her rightful place as her man's supportive helpmate." No wonder the feminist revolution was about to hit Hollywood films in a big way.

Times were changing and for the most part audiences would no longer accept such hypocrisy from their films and stars. Doris Day didn't write these silly late-1960s scripts, but as the star attraction and singular reason to see the films, she was treated as if she had. As a result, she was blamed for all of the films' shortcomings. When baby boomers jump-started the sexual revolution, they seemed to blame Doris Day personally for stifling sexuality, completely misreading her films in the process (the simpering *Touch of Mink* being the one film that unreels guilty as charged). It was a tough load for any individual to shoulder and may very well have contributed to her premature retirement from feature films.

There is only one word to describe Day's next film, *Where Were You When the Lights Went Out?*: terrible. Only *The Tunnel of Love* ranks lower among Day's thirty-nine movies. An ostensible farce, it doesn't register a single genuine laugh. By film's end, not only is the question, "Why was this film ever made?" lingering in the air, but what resonates most strongly with the viewer is the sense that the ever-optimistic and energetic Doris Day herself looks tired throughout, as if even she barely had the energy to put up with this silliness.

Like so many of Day's later films, the movie gets off to an awful start, with yet another third-rate title tune; here sung by the Lettermen, with a Vegas lounge act orchestration, it is so subpar that it makes the viewer pause. How could such a terrific singer and actress be so consistently stuck with such awful songs? The answer really does appear to be Day's statement that although Marty Melcher appreciated great music, "he just couldn't bring himself to pay Hank Mancini his fee." Net result? Inexpensive, i.e., inferior, songs that plodded along at a deadly pace. The issue of title songs is significant in Day's films because she is a first-class musical talent and the songs were supposed to get the comedies off to a buoyant start. Instead, it usually took the first ten minutes of the film just to overcome the leaden musical beginning.

Day here plays Margaret Garrison, a Hollywood and Broadway star who is married to architect Peter Garrison (Patrick O'Neal). Margaret wants to quit show business and have a baby, but Peter appears not only to be preoccupied with his own work but also to be a philanderer. When the 1965 New York City blackout hits, Maggie's show is canceled; unexpectedly returning home, she finds Peter entertaining another woman and flees to the supposed safety of their Connecticut home. Maggie mistakenly drinks a sedative and is innocently joined in bed by a similarly sedated thief, Waldo Zane (Robert Morse, the film's narrator). There are idiotic complications about the money Waldo has stolen, husband Peter is mistakenly arrested, Peter and Maggie reconcile, and nine months later their first child is born. It's all so horribly filmed, edited, and acted that if Doris's Margaret Garrison had ever seen this film, she'd not only have given up acting but would also never have to take a sedative again; no chemical ever invented could induce sleep as quickly as does this third-rate farce.

Day stated in her autobiography that she knew the script for *Where Were You When The Lights Went Out?* was bad, but she had been signed up in advance, without her knowledge, by Marty Melcher. Day, who had a very clear sense of which of her movies were first rate (asked in 1969 which of her movies she enjoyed the most she instantly responded "I liked *Love Me or Leave Me* and *The Thrill of It All*"—both of them first-rate films), was right on the money about the terrible *Where Were You When the Lights Went Out?* because the screenplay by Everett Freeman and Karl Tunberg is strenuously unfunny. Peter cheats on Maggie, then accuses her of cheating on him, and seems to spend his time flinging verbal barbs her way. This married couple certainly doesn't seem to be very happy, leading to the question, "Why are these two even together?" Not a good question for the audience to be asking about a film where one is supposed to spend the duration of the running time rooting for the husband and wife to realize their deep love for each other.

It is dispiriting to see Doris Day stranded in these circumstances. She is simply going through the motions, and her lack of enthusiasm shows. This actress who always gave 1,000 percent—mostly for the good, sometimes for the bad—has the air of just wanting it all to be over. The script is so flaccid that when Maggie becomes loopy on sleeping medication, she literally must say, "Hello, Peter, so you're here," ten times in a row. A scene that might be sporadically amusing for two minutes here takes up fifteen minutes of screen

The abysmal *Where Were You When the Lights Went Out?* From her expression, it looks like Doris has just read the script. Note the heavy-handed "joke" marquee. *Photofest*

time. Even Doris Day, a master of comic inflection, is helpless to ring any merriment out of the situation. She is forced to spend half of the movie in a pair of men's pajamas and is shown sleeping with her mouth open. It's a demeaning sight and situation—a Brand X sitcom that any one of a thousand other actresses could also have played. There is nothing unique that Doris Day can bring to the role. No one could.

This is one depressingly uninspired script. Just as happened with *Send Me No Flowers,* instead of developing real characters, the writers here resort to in-joke references about their star's persona as a means of characterization. Husband Patrick refers to Maggie as "a freckle-faced American sweetheart" and even repeats the tired Oscar Levant quip, "I knew her before she was a virgin." An even more shopworn form of humor is the fact that the play Maggie is starring in is called, what else, "The Constant Virgin." As in *Move Over Darling,* near the climax of the film there is a long and pointless slapstick car chase. Worst of all, however, is the fact that the movie ends, like so many other of Day's later films, with the leading man lying to Doris—and this time the lie is told by her husband. It turns out that Patrick cheated on Maggie previously, but since they weren't married at the time, that is presented as being okay. Patrick knows that Maggie didn't sleep with Waldo, but does he tell her that she's "innocent"? Of course not. That would interfere with what he wants. Never mind that just as at the end of *Send Me No Flowers,* we are shown a marriage based on lies and deceit. The depressing part of this is that the filmmakers clearly seem to think that it's all quite funny. The screenwriters can't even muster up the energy to craft an original ending, instead copying the climax of both *That Touch of Mink* and *Lover Come Back* by having Maggie rushed to the hospital to give birth. Just like that, we're supposed to think that all ends happily. Thank goodness Maggie's a mother now; at last she can cheerfully give up that awful world of starring on Broadway and in glamorous Hollywood films, and instead continue a marriage to a man who lies to her repeatedly. Who could resist that enticing setup . . . ?

Doris suffered from an extremely painful pinched nerve during the making of the film, leaving her in agony during much of the filming. It's an apt metaphor for the entire film, and one wonders what was worse for Doris Day herself—the pinched nerve, or actually having to film such a terrible script. Any way you look at it, *Where Were You When the Lights Went Out?* must have proved to be a truly painful experience.

After so many dismal films in a row, it is all the more ironic that Day's next film, *With Six You Get Eggroll,* proved to be the last feature film of her career, because in many ways, the movie could have and should have paved the way for a whole new set of films, ones in which she played a woman her own age.

In the movie, she plays Abby McClure, a fortysomething widow with three children who falls in love with and marries widower Jake Iverson (Brian Keith). Day is relaxed, confident, and in complete control—playing a woman her own age seems to have freed her. It makes her subsequent retirement from feature films all the harder to accept, because *With Six You Get Eggroll* really seemed to point the way to an entirely new phase in her career.

In a way, *With Six You Get Eggroll* is the movie showing the middle-aged Doris Day for which all of her fans had been waiting. Yes, the television sitcom aspects show, but damned if the whole thing isn't a lot of fun. To begin with, the technical credits land several levels above the recent bargain basement support Day had been receiving. The score was composed by Robert Mersey, who had been working extensively with Barbra Streisand ("He Touched Me"), and one of the two directors of photography was the top-notch Harry Stradling Jr. Best of all, the script is genuinely funny. It may have taken four writers—Gwen Bagni, Paul Dubov, Harvey Bullock, and R. S. Allen—but they got it right and allow their star to relax and have fun. (Interestingly, it is the first of Day's movies that Marty Melcher produced on his own since *Julie,* twenty years earlier.)

With Six You Get Eggroll combines the best of the two disparate Doris Day personae: She is a widow with three sons but at the same time she is a working woman who is running the family lumberyard. In fact, the audience's first glimpse of Day finds her wearing a hard hat and riding a lift. She looks great—competent, professional in a man's world, yet thoroughly feminine. Told by sister Maxine (Pat Carroll) that she needs a man, Abby simply retorts, "I don't need a man. I have a company to run and three beautiful children."

Of course she does end up with a man: chemical engineer Jake Iverson (Brian Keith). They tentatively arrange a date, and the evening is such a disaster that the audience of course instantly roots for them to get together. Bawling out her sons for making a mess, insisting that they put their retainers back in their mouths, Abby McClure is a harried woman who has forgotten how to date, and Day is utterly winning in delineating Abby's charming shortcomings. Jake's arrival is imminent, but her two young boys have filled the tub with paint, and she has cold cream on her face and a shower cap on her head—and this is the first sight Jake has of her as he arrives for the dinner party she is giving at her home. Jake is disconcerted, to say the least, especially when housekeeper Molly (Alice Ghostley) announces, "I have to put a roast on broil but your wig is on bake." Day's comic rhythms are so expert that the viewer is utterly won over, disastrous party or not.

Day and Keith make a terrific team, beautifully playing off of each other; her pep gives his laconic delivery some zing, and he calms her down through nicely calibrated understatement. After sorting out a rather large misunderstanding—spying Jake with a young woman, Abby does not realize that far from being a girlfriend, she is his daughter Stacy (Barbara Hershey)—Abby and Jake get back together. Jake is shown leaving Abby's house late one evening after one of their dates, but he then reverses course to go back inside. It's clear that they will spend the night together. Who would have thought it—this high-level sitcom of a movie is actually an adult love story.

Abby's teenaged son Flip (John Findlater) doesn't want Jake with his mother, and Stacy doesn't want Abby with her father, so what's the result? The two adults have to meet at the drive-in. Subsequently shown in their own beds, talking to each other via split screen (director Howard Morris's witty nod to the famous split-screen bathtub scene in *Pillow Talk*), they take matters into their own hands and elope (to the strains of the Hallelujah Chorus). How do their families find out? Running into Doris's bedroom, her youngest son screams out, "There's a man in Mommy's bed!" This is innocent feel-good fun in all the best ways.

The best scene in the film, one which is downright hilarious in its execution, occurs when the two families, now blended into one very uneasy large nuclear unit, go to the amusement park together. A nice friendly spin in the bumper cars of course turns out to be anything but a friendly family outing. The look of grim determination on Barbara Hershey's face as she rams Doris's car full on is matched only by Doris's look of surprise and anger. There isn't a shred of overacting here, and the slow burn she pulls off is every bit as hilarious as the expression on Brian Keith's face when Flip makes a point of barreling into his bumper car. Youngest son Jason (Richard Steele) happily exclaims, "I'm glad we're a family 'cuz with six you get eggroll," but he's about the only one who feels that way. Stacy won't accept the hat Abby buys her, and Flip purposely cuts wood when Jake is talking so that his conversation will be drowned out.

It is no wonder that when Jake and Abby try yet again to sleep together, only to be interrupted by a fervent cry of "Mommmeee!" that Abby wittily remarks in great frustration, "You know, you can grow to hate that word." Day's delivery of this funny line is classic: understated, wry, and right on the money. Freed from her run of horrible scripts, she's once again the expert comedian of yore. Day is even allowed a slight bit of bitchiness, as when sexpot neighbor Cleo (Elaine Devry), who has a yen for Jake, remarks in all studied innocence, "I was just walking down the street." Day, with equal innocence, remarks, "Yes, it's a nice night for streetwalking." This is exactly how a wife

Doris Day's last feature film, the genuinely funny *With Six You Get Eggroll. Photofest*

would react to such a challenge. Such true-to-life behavior is even carried over into the scene where Abby and Jake have their first serious argument: The argument is based on a real-life situation, the behavior of Jake's daughter Stacy. Jake and Abby argue about Stacy, yelling and screaming at each other. Both of them are right, and both of them are wrong; in other words, it's just like real life (except funnier). In fact, it's this spot-on comic writing in the first two-thirds of the movie that makes the last thirty minutes such a disappointment; it's as if the scriptwriters got everything right up to this point, only to find that they couldn't figure out how to resolve all of the complications.

Once again, the audience is subjected to a Doris Day movie that ends with a silly slapstick car chase, complete with chickens being dumped all over the road; it's like watching *That Touch of Mink* Part II, and Part I wasn't any good to begin with. There are ridiculous late-1960s stereotypes of hippies (played by Jamie Farr and William Christopher, both soon to find fame as Klinger and Father Mulcahy on the television series *M*A*S*H*), and the two families finally unite for a happily-ever-after life by joining together to beat up the chicken truck driver (Vic Tayback Jr.). Such nonsense is here doubly frustrating, because while the first two-thirds of the movie is character and plot driven, yielding some genuine laughs along the way, the silly car chase and cartoon villain represent recycled stick figures who never ring true.

But—two-thirds of a good movie is a much better ratio than Day's previous six films had yielded. It makes her subsequent retirement from feature films all the more frustrating because this movie clearly demonstrates that with good material she could still rise to the occasion—and then some. As it was, with Marty Melcher's death and the unexpected and imminent start of a five-year television commitment to film *The Doris Day Show,* the August 1968 release of *With Six You Get Eggroll* represented the end of Doris Day's feature film career.

Doris Day had come a long way from the overly bright ingenue who debuted in 1948's *Romance on the High Seas.* Possessed of a larger-than-life talent for musicals, comedies, and drama, she overcame the stock situations of clunky Warner Bros. musicals like *It's a Great Feeling* and *Lucky Me,* to soar in terrific comedies like *Teacher's Pet* and *Please Don't Eat the Daisies.* If she couldn't overcome the desperately poor scripts of such third-class fare as *Do Not Disturb* and *Where Were You When the Lights Went Out?* she positively triumphed with brilliant three-dimensional characterizations in *Love Me or Leave Me, The Man Who Knew Too Much,* and *The Pajama Game.* Fifty years on, these three first-rate films are still fresh and vital, and stand as monuments to the unique talents of Doris Day; no other actress in Hollywood history has ever triumphed so completely in musical drama, dramatic thriller, and musical comedy in a mere two-year span (1955–1957). Forthright, independent, aggressive yet utterly feminine, and blessed with a beautiful, indeed soulful, singing voice that could deliver a total characterization in three minutes of song, she stands as a uniquely American icon. Doris Day is a symbol of the post–World War II optimistic and idealized America that was to be the world's "good guy." Her likes—and that America—will never be seen again.

Recordings

I dig Doris Day!

—Sarah Vaughan

Doris Day had the talent to be a great singer, if only she had been given the right material. But when she started getting big, Columbia Records started giving her these crappy songs, which made her a big star, but it took away from her singing ability because everyone thought of her as a trite "Que Sera, Sera"–type of singer from then on. She just played it lightly, took it as it came. But she never really had the ambition to be that great. She just sort of floated along with whatever came up.

—Tenor saxophonist Ted Nash

I don't see my films—I see all the wrong things I've done and I turn them off. But sometimes a song will come on the radio—a song I've done a long time ago—and I think 'ahhh' and I'll listen—really listen—and I'll feel so good inside and say: "I did it."

—Doris Day

It's not correct to call Doris Day a good singer, because that isn't quite right—she is a great singer. No style except rock and roll is beyond her reach: pop, jazz—that's right, jazz—ballads, big band, you name it and she sang it, often brilliantly. The quality of her films may have varied widely, from brilliant to awful, but the quality of her singing never varied: It was always terrific. Listening to the full output of her solo recording career, which ran from 1947 through 1967 and resulted in a staggering six hundred–plus released recordings, is to witness the tentative beginnings, the growing confidence, and the full flowering of one of the last truly great exponents of the traditional American popular songbook. It is a body of work extraordinary in its breadth and depth, and, in the annals of American female pop music recordings, surpassed only by Ella Fitzgerald in terms of the sheer scope of its achievement.

Before branching off on her own as a solo recording artist, Day recorded forty-two songs with Les Brown (and his Band of Renown) during her two separate stints with the band. Remarkably, no fewer than twelve of these songs became top twenty recordings. Taken together, the resulting cuts form a fascinating preview of the extraordinary work Day would undertake at Columbia Records, because even at this early stage, it's all present: the flawless intonation, the jazz stylings, and most noteworthy of all, the intimate way with a ballad that results in even a casual listener thinking that Day is singing directly to him or her. The vocals may be occasionally tentative, but the talent and style are already present and accounted for.

The studio sessions for the first fifteen songs Day recorded with Brown occurred between November 1940 and April 1941, before she left the band for her disastrous first marriage to musician Al Jorden. These cuts adhered to a very strict formula: an introduction and first chorus by the band, which lasted for just over one minute, segueing into a vocal by Day of approximately one and one-half minutes, ending with a thirty-second coda by the band. It's a formula that brought Brown great success, and it never varied on any of these forty-two recordings. If it cut short any sense of exploration or surprise, it also proved to be a formula that, within its own limitations, worked extremely well.

On her very first recording, "Dig It," the influence of Day's idol Ella Fitzgerald is immediately apparent. There are definite jazz underpinnings to her phrasing, and her innate sense of swing instantly communicates itself. This Fitzgeraldian influence is particularly apparent on "Easy as Pie," in which she sounds remarkably like Ella herself as she tells her lover, "Let yourself go—baby don't worry, you can learn as easy as pie."

"Booglie Wooglie Piggy," a title redolent of the 1940s if ever there was one, requires Day to negotiate a tricky rhythm, which she does with ease. There are multiple numbers of '40s hepcat jive: "Beau Night in Hotchkiss Corners," "Alexander the Swoose (Half Swan—Half Goose)"—how did Day keep a straight face singing this gibberish? No wonder she accepted a lot of the junk foisted on her by Columbia Records during her solo years—she had already gotten used to it during her band days. In fact, one of the reasons for Day's laissez-faire attitude toward the recordings may have been this very background as a big-band singer. In the early 1940s, the "girl singer" was in no way a star. She was simply another member of the band, one who stood up to sing her vocals, and then sat down, quietly listening while the band played. It was a subservient position, made even more so by the reality of being the only girl in a band full of men. Coupled with Day's innate cheerfulness and desire to keep things sailing smoothly—perhaps a reaction to both her parents' unpleasant divorce and her first marriage to a pathologically jealous man—it is therefore not a total surprise to learn that Day often blandly accepted the second-rate material handed her, both on the movie set and in the recording studio.

There are mild surprises among these Les Brown tracks; one doesn't ordinarily think of Doris Day singing with the attitude required by "Keep Cool, Fool," but she does, and in its way, the song is a forerunner of "Georgia Garrett," the character she would play in her first film, 1948's *Romance on the High Seas:* This is a tough-talking, everything-under-control hepcat. Day sounds great on all of these cuts; she sings in an amazingly pure tone, but it's a lighter voice than the slightly husky, burnished instrument that became so familiar in later years. She is girlish rather than womanly, a fact made clear on one of the few ballads among the early recordings: "While the Music Plays On." Day sings here of "smiles through my tears," but while she sounds great, she also sounds downright cheerful, not the most appropriate sentiment for the song's message of lost love. Day is here too young and inexperienced, not yet the actress she would become, to convey the real morning of the song.

Which is why it is something of a shock to hear her next recording, made in

November of 1944—"Sentimental Journey." It's a shock because she has here been given a truly great song, and not only does the Brown band sound richer and fuller, but most of all, Doris Day is really digging into the song, fully exploring the lyrics. Three years older (still a mere twenty), she had been away from the band for three years because of her marriage. Doris had survived an abusive, jealous husband who beat her while she was pregnant, and such harrowing experiences clearly informed her reading of this ballad of yearning. She may eventually have grown tired of endlessly singing the song, but that reaction lay in the future. Here she sounds terrific—this is star-is-born kind of material. Nearly fifty years after recording the song, she recounted her initial reaction on being handed the sheet music: "That's a lovely title." Les Brown's immediate reply: "Wait till you hear it."

Brown was certainly right. Opening with a beautiful full-bodied orchestral sound dominated by the saxophones, "Sentimental Journey" manages the neat trick of graduating to full-blown wailing yet somehow still maintaining a, well there's no other word for it, "sweet" sound. Paving the way for Day's vocal, the band diminuendos until Day's first husky words are heard:

Gonna take a sentimental journey

This girl has grown up. A woman is now singing, and her slightly deeper voice gives the words an added texture. Every man or woman separated from a loved one during the Second World War could relate to this song, and Doris Day was the woman conveying those thoughts. Call it kismet, call it fate, but she was the right girl, make that woman, with the right song, at the right time. By the time she murmurs

Never thought my heart could be so yearny,
Why did I decide to roam?

all bets are off.

Recalling the song in the 1991 documentary *Doris Day: A Sentimental Journey,* Day herself shed tears: "The song was released in January nineteen forty-five. Just thinking about it makes me cry. The servicemen . . . That song said so much." Sixty years later, the song still sounds fresh, and its induction into the Grammy Hall of Fame in 1999 represents sweet artistic justice.

The years away from the band—away from show business—had clearly deepened Day's talents, because the numbers she now recorded with Les Brown represented a real step forward, and if not a quantum leap—that would come later with the concept albums for Columbia Records—they did represent a deepening of true artistic interpretation. On "My Dreams Are

Getting Better All the Time," she actually is phrasing the lyrics, telling the listener a story. "He's Home for a Little While," recorded in February 1945, speaks to the ongoing war separations, and Day employs a particularly nice vocal line on the key words "a little while"—her soldier love is home, but it's still just for a seeming instant. . . .

There are sweet Glenn Miller Band soundalike versions of "Taint Me" and "I'll Always Be With You," and even "list" songs like "I'd Rather Be With You," in which she favorably compares the charms of her love to those possessed by then current 1940s movie stars. However, it's in the ballads that one notes the real improvement in Day's singing. "Till the End of Time," most famously recorded by Perry Como, is the best early example of a Doris Day vocal persona that would recur with increasing frequency throughout the years, one that underlined a key aspect of her appeal: This was a girl who loved her man and would stay with him no matter what problems lay ahead. She was the girl that man wanted by his side, in good times or bad, because she'd stay during both:

Till the wells run dry
And each mountain disappears

Better yet is the September 1945 recording of "Come to Baby, Do!" a terrific Inez Miller/Sidney James song that Day rerecorded on one of her last Columbia albums, *Sentimental Journey* (1964). Her 1945 version of this sexy song is much better than anything she sang in the early '40s, yet it is still surpassed by her 1964 remake; this early, cheerful, easygoing version seems fresh and sounds great, but it is a youthful take on the lyrics, neither as sexy nor as knowing as the version recorded twenty years later.

As Day's star increased post "Sentimental Journey," so too did the quality of the songs she recorded with Brown. "The Last Time I Saw You" received a very subdued arrangement with a nicely controlled vocal from Day, and she applies a beautiful light touch to "You Won't Be Satisfied (Until You Break My Heart)." Even more noteworthy is her very satisfactory take on the Sammy Cahn/Axel Stordahl/Paul Weston classic "Day by Day," smoothly conveying the essence of this sweetly insistent love song:

I'm yours alone and I'm in love to stay
As we go through the years day by day

The melody suits her deepening voice perfectly, and she's interpreting the lyrics with much greater understanding. The only qualifying note is that at age twenty-one, she is still too young to mine the full meaning of a lyric extolling years of travelling through life together; one only need listen to her masterful treatment of the song on the *Day by Day* album to realize how much more she could still bring to this lyric.

Best of all of these songs was a stirring version of the Carl Fischer/Frankie Laine song "We'll Be Together Again." Only someone who has been knocked around by life and understands the ebb and flow of life experience could impart true quiet emotion to the simple, heartfelt sentiment that

. . . parting is not goodbye
We'll be together again.

Day may not capture every nuance of the song yet, but she is well on her way as an interpretive vocalist, and this stellar recording makes a fitting bookend to the equally great "Sentimental Journey" recorded exactly one year earlier.

War ended, Day continued to tour and record with Brown for one more year—1946. There were swing numbers—"There's Good Blues Tonight" delivered big-band swing with jazz undertones—the occasional silly novelty song like "The Deevil, Devil, Divil," and sweet love songs like "My Number One Dream Came True" and "The Whole World Is Singing My Song" that did little to test either Brown's band or Day's vocal prowess. In fact, what these latter two songs shared in common was the fact that as Day edged toward a fuller understanding of life's vicissitudes, these girlish expressions of contentment sounded pretty but didn't register particularly strongly. Doris Day was now capable of much more:

Don't ask me when or how or why
But if I'm here with you my number one dream came true

Well, that's nice, but so what? Any girl who can sing "Sentimental Journey or "We'll Be Together Again" with such knowingness should be singing better fare, and in her last few recordings with Brown, she did just that.

March 1946 brought her first of three recordings of Irving Berlin's "I Got the Sun in the Morning," but the band is the star here, not Day. There is great clarinet work and a driving arrangement complete with key changes, but she recorded the song to much greater effect on both her *Show Time* and *Annie Get Your Gun* albums twenty years in the future. Mel Tormé's (and Bob Wells's) instant classic "Christmas Song" receives a lovely reading, but this is a skating-over-the-surface picture-postcard version, completely surpassed by her 1964 Christmas album takes on "Have Yourself a Merry Little Christmas" and "Be a Child at Christmastime."

The two best Day vocals from the September 1946 sessions with Brown displayed the two different sides of her talent. The swinging Wolcott Gibert song "Sooner or Later" reveals not just her readily established sense of swing but also the fact that this is one sassy gal who is breezily and sexily confident of her own charms:

Sooner or later you're gonna be comin' around I'll betcha
You wait and see I'll betcha I'll getcha

Only someone as musically self-assured as Day could sail through such a rhythmically complex song with nary a stumble and plenty of attitude.

Finally, there is the last song Day recorded with Les Brown, the quintessential 1940s James van Heusen/Sammy Cahn ballad "It Could Happen to You," a companion piece of sorts to their sweet "Imagination." With a smooth Glenn Miller–like sound, the Les Brown band supplies Day with solid support as she, now a seasoned veteran at twenty-two, casts a knowing eye on love:

Keep an eye on spring
Run when church bells ring

Sustaining a beautiful flowing vocal line, she is acting out the lyrics, singing directly to one person, and if this version does not, understandably, achieve the depth and clarity of her '64 remake on the *Sentimental Journey* LP, it is a remarkable achievement for a twenty-two-year-old.

Her "apprenticeship" with Les Brown over, Doris Day embarked on a twenty-year solo recording career with one of the biggest labels in the music industry, Columbia Records. The result was a recording legacy of extraordinary range, power, and depth, spread over an astonishing six hundred–plus released recordings (there are, it is rumored, hundreds of others that have never seen the light of day).

Day's solo recording career can be roughly divided into two distinct phases. The early years, which lasted from roughly 1947 through 1956, found Day recording an enormous number of singles covering a wide range of genres and styles; in addition, during this same time, Columbia Records often released albums of songs featured in her movies, songs that were, for contractual reasons, rerecorded by Day, often in different versions from those featured in the Warner Bros. films. Phase two of her recording career, which ran from the 1957 release of *Day by Day* through the 1967 recording of *The Love Album*, saw Day at the peak of her powers, exploring the full range of the great American songbook in an often brilliant series of concept albums. It is these eighteen albums for Columbia that not only showcased Doris Day at her best but also provide her true recording legacy.

The bald statistics about Day's success as a singles recording artist are astonishing: She placed seventy-six singles on the charts, and no fewer than twenty-one of them hit the top ten. Seven claimed the number one position: "Bewitched, Bothered, Bewildered," "A Guy Is a Guy," "If I Give My Heart to You," "Love Somebody," "My Dreams Are Getting Better All The Time" (seven weeks at number one), "Secret Love," and "Sentimental Journey" (nine weeks at number one). Perhaps even more impressive, no fewer than nineteen of her singles spent at least twelve weeks in the top forty, with "Que Sera, Sera" charting for twenty-four weeks, and both "Secret Love" and "Sentimental Journey" taking up residence for twenty-eight weeks—seven full months of the year. In sum, Doris Day not only held the number one position on the singles charts for a total of twenty-six weeks during her career but also, according to Gary McGee's encyclopedic compendium of Day statistics, spent no fewer than 460 weeks in the top forty.

The formative big-band influences on Day's burgeoning solo career were, understandably enough, very clear in her very first efforts; whether on "I'm Still Sitting Under the Apple Tree" or "Tell Me Dream Face (What Am I to You)," one can still picture Day standing in the spotlight, front and center of the Les Brown Band. There is also an interesting recording of "Just an Old Love of Mine," written by Peggy Lee and husband Dave Barbour; if one listens to both versions of the song, the difference between the equally valid and effective approaches of these two brilliant big-band singers reflects the very differences in their personalities: Day's take is sweeter, less sensual, and more matter-of-fact.

Analyzed in chronological order, the Columbia singles are most interesting in light of their surprisingly strong jazz underpinnings. Just as proved to be the case with Day's early Les Brown recordings, the influence of Doris's singing idol, Ella Fitzgerald, is clear right from the start: "It Takes Time," "Someone Like You" (a song utilized in the film *My Dream Is Yours*), "A Chocolate Sundae on a Saturday Night," "My Young and Foolish Heart," and especially "Pete," a song Day included in her solo sets at the Little Club in New York City. In fact, one of the side benefits of watching Day play big-band singer Jo Jordan in *Young Man with a Horn* is the fact that it is the closest anyone will ever get to seeing exactly what the very young, very talented Doris Day was like in her earliest days as a solo artist in venues like the Little Club. Both at the Little Club and on these recordings, Day was backed by a small group, and her crystal-clear enunciation and clarity of tone, qualities she shared with Ella Fitzgerald and that played no small part in her extraordinary appeal, are immediately apparent.

Equally striking as the jazz currents running through these recordings is the sheer volume of songs: As she herself was to wonder in later years, "How did I ever record so many songs while making thirty-nine feature films?" Clearly, the formidable energy exhibited onscreen was not limited to the film set. Sheer energy alone, however, cannot account for the great success she found as a solo artist. Similarly, neither can sheer talent, plentiful though it was. Rather, although Doris Day's talent would have assured her success in any era, she was fortunate to be in the right place at the right time, hitting her stride just as a home stereo system became a feature of middle-class American life. By closely following voice teacher Grace Raine's advice always to sing as if to one person, Day managed to connect with the listener in an extraordinarily intimate manner. It was a style made for the hi-fi age: the listener alone at home with Doris Day crooning in his or her ear, sometimes upbeat, often sad, but always personal. Her persuasively gentle ballad singing was made for the microphone, just as proved to be the case with Bing Crosby and Frank Sinatra. It's a winning approach heard on her very early solo recording "When Tonight Is Just a Memory" and, in its way, this ballad serves as the prototype for all of the warmly enveloping ballads she would record so successfully in her career: As Day develops an audio characterization of the woman singing this song, all of the key elements are in place: She is intimate, suggestive, and supportive, in short, the woman of near fantasy you want by your side.

Right from the start of her solo career, Day began to record the numerous songs from Broadway shows that formed a major portion of her repertoire. She had a natural affinity for theater songs right from the start, because she treated each song as an actress, analyzing the character of the woman telling the musical story. As a result, theater and film songs felt natural to her—she could act out the lyric.

The first of these Broadway show tunes, "Poppa Won't You Dance With Me," a bouncy song from the show *High Button Shoes,* was written by Jule Styne, composer of "It's Magic." This was followed by the classic Gus Kahn song "Pretty Baby," which was featured four years after this recording in the film *I'll See You in My Dreams.* Day here manages the neat trick of appearing to be simultaneously maternal and sexy:

Won't you come and let me rock you
In my cradle of love.

This girl knows about sex and about comfort—a combination that contributed greatly to her appeal on disk.

One of the best of these singles was a wistful reading of the quintessential

1940s song, the James van Heusen/Johnny Burke "Imagination." Day's vocal here works on all levels; with her slightly husky two-octave range she produces a lovely sound, while at the same time she imparts a true understanding of the story these lyrics tell, the universal tale of unrequited love:

For example I go around wanting you
And yet I can't imagine that you want me too.

With songs like "Imagination" and "Sentimental Journey," Day became the female voice of the World War II generation; this war-weary generation had experienced separation and yearning on a global scale heretofore inconceivable. These were the most primal of emotions, and when the men and women of "the greatest generation" heard their feelings vocally expressed in the knowing, enveloping, intimate voice of Doris Day, they connected with the singer. She understood their lives and, as a result, they would never desert her.

Even though Day was beginning to delve into the Gershwin, Porter, and Kern catalogs that formed the basis of the classic American songbook, a full analysis of Doris's recording legacy reveals a great many songs that were simply awful. To wit: "Quiet Town in Crossbone County," a cross between hillbilly cornpone and 1940s tight vocal harmony, complete with snores and gunshots in the background!

After Day hit number one in 1948, courtesy of the bouncy "Love Somebody" with Buddy Clark, she recorded a series of ten further duets with Clark the very next year. Day's and Clark's voices blended extremely well together and their recorded output ranged from the silly "That Certain Party" and "His Fraternity Pin" to a terrific version of "I'll String Along With You." Given a superior song such as "I'll String Along With You," Day and Clark make a first-rate team, neither singer ever attempting to upstage the other. Clark's relaxed, mellow vocal, reminiscent of Bing Crosby, especially in the lower register, admirably complemented Day's smooth tones.

Three singles from this period shed fascinating light on Day's vocal development. On the beautiful Lew Brown/Sammy Fain ballad "That Old Feeling," she generates great emotional feeling; when she sings

There'll be no new romance for me
It's foolish to start

it's clear that this is a woman who still carries the torch, pure and simple.

"Pure and simple" are the exact words to describe Day's style on the down-in-the-depths ballad "When Your Lover Has Gone," famously interpreted by Frank Sinatra at his barroom-lonely best. Day is singing a song of misery, but she does not, will not, invest the song with the gut-wrenching emotion of a Barbra Streisand or a Judy Garland. Day sings this song out of great sadness, but she is contemplative of life's vagaries, not suicidal over them in her deft underplaying of Einar Swan's evocative lyric:

Like faded flowers
Life can't mean anything
When your lover has gone

Her recording is aided here by the beautiful conducting of key Sinatra collaborator Axel Stordahl. Day had first worked with Stordahl on *Your Hit Parade* with Frank Sinatra, but she was never comfortable with the live nature of that show, an only-one-attempt-to-get-it-right approach that did not fit in with her perfectionist instincts. In the controlled environs of the recording studio, however, she was free to record take after take, and meshed very well with the multitalented Stordahl. Doris Day worked with numerous conductors and arrangers during the course of her career, musicians of widely varying abilities. Stordahl was one of the best.

The third of these extraordinary singles, "You Go to My Head," found her working with George Sirvano as conductor; when she glides into the sublime title lyric extolling her lover's

smile that makes my temperature rise,
Like a summer with a thousand Julys

the listener capitulates. It's like hearing Day sing in whatever dreamlike vista one's imagination can conjure, because the vocal seems directed at you and you alone. Such intimate vocal stylings free the listener's imagination to roam—she's singing in whatever fantasy setting it is where love is deep, passionate, and, well, perfect. It's sitting fireside on a cold winter night, or by a moonlit lagoon, waves gently lapping the shore—it's wherever "Loveland," in Stephen Sondheim's memorable phrase, happens to be.

Doris Day is never desperate for love like Barbra Streisand—such all-out theatrics don't suit her more contemplative approach. In fact, when discussing Streisand in a 1968 *New York Times* interview timed to the start of her new television series, Day stated, "Streisand is great with the big orchestra. She can really belt. I'm not like that. I like the *simplest* form of music. I would prefer singing with just a guitar or piano. See, *I have to sing in somebody's ear.*" This extraordinarily beautiful approach—and it is one that only a great vocalist with total control over her instrument can ever implement—is best summed up by son Terry Melcher, himself an extremely successful songwriter/producer: "She can make a vocal sound like there's a smile or some kind of tear behind it. She can really create a visual effect with an audio art."

There were beautiful interpretations of classics like Rodgers and Hart's "Bewitched, Bothered and Bewildered," which held the number one position on the *CashBox* charts for four weeks, a recording that resurfaced a decade later on her best-selling *Greatest Hits* LP. The late 1940s also produced an extraordinary reading of the classic torch song "You're My Thrill," which became the title of her first nonsoundtrack solo LP (1949). (The album was subsequently repackaged with four additional cuts and released as *Day Dreams*.) This great song received a silken reading from Day that found her digging deeper in terms of the lyric, revealing subtler emotions.

With great material, Doris Day continued to evolve. Confronted with lesser material, she couldn't overcome the silliness—only Ella Fitzgerald, with her otherworldly sense of swing, could turn a ditty like "A Tisket, a Tasket" into a jazz playlet. Day couldn't defeat the awful pseudo-French requirements of "At the Café Rendezvous" from *It's a Great Feeling,* nor, for that matter, the pseudo-Spanglish of "It's Better to Conceal than Reveal." By the time of 1965's *Latin for Lovers,* however, an album that contained the only singing Day ever did in a foreign language, she had developed such style that she carried off an entire LP of Latin-inflected songs with ease.

At this early stage of her career, Doris was recording duets not just with Buddy Clark but also with myriad other partners, both male and female. Teaming with Dinah Shore, she sang the archetypal devoted little woman song "You Can Have Him" from Irving Berlin's *Miss Liberty.* With its lyrics extolling the woman's desire to

> *Close the window while he sleeps*
> *Cook a breakfast that would please him most*

it's a song very much at odds with Day's can-do, self-sufficient film persona.

Most fascinating of all, however, is the duet with Frank Sinatra on "Let's Take an Old Fashioned Walk," another song from the score of *Miss Liberty.* The duet represented a reunion of sorts, as Day had previously appeared in 1947 as a featured singer on the Sinatra-hosted radio program *Your Hit Parade*. On those live shows, they sang "Take Me Out to the Ball Game" and "There's No Business Like Show Business." Here, the duet with Sinatra clearly reveals why they were a mismatched team, a state of affairs also on display in their 1955 film *Young at Heart.*

Berlin's lyric begins with the words, "I know for a couple that seems miles apart"—Berlin sure has it right about these two, but not in the sense originally intended. Good as Sinatra and Day are as singers—and they are all-time greats—their styles are totally opposite. They both sound terrific, but these lyrics make no sense coming from such a pair. Sinatra is not exactly the man you associate with an old-fashioned walk. A jet-set trip to Peru in "Come Fly With Me"—you bet. An old fashioned walk around the block—no way. Sinatra is a self-described "twenty-four-karat manic-depressive," while Doris Day gets on with the task at hand, goes with the flow, and always projects an optimistic attitude. Their two personalities, on disk and film, are so larger than life that one can't help but react to the song with their disparate personae in mind. Day would enjoy a walk around the block, especially with several dogs in tow. Sinatra would stop in for a scotch at the nearest saloon and stay there until the wee small hours of the morning.

As Day's recorded catalog began to grow, it was unfortunately becoming apparent that many of the recording dates juxtaposed the ridiculous and the sublime in the very same session. In one 1950 recording date, working with the jazz great, trumpeter Red Nichols, Day could—and did—swing through "I Don't Want to Be Kissed by Anyone But You," but the first-class vocal is ruined by the inclusion of supposedly funny impersonations of foreigners—Frenchmen, Britishers, you name it, they're all on this record. Why the insistence on foreign accents when the vocalist in question was all-American Doris is anyone's guess. Talk about an uneasy fit.

If only Day had possessed the temperament—or is it the contract?—to refuse the nonsense forced upon her by various producers. On the one hand, she could ooze sex on record as on the hypnotic and sensual "With You Anywhere You Are." Just listen to Day caress the lyric, "Always like to hold you tight while the moon is hanging low." The promise of sex is heavy in the air. Yet at the very same session where she would record a gem like this, she also have to record a terminally dopey song like "Save a Little Sunbeam (For a Rainy Day)," complete with annoying talking interruptions from arranger/conductor Ray Noble.

Strangest of all, producers saddled Doris Day with songs in genres that made little or no sense in terms of her vocal style, to wit, country-western. Listening to these cuts, one's reaction is, well—as they say in the Wild West, "Oy vey." One country-western song, "Quicksilver," hit number twenty on the charts, but it's not a particularly adept song. Outfitted with a traditional country-western sound featuring steel guitars, it sounds good, but what does it all mean? These are not songs suited for Day's interpretive style of singing. She can't dig into these lyrics; there'd be no drinking of whiskey at the bar for this gal. Nope, she'd whip the lazy cowpokes into shape one-two-three and get them out in the sunshine to walk the dogs. Even fifty-plus years after these records were made, one reacts with more than a little disbelief to the studio personnel listing of "Doris Day and her Country Cousins." Who the heck was such pseudocountry music aimed at—aside from Doris's country-and-western-music-loving mother, Alma?

Yet shortly after this rather painful recording, Day triumphed, and then some, with the terrific tracks she cut for the film *Young Man with a Horn.* The album hit the number one chart position in the United States, and for once artistic and commercial success went hand in hand. Anyone doubting Day's jazz abilities need only listen to her opening attack on "I May Be Wrong (But I Think You're Wonderful)." Crisp, clean, and swinging, she nails every note squarely in the middle. At these same sessions she cut a slightly different version of "Too Marvelous for Words" from the one utilized in the film, and she scores very well indeed, even when paired head on with the flashy Harry James.

Day is at home with a jazz setting; the apprenticeship with the Les Brown and Bob Crosby big bands had taught her to listen to the musicians—when to attack the vocal line and when to swing lightly. In a way, Doris Day's very versatility as a vocalist has undercut people's ability to fully comprehend just how great a singer she was. Contrast the bright attack on "I May Be Wrong" with the seductive seamless vocal lines of "The Very Thought of You"; similarly, even a casual listener can realize how clearly she puts across the true meaning of "With a Song in My Heart"—crystalizing exactly what kind of love she is singing about. Such a combination of dramatic force and musical agility is no easy task when competing with Harry James's ornate solos, but Day is up to the task. No wonder jazz legend Sarah Vaughan exclaimed, "I really dig Doris Day."

And how did she follow up the total triumph of "Young Man with a Horn"? By having to record the terminally stupid polka "I Went a Wooing." On the face of it, Doris Day's boundless energy should have made her a natural singer of polkas. The problem was that she was saddled with a lot of bad polkas. "I Went a Wooing" is not exactly a polka in the same class as Richard Rodgers's "Shall We Dance." In fact, the lyrics for "I Went a Wooing" make one long for the subtleties inherent in "The Beer Barrel Polka" . . . Her follow-up polka recording? "Hoop-de-Doo," most famously recorded by Perry Como. It's a catchy tune, but its lyric content? Not exactly material to cause sleepless nights for Stephen Sondheim.

And yet—and yet—Day could follow these second-rate polkas with gems like "I'll Be Around" and "Darn That Dream." In these sessions she worked with the best musicians in Hollywood—Axel Stordahl conducting, Eleanor Slatkin on cello, Dave Frisina on violin—and Day was every bit their equal. Especially on "I'll Be Around," she gives the listener a three-act play complete in and of itself. Singing with an understanding yet persistent point of view, this girl next door will wait out her man's foolishness. As the title has it, her love will last, and she makes you believe that she's the right gal for, well, anyone and everyone who is listening.

As Day filmed musical after musical for Warner Bros., her recorded legacy kept pace, and her development as an artist accelerated. From the pleasant but forgettable Warner Bros. musical film *Tea for Two,* Day, working with Stordahl and both Felix and Eleanor Slatkin, emerged with a version of the title song that ensures one will never listen to the well-known ditty in the same way again. Underlying Day's interpretation is a very gentle sense of swing—the slowed-down yet syncopated rhythm of the isolated "lover's oasis" to which the lyric refers:

Nobody near us to see us or hear us
No friends or relations on weekend vacations

This is the girl with whom you want to be alone in that seaside cottage—and, not so coincidentally, the girl you want to take home to meet Mother.

Day's jazz roots emerged even more strongly in her work with the Page Cavanaugh Trio, most notably on "I Want to Be Happy." The vocal here is no mindless parroting of the well-worn standard. Rather, she slows down the tempo, taking it at a relaxed pace until the Cavanaugh trio, led by the vibraphone, accelerates the song into a duet between Day and the trio itself (which sounds strikingly reminiscent of the great Nat King Cole Trio). The resulting recording is up-tempo yet never races, and is exhilarating in its clarity. From his previous work accompanying Frank Sinatra and Mel Tormé, it was clear that Cavanaugh, himself a recording artist, possessed a great feel for sympathetic backing. Even on middle-tier songs such as "He's Such a Gentleman" and "I Love the Way You Say Goodnight," the interplay between trio and vocalist is always worth a listen, and Day's work with him on "Orange Colored Sky" may not be the equal of Nat King Cole's—whose is?—but it's a damn good try.

By this time, Day's enormous popularity as a recording artist was such that sound track recordings from her films routinely reached the top of the charts, no matter the quality of the film in question. Doris Day was the "it" girl of the moment, but because Warner Bros. owned the rights to Day's vocal performances on film, Columbia Records could not release those recordings; as a result, in order to take advantage of Day's soaring popularity, Columbia Records had Day rerecord the songs she sang in the films and released the results on Columbia LPs emblazoned with the film's title in large type. Such rerecordings often featured different arrangements and vocal takes, welcome evidence of Day's evolving search for an increased clarity and subtlety in her singing.

All of these musical sound track albums sold extremely well, even though their early 1950s release dates mirrored the beginnings of the rock-and-roll revolution. *Lullaby of Broadway* reached number one on the charts and was followed by *On Moonlight Bay* (number two) and *By the Light of the Silvery Moon* (number three). The songs in these films did not cover a wide enough territory to showcase Day's true versatility, but she invariably sounded good—make that great—and the public lapped it all up.

Continuing to record at a feverish pace, Day had to suffer through additional, and even more painful, polkas, the nadir of which were the unfortunately titled "Comb and Paper Polka" and "Pumpernickel." Suffice it to say that the combined singing and acting talents of Ella Fitzgerald and Meryl Streep would be helpless to make any sense of these extraordinarily insipid ditties. Wisely, in a total change of pace, Day next recorded three hymns. These are particularly interesting to listen to in light of her later (1962) LP of religious music *You'll Never Walk Alone.* Day has spoken publicly of her love of hymns, and even at this relatively early stage of her recording career, there are two interesting attempts at true spiritual depth with "The Everlasting Arms" and "David's Psalm," both written by Day's Christian Science practitioner, Martin Broones (the former song cowritten with Paul Francis Webster of "Secret Love" fame). Ten years later, at the time of *You'll Never Walk Alone,* Day achieves a fuller reading of such spiritually based lyrics—a decade of often tough life experiences bringing a greater maturity and perspective to the interpretation of the lyrics. At this juncture in her solo career, Day still sounds more at ease singing the secular "Christmas Story" (from the film *On Moonlight Bay*) but nonetheless, her attempts at religious music here form impressive testaments to her versatility.

Better still are the Broadway show tunes she was beginning to record in greater and greater number, witness "I've Never Been in Love Before" and "Bushel and a Peck" from *Guys and Dolls.* These two songs are, respectively, sung in the show by Salvation Army stalwart Sarah Brown and nightclub floozy Miss Adelaide, yet Day handles the contrasting vocal requirements with ease. She also covered two terrific Irving Berlin numbers from the Ethel Merman vehicle *Call Me Madam:* "It's a Lovely Day," which featured a

George Sirvano–led orchestra complete with wailing trumpets, and an even more noteworthy complete reworking of Merman's "The Best Thing for You." Great as Merman was onstage, she was not exactly subtle, basically bullying the listener into submission; she'd tell you what the best thing for you was, all right, and you better damn well do it. Day here turns the song into a tender ballad and is nearly maternal in telling her love, "After thinking it through the best thing for you would be me."

The recording sessions for Day's film *Lullaby of Broadway,* led by Frank Comstock (whom Day had known since her days with Les Brown), produced a standout version of "You're Getting to Be a Habit With Me," in which her very seductive vocal made it clear that the habit in question was *sex*. Just as she did with "Please Don't Talk About Me When I'm Gone" from the same sessions, Day here slows down the song so that the nearly erotic take on the lyric registers fully. Interestingly, after employing the same leisurely tempo to the beginning of "Somebody Loves Me," she then races into a full-out big-band rendition—trumpets blare, and you're listening to the golden-voiced kid on the bandstand all over again. Best of all on this sound track recording is her rendition of "Lullaby of Broadway." Although she was to rerecord the song again, delivering *the* all-time definitive interpretation of this show business anthem, it's still great fun here: With the very strange but somehow effective backing combination of the Buddy Cole Quartet with the Norman Luboff Choir, the song peaks with Day drawing out the evocative phrase "Sleep tight, baby—the milkman's on his way." "Baby" becomes a four-syllable word, drawing upon her lower register, and the effect is sexy and startling, an unexpected turn of phrasing that only a truly great vocalist could deliver.

Like all great artists, when Day rerecorded the song a mere twenty days later, once again with Frank Comstock at the helm, she had rethought and improved the vocal. So it was that on December 28, 1950, she recorded a version of this brassy paean to New York City that is nigh onto perfect. Working with brilliant jazz musicians like Harry James on trumpet and Louis Bellson on drums, and taking off from a swinging Jack Mathias arrangement, Doris Day here lets loose, and what a glorious, freewheeling sound it is. She may prefer ballads, but boy, oh boy she sure can belt when she feels like it. She really is the sound of 1950s America here—hands on her hips, she's game for anything. Playing off the clean sound of James's trumpet, she's ready for the "La-di-da and whoop-de-doo, the lullaby of Broadway." Propelled by Bellson's drums, she is freedom personified in urging all to "Listen to the lullaby of old Broadway." No other version of this song—not even the famous Count Basie—Tony Bennett version—quite lives up to this stratospheric recording.

The songs collected in the indispensable Bear Family Records boxed set titled *Secret Love* cover 1951 through 1955, and this encyclopedic collection makes it clear that these were the years of Day's true growth as a vocalist, years that led to the concept album masterpieces she began recording in 1956. In fact, one can sense Day's trajectory as an artist by listening to the very first cut contained in the "*Secret Love*"—boxed set, "It's So Laughable." It's a middling song, but when Day sings, "It's all laughable to everyone but me," she is so astonishingly intimate, so vulnerable and sexy, that an immediate connection is forged with her listeners, one that would never truly be broken again.

It was also at this time that the missing ingredient for the complete expression of Day's vocal capabilities was found—the addition of Paul Weston as arranger/conductor. Weston came to serve the role with Day that Nelson Riddle did for Sinatra and Peter Matz for Streisand: All three men were brilliantly talented arrangers, the best in the business, who intuitively understood what showcased their singer's strengths to best advantage. In the process of working together, these teams of singer and arranger created the true lasting legacy of each singer's vocal art.

Weston, who married the superb singer Jo Stafford, had written arrangements for Tommy Dorsey, Bob Crosby, and Phil Harris. At the time that his work with Day began, he was working as musical director of Capitol Records and also arranging for Rosemary Clooney and Ella Fitzgerald as well as wife Stafford. Weston seemed to possess an innate understanding of the female voice and for his sessions with Day, he came up with a very specific orchestral mix which he felt would showcase Day to best advantage: eight brass, five woodwinds, ten or twelve strings, a rhythm section, and seven or eight backup singers (usually the Norman Luboff Choir). The band Weston would assemble for Day's recording sessions at the Radio Recorders Annex was often loaded with all-star musicians, including trumpeter Ziggy Elman and saxophonists Ted Nash and Babe Russin. Musing about these sessions decades later, Weston stated, "I always felt [Doris] was a better singer than she thought she was. She was a very expressive singer. She could take a lyric and to some extent act it out, while never losing sight of the musical part. The music always seemed to come first with her. I always felt with Doris that I liked to give her a nice firm lower background musically with clarinets and sometimes saxophones and strings to sing against because her voice stood out so well that you would never want anything up high to clutter up whatever she wanted to do vocally."

Paul Weston "got" Doris Day. More than any previous or subsequent arranger, he knew how to make her voice "pop" on the recordings. Load up the lower musical background with clarinets and/or strings and then let 'er rip.

So it was that on May 15, 1951, in her first non-film-related session with Weston, Day brought her sound into the modern age in one fell swoop, via a brilliant take on the novelty song "(Why Did I Tell You I Was Going to) Shanghai." With all-stars Nash, Russin, and Elman on board, Day was off and running right from the start, sailing over the brass with a pure clean sound that's filled with joy:

Who-who-who-who's gonna kiss me, who's gonna thrill me
Who's gonna hold me tight

You can tell that these musicians, big-band veterans all, love Day, and vice versa—the support is so sympathetic yet so joy-filled that it really does represent the best of traditional American pop music.

The Weston sessions weren't all great—or rather the material wasn't all great—because further third-rate polkas such as "Ask Me—Because I'm So in Love" lay dead ahead. Did Columbia Records execs think that because of Day's German background she'd automatically take to polkas? Was it producer Mitch Miller's well-known love of novelty songs (e.g., Clooney's "Come On a My House") that forced this silliness on Doris? What the hell was everyone involved thinking? Whatever the reason, the recording of such songs proved to be a waste of everyone's talents.

Fortunately, the musicians Weston assembled were so great that even a fair song like "Got Him off My Hands" landed solidly, and on a good song, like the Harry Warren/Johnny Mercer ballad "Baby Doll," Day sails through like the first-class artist she had become. On slower-tempo songs, Weston builds on his big-band roots, crafting a Tommy Dorsey–like smooth trombone sound to accompany Day's sensual crooning:

Honey, there's no use talking
You're a wonderful baby doll.

It is actually Day (and not a man) who is here taking control. Telling her love that there is no use in his even trying to talk, she is both in charge of her love and having fun at the same time. With such first-class material, she could alternately express longing, a deeply felt love, or even a near maternal protectiveness—her voice really was capable of this range of emotions.

Weston also conducted Day's recording sessions for the songs used in her excellent biopic *I'll See You in My Dreams.* In pure vocal terms, there are no fewer than three standouts here: the first is a sexy "It Had to Be You," in which Doris sings the famous words, "For nobody else gave me a thrill, with all your faults I love you still," in an astonishingly pure voice. The next gem is

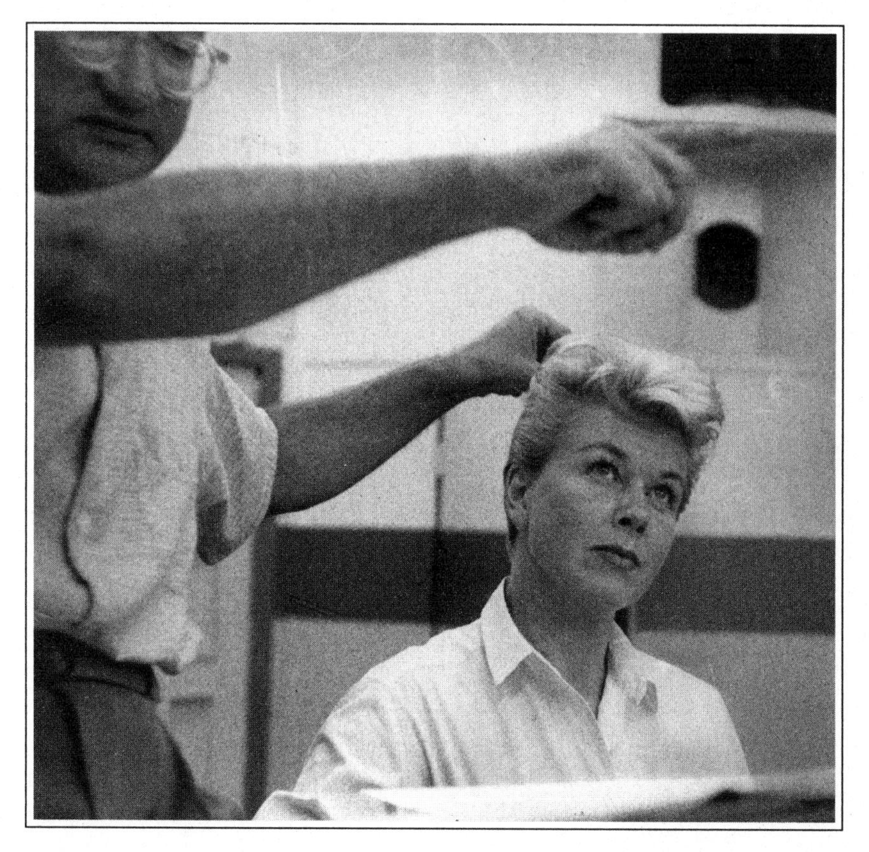

Listening to a playback with the great Paul Weston. *Photofest*

a reading of the well-worn standard "My Buddy," on which Day's vocal not only points up her extraordinary capacity to act out a song but also forms an interesting basis of comparison with Barbra Streisand's version on her *The Way We Were* album. With Streisand one is awed by the vocal purity and the long seamless lines spun out without a break. With Day the listener simply thinks of the buddy about whom she's singing. Finally, on "The One I Love Belongs to Somebody Else," Weston builds a veritable cushion of strings on which Day floats her vocal. It's a beautiful match of music, voice, and arrangement, and smooth sailing all the way.

Still churning out singles by the dozens in the 1950s, it's interesting to note how many duets Day recorded during this period, and with a diversity of partners—male and female—who ran the gamut both in terms of suitability and talent. The "Ain't We Got Fun" duet with Danny Thomas from *I'll See You in My Dreams* works well, not because Thomas is a great singer but because Day carries him along, and because the sometimes annoying and saccharine Norman Luboff Choir here actually supplies backing vocals that provide rhythmic underpinning (in point of fact, this sound track topped the charts in the United States).

Yet at the same 1952 sessions where Day recorded the songs from *I'll See You in My Dreams,* she also sang duets with Frankie Laine that were, in a word, awful. It's not that Laine is a bad singer; it's that his style is so opposite of Day's. "Sugar Bush," which, incredibly, became a top ten hit, is most noteworthy not for the singing but for the hand claps accompanied by xylophone. One has to hear this nonsense to fully believe it, yet this cut is actually better than another of their duets, "How Lovely Cooks the Meat"—yep, that's the real title, and unfortunately it tells one everything there is to know about the duet. In this song about food preparation, Doris is stylistically singing a lullaby, Laine is still singing "Mule Train," and they actually have to wrap their tonsils around lyrics like

the stove is much too hot
The steak has a big black spot.

With songs like this, it's a wonder the West was ever won.

After these sessions with Laine, a veritable who's who of 1950s popular male singers made the trek to the recording booth with Day. It's as if the Columbia Records execs tried out her duet capabilities with every singer they could think of and just hoped that one of the combinations would stick, the way it had with Buddy Clark. This was not exactly an approach to ensure first-class artistic expression, a fact borne out by the lackluster results. There is a duet on "A Little Kiss Goodnight" with Guy Mitchell, a song striking only for Mitchell's interpolated patter of calling Doris "Dodo" in the middle of the song. "No Two People," by Frank Loesser, featured Donald O'Connor as Day's duet partner, but good as O'Connor could be onscreen, he was not in Day's class as a vocalist. Most ill fitting of all were a half dozen duets with the popular Johnny Ray. Again, it's a case of ill-matching styles: Johnny was all overwrought emotion, Doris just the opposite. Ray had the vocal power, without the true understanding of the lyrics, but both singers were hampered by terrible songs such as "Ma Says, Pa Says" and especially "Beautiful Music to Love By," a second-rate song featuring a mind-boggling marimba accompaniment that manages the neat trick of sounding like an organ playing in a funeral home.

The duet sessions were nearly over, thank goodness, but take a look at the variety of partners: Frank Sinatra, Dinah Shore, Buddy Clark, Donald O'Connor, Frankie Laine, Guy Mitchell, Johnny Ray—all A-list singers, with the exception of O'Connor, but it's actually Day's work that one remembers from the sessions. She always blended her voice effectively with her partner's, but so distinctive and singular is her sound that one ends up wanting nothing so much as the chance to hear her sing the song by herself. It's the same principle as with Sinatra and Streisand: Like Day, they both recorded many duets, but with those voices, and those personalities, they, like Doris Day, function better on their own. Talent that unique shines best when left alone.

It's no surprise, then, that the best songs from this period were Doris's solo singles. "Who Who Who" is a semi-obscure song, but in Day's swinging rhythmic attack, one can really hear the big-band singer with the jazz roots. Similarly, it's a measure of Day's growth as an artist, of the singing actress she had become, that she can take a song like "My Love and Devotion" and invest the lyrics with a sense of genuine yearning. "My Love and devotion are yours till I die": Day croons the words with such understated intensity that the depth of her commitment rings through loud and clear.

Commitment? Try listening to Day's version of "A Full Time Job," where she sensually whisper-sings the words

I want a full time job making love to you
I'll do anything you want to do

After listening to this recording, one can only ask: —What made people think that this woman was America's perennial virgin? Well, the answer, of course, was that the films made people think that way, never the recordings.

Best of all during these early/mid-'50s sessions are three huge hits: "A Guy Is a Guy," a reworking of "It's Magic," and "When I Fall In Love"; it's only fitting that all three songs ended up on the multimillion-selling LP *Doris Day's Greatest Hits.* "A Guy Is a Guy," guitar player Oscar Brand's adaptation of an eighteenth-century English tavern song, was recorded in February 1952; it does read as ridiculously sexist now, what with the singer's parents' "agreeing" on "the married life" for her, but it's an infectious tune and Day invests the lyrics with such knowingness that one doesn't really believe she'd be anyone's simpering mate. When her lover asks her for a goodnight kiss in the daytime, she blithely sings that

I would have told him more except
His lips got in the way

Listen to her voice sliding down the scale on the phrase "in the way"—this girl is talking about *sex.* No ifs, ands, or buts.

"It's Magic," recorded on June 4, 1952, with Percy Faith leading the orchestra and Buddy Cole on piano, is a superior reworking of a song that was great when first recorded four years earlier for the film *Romance on the High Seas.* Day has rethought the lyrics, rephrasing the vocal line to even greater effect: spinning out long, flowing vocal lines, backed by a legion of strings, she yearningly tells the listener

When we walk hand in hand
The world becomes a wonderland.

This is great singing—the single best recorded version of a terrific song that still resonates fifty years later.

Finally, there is "When I Fall in Love," a Victor Young/Edward Heyman ("Body and Soul") song that registers as the quintessential Doris Day ballad of longing; when this woman falls in love, "it will be forever, or I'll never fall in love." Day is here singing with great intensity, but she never overstates, a key reason why the recording has not dated.

For every "When I Fall in Love," however, there were pointless novelties like "A Purple Cow," a prime example of '50s pop novelty songwriting at its worst. Patti Page may have had success with the treacly "How Much Is That Doggie in the Window," but when Marty Melcher first brought "A Purple Cow" to Doris, her reaction was immediate: "I hated it." But record it she did. For Doris Day to go from "It's Magic" to

I never thought I'd see a purple cow
I never thought I'd hear a butterfly meow"

well, that's a journey in reverse, big time.

It was right after these sessions, which fortunately all had the saving grace of the great Paul Weston at the helm, that Day filmed and recorded the songs from *Calamity Jane.* Whatever its merits and flaws as a film, *Calamity Jane* did possess the best original score composed for any Doris Day film musical, the kingpin number, of course, being "Secret Love." Day's antennae for a great song, which unfortunately were often overridden by both Marty Melcher and Mitch Miller's insistence on chasing novelty hits, were right on the money regarding "Secret Love." Her reaction to the Sammy Fain/Paul Webster composition was immediate: "When I first heard Sammy Fain sing that song for me in my house in Toluca Lake, I just about fell apart. I loved the whole score so much I was just dancing around the house." Immensely aided by the first-rate arrangement by Frank Comstock, the single topped the charts in the United States for four weeks, placed on the UK charts for an astounding twenty-nine weeks, and was instrumental in making Day a huge star in England, where her loyal following continues to this day.

"The Deadwood Stage" from *Calamity Jane* is such fun to watch on the screen, with Day's athleticism, as she drives a stagecoach over the open Western landscape, perfectly complementing the rollicking tune, that only in listening to the recording does one realize how carefully calibrated the vocal really is.

When Doris reaches the words "A beautiful sky, a wonderful day," she opens up on the word "sky" to a full-throated cry of freedom, which induces that same feeling in the listener. It's no accident that the sound track album reached number two on the charts in the United States.

In the middle of the *Calamity Jane* recording sessions, Day tested her own versatility by recording both the novelty song "Choo Choo Train," which reached number twenty on the charts, and the religious "This Too Shall Pass Away" by Ervin Drake, Jimmy Shirl, and Irving Graham. On this beautiful contemplative track, Day counsels patience and faith in the middle of life's "bleak and cold" misfortunes:

Be brave, be patient, and behold
This too shall pass away

This is sung with such tenderness and inherent understanding of life's upheavals that one is again reminded of a key component of Day's appeal: You want this woman by your side because she'll stay put through thick and thin. To have delivered such an introspective, spiritual performance in the middle of recording the rollicking score for *Calamity Jane* is extraordinary.

Edging toward the full-blown masterpiece that was *Love Me or Leave Me,* Day recorded the sound track to the mediocre *Lucky Me,* which at least preserves the one truly good song in the score, the top twenty hit, "I Speak to the Stars." The song works better on record than on film because one is not distracted by the surreal film setting of Day vocalizing underneath a see-through crystal tree (!); instead, one can concentrate on the song's beautiful ending, where Day effortlessly negotiates the key change from minor to major, intimately murmuring the phrase "I'm in love" three times in a row. It's a wonderfully evocative coda to the piece, and it is only the munchkin-sounding backup chorus that keeps the song from a place in the top tier of her recordings.

1954 found Day working for the first time with Frank DeVol who was, over time, to develop into her best arranger of up-tempo songs, as evidenced by her extraordinary 1959 *Cuttin' Capers* album. Here, however, faced with a number of mediocre songs like "Jimmy Unknown" and "Someone Else's Roses," their debut together was not auspicious; Day unfortunately still had to record a number of silly novelty songs, and it was more than apparent that this most intimate and interpretive of vocalists had absolutely no affinity for such insipid fare. Her first collaboration with DeVol, "Kay Muleta," appears to be Day's answer to "Mambo Italiano" (Rosemary Clooney) and "Poppa Loves Mambo" (Perry Como). Listening to three "white-bread" singers, who were all of course superior artists, try to enliven such "ethnic" offerings is a slightly surreal experience. Clooney and Como had greater success with their mambos than did Day, simply because their songs were better. Doris's "Kay Muleta" appears to be a mambo love song in which her suitor literally falls off the balcony. "As Time Goes By" it ain't.

In July 1954, Day reunited with Paul Weston and recorded another top-of-the-charts hit: "If I Give My Heart to You." Rising to number one on *CashBox,* and eventually ending up on Day's *Greatest Hits* LP, it's a first-rate medium-tempo cut, and for once the vocal backing fits the song. Day's vocal here is framed by a repeated "Ba Ba Ba Ba Bum" bass chorus from the Mellomen, a backing that turns the ballad into a gently rhythmic tune outfitted as an interesting conditional love song: "If I give my heart to you, will you still be true?"

This was followed by a number of mediocre songs from the film *Young at Heart,* such as "Till My Love Comes to Me" and "You My Love"—songs that didn't register even with Doris Day and Frank Sinatra to sing them! (The sound track from the film peaked at a chart position of number fifteen.) If these two superstars couldn't make the songs click, no one could. Perhaps it's a sign of the ongoing search for novelty hits that "Ready, Willing, and Able" from the same film tried to build on the Rosemary Clooney hit "Come on a My House" by once again utilizing a harpsichord as the predominant backing instrument. It didn't work.

1954 had seen the true jump start of the rock-and-roll revolution with the overwhelming success of "Rock Around the Clock" by Bill Haley and the Comets. The large record companies had absolutely no idea how to deal with this phenomenon called rock and roll; this was a new style of music for which the big-band-trained executives and arrangers at Columbia Records were ill equipped to deal. No surprise, then, to see this uncertainty in the songs Day was forced to record at this time. Frank Comstock arranged the Otis Williams and the Charms song "Two Hearts, Two Kisses, Make One Love" for Day, and while the September 1955 recording date did boast Paul Weston at the helm, it's clear that Day and rock and roll are an ill-matched pair. Day and Comstock are trying for the Bill Haley sound here, but it can't happen with Day: Her articulation is too clear, the sound too clean ever to register with any of rock's primal force. Similarly, the third-rate "Ooh Bang! Jiggly! Jama!" by Bob Merrill is all wrong, beginning with the title. In an example of the extent to which the record companies had been caught off guard, they had here turned to a Broadway composer/lyricist, the author of "How Much Is That Doggy in the Window," to pen a rock-and-roll song for Doris Day. The result is a total mismatch of composer, song, and singer; Doris Day can be very sexy, but she is intimate and seductive, while rock music revolves around a gut-level in-your-face kind of sexual energy.

In a similar vein, "Whad'ja Put in That Kiss" features a pseudorock Jerry Lee Lewis piano, and even has the great Irv Cottler on drums, but from beginning to end the song goes nowhere. More attempts all fell flat: "Live It Up" with a simple three-chord guitar riff, and "I'm a Big Girl Now" are painfully thin attempts to fit in with the times. It's like listening to Barbra Streisand's attempts at rock singing, although Day's vocals are not as unremittingly earnest as Streisand's. Doris Day didn't even really change her vocal approach with these rock-lite songs—she just plowed ahead, singing in her usual style; fortunately, she attempted, or rather, was forced to attempt, this stylistic change to rock on far fewer songs than Streisand insisted on. It's no accident that ultimately these two brilliant vocalists had their biggest artistic successes by pursuing their own vision in songs most closely suited to their musical roots: Streisand with the Sondheim-oriented *The Broadway Album* and Day with her Paul Weston–arranged *Day by Night*. Doris Day's talent allowed her to be many things—actress, singer, dancer, comedian—but rock-and-roll singer was definitely not one of them.

The silly rock attempts are what made the overwhelming success of *Love Me or Leave Me* an even sweeter triumph. It's not just that the film represents Day's greatest musical performance as an actress—it's that the sound track represents her most versatile performance as a singer. Rarely has a single performer been called upon to carry an entire film vocally while running such a gamut of styles: "Everybody Loves My Baby" is quintessential 1920s flapper music; Irving Berlin's "Shakin' the Blues Away" personifies Broadway belting; "Ten Cents a Dance" is tough-dame Rodgers and Hart styling; "You Made Me Love You" registers as the quintessential torch song. It is not an exaggeration to say that Day is flawless here—not one vocal mistake on an incredible lineup of songs and styles. Recorded in a mere ten days, the album peaks with Day's sublime vocal to "It All Depends on You." Accompanied only by the piano of Milton Raskin, she is here not being masochistic, not playing the victim, but rather simply expressing—murmuring, almost—an acceptance of what life has brought her. This is the definitive interpretation of a classic song. Then again, maybe the peak of the album is "I'll Never Stop Loving You," a melting ballad that seems tailor-made for the trademark intimate, seductive Day style. It's a style that here suggests Ruth Etting but never imitates her; Day is actually a richer, more powerful vocalist than Etting. For once, the sales success of an extraordinary LP matched the artistic achievement it contained: This LP spent seventeen weeks at number one on the charts, ranking as the third most successful LP of the decade, topped only by the *South Pacific* sound track and Harry Belafonte's calypso album. It's a success totally deserved, and its cover photo of Day in the low-cut blue spangled gown she wears in the "Shakin' the Blues Away" production number remains iconic to this day.

The years 1956 through 1959 found Doris Day at her peak, both artistically and commercially. Gone were the days of recording random singles, of having inferior material foisted upon her in Columbia's search for a novelty hit. Instead, in these years Day recorded one extraordinary concept album after another, all of which featured brilliant interpretations of classic American popular songs. The first was the Paul Weston–helmed *Day by Day*, but even before those sessions began, there was the little matter of a single titled "Que Sera, Sera."

With its distinctive mandolin backing, "Que Sera, Sera" resonated with audiences from the moment they first heard it in Hitchcock's *The Man Who Knew Too Much*. Sung twice in the film—first as a lullaby to Day's son and then as a means of helping that young boy escape captivity—the Ray Evans/Jay Livingston song has a singsong melody line that recalls any number of sweet childhood tunes. Ironically, Day herself confessed that the first time she heard the complete composition, which was to become her theme song, she didn't particularly like it: "I thought it was a cute, bouncy tune, but most singers prefer more substantial ballads." However, this childlike ditty contained a melodic hook that stuck in the listener's brain after even one hearing, and aided by a terrific Frank DeVol arrangement, the melody landed. Add in a lyric that complemented the simple melody with a laissez-faire philosophy, and one couldn't forget the song, even if one wanted to. Most people didn't. This song, which ranked second on the *Billboard* charts for three weeks, became Doris Day's unquestioned theme song, because the laissez-faire lyric came to embody her own personal philosophy of life:

Que sera, sera
Whatever will be, will be

The song's lyrics form an ironic juxtaposition with Day's persona of a determined, self-sufficient woman, but then again, she is a self-confident woman who still always left all of the business decisions to husband Marty

Melcher, a move that does speak to a "que sera, sera" philosophy. Day came to utilize this song as the theme for all five years of her television series, sang it in other movies (e.g., *Glass Bottom Boat*), rerecorded it on her children's album, and used it as the introduction to her autobiography. With all of the twists and downturns Day's personal life has seen—the violent first husband, the failed marriages, her son Terry's untimely death—it's a philosophy that seems to have brought her comfort and functioned as a survival mechanism. (Lost in the hubbub surrounding "Que Sera, Sera" was another Evans/Livingston song from *The Man Who Knew Too Much,* "We'll Love Again." This is an undiscovered gem from Day's recording output, a beautiful, plaintive melody combined with a wistful lyric that together conjure up a nearly palpable elegiac air.)

Signing a then-record $1 million contract with Columbia Records in 1956, Day first recorded the theme song from her film *Julie* and found herself with another hit, but even such a hit single paled in comparison to the series of extraordinary concept albums that began with *Day by Day* (1956). This represented her first non-film-related studio album, and to put it succinctly, she hit a home run in her very first time at bat. It has been reported that the final selection represented a mix of songs that Columbia wanted Day to record and songs she herself selected. Whatever the provenance, the result was electrifying.

Rising to number eleven on the *Billboard* charts, this masterpiece—and that is not too strong a word—found Day working with Paul Weston and an array of musicians who represented the cream of the big-band veterans: Barney Kessel on guitar, Alvin Stoller on drums, Ted Nash on sax, Babe Russin on sax, and Frank Flynn on vibes. Weston understood Day's vocal lines so thoroughly, and here was presented with such first-rate American classic pop songs, that together vocalist and arranger soared on the album's twelve cuts. Filled with gems from the golden age of the great American songbook like "The Song Is You," "Gypsy in My Soul," and Autumn Leaves," the LP is so consistently first class that it is hard to pick out a particular standout cut. "Gone With the Wind" captures a heartfelt air of regret, "Day by Day," by Axel Stordahl, Weston, and Sammy Cahn is spun out with long vocal lines featuring seamless phrasing, while "But Beautiful" features a George Epps guitar accompaniment that quietly echoes and even supplements her flowing vocal line. Among this plethora of riches, the best cut of all may be the Victor Schertzinger/Johnny Mercer standard "I Remember You." Day turns in what very well may be the definitive interpretation of this song, just as she did with the up-tempo "Lullaby of Broadway." In just three minutes, Mercer's nigh-perfect lyric conjures up love, nostalgia—the whole damn shooting match—and together Day and Weston capture every last one of these sentiments:

I remember too a distant bell
And stars that fell like rain out of the blue

This is singing of such extraordinary expertise that it is difficult to believe that the entire album was recorded in less than one week. When one remembers that there was no multitracking in those days—everybody was playing and singing at the same time—the end result registers as an even more impressive achievement.

Day's sublime artistry here results from the fact that the effort to create a musical or emotional statement never shows, yet both occur. In the words of critic Will Friedwald, it's "a kind of instant, chemical reaction that just occurs naturally when all the right ingredients are mixed together. . . . This is perhaps what distinguishes Day from her peers and colleagues: as great as Ella Fitzgerald, Peggy Lee, Rosemary Clooney, Jo Stafford, and Judy Garland are, to name only five, all of them communicate something of the effort that goes into producing beautiful music. With Day, it just seems to exist, a product of nature that has nothing to do with the machinations of mere mortals, even herself. Just as much work went into her singing as any of these other great divas of jazz and pop, it's just that Day makes the process that much more invisible."

In a fascinating anecdote that says volumes about Doris Day's own personality and about her desire to create a positive and harmonious atmosphere when she worked, she revealed that on her way to recording sessions, "I liked to bring in donuts and coffee cakes. I would go by this smashing bakery in Beverly Hills and bring in all this stuff. We had a big coffee urn in the studio and everyone had a good time." It's hard to think of more unstarlike behavior than this; it's just a tad on the difficult side to try and picture the Barbra Streisands and Bette Midlers of the world stopping off at the local deli on their way to the recording studio in order to bring everyone a nosh. (Day was not, however, immune to criticism that would seem to negate this donut–buying den mother image. In a 1963 article titled "The Girl Next Door," journalist Richard Gehman quotes an unnamed director who "has worked with Miss Day and says . . . she's hard to work with . . . she's very very aloof as far as the crew is concerned. It's not that she's mean exactly. It's more that she terribly resents any invasion of her precious privacy." It's a minority opinion, to be sure, but one that exists nonetheless.)

Okay, the recording of junk wasn't quite over just yet, because this masterpiece was followed by a number of 1956 and 1957 singles sessions with Frank

DeVol that featured subpar material. "Today Will Be Yesterday Tomorrow" is a fun, bouncy number but pales in comparison to "Day by Day"—it's notable only for Day's vocal byplay with legendary trumpeter Harry "Sweets" Edison. "Nothing in the World" contains the first instance of Day singing counterpoint with herself, a technique she later perfected in the smash single "Everybody Loves a Lover." Worst of all are two grade-Z ditties that contain nary a shred of worthiness: the awful "Twelve O'Clock Tonight" and the aptly titled "Rickety Rackety Rendezvous." There was nothing authentic or interesting about either song, and one wonders: Who ever thought Doris Day could sing rock and roll? This third-rate rock material surely rated as one of the reasons why Paul Weston and Mitch Miller clashed. Miller, who produced many of these sessions, had been promoted by legendary Columbia Records executive Goddard Lieberson to a position where he possessed authority over album projects. In his pursuit of novelty hits to push the album sales, Miller clashed with Weston, who preferred material of a more classic nature. In this battle of bottom line versus artistic merit, it's no surprise that it was Weston, not Miller, who eventually left Columbia.

In June 1957, Doris recorded the sound track to *The Pajama Game*. In those far-off days when musical comedy scores could still meet with chart success, *Pajama Game* hit number nine on the *Billboard* charts. This was classic American musical comedy theater, with material ranging from the tender "Hey There" to the brassy "There Once Was a Man." Listening to the buoyant "I'm Not at All in Love," one realizes how great Day would have been on the Broadway stage. She could belt it out to the second balcony and still emote like the terrific dramatic actress she had become. It's heresy to suggest, but did Ethel Merman or Mary Martin ever combine the dramatic and the musical in one such complete package? Certainly neither one ever did so on film.

If there is one album to pick as the definitive Doris Day LP, it would be her successful follow-up to *Day by Day* titled, what else, *Day by Night.* Hell, it's not a follow-up—it surpasses its predecessor and ranks as the single best album Day ever recorded. This collection of twelve classic popular songs by the likes of Howard Dietz, Arthur Schwartz, Cole Porter, and Mitchell Parish will be listened to as long as people listen to the golden-age American songbook. It's that good.

This is a concept album in the best senses of the term: Nearly all of the songs date from the 1930s, and more important, all revolve around the idea of romance in the nighttime. This mood of dreamy romance is established with the evocative cover shot of Day in profile, head tilted to the sky—you sense the romantic yearning, and mood is created with the very first cut—"I See Your Face Before Me." Playing all twelve cuts, one right after the other, a listener is left with exactly one question: How could an album this brilliant be recorded in exactly three days? The only possible answer is that the artists involved were extraordinary musicians of the very highest caliber and training, musicians who could make this happen quickly and flawlessly; it's a method of recording unthinkable in the twenty-first-century era of spending months and sometimes years in the recording studio on one CD.

It's therefore no surprise that the musicians on this album read like a who's who of big band alumni: Ted Nash, Babe Russin, David Frisina and, importantly, Paul Smith on piano. Smith, who worked for many years with Ella Fitzgerald, supplied Day with the gentle but solid backing that provided the foundation for her evocative interpretations. On "Dream a Little Dream of Me," there is an interlude of Smith's piano playing—it's really soft jazz—that seamlessly gives way to swelling strings and Day's vocal. She nails every note right in the center, and then at the end of the song the piano comes back for a brief coda. Together, Day and Smith have wrought a perfect little three-act play. On "You Do Something to Me," Weston employs beautiful muted trumpet underscoring, and on "Moon Song," a noodling sax that complements, but never overwhelms, Day's final sustained notes. This is singing of extraordinary intimacy, as seductive as anything Peggy Lee ever sang—just not as overtly sexy. "Close Your Eyes," featuring an arrangement propelled by sax and light but insistent drums, finds Day singing to her lover of the need to

Close your eyes
When you open them dear I'll be near . . .

It's an overtly sensual vocal in which Day is imparting secrets, taking her lover, and the audience, into her confidence.

"Soft as the Starlight," which was used a decade later in the film *The Glass Bottom Boat* (and the British single edit of which resurfaced on the 2004 CD release of *Young at Heart*), really is, as Joseph Laredo called it in his excellent Day discography notes, "achingly beautiful." On an album without even one less than brilliant vocal, there are two cuts that stand out: the first is the aptly titled Tom Adair/Matt Dennis song "The Night We Called It a Day," which features a Day vocal floating on ever rising strings. Doris's subtle shadings, tinged with sadness, instantly evokes the mood of a melancholy night when her lover has "called it a day":

There was a moon out in space
But a cloud drifted over its face

This is a song of regret and resignation, filled with the vulnerable imagery of nighttime. It's the type of song that a Barbra Streisand would bitterly tear into, acting the hell out of it. Day reads it as a woman accepting fate and moving on, an interpretation that results in a recording all the more devastating for this understated approach. Best of all is the sexiest cut on the album—"Moonglow." Sexy? Hell, here Day practically radiates sex. With terrific sax accompaniment by Ted Nash, Day spins out lyricist Eddie deLange's vivid imagery of "heavenly songs" and floating through air. These are images which call on the listener's every romantic instinct. At song's end, Day whispers

I'll always remember
That moonglow gave me you

By the time she purrs this final line for the third time, it is apparent that this woman is on her way to bed, and not to sleep. The strings rise, Day whispers the words, and as Nash's sax coda provides velvety underscoring, one realizes that this is perfect pop singing and arranging. In fact, this must be the exact album John Updike had in mind when he stated, "I do think she's a terrific singer. You feel she's this kind of ideal woman singing these words."

There is no way that Day could ever top this collection with another album of ballads, and wisely, she didn't attempt to do so. Instead, teaming up with DeVol, she created *Hooray for Hollywood,* a (unusual for 1958) double album, and one that ended up being first rate.

Day's track record with DeVol over the years was variable, working very well together on the up-tempo numbers but stumbling when faced with the awful title songs from her later films. DeVol, whose background was with the big bands, worked extensively at both Capitol and Columbia, was married to big-band star Helen O'Connell, and over the years undertook a great deal of work on solo recordings with the likes of Vic Damone, Robert Goulet, Tony Bennett, and Ella Fitzgerald. Where DeVol succeeded so well with Day was in the up-tempo numbers—he loosened up her approach and brought her back to her big-band roots. DeVol understood light swing and produced genuinely first-rate work on the entire double disk. The songs contained herein are all certified winners, proof that when Day was freed from novelty schlock, she was as good a vocalist as has ever been produced in the United States.

On "I've Got My Love to Keep Me Warm," she expertly rides the rhythms of the melody, while she tackles "Let's Face the Music and Dance" in a completely unexpected manner, eschewing the melancholy and giving the Berlin tune a lightly buoyant feeling. Day and DeVol turn in expert readings of "It's Easy to Remember" and particularly of the Rodgers and Hammerstein classic "It Might as Well Be Spring"; on the latter song, Day plumbs the depths of the lyrics as well as Barbara Cook does in her extraordinary version. When Day reaches the phrase "Walking down a strange new street," she bends notes on the word "new" with an ease that only the very best singers possess.

There are terrific renditions of the Gershwins' "A Foggy Day" and "Our Love Is Here to Stay," the latter featuring a male backing vocal group that for once doesn't intrude and indeed provides nice rhythmic counterpoint. The string-laden "Three Coins in the Fountain" almost redeems the bathos of that syrupy Styne/Cahn song, generating some nearly real emotion, and there is an extraordinary take on Porter's "In the Still of the Night." Day and DeVol team particularly well here, with a lovely section sung to the words

Like the moon growing dim, on the rim of the hill
In the chill, still of the night

She quietly sings Porter's evocative nighttime imagery, accompanied by strings, harp, and a muted chiming clock to paint a picture of a fading moon and conjure the sense of nighttime so crucial to the song's effectiveness.

Nice versions of "You'll Never Know" and "I Had the Craziest Dream" complete disk one. On the latter song, it is particularly interesting to compare Day to Helen Forrest, a big-band vocalist who helped make the song popular in the original and well-known Harry James version. Or, more particularly, one can't help but compare Day's rendition to the one Forrest essayed when she sang the song in the film *Springtime in the Rockies.* Forrest was a terrific singer, one of the very best from the big-band era, but she appeared vaguely ill at ease on film, and one instantly sees why Day became an enormous movie star and Forrest never could have.

An odd side note to this superb two-disk outing is the fact that in the midst of recording these classic Hollywood songs, Day recorded three tracks for single release. The first, Joe Lubin's title song to *Teacher's Pet,* is a fun ditty whose insistent rhythm, like that of "Que Sera, Sera," instantly lodges in the brain. In this joyous, guitar-driven reading, for once the accordion and male chorus work, and the song perfectly fits the mood of the excellent film. Even at this highly successful juncture of her career, Doris was still being saddled with some awful songs, to wit, another pseudorock number titled "Walk a Chalk Line"—surely Day herself must have disliked this song, because at the very best it shows in the subpar vocal. Even more substandard was "Run Away, Skidaddle, Skidoo," from the grade-Z film *The Tunnel of Love.* The title states exactly what the listener wants to do after having to endure this song. The most generous assessment of this terrible recording is that if Day were recording today, with the power that stars can now wield over their own careers, she would never agree to sing such an inferior song.

The midsession singles interruption over, Day was back at work on the remaining tracks for the *Hooray for Hollywood* album: "Pennies From Heaven," "Easy to Love," and the Arthur Schwartz/Leo Robin "Oh, But I Do," whose lyric seems to echo Day's perception of the disparity between the real Doris Day and who she appears to be.

The public may not think Doris Day gets blue,

Oh, but I do
First I'm singing, then I'm sighing.

There is a nice take on the Dorothy Fields/Jerome Kern "The Way You Look Tonight," an approach that reads like a buoyant acceptance of love. Day here reaches terrific interpretive heights; note the phrase "never, never change," the vocal blending seamlessly with the bass and muted trumpet—a particularly effective combination among the all-out orchestration heretofore employed. "Night and Day" strikes a particularly effective note, with Doris digging deeper lyrically here—one genuinely gets a sense of obsessive love, love that is brooded over "Day and night, 'neath the moon and under the sun." It's an intense approach that makes her rather surface treatment of "Blues in the Night" all the more surprising. No one has ever thought of Doris Day as a blues singer, and she is not by nature a wrench-your-guts-out type of artist, but she could have delved deeper here and called on her own sense of personal pain. Instead, she employs a lighter than usual approach to the song, and even though she effectively plays with the final notes of the phrase "blues in the night," giving the word "night" a minor key, jazzy feel, she could have done better. (The only other less than satisfactory song here is the Rodgers and Hart "Soon"; it's not so much that Day's singing is bad as that the male chorus interferes with the song's effectiveness.)

But these are minor quibbles, and the album is best summed up by three disparate and equally terrific cuts. The first two, "Over the Rainbow" and "That Old Black Magic," are indelibly associated with two Hollywood icons: Judy Garland and Marilyn Monroe. There are in fact many similarities between Day and Garland; both were top-notch singers as well as movie stars, both reached unprecedented heights of popularity in the 1950s, and both had substantial personal problems. Day wrote movingly of her relationship with Garland in her autobiography, citing the fact that contrary to their images, both women experienced feelings of insecurity that resulted in nervous breakdowns. Day, however, proved to be the more resilient of the two women, a fact which is borne out in her interpretation of "Over the Rainbow." One of the greatest songs ever written, the Harold Arlen/E. Y. Harburg classic will always—and rightly—be associated with Garland. However, in listening to Day's version, one fully understands the differences between the two women: Garland, ever vulnerable, truly looked for the better life over the rainbow, packing a powerhouse punch into her plaintive question at the end of the song: "Why, oh why, can't I?" Day approaches the song as if ruminating on the possibility of a different, better life and appears to shrug her shoulders, as if to musically state, "I best get on with my life—nothing else to be done."

Similarly, "That Old Black Magic," which Monroe performed so memorably as the second-rate chanteuse Cherie in *Bus Stop,* here receives what may be the sexiest performance of Day's entire career. DeVol's extraordinary arrangement is first propelled by bongos and guitar, gradually adding in bass, trombone, and sax. Day begins with a sexy insinuation, rises to an all-stops-out vocal, and then descends back to whispered nothings:

In a spin, loving that spin I'm in
Seeking that old black magic called love

Whew—this recording is downright erotic. Monroe's version was purposely touching in its desperation. Surprisingly, it's Day's version that registers as all-stops-out sexy.

Finally, Day delivers what must stand as the single best ever recording of "Hooray for Hollywood," an opinion held by the song's composer, Richard Whiting, who stated quite simply, "No one can sing my song better." Day combines her consummate singing and acting ability into one brilliant package, communicating what Johnny Mercer's hilarious and extraordinarily cynical lyric is really all about. This song does not represent a mindless rah-rah cheer for Hollywood—far from it. It's a clear-eyed look at what so often proves to be the empty interior behind the set's shell:

Hooray for Hollywood
Where you're terrific if you're even good"

That line alone sums up a year's worth of press agent flackery, and Day nails every last bit of the sardonic humor, really tearing into the classic lines,

See Mr. Factor
He makes a monkey look good"

It's as if Nathanael West's *Miss Lonelyhearts* has been boiled down to a three-minute popular song, and Doris Day gets it. Big time.

She continued her superb collaboration with Frank DeVol with the May 1958 recording of one of her signature songs, "Everybody Loves a Lover." The song, which garnered Day a Grammy nomination as Best Vocal Performance—Female (incredibly, one of only two Day ever received), rose to number six on both the *CashBox* and *Billboard* charts, and it was Day's last top forty single in the United States. DeVol cannily arranged the song to feature guitar, trombone, and prominent finger snaps, further devising the missing ingredient that made the bouncy tune a big hit: He added a double-tracked vocal, so that Day dueted with herself in counterpoint. One only has to listen to the alternate take featuring a single-track vocal in order to understand exactly how the double track made the song a very big hit; without Day's duet with herself, there is no pep or bounce to the rollicking melody.

In typical fashion, this great song was etched on disk in the same three-month period when Day had to record no fewer than four mediocre songs as singles: "The Tunnel of Love," an at-best passable song from the awful film of the same title; the juvenile "Kissin' My Honey"; Joe Lubin's "Possess Me," which ended up in the *Pillow Talk* film; and the terrible "That Jane From Maine" from the terrific film *It Happened to Jane. It Happened to Jane* is a bad title for a film, "That Jane From Maine" is a bad title for a song, and it's no surprise that one listen to the recording confirms the suspicion that "That Jane from Maine" is a downright terrible song.

The clickety clack of the railroad track
Will clickety clack to bring him back

Awful.

This nonsense is all forgotten, however, in the wake of Day's follow-up masterpiece with Frank DeVol, the up-tempo feel-good concept album *Cuttin' Capers.* Once again, it's the combination of top-drawer songs with terrific arrangements that allows Day the room to swing, and swing she does. The album opens with the smartly arranged title song that lets the listener instantly know what he or she is in for—unadulterated high spirits. Day is back with the big-band sound, now updated to the late 1950s. Listen to the beginning of the album-opening title song:

Hey look at me [Day's vocal is here followed by a big-band blast]
Can't you see [another orchestral blast, featuring an all-out brass attack]
I'm in love, I'm in love, I'm in love

The tone is set instantly; Doris Day is here singing about love—not quiet and contemplative as on *Day by Night* but heart-on-the-sleeve, having-a-good-time kind of love. Day's following *Day by Night* with *Cuttin' Capers* is a display of versatility akin to Sinatra recording the brilliantly boozy *In the Wee Small Hours* after the equally dazzling up-tempo *Songs for Swingin' Lovers.* Doris Day's work on *Cuttin' Capers* is the fulfillment of her own astute self-assessment that singing "gives me a sense of release—it makes me happy and I think that the people who listen to me instinctively know that."

On "Why Don't We Do This More Often," Day is backed by some terrific musicians—Alvin Stoller on drums, Joe Mondragon on bass, and Ray Sherman on piano—musicians who really formulate the gentle yet distinctly jazzlike foundation of the arrangement. When Day musically asks the title question and follows it with the words, "You can never, ever overdo a good thing," you know that this girl is looking for a very good time, and it's not at the library.

There's a swinging version of "Fit as a Fiddle," and a great take on the Gershwin/Harburg/Arlen "Let's Talk a Walk Around the Block"; on the latter song, Day, lyrically enumerating of all the sites around the world that she will see with her love, positively rips into the lines

Then Vladivostock
Where Bolsheviks flock

Day is communicating such a feeling of joy and release, such a genuine sense of freedom, that on these two lines she lets loose with a full-throated vocal that would make even Ethel Merman pause in admiration.

A shimmery version of "I Feel Like a Feather on the Breeze," a joyous "Get Out and Get Under the Moon," and three further extraordinary cuts complete this remarkable LP: When Doris Day sings "I'm Sitting on Top of the World," she sounds like she is doing just that. It's what America was doing at this time of Ike—America was the good guy off to make the world a better place and, most important, a majority of Americans believed in that myth. It's that self-belief that allowed Americans to strive for the suburban lifestyle with unfettered heart and no trace of ironic self-doubt: Americans believed that they were sitting on top of the world, heading to the promised land of the "nice" wide open suburbs, and generally living in the best place on the planet. Doris Day expressed that unbounded self-sufficiency and optimism in her best films, and she certainly does it to a fare-thee-well on this up-tempo masterpiece.

When Doris Day here directly takes on the oft-recorded "Makin' Whoopee," she does for this song exactly what she did for "Hooray for Hollywood"; she makes the listener realize what the song is really all about. There is subversive lyric wit at work here, and a superb singing actress is giving you the lowdown: This marriage is not going to be all roses. Delivering every last measure of bite found in the lyric, Day concludes by counseling the listener:

Day on Day: "I really like to sing; it gives me a sense of release, another dimension." Recording session, 1959. *Photofest*

You better keep her
I think it's cheaper
Than making whoopee.

Whew. This couple is in for it.

Any doubts about how great this particular recording is? Just listen to the alternate take made at the same session: The big band really wails; Day sounds great but she can't give the lyrics the same amount of attention with such a driving arrangement. As a result, the song simply can't register as strongly. The released take works beautifully precisely because it marries her singing and acting abilities so well, and the essence of the lyric comes through loud and clear.

Ending with the breezy "Let's Fly Away," this concept album has worked in toto: At the start the listener was invited to join the singer in "Cuttin' Capers," and at the end the listener is enticed to fly away with the singer—the promised land of freedom, joy and, not so incidentally, sex is just around the corner. Doris Day is really at her peak here, as she sings the penultimate lines:

I'll take up all your time
Compromising you

She swoops down into her lower register on the word "you" and then very sexily pleads "let's fly away" no fewer than three times.

You'd have to be dead not to want to fly away with this woman. She is that good.

After this first-rate release, it was back to recording a series of singles, mostly related to her films: The best of these recordings is the great "Any Way the Wind Blows" from *Please Don't Eat the Daisies,* a track that is highlighted by some first-rate slide trombone work. In the exact reverse of what happened with "Everybody Loves a Lover," here one listens to the difference between the single- and double-tracked vocal versions and realizes that the single vocal works better. Day is in excellent voice, and her high spirits perfectly express this paean to the "highs, lows, ins, and outs" of love. The only quibble with the use of the recording in the film is that in *Please Don't Eat the Daisies* Doris Day is presented as the quintessential suburban housewife next door, but one quickly realizes that no girl next door sings this beautifully—never has, never will.

These singles sessions included two more mediocre songs from *It Happened to Jane*—a new version of the title tune and the bland Cub Scout hymn "Be Prepared"—as well as the so-so Lubin/Roth song "Inspiration," which was utilized in *Pillow Talk*. It's not a great song, but it does possess the singular advantage of functioning as an amusing plot point in the film; playboy songwriter Rock Hudson serenades an endless procession of women by singing "Inspiration" to them over the phone, simply inserting their first names into the appropriately available spot in the lyric. Much better than "Inspiration" was the bouncy title tune to *Pillow Talk*. It's a slight but fun song, capped by Day's exclamation at the song's finish that

A break in the "Pillow Talk" recording session. Husband Marty Melcher is on Doris's right. *Photofest*

There must be a pillow talkin' boy (for me)
THERE MUST!

This woman wants a man. *Now.*

So extensive was Day's popularity as a vocalist by now, that in 1959, at the height of the cold war, the *World Telegraph* newspaper reported in "From Pinsk to Omsk They Love Doris Day" that Doris was "the most popular American singer in Russia."

Almost all of these singles ended up on Day's 1960 album *Listen to Day,* a mixed bag that peaked at number twenty-six on the charts. This was not a concept album, and it shows; there is no flow to the songs, no logical progression, and most of the songs are simply second rate. Yes, "Pillow Talk" and "Any Way the Wind Blows" are great fun, as is Rodgers and Hammerstein's "I Enjoy Being a Girl," which bolts off to a racing start and then melts into a relaxed swing version that Day sings with a knowing smile in her voice. But—and it's a big but—*Listen to Day* was a promotional album available for only a short time in 1960, one hastily put together to capitalize on Day's extraordinary popularity. Anything she touched at the time turned to gold, and by this time her record sales had exceeded sixteen million units. The problem is that this album features too many mediocre songs, no fewer than four of which were featured in *Pillow Talk:* "Oh What a Lover You'll Be" complete with a grating organ accompaniment, "No"—again with the obtrusive organ, "He's So Married," and "Possess Me." Aside from the title tune, none of these songs needed to be released on an album, but Day hit the recording jackpot again with her next release—*What Every Girl Should Know.*

What Every Girl Should Know, which features lushly detailed charts and remarkably sympathetic conducting by Harry Zimmerman, mixes a few up-tempo tunes with a plethora of ballads. In many ways, this album seems to fit the total Doris Day vocal persona most accurately—contemplative, occasionally upbeat with a hint of jazz stylings, and most of all, intimate.

It's this sense of intimacy that is a key part of Day's appeal to men. When Day sings of learning how to make a man laugh and how to make him cry, concluding that these are "little" things "every girl should know," many a man would respond favorably.

The problem of course is that these very lyrics are an example of why Day seemed to inspire such contempt from the baby boomer audience. As they discovered feminism and irony, they were incredulous that she could sing of such seeming submission; never mind the ethos of the times, they blamed Day as if she had written the lyrics herself. Doris seems to have been attacked much more strongly than were other female vocalists singing similar fare, precisely because she projected such a strong personality. Somehow the viewing and listening audiences simply assumed that such an assertive and forthright woman controlled the entire finished product herself. In the view of these critics, it was all Doris Day's fault.

This misreading of Day precluded an understanding of what else remained on this great album. For starters, there is a melting rendition of Duke Ellington's "Mood Indigo," with Paul Smith on piano, a version so steeped in the aura of nighttime melancholy that it easily conjures up visions of Day sitting by the window at night, ruminating over her misfortune at love. With her great rhythmic attack, she's blue but not overly distraught, striking the same note of resignation and contemplation that she did with her version of "Over the Rainbow."

There's also a great subdued swing version of "My Kinda Love"; a lush orchestral reading of "Something Wonderful," complete with strings, viola, and harp, culminating in a near palpable release at song's end; an up-tempo "When You're Smiling"; and two songs freighted with meaning for anyone aware of Day's personal life. The first of these, Rodgers and Hammerstein's "A Fellow Needs a Girl," from *Allegro,* presents the picture of a totally supportive woman, a helpmate always ready to listen to her man:

To sit by his side . . .
And agree with the things he'll say

What, one wonders, did Doris think of when she recorded this song? It is so mood laden, and she, ever the singing actress—did she think of her own personal life? The first husband who beat her when she was pregnant? The second husband who simply walked away from becoming Mr. Doris Day? One wonders.

Similarly, Rodgers and Hammerstein's "What's the Use of Wond'rin' " almost certainly must have struck a chord with Day's "Que Sera, Sera" personal philosophy of life. Her connection with the material shows in her murmured answer to the song title's question. There's no use in "wond'rin" about the ending because

He's your fella
And that's all there is to that.

Que sera, sera, indeed.

In fact, the only thing that keeps this terrific album from joining the very top echelon reserved for *Day By Night, Cuttin' Capers,* and *Hooray for Hollywood* are two songs that aren't up to the standard set by the rest of the album: "Not Only Should You Love Him," similarly themed to "Something Wonderful" and "Mood Indigo," but not of the same caliber; and "The Everlasting Arms," a spiritually based song that rests uneasily alongside all of the show tunes present on the disk, thereby upsetting the flow of the album.

Finally, and of greatest interest, there is "What Does a Woman Do," the vocal version of the love theme to the film *Midnight Lace* (produced by Marty Melcher in conjunction with Ross Hunter). This Maxwell Anderson/Allie Wrubel song is the last song Day recorded in the decade she owned—the 1950s. It resonates with all sorts of implications in Day's personal and professional life, especially in terms of husband and manager Marty Melcher. Indeed, it's almost a microcosm of the complex layers of their relationship, layers that informed both her movie and recording careers.

Doris Day loved and supported Marty Melcher as he did her, but for all of the independence she exhibited onscreen, she purposely left all of the career-based business decisions to him. She wanted to feel protected from any business considerations and Melcher was happy to comply. This excessive reliance on others resulted in Day's having to record second-rate material she couldn't abide

("A Purple Cow") because Melcher had already chosen them. Melcher didn't have to pay a great deal of money to unknown (read, inferior) songwriters and could, at the same time, control the publishing rights to the songs in question. In the end, this approach to business simultaneously helped Day, freeing her to concentrate solely on the artistic matters at hand, and also hurt her—the recording of second-rate material resulted in lessening audience interest. In purely financial terms, it led to utter disaster, with Melcher and business partner Jerome Rosenthal losing Day's entire multimillion-dollar portfolio through misguided investments, ultimately leaving her half a million dollars in debt. In fact, her hands-off approach to business led the judge who ruled in Day's favor in her lawsuit against Rosenthal to admonish her for her "excessive naïveté."

With this background in mind, how then did Day approach the recording of a song such as "What Does a Woman Do?"? Here are her own words from her autobiography: "Who was Marty Melcher? Was he in league with Rosenthal? Who was this man I had lived with all those years—fool or thief or both?" Perhaps the best take on this question comes from one who knew Melcher and viewed him from both a professional and personal perspective: Ross Hunter, who produced three Day films with him. In Hunter's view, Melcher was determined to succeed as his own man, separate from his wife's star status, and as a result made foolish decisions and became involved with Rosenthal. Yet Hunter reasoned, "I do think that Marty loved Doris. I don't think he meant her any harm."

So then, what must Day have been thinking when she sang the following words? At the time of this recording session, the Day/Melcher marriage had already had its share of ups and downs, but the extent of Melcher's fiduciary malfeasance was unknown. For better and worse, Doris decided to stay with Marty until the day he died. Therefore, perhaps the more pertinent question becomes, what does she think if and when she hears the song today? Whatever her reaction, Day's attraction to the song can't help but be read as a partial self-portrait, a bit of self-recognition that undoubtedly helped inform her beautifully subdued and sympathetic treatment of the lyric: Day is in great voice here, but nice as the gentle and flowing melody line is, it's the lyrics that linger in the listener's mind:

What does a woman do, when her man is wrong
Judging from me and you, she goes along, she goes along

Layers upon layers upon layers, personally and professionally . . .

After the release of "What Every Girl Should Know," Day returned to the studio early in 1960 to record three country songs: "The Blue Train," "Daffa Down Dilly," and "Here We Go Again." All were a product of Day's first recording sessions with Neal Hefti (who went on to conduct her *Bright and Shiny* album), and all three are marred by faux-country arrangements. Was an entire album of country songs planned at this point? If so, based on the evidence of these three songs, it is better that it never happened. Country music is one of the few forms of music that don't seem natural in Day's hands. She can sing ballads, jazz, big-band standards, up-tempo belters, religious songs, indeed, she can sing almost anything beautifully and with great conviction—except for rock and country music. Those two forms simply do not reside in her soul. What always was in her musical soul, however, was a love for Broadway show tunes, and this led to another concept masterpiece, the *Show Time* album with Axel Stordahl at the helm. Together, Day and Stordahl created an album without one weak cut. In the parlance of 1960, the year the album was recorded and released, it's a wow.

Like all great concept albums, *Show Time* sets its theme and tone right from the opening track, a terrific up-beat Joe Lubin composition titled, what else, "Show Time." The song functions as a vocal overture—Day here sings snippets of the songs that are to follow on the album. When she hits the last phrase, "Showtime on Broadway is just about to begin," in effect the curtain is rising. As son Terry said, Doris Day is able to create a visual effect with an audio art.

What's most noteworthy about the album is how relaxed Day's singing is. "On the Street Where You Live" has a slight jazzlike feel to it, "When I'm Not Near the Boy I Love" positively lilts, and there is a knockout version of Cole Porter's "I Love Paris." Starting out in its famous minor key, shifting to major on the phrase "I love Paris every moment—every moment of the year," the song—and Day—set sail on this very phrase, carrying the listener along for the ride. Just like Day, Stordahl is at the top of his game here. Strategically placing Marty Cobb on bass and Milton Holland on drums, the song unfolds in patented Porter "list song" fashion; as Porter ticks off the seasons, each is underscored by different instruments.

Paris in the fall [bass and brush cymbal]
Paris in the summer [strings swelling underneath the melody line]
Paris "when it sizzles" [—at which point the brass section is fully introduced]

And then Doris Day lets loose on an open-voiced cry of

I love Paris every moment of the year . . .
Because my love is near

This last phrase floats on strings and the bass plunks out the final notes. It's not just a mini-play complete with rising action, conflict, climax, falling action, and resolution. This is pop singing of the very highest caliber.

There isn't a weak cut on the entire album, and the lingering reaction is a realization of how great Day would have been onstage in many of the classic Broadway musical roles. It may be the character of Curly, and not Laurie, who typically sings *Oklahoma!*'s "Surrey with the Fringe on Top," but Day's version really does succeed in conjuring up visions of the great outdoors. And what a terrific Laurie she in fact would have made in *Oklahoma!*—the archetypal Midwestern female musical character being played by the archetypal Midwestern actress/singer. To say it's a fit is an understatement, a fact borne out by the album's terrific version of "People Will Say We're in Love."

There is a lovely double-tracked vocal to "Ohio," from *Wonderful Town,* a recording that brings out all of the wistful quality inherent in that nostalgic valentine to hometowns and growing pangs. Again Day could have played either leading female role in the musical, although she's too pretty by half to be believable in the role of an intellectual plain Jane who couldn't land a man. There's a very intimate version of "I've Grown Accustomed to His Face" from *My Fair Lady,* and two extraordinary songs from *Annie Get Your Gun.* As if *Calamity Jane* weren't evidence enough, these two cuts prove that Doris Day would have made a top-drawer Annie Oakley; she turns in a typically silken reading of the ballad "They Say It's Wonderful," and it's a safe bet that Ethel Merman and Betty Hutton never sounded this tender. Even better is "I Got the Sun in the Morning," which has here been orchestrated to a fare-thee-well. The vocal begins accompanied only by a piano, but soon thereafter the trumpets and trombones snake in, and then her purred insinuation is walloped forward by an orchestra blast as she lets loose vocally on the open-hearted phrase "Sunshine gives me a lovely day." Make that Day. This is an outdoors gal exulting in the freedom she enjoys, and it makes a fun contrast to Merman's terrific and well-known version of Annie Oakley, an Annie Oakley who'd yell at the sun and the moon, "Hey, get out here—*Now*!"

In an album of continuous highlights, best of all is the tour de force on "A Wonderful Guy" from Rodgers and Hammerstein's *South Pacific.* This one cut is a perfect blend of arrangement, singer, character, and star persona. Such synchronicity usually happens only once a generation—Streisand in *Funny Girl* achieved the same miraculous blend—and when it does, one can only shake one's head in admiration. The sunshiny, always optimistic Doris Day is singing the always optimistic Nellie Forbush's anthem to love: "I'm as corny as Kansas in August, I'm as normal as blueberry pie." *South Pacific* was *the* musical of post–World War II America, blending romance, tragedy, and a questioning of racial attitudes into a full-scale love letter to the America that could be in the aftermath of the war. There was no one, absolutely no one, who exemplified these quintessential American attitudes better than Doris Day, and with her extraordinary singing and acting abilities, it was a huge loss when terms could not be successfully negotiated for her participation in the film. Just as audiences never got to see superstars Sinatra and Streisand in musical roles they were born to play—Sinatra in *Carousel* and Streisand in *Gypsy*—audiences were cheated of Doris Day in *South Pacific.* This one cut lives on as evidence of what could have been.

Day's next album, *Bright and Shiny,* conducted by Neal Hefti, was recorded in December of 1960. Day came to work with Harbert because she had admired Sinatra's recording of the Harbert-composed "This Was My Love." Harbert became Doris's rehearsal pianist and accompanist, writing songs for her until 1963. With Harbart conducting, the arranging was left to Neil Hefti, a highly respected jazz-oriented arranger known for his work with Count Basie and Sinatra. The collaboration produced a good, but not great, album. Doris Day is at her best in an intimate, soft-sounding atmosphere and is not shown to best advantage in a vibes-heavy setting such as the one Hefti here concocted. She can sing this type of music, and sing it well, but Ella Fitzgerald, Sarah Vaughan, and Peggy Lee are all better at it.

Bright and Shiny is one of Day's three most jazz-oriented albums, along with *Young Man with a Horn* and *Duet.* Hefti and Harbert recruited a top-flight cast of jazz musicians, including Red Callender on bass, Shelly Manne on drums, and Jimmy Rader on piano, with Hefti's arrangements featuring a stripped-down sound without any strings. The songs chosen are, for the most part, first rate: "Happy Talk" from *South Pacific,* a racing version of Cole Porter's "Ridin' High" featuring vibes and horns, the Gershwins' "Clap Yo' Hands," and a nicely contented reading of the usually boisterous "Singin' in the Rain." Even better, there are relaxed readings of "On the Sunny Side of the Street" and particularly "I Want to Be Happy," a cut that contrasts interestingly with her vocal on the same song in the film *Tea for Two.* Here Day is singing with vibes and muted trumpets, and achieves a very relaxed, flowing tempo.

The problems—and they are not huge ones—arrive with the lesser-known songs. They're less well known for a reason—they're just not as good as the "Ridin' High" and "Clap Yo' Hands" of the world. "Stay With the Happy People" is a second-tier Jule Styne song, and along with other mediocre songs like "Twinkle and Shine" and "Bright and Shiny," it suffers from an overly liberal application of mandolins and organ. A warm voice like Doris Day's is not best served by the brighter sound of vibes and mandolins.

In essence, the mixed virtues of the album are encapsulated in one cut—

"Make Someone Happy" by Styne, Betty Comden, and Adolph Green. Stripped of the surrounding context of the show from which it came (*Do Re Me*) the spoken introduction of the song's initial lyrics sounds silly, but with this introduction out of the way, Day settles into the album's highlight, singing the incisive lyric about the fleeting nature of fame with perfect understatement:

Where's the real stuff in life to cling to?
Love is the answer

She imbues these words with multiple shades of melancholy; it's terrific singing and redeems everything else on the album that isn't quite up to her high standards.

The flawed but pleasant *Bright and Shiny* was followed by one of the last of Day's concept masterpieces, *I Have Dreamed.* Working with Jim Harbert, Day chose beautifully crafted classic pop songs whose languid melodies are perfectly matched by literate, occasionally complex, lyrics. Such multilayered lyrics gave her a chance to convey genuine emotion in her meticulously planned but seemingly effortless vocals. In fact, hearing her create such full-bodied characterizations makes one realize how beautifully she could have sung many of Stephen Sondheim's multi-layered compositions. Just for starters, she would have made a startlingly effective Sally in *Follies,* investing that wistful, self-deluded member of the World War II generation with tremendous pathos in songs such as "Losing My Mind" and "In Buddy's Eyes."

I Have Dreamed hit a respectable but not terribly impressive number ninety-seven on the charts, but forty-five years later, the album stands as an extraordinary work of art. Inconceivable in this day and age of multimillion-dollar, multiyear recording projects, Day recorded this entire album in three days; it took no more than ten hours of studio time to record an album with nary a false step, an album that can stand comparison with the best of any of those released by Frank Sinatra, Ella Fitzgerald, Rosemary Clooney, or Tony Bennett.

It's not just that the concept of an album devoted to songs about dreams is a good one; it's that the idea and imagery associated with dreams and yearnings provide the perfect vehicle for Day's intimate singing. Opening with Harbert's own lovely composition "I Believe in Dreams," the album unfurls smoothly with the likes of "Time to Say Goodnight," "My Ship," and a version of "I'll Buy That Dream" that sounds so comforting and warm that it could rank as any husband's dream marriage; actually, make that fantasy marriage, because no real-life marriage could ever be this good.

Rehearsing for a 1961 recording session. *Photofest*

Here, the flute underscoring, muted trumpets, and gentle sweep of multiple violins all work to float Day's "smile in her voice" vocal, effortlessly lifting the listener to the dream world of "a sky full of moon and a sweet mellow tune" right along with the amazingly relaxed singer. It's as if, through her vocal art, Doris Day distills the complexity of marriage into a warm, all-enveloping relationship that manages to seem both comfortable and comforting at the same time. It may not ever happen quite that way, but it sure sounds great.

"Someday I'll Find You," Noel Coward's evocative musings on the elusive nature of love; "All I Do Is Dream of You"; even the album's only second-tier song, "Periwinkle Blue"—all are arranged and sung in artful fashion. In an album of continuous highlights, there are, however, four extraordinary cuts that rise to a different level entirely. There is a reworking of the Livingston/Evans ballad "We'll Love Again," composed for *The Man Who Knew Too Much,* and the result is a vocal that brings out all the qualities of separation and longing inherent in this near-perfect marriage of words and music. Over the course of repeated listenings, it becomes clear that Livingston and Evans are to Doris Day what Alan and Marilyn Bergman/Michel Legrand are to Barbra Streisand and Van Heusen/Cahn were to Sinatra—brilliant artists who instinctively understand the style and sound of the star for whom they are writing. As evidenced by "Que Sera, Sera" and especially "We'll Love Again," Livingston and Evans "get" Doris Day in a way no other composer/lyricist team ever did.

We'll kiss again and again—and again
Darling we'll love again—somewhere.

If this song had been written fifteen years earlier, it would have become as anthemic and redolent to the World War II generation as, well, "Sentimental Journey."

There is a brilliant arrangement of "All I Do Is Dream of You," which completely transforms a song usually associated with the famous up-tempo production number seen in *Singin' in the Rain.* Here, Day begins with a simple piano accompaniment, until she reaches the lines

And were there more than twenty-four hours a day
They'd be spent in sweet content, dreamin' away

It's at this point, with the piano still in the forefront, that the strings float in, and when Day subsequently reaches the words "Mornin', noon, nighttime too," on the word "nighttime" her voice drops with an extraordinarily sexy intimacy. The arrangement circles back to the sound heard in the opening bars, and the recording ends just as it started—Doris Day singing with nothing but a piano as accompaniment. This is not just terrific pop singing—it is smart, state-of-the-art arranging.

"You Stepped Out of a Dream," another popular classic best known from *Singin' in the Rain,* is presented in a similarly smooth arrangement. Opening with a solo piano, the recording then adds Day's vocal to the mix, but this time the blend has an entirely different sound: Day's vocal echoes as if from a dreamlike distance, right up until reaching the line "Could there be eyes like yours," at which point her voice sails to the forefront on the word "eyes." It's a startling yet very smooth effect, and the cut receives a lovely boost both by the use of the oboe, which echoes her vocal line, and by a veritable sea of violins.

Best of all, and one of the greatest cuts Day ever recorded, is "I Have Dreamed" from *The King and I.* The first-rate arrangement utilizes a single oboe to great effect throughout, echoing the wistful longing quality inherent in the lyric:

I have dreamed every word you'll whisper . . .

When Day reaches the climactic lines of "I will love being loved by you," she seamlessly spins out the final note, supported by harp and strings, until all that is heard is the echo of a solo oboe. This is singing and arranging of such a high standard that only the song's composer, Richard Rodgers, could sum it up properly. Writing to Day and Harbert, Rodgers stated simply, that theirs was the most beautiful version of the song he'd ever heard.

In November of 1961, Day spun her recording career off in a highly unexpected and rewarding fashion by recording an album of duets accompanied only by André Previn on piano, Red Mitchell/Joe Mondragon on bass, and Frank Capp/Larry Bunker on drums. It's a startling display of versatility that came about, in Jim Harbert's words, because "I knew that André admired Doris, and I also knew that Doris was going through a period where she didn't feel like working with a big orchestra." Recorded in just two days, the album exudes the sense of a great vocalist going back to her roots. In effect, it's a 1961 version of *Doris Day Unplugged.*

Freed from the interference of overly controlling producers and artists and repertoire (A&R) men, Day once again chooses A-list songs from start to finish: "Remind Me"; "Yes," in which she is accompanied only by Previn's piano; "Control Yourself," with full-out jazz playing in the nonvocal interludes; "Wait Till You See Him"; and "Nobody's Heart." The most interesting cuts tend to be those that most clearly showcase Previn's sympathetic support: on "Fools Rush In," his firm chords provide the foundation for Day's singing, and on "Daydreaming," an upbeat Previn composition, his ascending three-chord progression, which is heard every time she sings the title words, provides a clear flavor without ever overtly calling attention to itself. There is a nicely understated "Falling in Love Again," which exudes none of Dietrich's world-weary ennui, and a jazzier version of "Close Your Eyes" than that heard on the *Day by Night* album. It's an equally valid reading of the classic song, but absent the strings, some of the seductive nature of her original version is missed.

The album's single best cut is Rodgers and Hart's "Nobody's Heart," a reading that is murmured so quietly, with such intense vulnerability, that a feeling of wanting to protect the singer is engendered in the listener. It's not that Doris Day cannot take care of herself—she can. But just as happened with her film roles, she is so straightforward, so without guile, that one can't help but feel that she deserves better than this, she should not be treated this way. In that dichotomy between Day's self-assurance and her vulnerability lies a key reason for the success of Doris Day's ballad singing.

In this song "nobody's heart" belongs to her—the moon is "just a moon." Halfway through the song, the piano modulates but the mood lingers; this singer may be vulnerable, but she won't collapse.

I may be sad at times and disinclined to play
But it's not bad at times to go your own sweet way

Which she does. Beautifully.

Day followed up this experiment with another one-hundred-eighty-degree turn, by assembling a song collection entitled *You'll Never Walk Alone.* Recorded in November of 1962, this mixture of religious and secular songs contains fine performances but is often marred by the arrangements. The sessions were led by the excellent Buddy Cole, and his organ playing governs throughout—too much so. "I Need Thee Every Hour," "Abide with Me," and even "Be Still and Know" are all dominated by Cole's organ. So slowly paced is the accompaniment, so nearly dirgelike the pace, that one is instantly put in mind of a funeral parlor—not the optimum reaction to such inherently moving material.

Better are songs like "In the Garden," which added strings, flutes, bass, drums, sax, and cellos and thereby gave the album a much needed jolt of variety. Martin Broones provided a new setting to "The Lord's Prayer," and Day delivers a nice performance of "Walk with Him," delivering the sense of peace and rest outlined in the lyric:

Stand with him atop the mountain high
Peace of mind and love will walk beside you as the days go by . . .

There is a nicely understated version of "You'll Never Walk Alone" that eschews the normally stentorian approach of an ever-building chorus. Instead, with strings and gently plucked guitar, a framework is provided for Day's very maternal vocal, enfolding the listener with her voice and, metaphorically speaking, into her arms.

At this point in her recording career, Day was clearly trying to explore new settings. She was extraordinarily popular as both film actress and recording star, yet she was tired of her usual fare. Such restless experimentation oftentimes reveals a feeling on the artist's part that something is missing—"Is that all there is?" as Peggy Lee sang so memorably. So, when Day looked back on this recording and stated, "My favorite things are hymns. I enjoyed singing hymns more than anything," one wonders on how many levels she was operating when she sang "If I Can Help Somebody"; was she analyzing her own career, her very raison d'être? She clearly was not oblivious to the fact that for all of her extraordinary popularity and intermittent acclaim, she was not a critic's darling. She was too popular and straightforward for that. What then did it mean to her when she sang:

If I can cheer somebody with a word or a song . . .
Then my living shall not be in vain.

This was music to which Day related strongly, given her own spiritual quest and evolution. Such songs are a long way indeed from the youthful recordings of wacky novelties like "Tacos, Enchiladas, and Beans." . . .

Sandwiched in between these wildly different concept albums was the full-scale recording of the sound track to the 1962 film *Jumbo.* Listening to the songs on their own, removed from the often overwhelming context of the motion picture screen, once again brings home just how adept Day was at blending the large-scale up-tempo production numbers like "Circus on Parade" and "Over and Over Again" with classic ballads such as "Little Girl Blue" and "My Romance." Each and every one of the ballads can be considered a great song, and they are all given fully considered dramatic readings, yet surprisingly, the highlight remains a duet with Martha Raye on "Why Can't I." Their voices blending with surprising ease (Raye was a much better singer than anyone ever gave her credit for, witness her classic take on "Body and Soul"), the duet ends with wistful harmony that perfectly underscores the plaintive question of the title. In fact, the sound track, just like the film, is marred only by the last number, "Sawdust, Spangles and Dreams," a ponderous top-heavy production number that ends both the film and recording in plodding fashion.

Interestingly, in 1962 Day also recorded another Broadway score in toto,

Irving Berlin's *Annie Get Your Gun.* This was not planned in conjunction with any proposed film or Broadway staging of the classic show but rather existed sui generis. As such, the recording, which costarred Robert Goulet, is complete unto itself, and to use the show's vocabulary, hits a bull's-eye from start to finish.

According to Joseph Laredo's production notes from the *Move Over Darling* boxed set of Day's recordings, Doris and Robert Goulet recorded their vocal tracks to a solo piano accompaniment, with the full orchestral backing added at a later date. Be that as it may, the pieced-together nature of the recording is nowhere evident, because this is one hell of a seamless ride for the listener, beginning with the brilliantly arranged (by Philip Lang) overture, which spells Broadway in capital letters. It's not only Day who is terrific here; the recording also represents the best, most sustained singing Goulet was to perform in his entire career. In "The Girl That I Marry," he isn't just vocalizing in stentorian fashion to show off his impressive pipes; he's really paying attention to the lyrics. It's a performance he sustains throughout, from the virile, all-encompassing sound of the witty and chauvinistic "I'm a Bad, Bad Man" to the tender "They Say It's Wonderful," which he ends as a beautifully sung duet with Day.

As for Day herself, there isn't one false step or note here. In her character-defining "Doin' What Comes Naturally," she has great fun with the tricky, intricately rhymed Berlin lyrics

You don't have to go to a fancy school
Not to hitch up your bustle to a stubborn mule

Any listener knows that Day could, in fact, hitch up her bustle and then march right off to a fancy ball. Even on disk, one realizes that she is a much more athletic and Midwestern outdoors gal than the great, quintessentially New York Ethel Merman ever could be. On "You Can't Get a Man With a Gun," Day tears into the clever lyrics that wittily echo the larger-than-life, assertive Doris Day screen persona:

If I went to battle with someone's herd of cattle
You'd have steak when the job was done . . .

Ending the song with open-voiced belting that never loses its pure tone, Day is here essaying her quintessential character, a tomboy who turns feminine and captures her man yet never loses her independent streak.

"I Got the Sun in the Morning," which features an ever building chorus in the background throughout, receives a different reading from the slightly jazzier version on the *Show Time* album, and there is a terrific playful duet with Goulet on "Anything You Can Do" that plays right into the hands of Day's assertive personality. It's a battle of the sexes in which Day's Oakley confidently asserts that she can sing higher, buy cheaper, say anything softer, and hold any note longer than can Goulet's Frank Butler; he smartly concedes on the last claim as she effortlessly holds the final note of "Yes I can" for multiple, and seemingly endless, counts of four. This is Berlin at his funniest and finest, as the characters sing their challenges to each other:

Frank: I can jump a hurdle
Annie: I can wear a girdle

There is a sense of such playfulness between Goulet and Day that it makes her best work on the recording, two extraordinary solo takes on masterly Berlin ballads, all the more impressive. On "I Got Lost in His Arms," surely one of the best ballads ever written for the Broadway stage, there is a melting arrangement of strings and vibes that effortlessly supports Day's ruminative reading of the lyrics, lyrics that express her surprise and delight at falling in love. Doris/Annie's heart may be "foolishly . . . jumping all around," yet she realizes

I got lost
But look what I found

Day's singing is so pure and unforced that it sounds like a private conversation which she is having with herself, as well as the listener. This is singing of the first rank, and yet even this doesn't quite equal the heights she hits in "Moonshine Lullaby."

A lullaby that Annie sings to her brothers and sisters, "Moonshine Lullaby" does not constitute one of *Annie Get Your Gun*'s showstopping belters. Indeed, it usually functions as a sweet depiction of Annie's motherly relationship to her younger siblings. In Day's hands, however, the lullaby turns into a tender statement that could apply just as easily to Annie's lover as to her siblings. In a recording career replete with sensual performances that are startlingly confidential in tone, this may stand out as the most intimate vocal she ever recorded—partially because it is so unexpected, and partially because it is simply so damn beautiful. Lang here turns in a multilayered orchestration, highlighted by a haunting clarinet:

Bye bye baby, stop your yawnin'
Don't cry baby, day will be dawnin'

Joined by a subdued and beautifully deep-voiced harmonizing male quartet, Day lulls her loved one toward dreamland, until she ends with a final murmured "with a moonshine lull-a-bye," bending the notes on the final syllable until the only possible response on the part of the listener is total capitulation. Listen to this cut again. And again. Like the very best popular recordings, it doesn't diminish but rather grows deeper and richer with every repeated listen. If, as is claimed, musical comedy, along with jazz, really is America's native musical art form, then Day here reigns as nothing short of a leading practitioner. Her performance of this entire score is a master class in and of itself.

Having shoehorned in these sound track recordings after her unusual and intermittently successful album of religious songs, Day next recorded three singles in quick succession. The first, "Let the Little Girl Limbo" by the successful Brill Building team of Barry Mann and Cynthia Weill, is one of the true oddities of Day's recording career. Sounding a great deal like Eydie Gorme's "Blame It on the Bossa Nova," which had been written by the same team, "Let the Little Girl Limbo" is a ridiculous but catchy tune that perfectly fit the AM radio ethos of the time. Who knew that Doris Day ever recorded a limbo song? (An alternate take on the song, featuring a double-tracked vocal, results in a truly bizarre listening experience; not only is one listening to Doris Day, of all people, sing a limbo song, an event disconcerting all by itself, but on this version she does so with a vaguely Caribbean/calypso accent. Strange indeed.) Day was to return to Mann and Weill with her June 1964 recording of their "Oo-Wee-Baby," a cut that succeeded only in showing that even such softer-sounding early rock songs were simply not natural fits with Day's acting-oriented approach to singing.

Day then recorded two songs from the film *Move Over Darling:* "Twinkle Lullaby" and the great title tune. "Twinkle Lullaby" delivered exactly what the title said—a lullaby—and a fairly generic one at that—which works within the context of the film when Day sings it to the children who don't recognize her as their own mother. The title tune from the film provided Day with the last hit single of her career, and while it may not be a great song, it is a great recording, thanks to the work of Terry Melcher. Terry, who was soon to find big success producing records for rock groups ranging from the Byrds to the Beach Boys (even cowriting the Beach Boys' last hit single, "Kokomo"), also produced records for the Mamas and the Papas, Glen Campbell, Bobby Darin, and Randy Newman. Here, Melcher rewrote the existing first version of the song, brought in the then-unknown Leon Russell (piano) and Glen Campbell (guitar) to play on the recording, and ultimately ended up producing a Day single that sounded very much like those put out by the girl groups (e.g., the Ronettes) that were so popular at the time.

When looking back on his own career years later, and how this single recording impacted his work, Melcher gave much of the credit for his success to producer Jack Nitzche: "Jack Nitzche was the first guy with any kind of an ear, with credibility 'on the street,' who decided that I had some talent. He kind of invented orchestral rock. He was instrumental in creating the Phil Spector sound, arranging for groups like the Crystals and the Ronnettes." Melcher took the lesson to heart and here created an infectious and sexy single that featured a Spector-like layered chorus. Modestly successful in the United States, the song climbed all the way to number eight on the charts in the UK; the recording also remains the answer to what is perhaps the most unexpected piece of Doris Day recording career trivia ever to come down the pike: What Doris Day single became a top ten hit in England despite being banned for its suggestive lyric? That's right, Doris Day was banned for being overly suggestive. Next thing you know Mary Poppins will be appearing topless in a movie—wait a minute, that did happen, in 1981's *SOB.* Talk about your good girls going wild; good thing Doris and Julie never went on spring break together. . . .

Fresh from this success, Melcher produced the December 1963 recording sessions for his mother's next album, *Love Him!* It was Terry's idea to bring in Tommy Oliver to conduct and arrange the sessions, and clearly it was a happy collaboration, as Oliver was asked to work with Day again on her 1975 television special *Doris day toDay.* When asked about Day, Oliver stated simply, "I absolutely adored her. She is just a really nice, very talented human being." Oliver gave Day a big orchestra—sixteen chairs—and in his own words; "It was a little different sound for her. Very, very lush."

Under the influence of her son, Day applied this lush sound to a surprisingly eclectic array of songs; the decades-old "Can't Help Falling in Love," which had experienced a resurgence in popularity due to Elvis Presley's hit recording from his 1961 film *Blue Hawaii,* is here rendered with myriad strings and a large backing vocal chorus. There is an unexpected take on the standard "A Fool Such as I," which had been covered by both Bob Dylan and Elvis Presley, and a cover of Brenda Lee's hit "Losing You" (these latter two recordings were big hits in Asia). There is, as well, a very interesting recording of the album's Mann/Weil title tune "Love Him"; Oliver's arrangement granted a bolero feel to the recording, an effective fit with the oddly interesting lyric:

Be the girl I couldn't be
And love him—love him for me

Hmmm . . . Doris Day, the girl who continually promised "I'll Be Around," the girl who personified a quietly subdued yet sexy acceptance of managing with the cards life dealt her, the woman who would stick by her man no matter what—well, according to the lyrics of this song, she'd no longer be singing "I'll be around." It's almost as if Day, the older woman, is passing on her life experience and wisdom to a younger woman, passing the torch both literally and figuratively.

Asked if it was odd to produce an album featuring his mother singing love songs, Melcher replied, "I'm not sure who else has ever done that. It was different, but it wasn't too tough, because I felt like I knew what I was doing." It also helped that Terry Melcher, an acclaimed musician himself, possessed great respect for Doris Day the vocalist: "I really think she and Ella Fitzgerald were all by themselves in their ability to bring magic to a lyric." This sentiment was returned in full measure by his mother: "He and I are such good friends and I just love working with him. We're not like mother and son really, we're more like best friends. We have a great time together. We laugh a lot." The result of this mother/son collaboration was a good album, but one that doesn't qualify as great simply because of the uneven quality of some of the songs.

On the plus side, there is a lovely, subdued "Softly, As I Leave You," country-sounding "Losing You" replete with cascading strings, and a strikingly low-key version of "Since I Fell for You" featuring nice sax and trumpet work. In fact, this cut plays to Day's two biggest strengths by applying the roots of her big-band sound to her favorite type of song, a lush ballad; the mixture ends with an interestingly moody and minor-key saxophone accompaniment to the song's last words: "I get the blues most every night since I fell for you." She is also right at home on the Broadway ballad "As Long as He Needs Me," turning in an interpretation that is not so much masochistic, as it is in the context of the show *Oliver,* but rather registers as the voice of a woman who is quietly accepting her partnership with the man in question; she loves him and that is how it will always be. No use fighting fate. This is terra firma for Doris and it shows in her sensitive handling of the lyric.

Day worked with top-drawer musicians on this recording: Irv Cottler on drums, Bud Shank on sax, and on certain cuts these cream-of-the-crop musicians are able simply to let loose and wail. On "Funny," Shank's crisp sax solo is supported by the brass section building up steam underneath, a mix that climaxes when a full vocal chorus joins in to create, in the famous Phil Spector phrase, a wall of sound.

The problems with the recording revolve around such a great production being lavished on second-tier-songs like Tommy Oliver's own "Moonlight Lover," a song "suggested by" a Chopin prelude. This song is similar in quality to "Rainbow's End"—no matter how great the production, these just aren't particularly interesting songs.

Although the positive outweighs the negative on this recording, perhaps the variable quality is perfectly encapsulated in one cut: Willie Nelson's "Night Life," one of the first pop recordings of a Willie Nelson song ever made. One never thinks of Willie Nelson and Doris Day inhabiting the same universe, but there have been stranger bedfellows: Cole Porter and Roy Rogers on "Don't Fence Me In" immediately come to mind. At any rate, Day does well by Nelson, but only after overcoming the song's introduction. To begin the cut, Tommy Oliver wrote a spoken introduction (he wrote it in the car on his way to the day's recording session). Day is first heard speaking over the sound of traffic and daytime noises, and when this segues into a moody sax accompaniment to the words "Darkness comes and spreads its familiar sound of quiet," one senses that the borderline of camp territory is fast approaching. But the borderline is never crossed, and instead, as she intones "sad, sensuous—this is the sound of night. This is the sound of nightlife," she glides into a vocal and arrangement that are so good, so moodily intimate, that you forget everything that has come before. Guided by Cottler on drums and Shank on sax, she delves into some much darker territory here:

Oh, the night life, it ain't a good life
But it's my life.

John Updike, in his fascinating essay lauding Doris Day, states that her idol, Ella Fitzgerald, takes her voice to "dark sweet places" to which Day's doesn't travel—implying that Day, unlike Fitzgerald, did not have the resources to vocally explore these darker territories. Actually, that may not be completely accurate; Day did have the resources to do so, but throughout her career she steadfastly chose not to explore such provinces. On this one cut, working with great musicians on a terrific Willie Nelson song, she does in fact probe the bleakness inherent in the material. The results are brilliant, and artist and audience are all the better for it. If only she had investigated such territory in even greater depth.

In June of 1964 she recorded *The Doris Day Christmas Album* and the finished product was pretty damn spectacular. Once again, it's the material that made all of the difference: Working with arranger/conductor Pete King, Day recorded ten top-notch Christmas songs (the CD reissue of the album was subsequently fleshed out with five additional early Christmas recordings), and the result was an album without one weak cut. In song after song, she succeeds in creating a glowing mood of contentment; with her soft fluid vocals, one can nearly visualize a landscape covered by silently falling snow.

The songs on the LP range from the Judy Garland classic "Have Yourself a Merry Little Christmas" to "The Christmas Song" and Irving Berlin's "White Christmas." What Day accomplishes with remarkable effectiveness on this album is to evoke childhood, the innocence and fleeting nature of a cocooned existence, which is at its most pervasive at Christmastime itself. Listen to her take on Victor Herbert's "Toyland," a song never previously examined with such emotion. When Day reaches the lines "Once you pass its borders, you can ne'er return again," the undertow of sadness is palpable. It's not just toyland that's receding—it's childhood itself. There is a wistful reading of Martin Broones's "Be a Child at Christmas Time" and an exceptionally moving version of "I'll Be Home for Christmas." The song's last line, "I'll be home for Christmas if only in my dreams" evokes a sense of longing both in those who won't be home for Christmas and those who never experienced the idealized holiday gatherings limned in so many of these seasonal favorites.

Among so many first-rate cuts, three stand out. The first is "Winter Wonderland," in which the soft cushion of strings on the words "Later on we'll conspire, as we dream by the fire" produces the very picture of the fireside spoken of in the lyrics. Day sings with such intimacy on this cut that jazz critic Gary Giddins, writing in *The Village Voice,* was moved to refer to the recording as "strangely erotic." The second is a deftly sung version of the Claude Thornhill big-band classic "Snowfall," complete with tinkling piano, descending strings, and gently plucked bass and guitar that aurally illustrate the "snowfall, snowfall, glistening snowfall" painted in the lyric. Finally, Day and King deliver a version of the Styne/Cahn classic "Let It Snow!" which gently swings with the jazz piano of Buddy Cole. Listening to this cut is a total kick, and it's the perfect song with which to close the LP, evoking, as it does, firesides, contentment, and a sense of keeping the world at bay.

After tackling Christmas standards, religious songs, and Broadway show tunes, Day yet again struck out in a completely different direction, next recording an album of children's songs titled *With a Smile and a Song.* It's a concept that makes perfect sense, not only because Day so often portrayed the ideal mother onscreen (*Please Don't Eat the Daisies* and *The Thrill of It All*) but also because the optimistic philosophy espoused in the majority of these songs is a perfect fit with Day's own sunny outlook on life.

"Zip-a-Dee-Doo-Dah," an upbeat song from Disney's *Song of the South,* presents exactly the kind of cheer and uplift that people stereotypically associate with Doris Day; singer and song here represent a perfect fit, just as proves to be the case on "With a Smile and a Song" from Disney's *Snow White.* Day delivers a nicely understated version of this song, which represents a cheerful outlook similar to Day's own:

There's no use grumbling when rain drops come tumbling
Remember you're the one who can fill the world with sunshine.

Day, who had so often recorded Rodgers and Hammerstein to great advantage, here essays *The King and I*'s "Getting to Know You" from the viewpoint of an All-American (not British) teacher. The Jimmy Joyce children's chorus joins in with Day the second time she reaches the words "getting to know you," and since Day, aided by a fitting Allyn Ferguson arrangement that emphasizes flute, has already established the child-friendly tone of the recording, the fit with the children is a nice one. There is no sense of, "Hey, where the hell did those kids come from and why are they singing with Doris?"

The "Sleepy Baby" lullaby is sung in the gentle tones of a mother lulling a child to sleep, and there is an interesting new look at "Que Sera, Sera," with the children often taking the verse—"Since I was just a boy of two"—and Day herself singing the chorus—"This was my teacher's wise reply—Que sera, sera." As a result, the lyric becomes a dialogue between teacher and child. It's a worthwhile new look at an iconic song because this lyric makes sense when sung from such dual viewpoints. Frank Loesser's "Inchworm" receives a terrific, gently swaying vocal, with strings swelling up during the section that enumerates the mathematical possibilities: "two and two are four, four and four are eight"; most interesting of all, this is the one cut on the recording where the arrangement underlying Day's characteristically warm and confidential singing contains a nearly bittersweet tone. These are terrific arrangements—sweet, subtle, and entirely in keeping with the nature of the material. In fact, there is only one second-tier song in the collection, "The Lilac Tree," which contains children singing in French. Considering Day's bad luck with French in such films as *It's a Great Feeling,* it's just as well she didn't try the French herself.

Completing the recording are two renditions of anthemic odes to childhood. "Do, Re, Me" from *The Sound of Music,* a song that has no hidden depths for a singing actress to explore, is a natural fit with and for children, and once again causes one to wonder which of the conflicting versions regarding the reasons for Day not playing Maria Von Trapp in the movie is true: Did Doris herself turn down the role, claiming that she was too American (a wise self-criticism—after all, no one particularly buys Julie Andrews as an American), or did Marty Melcher reject the role on her behalf? Perhaps it was the filmmakers and Rodgers himself who nixed the idea of Day, especially after the lackluster box office returns on *Jumbo.* At any rate, she delivers a very nice take on the song, a vocal that is only slightly less enjoyable than her terrific rendering of "High Hope." Indeed, that song appears to be tailor-made for Day's clean notes, optimistic philosophy, and generally infectious spirit, and it's no accident that Day's version featured prominently in Dream Works Pictures animated hit *Antz.*

By the time of her next recording sessions, September 1964, the landscape of pop music had been irrevocably altered. Spurred on by the Beatles and the subsequent "British invasion" of the American music scene, rock music now dominated the charts. The era of the classic American songbook was drawing to a close; the days of artists such as Sinatra, Fitzgerald, Day, and Bennett topping the charts proved to be the exception, not the rule. As such, it made a curious kind of sense that Day returned to her big-band roots for the nostalgic *Sentimental Journey,* arranged and conducted by Mort Garson (composer of "Our Day Will Come"). Recorded before, but released after *Latin for Lovers, Sentimental Journey* is an interesting album most notable for its unmistakably elegiac tone.

All of the songs on *Sentimental Journey* had been written at least twenty years previously but were here outfitted with contemporary arrangements that suggested, but did not slavishly imitate, the original versions. The result is a combination of song and arrangement that works well for the most part but doesn't strike a consistent enough tone to land in the top rank of Day's concept albums.

Several of Day's key songs are here revisited, a practice Sinatra also undertook at this time with his albums *I Remember Tommy* and *Songs for Swinging Brass.* In Sinatra's case, the reworked songs emphasized the shift in his singing from smooth ballads to punchy brass-driven vocals. For her part, Day looks again at "I Remember You" from the *Day by Day* album and revisits her iconic "Sentimental Journey." At this stage of her career, Doris Day preferred arrangements featuring extremely slow tempos, but on "Sentimental Journey" she actually sings at more of an up-tempo clip than she did in 1944. There are second looks at "It Could Happen to You," "I'll Never Smile Again," and "It's Been a Long, Long, Time," all of which had been recorded with Les Brown. These are all nice contemplative ballad readings, although on "It's Been a Long, Long Time" it's impossible not to miss Harry James's original recording with its full-bodied trumpet kicking in at the end of the vocal and propelling it forward. One particularly nice cut, "At Last," features a standout arrangement by Garson that blends seamlessly with Day's singing: At first Day is accompanied just by a piano, after which the arrangement adds strings and chorus, rising to a smooth liftoff when Day glides into the words "at last," alongside a beautifully muted trumpet.

If the album never takes off into the stratosphere of her best recordings, there are also no genuinely weak cuts, and there are two numbers that truly stand out. "I'm Beginning to See the Light" brings Doris back to her jazz-influenced roots and features a terrific introduction where Day sings to the accompaniment of just a brushed drum; the bass is added to the mix next, and then the piano, all of this culminating in the addition of strings, until a terrific syncopated rhythm is achieved. This is a real musician singing with her fellow big-band veterans and they are all totally simpatico. Even better, however, is "Come to Baby, Do" with its gently up-tempo and hypnotically insistent rhythm:

I want to love, love, love, love, love you the way I want to
I want to try, try, try, try, try to make you understand . . .

With its insinuating rhythm and sensual wordplay, it's a song one might associate more readily with a Peggy Lee, but Day is here assured, playful, and sexy, delivering a performance every bit as complete as any of Lee's.

Joseph Laredo, in his liner notes to the *Move Over Darling* boxed set wrote that there is a sense of melancholy to this LP; the listener senses that events have come full circle and that Day is nearing the end of her recording career: "It is simultaneously an exercise in wistful nostalgia and a celebration of timeless music." Yes, but while Doris is clearly looking at her past, examining her "sentimental journey" that has now come full circle, she is not doing so as Norma Desmond in *Sunset Boulevard,* or even as a past-her-prime singing diva dragging the listener along on one more trip down memory lane. Rather, with her forward-looking philosophy, Day is simultaneously looking at her past and gazing to the horizon. For a woman with such a legendary past, she continued to remain remarkably forward looking in both action and philosophy.

Working once again with Mort Garson, Day recorded *Latin for Lovers* in November of 1964. Nearing the end of her recording career, she was still functioning at an extraordinarily high level and succeeded in recording this A-list album in the amazingly short time of ten hours, spread over three days. This album stands as yet another example of Day's overlooked versatility, and it is worth noting that she was here exploring Latin music three years before Sinatra's seminal recording of *Francis Albert Sinatra and Antonio Carlos Jobim* and thirty years before Rosemary Clooney's *Brazil* album.

The album is extremely sensual, filled with beautiful melodies complemented by lyrics replete with romantic imagery. Ironically, while the finished recording often proved to be brilliant, Day was not at all certain of the undertaking: "When they first had a meeting and called me in to see if I wanted to do a bossa nova album I said 'oh no. I don't think that's for me at all! . . . Well it turned out to be one of my favorite albums and I'm so glad that the fans really enjoy what I enjoy doing."

The reason the album holds up so beautifully forty years after its initial release is that not only are the songs of an extremely high caliber but also that this quiet, gently sensual music plays directly to Day's strengths as a singer: This is intimate music with a bedrock structure of soft jazz rhythms. The Jobim tunes "Desafinado" and "Quiet Nights of Quiet Stars" receive beautiful readings, as does his "Meditation," a cut featuring the hushed plucking of the backing guitar. Accompanied by a flute overlay and the quiet sweep of the strings, Day murmurs, "I will wait for you, meditating how sweet life will be when you come back to me." Sexy, constant in her attention, and downright erotic at times, Midwestern Doris Day appears to be right at home with the Latin rhythms she had never before attempted. Talent such as hers shines through no matter the setting or provenance, and far from breaking when tested, becomes enriched.

The complete LP showcases up-tempo vocals on "Dansero" and "Por Favor," the latter featuring a cha-cha tempo that Day handles with ease. Garson's "Our Day Will Come" is sung in very relaxed fashion, and on "Be True to Me" Day sings in Spanish—the first and only time she ever recorded in a foreign language. Day actually sounds very at ease with the Spanish lyrics and definitely far more at home than she ever did in the unfortunately Americanized versions of French she was saddled with in several movie production numbers (just try watching "That's What Makes Paris, Paree" in *April in Paris. . . .*).

The best of all the up-tempo numbers is the insinuating "Perhaps, Perhaps, Perhaps," which received a fresh jolt of popularity when featured prominently in the hit 1992 film *Strictly Ballroom.* It's a joyously suggestive song in which Day is, however playfully, the sexual aggressor:

If you can't make your mind up
We'll never get started . . .

On this last of her concept masterpieces, two cuts linger on in the listener's memory. The first is "Summer Has Gone," a somewhat unknown gem of a song by Frank Comstock and Gene DiNovi. Day is singing with great depth of feeling here, exploring broken romance with a rawness not usually associated with her. Without ever becoming overwrought, she mines every possible emotion from the highly evocative lyrics:

Seagull cries on rainswept beaches
Tear washed eyes and pain love teaches

No cheerful optimism here. This is love gone wrong, and Doris Day gets it. Big time.

The second standout cut, Jobim's "How Insensitive" (written with Norman Gimbel and Vinicius de Moraes) is handled with such melancholy understatement that by the end of the track it is clear that Day's version can stand side by side with Sinatra's masterful take on the same song. Doris Day knows how to sing not just to only one person, but crucially, as if you, the listener, are the only person who matters to her; in this tale of a broken love affair, she delivers the vocal equivalent of a full-blown existential drama, vocally shrugging her shoulders as she murmurs what else "can one do when a love affair is over." Doris Day—existential? You bet.

How he must have asked
Could I just turn and stare in icy silence

This is so far from stereotypical sunshiny Doris Day territory—that is, so far from the stereotyped screen image of Doris Day—that it's never Doris Day one sees in the evocative setting painted by the lyric; instead, it's Jeanne Moreau, puffing a cigarette in her world-weary seen-it-all fashion, as she walks on a fog-shrouded beach. . . . Day was nearing the end of her recording career, but she here saved one of her very best for last.

After making these last two albums, Doris undertook only four more sessions (between May of 1965 and November of 1966) while still under contract to Columbia Records. A total of ten songs were recorded, most of them random singles from her various films. None of the songs were aimed at album release, and it is just as well. To be charitable, none of the songs were very good. In fact, in this collection of songs from the films *Do Not Disturb, The Glass Bottom Boat*, and *Caprice,* the only one of any interest is "Sorry." It's not a first-rate song, but it does contain a lyric by one of the all-time greats, Johnny Mercer, and the recording of Mercer's ballad on May 8, 1967, became the last Doris Day recording to be released by Columbia Records. Said Terry Melcher, "Her contract with Columbia expired in 1967. She wasn't happy with the songs she was singing. The recordings were just kind of tossed in between the movies. For me the only really sad part of Doris's career is the fact that the movies became so big and so important that for some reason they took precedence over the music. It's a shame, because she's one of the greatest singers that ever lived."

And what exactly were the songs in question like? Bad and boring. It's not just that the melodies were tired and uninteresting; it's that the lyrics were so second rate and nineteenth century in outlook. Doris Day is far too assertive and interesting a woman for the nonsense of the simpering "A Whisper Away" (which actually remained unreleased until the Bear Family set compilation of the 1990s). The nadir of these marriage-is-everything songs is "Catch the Bouquet," which is juvenile in the extreme and which Day (or anyone else) is helpless to redeem:

Catch, catch, catch the bouquet and you'll
Be, be, be happy some day

What? Did anyone writing, producing, or arranging this song ever look at a Doris Day movie and realize for whom they were writing? Unless they screened only *That Touch of Mink,* the answer appears to be no, and these last sessions are a waste of Day's abilities.

"Do Not Disturb" from the film of the same title is a guitar-and drum-driven tune that is somewhat catchy but also meaningless. "Au Revoir Is Goodbye with a Smile" is a simply awful song that was shoehorned into *Do Not Disturb,* complete with clichéd accordion music, for no discernible reason. "Every Now and Then," with its cascading strings, sounds like a reject from a recording session of the then popular Connie Francis, and "The Glass Bottom Boat" from the film of the same title is grade-Z material complete with obvious and thudding nautical sound effects like foghorns. Doris Day, who recorded brilliant material like "Sentimental Journey," "I'll Be Around," and "Stars Fell on Alabama," now had to record a song whose lyrics sound like a call for an underwater shindig:

Spiny crabs and whitefish too
Will all be there—what a hullabaloo.

This is disheartening in the extreme, and, if it's disheartening for the listener, what was it like for Day herself?

To say "There They Are" and "Sorry" are the best of the bunch is truly to damn with faint praise, and it is only the latter song that even momentarily arrests interest, mostly because of an ending on which Day reaches up for a high note à la Ella Fitzgerald, a move that surprises and pleases precisely because it is so unexpected.

The contract with Columbia having expired in May of 1967, Day was now a free agent. Said son Terry, "She felt that what she loved to do was not terribly relevant as far as recording for Columbia Records. She just felt around '67 or '68 that the ballads and the Broadway-type tunes were not relevant. She wasn't bitter about it. She really loved the new music. She loved Motown records. She thought, 'Well, that's terrific. Now this is going to happen and I had a wonderful time.'" But first, before the curtain was drawn forever on the recording career, Day herself booked studio time, hired her (soon to be) television show casting director Don Genson to produce, and engaged Sid Feller to arrange and conduct. Both men were inspired choices: Genson, who worked for Day's Arwin Productions, thoroughly understood her style, and Feller, who had arranged and conducted many of Ray Charles's albums of standards, was thoroughly grounded in the world of the great American songbook. As Will Friedwald points out in his liner notes to the U.S. issue of *The Love Album,* Feller smartly employed a rhythm section with a string quartet, having a woodwind player doubling on sax and flute—a classical rather than jazz style of recording.

The songs Day chose were her personal favorites, songs the record company had deemed "not commercial" (the very fighting words that had spurred Streisand's return to her roots for the triumphant *Broadway Album*). Working with the very best studio musicians of her generation—Barney Kessel on guitar, Irv Cottler on drums—Day recorded *The Love Album* and ended up with nothing short of an autumnal masterpiece.

Mother and son provide fascinating background on the evolution of this last recorded album. Said Day, years after the fact: "I love these slow tempos. That's the way I really enjoy singing more than anything. You usually can't get away with it, because the producer will invariably come out of the booth and say 'You have to pick it up! People will go to sleep!' They didn't think it was commercial and they're so afraid not to be commercial. I got to the point where I said 'I don't want to hear that word again!'" Added Terry: "So she picked some of her favorites, had all the songs put way back in tempo just the way she really likes them, and made that record in two days."

What then happened is the stuff of legend or, at the least, very interesting backstage gossip. Without the backing of Columbia Records, the masters were kept in Marty Melcher's office. In the aftermath of Melcher's unexpected death, the shocking discoveries of Jerome Rosenthal's financial malfeasance, and Day's all-consuming work on television's *The Doris Day Show,* the tapes, hard as it is to believe, were forgotten. Years later, when approached about a possible return to the recording studio, Day's response was to wonder what had happened to the tapes for the unreleased *The Love Album.* They were rediscovered by Terry, who oversaw the cleaning up of the static-ridden originals and personally prepared them for release in Great Britain in 1994 (a United States release finally occurred on Concord Records in 2006). So it was that an album recorded in 1967 came to be released twenty-seven years later, twenty-seven years after her last Columbia recording had been released. Incredibly, the album hit the charts in the UK and rose to number sixty-five, an impressive feat for a sixty-nine-year-old singer of standards who hadn't been professionally active for two full decades.

Was this a case of simple nostalgia? A pat on the back for a former superstar? The answer: an emphatic no. The album sold for one very simple reason—it contained some truly great singing from Doris Day. It proved to be quite a way to end her recording career, even if release of the recordings was delayed for almost three decades.

Day was certainly not exaggerating when she said that she liked slow tempos—all of the ballads on this album are taken at an extremely slow pace, yet so evocative are her sound and phrasing that the result is anything but boring. There is a string-drenched take on "Snuggled on Your Shoulders" and a seductive and very slow-tempoed "Life Is Just a Bowl of Cherries," an approach that underlines the lyrics' laissez-faire attitude to which Day could relate so well. Digging deep into the lyrics, she brings forth a romantic, wistful reading of Irving Berlin's "All Alone," as well as a contemplative "Are You Lonesome Tonight," the decades-old standard repopularized by Elvis Presley. The titles alone fully speak to the elegiac nature of the album: "Faded Summer Love, "Oh How I Miss You Tonight," and "For All We Know." The last song in particular receives a calm, considered reading that could have come only from a woman who has lived a full life and taken a few rough knocks along the way:

Tomorrow was made for some
Tomorrow may never come

Well—que sera, sera . . .

There isn't a weak cut on the entire album, and what could have dwindled into a lugubrious farewell instead registers as a perfect summation of the extraordinary vocal talents possessed by this most underrated of all pop singers—underrated, that is, in spite of gold records and chart-topping successes. Long after the album stops playing, two cuts linger in the mind. The first is the beautiful "Sleepy Lagoon" by Jack Lawrence and Eric Coates, in which Day's languorous reading perfectly suits the dreamlike quality found in both the melody and the nearly visceral lyric:

The fireflies' gleam reflects in the stream
They sparkle and shimmer

This is poetry, pure and simple, and Day paints the picture perfectly in her increasingly husky voice: After listening to this vocal unfurl, one can nearly picture the singer lying in a boat, hand trailing in the water, contemplating the scene around her. . . .

Perhaps best of all, there is an extraordinary take on "If I Had My Life to Live Over," a song to which Day brings all of her considerable intelligence and vocal expertise, folding it into a medley with "Let Me Call You Sweetheart." Sweet as this very last song is, it's the former song that one remembers:

I'd meet you when school days were over
We'd walk through the lanes that we know

The listener knows that Doris Day never did have those carefree schooldays. She was on the road with big bands by age sixteen, performing for students her own age at their high school proms. She is here singing about what might have been, about the "what ifs" in her own tumultuous life. It's why the song resonates so deeply; being the actress that she is, Day is simultaneously making this first-rate material both personal and universal. As Don Genson wrote in the album liner notes, "Someday over a drink I'll ask her what she was thinking when she recorded these songs. . . . Being in the studio control booth, listening to Doris, I became aware that something very different was taking place. Something so unique that even now, I can still feel the goosebumps as the sound of her voice and the orchestra joined together to create what I thought was the ultimate, intimate musical experience."

Genson is not indulging in hyperbole—the sound really is that intimate, and the listener almost feels that he or she is intruding on the singer's most private thoughts. What Day has here achieved, imparting a rueful acknowledgment of all of life's ups and downs, the hard-won wisdom accumulated over the course of an entire life, is the work of a master. Like the very best in any field, she has stripped away everything extraneous. She is incapable of telling anything but the unvarnished truth, both good and bad. In short, Doris Day, the unceasing optimist, has grown up. Beautifully.

Television

The Doris Day Show makes *Family Affair*
look like a meeting of the Mafia.

—Los Angeles Times
on season one of the sitcom

As in films, Miss Day here displays her usual
talent for somehow squeezing the corn juice out
of a square role. She is evocative and believable and, in
fact, the whole show is well cast. The locale . . .
[however] would seem to be somewhere between
Green Acres and Petticoat Junction.

—Variety, *September 25, 1968*

Miss Day is still a one-note (poignancy) actress.

—Variety *review of season three of*
The Doris Day Show, *September 23, 1970*

Acting with Doris Day was the most comfortable
acting I've ever done. She's so natural. . . .
She was a kind of genius.

—Larry Storch, "Duke the boxer" on
The Doris Day Show

When Doris Day completed the highly successful five-season run of her CBS television sitcom titled, what else, *The Doris Day Show,* she had accomplished something unequaled by any other entertainer in show business history: She had now triumphed as a motion picture star, highly successful recording artist, and star of a hit multi-year weekly television series. Many Hollywood legends had foundered when attempting to navigate the strange terrain of a television series: Henry Fonda, Shirley MacLaine, Bette Midler, and James Stewart all failed in their TV series, and in Midler's case, the failure occurred in a hail of bad publicity regarding her relationship with CBS. No other star—not Sinatra, Streisand, Bing Crosby, Lucille Ball, or Elvis Presley—had ever conquered movies, records, and series television so successfully. Sinatra and Streisand had certainly succeeded in Emmy Award–winning variety specials, but these were one-time events that served their edgy personalities well. Theirs were not necessarily personalities that America wanted to invite into its living room every week. Day, every bit their equal as singer and actress, succeeded as a sitcom star precisely because her warm personality translated to the small screen; she was ingratiating and charming, and came across as the perfect all-American mom who could solve any problem in twenty-two minutes plus commercials.

Day instinctively knew how to scale down her performance for the small screen, no easy feat for a larger-than-life icon—try picturing Carol Channing in your living room every week. . . . It's not that *The Doris Day Show* was a great sitcom—not by any stretch of the imagination. But Doris herself was charming, and not so incidentally, the five-year run of the show restored her personal fortune after suffering from the disastrous financial manipulations of Jerome Rosenthal. The television series provided her with financial security for the rest of her life and brought her a brand-new burst of fame. Thirty years into her career, she was as big as she ever had been.

When analyzing Doris Day's television appearances throughout the decades, one aspect stands out above all others—even at the height of her feature film popularity, she very rarely appeared on television. This woman had neither the need nor the desire to take part in the talk shows or variety series that dominated the airwaves during her 1950–1967 heyday. Any variety show in the land would have given its eyeteeth to have landed the biggest box office attraction in the country as a guest, but Doris wasn't having any of it. Thus it was that before the weekly grind of filming a television series began in 1968, she undertook only a handful of television appearances, appearances all the more noteworthy because they were so rare. In fact, before the sitcom, and aside from one 1956 appearance on *The Ed Sullivan Show* and three appearances as a presenter on the Academy Awards show, the only time Day materialized on national television, or rather, the only sightings still extant today, were a pair of guest-starring gambits on the television game show *What's My Line.*

Incredibly enough, her initial appearance on *What's My Line,* June 2, 1954, constituted her first national television appearance. Timed to coincide with the premiere of the motion picture *Young at Heart,* it found Day before a panel of blindfolded celebrity judges who were given up to ten questions in order to guess the identity of their mystery guest. Day, answering the questions in a squeaky cartoon voice, fooled the panelists until the eighth question, when Arlene Francis correctly guessed her identity. Day looked thoroughly at ease on camera, albeit momentarily nonplussed by the question, "Is your name alliterative?" At the end of her appearance she was presented with a gold record for her recording of "Secret Love."

Three years later, on September 8, 1957, she paid a return visit to the program, an appearance this time tied in to the release of *The Pajama Game.* Day employed the same squeaky voice but this time to no avail, as the panelists guessed her identity without asking any wrong questions along the way; well, Day was, by this time, the biggest female recording star in the land and was well on her way to her perch as the top box office attraction in the country—she was not exactly an unknown personality. Decked out in a dress and white gloves, Day charmed both the panelists and studio audience; in her forthright, sincere manner, she ended her guest-starring stint by stating simply, "I love New York. I always have." And, for nearly twenty years, that was the end of Doris Day's promotional talk show appearances.

In fact, this proved to be Day's final television appearance of any kind until the September 24, 1968, premiere of *The Doris Day Show* series. Which makes it all the more ironic that just a few months before this broadcast, Doris Day not only had no interest in television appearances, she actually had no idea that she would be appearing as the star of a network television series.

Imagine for one moment that you're Doris Day. Your husband, and not so coincidentally agent, of nearly twenty years, Marty Melcher becomes sick. Once he falls ill, Marty grows weaker and thinner, taking to bed for three months, strictly following his Christian Science beliefs, and refusing to see a doctor. Ignoring pleas from friends and family, he finally acquiesces to see a doctor with whom he used to play tennis. Diagnosis? An enlarged heart that should have and could have been treated months earlier. Listless and resigned, he falls into a coma and dies on April 30, 1968, leaving you with an overwhelming sense of being alone: In your own words: ". . . in my aloneness he was my father and I was a ten-year-old child. And I loved him very much."

Your shock at his death is increased when your son Terry informs you that every cent of your multimillion-dollar fortune has been lost, and you're a half million dollars in debt. You're not only grappling with the loss of your spouse but also trying to understand how and why he lost all of your money. How could this have happened? (It is only with the passage of years that Day came to the thoroughly reasoned yet sad conclusion that "I think Marty just trusted the wrong person. Completely.") Stupefied, uncomprehending, you later write that there's one other piece of news your son has to deliver: Your deceased husband has signed you for a five-year run as the star of a sitcom on CBS television. Shooting starts on June 15, 1968, exactly six weeks hence. Oh.

It doesn't matter—for now—that it is an extraordinarily lucrative deal granting you outright ownership of the negatives to the show, the control of all rerun rights, and even further hefty remuneration to make movies for CBS television. What matters now is that you have to start filming immediately, filming a show you knew nothing about and whose very concept you instantly dislike. In fact, in your own, rather chilling words: "I had lost three things: my husband, my life's savings, and my freedom—for television was much more rigid and confining than Warner Bros. ever was."

You'd have every right to try and bail out of this commitment, and chances are you'd succeed. But you don't, because, in the Doris Day worldview, "A deal's a deal." (Remember, you're the woman who subsequently turned down a $1 million offer for one day's work for a television diet commercial, a million dollars for eight hours of work at your very own home. Why turn it down? Because you've "never had a weight problem so it wouldn't be right.") You go back to work and discover that in the midst of your depression, because there is no other word for it, work proves to be your salvation. Just getting to and from the set every day feels like a victory in and of itself. And so you go to work, and by dint of sheer effort, you make the damn show start to work. And that's another miracle, because boy, oh boy, you don't even like the concept for the series, let alone the scripts.

And that's a dislike shared by first-season television viewers across America—with good reason. The basic premise of the show gave viewers a widowed Doris Day (Doris Martin in the series), a successful journalist who had given up her career to move back to her father Buck's (Denver Pyle) farm in Cotina, California, in order to raise her two young sons Billy (Philip Brown) and Toby (Tod Starke). Rounding out the extended "family" were goofball handyman LeRoy B. Simpson (James B. Hampton) and acerbic housekeeper Aggie (Fran Ryan).

Airing on Tuesday nights at 9:30 P.M. and functioning as lead-in for *60 Minutes* (!), *The Doris Day Show* ended its first season ranked thirtieth in the Nielsen ratings. It's actually a bit of a shock in the year 2006, when the ribald and very gay sitcom *Will and Grace* occasionally aired at the family-friendly time of 8:30 P.M., to realize that the made-for-family-hour *Doris Day Show* was originally aired as late as 9:30. Whatever the reason for its relatively late slot on the schedule, the opening credits of the show immediately told the viewer exactly what was to follow: With Doris warbling "Que Sera, Sera" over the credits, the sun-dappled shots of pastoral images make it clear that there will be plenty of animals, as well as plenty of three-generational family closeness. Day herself sports a blond/silver pageboy hairstyle, a still terrific and trim figure (forty-five years old at the time of filming she looked sensational), and what are unquestionably the most luxurious false eyelashes found on any working farm.

In the sponsors' greeting that Day filmed as a promotion for the series, she stated, "The situations [on the show] are real—we want to bring reality to everyone." Well, that didn't exactly pan out. The aim was, as Rose Marie (Myrna Gibbons) later stated about ensuing seasons of the show, to avoid a nonstop series of one-liners, and instead have the jokes come out of the situations themselves. Said Rose Marie, "The comedy we did was family comedy. It was just wonderful. We don't see that today." As the show entered its second and third seasons, that did come to pass with increasing frequency, but even in the very uneven and often ridiculously plotted first season, it's clear why CBS had faith in the show and why it stayed on the air a full five years: The magic of Doris Day translated just as well to the small screen as it had to the larger-than-life movie screen. The exotic may have played well in the movie theaters of the 1950s and 1960s, but when it came time for weekly series in those precable television days, America wanted comfort, familiarity, and reassurance. And Doris Day provided them in spades, even when saddled with plots that, in the words of the *Los Angeles Times* made "*Family Affair* look like a meeting of the Mafia."

The plots of the first season's episodes would not, to put it kindly, tax the concentration of any five-year-old. In fact, the five-year-old would run circles around the screenwriters. For starters, Doris and father Buck are never glimpsed working on the farm—the farm appears to miraculously run itself. Yet somehow in the midst of this silliness, even in the very first episode where Doris's sons take her out to a restaurant for her birthday dinner without enough money to pay, the viewer is willing, albeit grudgingly, to go along for the ride. One smile from Doris over the birthday cake, a smile of such warmth that you believe she actually is mother to these sons, and one forgives all the nonsense that has gone before. This key ingredient is helped by the fact that both Philip Brown and Tod Starke, as Billy and Toby, are naturals on camera and evince a real rapport with Doris. Starke especially, with his one missing front tooth and a hoarse little boy's voice, brings a sense of believability to all of his antics. He is not a child actor in capital letters and in fact delighted Day off camera by greeting her every day with a cheery, "Good morning DorisDay"—to his mind, her one and only name was a run-on "DorisDay." (Tragically, Starke was killed in a motorcycle accident at age twenty.) Brown has described a genuine rapport with Day that extended for years after the show ended, as exemplified by the fact that he still called her on Mother's Day to wish her a happy day. (In the interviews included in the DVD release of the show's third season, the now forty-eight-year-old Brown muses that he was born at the wrong time, firmly believing that he would have made a terrific real life husband for Day!)

It quickly became clear in season one that the style of the show would be to tuck little lessons into the simple homilies that doubled as plots. In episode three, the boys star in a television commercial for milk and are allowed to choose classmates to play their sisters. Toby chooses a young black girl as his sister, much to the chagrin of the sponsor. Doris of course comes to the rescue—as if racial prejudice had a chance in the face of Doris's all-American sense of justice. Free milk at snacktime for two hundred well-fed middle-class children is not exactly *Love Me or Leave Me,* but it doesn't really matter. The stakes themselves are smaller on sitcoms, and Doris Day's natural warmth shines through. She is the ideal mother: beautiful, fun, understanding, and always able to spare time for a game or two with her sons. Good thing she has that magically self-running farm. . . .

In episode six, "By the Old Mill Steam," there are twenty-plus minutes of nonsense to suffer through, absolute gibberish about spinster con artists who in effect steal a valuable table from Toby and Billy. But one does suffer through this very nonsense, and then some, because at the end of the show, Doris, quietly lounging on the front porch of her home, briefly offers up part of a song. It's a quiet night, and in the beautifully lit shot, Day's singing generates such genuine emotion that in the end it's all one remembers about the episode.

Interestingly, the very next episode was actually intended to be the series opener, but it surfaced only a full seven weeks into the run. Written by none other than James L. Brooks, it sent Maggie Welles, Doris's former boss at *Today's World* magazine, out to the farm in order to lure Doris back to work. Will Doris take the job? Of course not—this all-American mom knows what's important in life. Why take a fabulous job in New York City, one complete with excitement, money, and a great wardrobe, when you can stay on the farm and chase animals around the barnyard? No wonder Day didn't love the initial concept for the series.

The participation of Brooks is of note, because Brooks, who went on to an Academy Award–winning career with *Terms of Endearment* and *Broadcast News,* soon became a key player in the success of *The Mary Tyler Moore Show* on television. It all makes a perfect kind of sense: Doris Day portrayed America's favorite high-powered career woman in her films of the early 1960s, films which paved the way for Mary Tyler Moore's groundbreaking portrayal of Mary Richards, America's favorite hardworking, happily unmarried television career woman. Without Day's film work, Moore's television character would not have seemed so logical an evolution, nor would the audience have so willingly accepted Doris Martin's season two evolution into working mom. As actor James B. Hampton (LeRoy B. Simpson) opined, "Doris recognized that there were a lot of working moms; before the *Mary Tyler Moore Show*—she pioneered that. . . . She also got to wear a lot of better clothes in the city than when the show stayed on the farm!"

Actually, the interest inherent in Maggie Welles tempting Doris back to work lies in the fact that it pits the two aspects of Day's persona against each other: highly successful go-getter career woman versus idealized loving mom raising her boys on the farm. This dichotomy—and the appeal of both personae—is apparent in episode seventeen, "The Flyboy." On the one hand, the episode revolves around an Air Force pilot betting that he can wrangle a date with Doris. When she subsequently does appear as his date at a dance, she is all dolled up and looks every inch a knockout. On the other hand, earlier in the same episode she is shown in the barnyard, holding and feeding pigs. Such extremes of behavior seem natural with Day, and just as proved to be the case in her movies, it is very clear here that no other television star of the time could have presented this dichotomy so believably. Angie Dickinson (Police Woman) raising two boys on the farm while tending pigs? Not in this lifetime. At the end of this will-Doris-go-back-to-work episode, her role as full-time mom has won out, but only for the remainder of season one.

It was also at this time, in the middle of season one, that housekeeper Aggie simply disappeared, with no explanation ever offered. One week Aggie was dispensing wisecracks along with her home cooking, and then presto-changeo, episode seven opens with a credit for Naomi Stevens as new housekeeper Juanita. Huh? Where's Aggie? How did Juanita get to the farm? By parachute? Evidently such questions didn't matter to the CBS executives. Sitcomland had its own logic—or lack thereof. So it was good-bye Aggie and hello Juanita. Of course any concerned viewer would like to have called Juanita aside and given her a little piece of advice—don't get too comfortable on the farm, what with changes ahead and all. . . .

As the season unfolded, sweet life lessons continued. In episode twelve, "Let Them Out of the Nest," Billy and Toby take over their neighbor's egg route. Not only do the boys learn responsibility and the importance of fulfilling job requirements, but even Doris herself has a little lesson to learn: trust her boys and let them take responsibility for their own actions. Says father Buck as he gently counsels daughter Doris, "It's a joyous adventure. Let them learn." This was comfort food television, pure and simple, and especially welcome in the tumultuous first season year of 1968, a year that saw the assassinations of Martin Luther King Jr. and Bobby Kennedy, convention riots in Chicago, and the escalating protests about the war in Vietnam.

What had become crystal clear by this point in the first season was that whatever success the show enjoyed came about because of the undiminished appeal of Doris Day, and because Doris and her boys actually appeared to be somewhat recognizable human beings—recognizable even if more than a bit idealized. By way of contrast, the villains of each episode were relentlessly cartoonish; in episode eleven, the boys learn that ducks, like all wild creatures, should be allowed to run free and not be harmed by the poacher Tyrone Lovee (Strother Martin). Nice lesson, but not one even a five-year-old is likely to take seriously when the villain in question is so one-dimensional and silly that he makes Pa Kettle sound like Jean-Paul Sartre by comparison.

Similarly, LeRoy the hired hand (James Hampton) is a cartoon himself—hopelessly inept, a golly-gee-whiz man-child who, much to Buck's chagrin, can bungle even the smallest repair job. But Doris sees LeRoy's essential goodness, soothing Buck and making LeRoy feel like a real part of the family. A few minutes of watching Doris in such action and it all becomes clear: This sitcom is a throwback to the 1950s and should in fact be titled *Mother Knows Best.*

Doris can solve any problem, outsmart any poacher, and still get in some high-level physical clowning, all in the space of a half hour minus commercials. When, in episode thirteen, LeRoy gives Doris a very loud chiming clock, she becomes sleep deprived; in a display of Lucille Ball–like slapstick clowning, she tumbles out of bed because the clock is chiming so loudly, falls into deep sleep at meetings, and as a result has to be bodily carried out of the room by her father. It's like watching the physical clowning in *Caprice* all over again—and while Day's shtick is great, the script is unfortunately about as believable as that found in *Caprice.*

With hindsight, it's also evident in watching the episodes from season one that Day was still recovering from her personal tragedies and needed occasional time off. In episode fourteen, she is reunited with guest star Mary Wickes from *On Moonlight Bay* and *By the Light of the Silvery Moon;* Doris Martin is away on a trip and shows up only halfway through the episode. The grueling television production schedule clearly took a toll on Day, but she trudged ahead, finding some comfort in the routine of work and in the knowledge that she had a purpose—that so many livelihoods depended on her efforts.

This constituted an admirable, nearly Herculean effort on Day's part, because some episodes were, well, nothing short of awful. To wit: In episode nineteen, "Love Thy Neighbor," Doris drives a jeep and tries to fix a tractor (just as she fixed the car in *By the Light of the Silvery Moon*). Admirable self-sufficiency indeed. The problem, however, is that she is displaying this competence while pursuing her archenemies, the hillbilly poachers. In response to such exertions while chasing cartoon evildoers, one can only ask, "Who thought this stuff up?" Surely Doris Day deserved better, deserved a foil who actually resembled a real human being. Was it a conscious decision that the villains always be stick figures?

Maybe not, because in episode twenty, "The Con Man," guest star Joseph Campanella actually portrays a semibelievable con artist. Campanella's character of Roger Flanders is on the verge of defrauding Cotina residents out of their life savings by promising to build them a community center. His character is sketched in only by broad strokes, but at least Campanella is a flawed, recognizable human being, and there's even a hint that he and Doris find each other attractive. Of course, once Doris gets wind of his scheme, it's all over for

Flanders. It's like Doris battling railroad tycoon Ernie Kovacs in *It Happened to Jane*—no contest—and needless to say, Doris gets this con man to change his stripes. Just goes to show you—you might be able to fight city hall, but not Doris. She goes into battle, and all of a sudden the con man's life is changed, the townspeople's money hasn't been lost, and there's going to be new convention center in town. Not a bad list of accomplishments, considering Doris managed all of it in twenty-two minutes.

The quality of the first season's episodes varied widely from bland ("The Musical") to terrific ("The Baby Sitter") to horrible ("The Still"). In "The Musical," the plot finds Doris directing the school musical, and the viewer waits in the hope that she will sing or dance. No such luck. Instead, she battles a principal who deems the 1960s dances "too suggestive." Solution? Doris just choreographs the children so that they showcase the evolution of dance from the Charleston that the principal once favored, right up to the current groovy go-go dancing of the 1960s. Doris rolls up her sleeves, turns into George Balanchine, and lickety-split the principal changes his mind while everyone munches on milk and cookies. Never mind the hilariously overchoreographed dance sequences here, sequences that make one thing very clear: These schoolkids definitely need a vacation—fast. There are no real worries here. Doris just tells the principal, "We need to give children freedom to grow—they're just flexing their muscles," and everything is solved.

Some of the plots are so ramshackle that "abysmal" seems too kind a word to describe them. For example, in "The Still," two old women possess an illegal still. Doris takes their bottles of homemade moonshine away from them in order to prevent them from being arrested; of course it's Doris herself who gets a flat tire on her "getaway," and when the police find the bottles of illegal hooch in her car, she ends up in jail. This is the height of nonsense, complete with a cartoonlike speeded-up car chase and heavy-handed 1960s secret agent music. There isn't one believable line or situation in the entire episode. In short, it's an episode that sums up everything that was wrong with the first season.

Yet occasionally it all came together, and came together very well, as in "The Baby Sitter," an episode that featured a troublemaking tomboy played by none other than the very young Jodie Foster. The situation is actually realistic, or rather, sitcom realistic; Doris fills in as a babysitter in order to help out a young family, and in the process she must charge through an ever-increasing mountain of Lucy-like physical shtick. The children in her charge place marbles in the dishwasher, put shoe polish in the bathtub, shoot arrows into Doris's forehead, tie her up with rope, and lock her in the closet. Even with all of these outrageous situations, Day plays it realistically—no triple takes, just a growing exasperation and befuddlement as to how she has landed in this situation. It's a befuddlement that makes the situation hilarious, and even believable, the television equivalent of her hilariously inept television commercial in *The Thrill of It All.*

In the final episodes of the season, the self-sufficient Doris Day of Hollywood fame begins to emerge, and the show starts to improve. In episode twenty-four, our first glimpse of her is prone under a jeep that she is repairing. She is sprayed with a hose and falls backward into the mud; she even swings a sledgehammer. This is all very physical, but somehow there is nothing butch about any of it. She's strong but always feminine—then, again, the noticeably false eyelashes while she's swinging the sledgehammer do tend to soften the action.

Real-life animal lover Day is glimpsed in "The Tiger," an episode that used a real tiger to recount its story of a tame tiger who escapes captivity and ends up both in Doris's truck and then in her house. What does she do about the tiger in her house? What any sensible gal would—she finds father Buck, together they calmly discuss the fact of the tiger being in her kitchen, and then she feeds the tiger milk. . . . When the tiger escapes, Doris and nitwit LeRoy hop into the jeep in order to save the beast from hunters and Doris ends up saving the tiger by lassoing him and purring endearments to him. This is all silly, if a little disconcerting, but once again one's reaction is, "No other actress would have even attempted this gig as a combination tiger tamer/animal rights activist." The 1960s were also the heyday of Elizabeth Taylor and Julie Andrews—excellent actresses both—but one can't exactly picture either one of them chasing after a tiger. Then again, maybe Julie could have sung a lullaby to the tiger and Liz could have knocked him unconscious with a jewel—that's the level of believability engendered here.

In another parallel with Doris's feature film oeuvre, where many of her films doubled as fashion parades of form-fitting Jean Louis gowns, here the first-season episode "The Date" turned into the first-ever display of a recurring motif of the show: When in doubt, drum up an excuse for Doris to model different outfits. Thus, this episode was ostensibly about Juanita's date, but it quickly developed into a searching attempt to answer one all-important question: How many outfits could Doris wear in a single episode. The answer? A world record's eight outfits in one half hour, ranging from orange dress to pink robe to blue turtleneck complemented by matching blue slacks. Good thing that farm ran itself—Doris was way too busy changing clothes to spare time for chores. If there was anything like, say, milking cows, feeding animals, or harvesting crops to do, why, then Doris wouldn't have been able to put on a one-woman fashion parade that would have made Coco Chanel envious. In Cotina, California, no less.

It's all silliness, of course, but in its own cuckoo way, it's fun. Day looks great and it's just an updated way of watching a star strut her stuff. It's not acting, it's not singing, but it's audience-friendly. If only the fashions were a little wackier, discerning viewers could give Doris the credit for starting the twenty-years-in-the-future cutting-edge displays of "vogueing." Those "fierce" gay men in Harlem strutting their stuff on nightclub runways didn't have a thing on Doris.

The first season ends with a truly terrible episode, "The Relatives," where LeRoy's cousins visit the Martin farm. Turns out LeRoy is the smart one in the family—a very bad sign. When Doris ends up with scrambled egg all over her face, not to mention hanging on the back of her bedroom door, it's clear to everyone that a change needs to occur. And fast.

Everyone got the message—and quickly, at that—because by season two, Doris had moved to San Francisco, the hillbillies had fled to the hills, and career gal Doris was back in her natural milieu—the big city. This was going to be character-driven comedy about the metropolitan workplace and a lot less claustrophobic than life on the farm. Doris Martin's life in the second season did not exactly reek of Ernst Lubitsch sophistication, but it sure beat the hell out of chasing pigs around the barnyard.

Sure enough, as soon as the credits rolled for the first episode of season two, you knew you were in for a different *Doris Day Show.* Rather than titles unfurling over pastoral images, Doris is shown leaving the farm in her convertible while, to the tune of "Que Sera, Sera," she crosses the Golden Gate Bridge into the glamorous Oz-like city of San Francisco. These credits prefigure the famous opening credits for *The Mary Tyler Moore Show,* with Mary whirling around Minneapolis to the tune of "Love Is All Around." Nobody remembers the salient fact that Doris got there first.

The difference between *The Doris Day Show* and *The Mary Tyler Moore Show,* of course, is that Doris may be a working gal, but she is an executive secretary at *Today's World* magazine, not a (low-level) executive like Mary Richards. With Doris's new job came new boss Michael Nicholson (McLean Stevenson) and a new comic sidekick—her fellow secretary, the man-hungry Myrna Gibbons (played by Rose Marie of *Dick Van Dyke Show* fame). Rose Marie's Myrna functioned in some ways as Doris's alter ego—she was loud, outspoken, and man crazy, and said whatever popped into her mind. Not particularly interested in her secretarial work, she was after some fun while she could grab it. She was the goofy sidekick that made Doris's character the warm center of the show—Rhoda and Phyllis rolled into one to complement Doris's Mary Richards. Rose Marie proved a welcome addition to the cast, but the new series format still struggled to gain its sea legs: Father Buck and sons Billy and Toby were relegated to cameo-type appearances, and LeRoy and Juanita disappeared altogether. Sure was tough to be a housekeeper on that farm—whether sharp-witted Irish Aggie or warm maternal Chicana Juanita, they disappeared with alarming frequency, no explanation provided. Guess they moved to the back forty acres and made moonshine with the hillbillies. . . .

The second season's switch in concept happened for a reason that looms large in any examination of Day's career: For the first time in her storied professional life, Doris Day herself took charge of the work. She would implement the changes that she instinctively know would showcase her persona to greatest effect. Doris Day hired new producers (the late Marty Melcher continued to be listed as an executive producer throughout the series's five-year run), employed new scriptwriters, and teamed up with the reconfigured staff to find the new locale and concept for the show. Doris Day was in control; Marty Melcher wasn't around to make the final decisions, and not even trusted son Terry, an executive producer of the show, had the final say. Doris Day had taken charge of her own career for the very first time. Involving herself with every aspect of the production, from writing to wardrobe, Day even broke her long-standing self-imposed taboo dating back from her earliest days at Warner Bros., and actually watched the daily rushes. If the resulting half-hour episodes were not exactly a threat to *Citizen Kane,* they certainly represented a quantum leap forward from the first season, and the switch paid off in the ratings: Moved by CBS to Monday nights at 9:30 P.M., in its second season *The Doris Day Show* achieved the highest rankings of its entire five-year run, finishing the 1969–1970 television season as the tenth highest rated show on the air.

What's most noteworthy about the early season-two episodes is how retro they remain in many ways. In the fifth episode, "The Chocolate Bar War," the magazine's conservative financial backer Mr. Fletcher matter-of-factly says to Doris, "Thanks for all that good coffee. I wish my wife had your touch with the percolator." All that's missing is Mr. Fletcher calling Doris a "pretty young thing" and patting her on the rear. (Speaking of time capsules, in that same episode, Doris hides in a closet to avoid Mrs. Fletcher, with whom she has tangled over their respective sons' selling of chocolate bars—you can see the level of plot sophistication at hand here. . . . Upon finding Doris hidden away among the coats, Mr. Fletcher loudly says to Doris, with a total lack of irony, "Doris, come out of the closet.")

By episodes six and seven, there have been almost no signs of either Buck or the two boys—aside from an episode where Toby's pet frog gets into Doris's purse and ends up on the head of a banking executive—but the stereotyping remains. Intrepid Doris has landed the serialization rights for a bodybuilder's new fitness book, just as she obtained Mr. Fletcher's vital financial backing for the magazine, but there is no reward—she remains a secretary even after landing this coup. Forgoing any display of unseemly ambition, Doris brings Mr. Nicholson's lunch to him on a tray, blithely stating, "Mr. Nicholson, I'm just a secretary," with absolutely no trace of anger at her continuing low-echelon status.

What also hasn't changed in the urban setting is the nonstop fashion parade. Although Day sports somewhat unflattering long hair throughout much of season two, she still appears trim, healthy, and occasionally quite glamorous. Before Cher riveted millions of viewers on *Sonny and Cher Show* with her flamboyant one-of-a-kind gowns, Doris was changing clothes with equally dizzying frequency, only her togs were made for everyday work and leisure. Unlike Cher's not-from-this-universe fashions, Doris modeled clothes that women could really see themselves wearing; Doris was still the woman next door and this helped to cement her small-screen appeal.

Of course, not all of the outfits exactly fit one's notion of everyday wear; on the aforementioned "Health King" episode, Doris jogs with the bodybuilder in the eye-popping ensemble of tight shorts, yellow turtleneck, matching cap, blue kneesocks, and sneakers! Not exactly the outfit Wilma Rudolph wore while running her way to all those gold medals. Then again, Wilma didn't have to save the all-important *Today's World* fashion spread by singlehandedly modeling every design by the world-renowned designer Montaine; that's right—after some mind-numbingly stupid high jinks involving Doris having to stop models from eating and thereby gaining weight, the only solution to the lack of models is of course to have Doris wear every single outfit herself, from pink coat and black ruffled minidress to powder blue maxicoat and white formal gown. This nonstop couture version of the Summer Olympics is all presented to orchestral music culled from Doris Day recordings such as "What Every Girl Should Know," "Pillow Talk," and "The Best Christmas Present of All" (a great deal of care went into selecting the music played throughout the show, and the music chosen throughout all five seasons was consistently top-notch). Yes, this fashion parade is silly, but it's also a sure-fire audience pleaser. Doris was known for the terrific clothes featured in her movies, and these slightly surreal fashion show episodes are simply a case of giving the public what it wants.

Occasionally, this feel-good oasis of calm projected by the show actually contained traces of believability. In episode ten, "Togetherness," Doris feels guilty that work is preventing her from seeing enough of her boys, so she plans a weekend full of family activities, a nonstop whirl of picnics and ball games, when all the boys want is to spend the time with their friends. This *is* realistic—it's a reaction common to many children. Similarly realistic is the depiction of Doris Day's extraordinary energy. In this "Togetherness" episode, Doris Martin's relentless activity exhausts her father, her two sons, and even the family dog. In fact, it is this unceasing energy and optimism that Day's critics found not just exhausting but slightly unreal.

Episodes that featured byplay between Day and Denver Pyle played particularly nicely; Day's oft-spoken affection for Denver is palpable onscreen (it is also interesting to note that the onscreen Doris Martin called her father "Buck" as often as "Dad," just as Day's son Terry referred to her as "Doris" more often than "Mom"). In episode twelve, "You're as Old as You Feel," Doris consoles her father, who has begun to feel old and as a result has begun acting like an old man. Doris's brisk solution: "You're only old if you think old." Aging parents, fashion show disasters, workplace conflicts—you name it and Doris can solve it.

The best of these season-two episodes—actually, the operative word is "nicest"—is in many ways the simplest: "A Two Family Christmas." In this installment, the magazine's second-in-command, the woman-chasing Ron Harvey (Paul Smith), and the man-crazy Myrna (who "favors" us with an endless and markedly subpar Jimmy Durante imitation) have too much to drink at the office Christmas party. That's no problem for Doris—she invites them to the ranch for a real family Christmas. Yes, it's a cliché—lonely urbanites learn the true meaning of Christmas from "real," i.e., country, folk—but damn if it doesn't work here, and it works solely because of Doris Day. Near the climax of the episode, all seven actors onscreen gather around the piano to sing. Doris, the only singer in the bunch, not only sounds great but also lovingly holds her onscreen son, young Tod Starke, while singing. It's a doubly interesting moment, because Doris Day and Doris Martin have blended into one here, a fact that is highlighted when Doris Day addresses the camera directly to "wish everyone happiness, peace, and much, much love. Merry Christmas, everyone." This works because just as Doris Day sings directly to listeners, she here speaks directly to them, making them feel that she is addressing each of them individually. She is truly sincere and utterly without guile or irony, because these are heartfelt wishes. You can't fake this sincerity—the camera would pick it up instantly—

and it's a big reason why she remained a star of the highest rank for thirty years.

Throughout the five-season run of the show, old friends of Day's would turn up in various guest-starring roles. There is a two-part second-season episode starring Day's childhood movie star idol, Lew Ayres, in which Ayres plays William Tyler, a Howard Hughes–type millionaire who lives like a vagrant. Doris, thinking he is a down-on-his-luck vagabond, arranges a job for him, a turn of events that lays the groundwork for a two-part episode in season three in which Tyler hires Doris as his globe-trotting assistant. Even more notably, when Colonel Fairburn, the owner of *Today's World* magazine, shows up at Doris's house, he is played by Edward Andrews of *Send Me No Flowers* (Rock Hudson's doctor) and *The Thrill of It All* (the father-to-be).

Andrews, in fact, returned for the final two episodes of season two. In the first he hired prissy, overbearing Billy DeWolfe as an efficiency expert charged with overhauling the office. In the second season's final episode, the colonel develops a crush on Doris and wants her to work as his secretary. There is no sign of Buck or the boys in either episode, as those characters became increasingly marginalized. Instead, Doris gently shows the colonel that he is acting like an old fool. This is all standard sitcom nonsense, but Day makes it work. She quietly turns down a gift from the colonel; it's a serious speech, but Day undercuts any tendency toward bathos by settling in for this serious talk only to discover that she is sitting on . . . a golf ball. It's a tension breaker—a recognizably human moment—and helps the audience accept Day's denial of her boss. Day calibrates this standard sitcom speech beautifully, complete with pauses, hesitations, and earnestness, but none of the thought or effort shows. It's all blended together for maximum believability, no easy feat in a sitcom. Colonel Fairburn is a cartoonish buffoon, but Doris treats him with courtesy and dignity; she herself is never a cartoonish figure, and as a result of her unceasing warmth and sincerity, the audience accepts her and cares about her.

The most noteworthy appearance by one of Day's feature film costars was that of Billy DeWolfe, who went on to become a series regular during seasons three and four. In "Doris Versus the Computer," directed by Denver Pyle (Pyle directed ten episodes throughout the run of the show), as well as in "The Office Trouble Shooter," DeWolfe turns up as efficiency expert Mr. Jarvis. Jarvis insists that Doris Martin has never paid her electricity bill, a computer-generated error that leads to chaos for all involved. This particular rant against computers was old news even in 1970, but it doesn't matter; Day and DeWolfe still play off of each other with great timing and affection. One does have to suffer through idiotic nonsense featuring hippies who join Doris in picketing the electric company, but at the same time there is compensation in the form of further evidence of the great byplay Day enjoyed with her two "sons" even in their increasingly infrequent appearances. When Doris has a headache and needs to lie down, young Toby stands right next to her, and in an ear-shattering caterwaul bellows upstairs to his brother, "Don't yell, Mom has a headache." It's the way children really do act with their parents and siblings, and provides a chuckle of recognition that more than makes up for the buffoonery of the cartoonish hippies.

In a dizzying change of pace, goofy farmhand LeRoy B. Simpson turns up for the first time all season, seventeen weeks into the run. Where does he turn up? Running a gas station. There's no mention of his previous life on Doris's farm, but all of a sudden his wife is giving birth so Doris and Myrna have to take over the gas station while LeRoy goes to the hospital. There's some gibberish with a convict who pulls a gun on Doris, but that's no problem for our executive secretary/mom turned gas station mechanic. She just yells at him about her bad day, and this wanted criminal is taken care of one-two-three. No, the interest here lies in watching Doris in action at the gas station. She changes from her color-coordinated shorts and kneesocks into overalls and she's off and running: changing oil, sliding underneath trucks, wrestling with tires—nothing fazes her. Now picture her fellow movie queens from the early seventies undertaking these tasks: Elizabeth Taylor? Audrey Hepburn? Barbra Streisand? No one else could do this. And certainly they couldn't undertake the feat in a grease monkey's coveralls and accessorize it with a hair ribbon. Tough, practical, and utterly feminine. Pretty good combination, and pretty symbolic of a lot of harried overscheduled moms.

As the season wound down, Juanita disappeared from even the credits—maybe not such a bad thing for her because boy, oh boy did these 1970 episodes contain some slapstick stinkers. For every truly funny episode there were episodes so illogical, so preposterous and silly, that it's a wonder Day could even muster the energy to say the lines. An exaggerated criticism? Just think about the installment where Doris is taken hostage by a mobster who makes his entrance via a painting scaffold outside the window, complete with stereotypical gangster clothes straight out of *Guys and Dolls*. Poor Kaye Ballard is on hand as the mobster's wife, portraying a woman who is so browbeaten that when he hits her out of anger, the action is played for laughs. This manages the neat trick of being simultaneously stupid and offensive.

Season Two of *The Doris Day Show,* episode entitled "The Gas Station." Doris Martin (Day) and comic sidekick Myrna Gibbons (Rose Marie) run the garage *and* manage to thwart a crook. All in twenty-two minutes, plus commercials. *Photofest*

When Doris refuses to cooperate in writing the mobster's memoirs, she yells at him and tells Kaye to stand up for herself. Doris acts like a marriage counselor for Mr. and Mrs. Mobster, then tries to escape and ends the episode by watching as Myrna arrives on the scene dressed as a French hooker. . . .

It's a tribute to Day's appeal that her fans stuck with her through this thoroughly unfunny mess, because it wasn't the only episode that struck such discordant notes. What were viewers to make of "A Woman's Intuition," wherein Doris's intuition tells her not to travel on a certain flight to Florida; taking an alternative, low-budget flight instead, she lectures her scared seatmate on the power of positive thinking in order to conquer his fear of flying (ironic in light of Day's own well-publicized fear of flying). What does the scared passenger do? He hijacks the plane to Cuba, of course, where the Cuban general in charge is played by that well-known Latino actor Bernie

Kopell of *Love Boat* fame. . . . This is an episode of such overwhelming dumbness that it manages to insult everyone in sight, almost arousing sympathy for Castro's military leaders.

Even "Doris Meets a Prince" is an improvement on this silliness and is vaguely amusing in the can-you-believe-this-nonsense? manner with which one views her earliest Warner Bros. musicals. The prince in question falls for Doris—of course he does, who wouldn't? What does Doris do to seal the deal? She invites the prince home for dinner, serves beef stew and cold beer (with "Summer Has Gone" from *Latin for Lovers* playing in the background), and he promptly proposes to her. This is fantasy time, but Doris is exactly the gal for this kind of American-style Cinderella nonsense. It's only in the plot's denouement that one fully bursts out laughing unintentionally; it turns out that Doris doesn't have to decide whether she wants to become a princess, because there has been a revolution at home. The prince is deposed, so there's only thing for him to do—you've got it—he opens a restaurant at a location Doris recommends. All ends happily as the accordion player in the background serenades the patrons with "Que Sera, Sera." Either the prince has a thing for accordions, or he's a Hitchcock fan. Either way, for this particular prince, running a country is out and slinging hash is in.

Maybe Denver Pyle and the boys disappeared whenever it was Pyle's turn to direct, but unfortunately Pyle did function as director of two episodes featuring Larry Storch as Duke the Boxer, episodes that rank right up there—or down there—with the Kaye Ballard mob episode as the nadir of the series. Somehow or other, the writers thought it would be funny to have Doris land an exclusive interview with prizefighter Duke on the eve of his big fight. Doris doesn't know much about boxing, but it turns out title contender Duke only wants to dance—that's right, dance—in the deserted mining town where he's training. Doris eventually has to be helicoptered to Duke's title bout midfight (shades of her inspiring Ronald Reagan at the climactic World Series game in *The Winning Team*), and for all her troubles, Duke still gets knocked out. Not a believable line or situation in the entire episode, so what do the producers do? Bring back Duke for a second episode where he opens his own dance studio. It's an equally ridiculous setup but possesses one advantage over Duke's first episode. Doris fills in as a guest dance instructor and the audience, grateful for any musical display by Doris, watches with bemusement as the still sexy Doris demonstrates the fox-trot and cha-cha with a series of increasingly out-of-shape and uninspired partners. Somehow, through a combination of facial expressions, slow burns, and stammered responses to outrageous requests, Doris Day not only injects a note of believability into these ridiculous situations but even makes the audience root for her.

Forget the mobsters, forget the boxers—better just to concentrate on the single best episode of the second season, in fact, the best episode of the entire first two seasons and one cited by Day herself as a personal favorite. In "Doris Strikes Out," Day blends her career gal and ideal mother personae while simultaneously mixing her love of the outdoors with her comic affinity for urban settings. The end result is genuinely funny television. The plot setup has grandfather Buck hurting his back and therefore unable to umpire the boys' ball game. He volunteers Doris to take his place, even though she has a date with a French movie star for the premiere of his latest movie spectacular (hey, it's a sitcom . . .). Momentarily nonplussed, Doris does what comes naturally. Leaping into action, she bounds up the stairs two at a time and changes into her umpiring gear—surely the world's first umpire to sport a pink jersey. Fearing the game will run too long and cause her to miss her date, Doris Martin begins to umpire in her own idiosyncratic fashion, and genuine hilarity ensues. To speed up the game she calls strikes even when the pitch hits her own son, and at one point she calls a strike even before the pitcher has let go of the ball. This is one ump who actually runs the bases herself, in point of fact running the bases faster than do the players! All of the baseball high jinks are executed with superb comic timing until the game ends, whereupon Doris rushes back to the house, changes, and arrives at the premiere looking glamorous. The capper to this full-out comic display is delivered in nicely understated fashion: Exhausted from the baseball game, Doris falls asleep during her date's own film. Only Doris Day could have believably managed such a quick transformation from baseball umpire to glamour girl, and if that French movie star has any sense he'll forget that she fell asleep during his film (besides, the movie looks like a stinkeroo). This woman is worth keeping around, whatever the terms.

In overall terms, the quality of season two varied wildly as the producers and Day herself struggled to free her from the confines of the farm and set her loose in the big city. It's a half-and-half enterprise; the effort shows in the dopey plots, but they're edging forward here because they all realize something key—Doris Day is a self-proclaimed outdoors woman, a lover of nature, animals, and the early morning hours, but in her work, she shines brightest in an urban setting, strutting her stuff as a successful go-getter who can hold her own—and then some—with any man who crosses her path.

This disparity in Day's persona becomes particularly clear when seasons one and two are viewed back to back on DVD reissue. Unfortunately, Doris herself sheds no light on this disparity because just as happened when the DVDs of her feature films were issued, she did not participate in any way with the DVD release of the first three seasons of her series. There are no funny stories, no running commentary, no nothing. From the perspective of today, Day's nonparticipation in the release of the DVDs confirms what one has always suspected: It's all in the past and can stay there, as far as she's concerned. It was a great time, but her interest is in what lies ahead. Day's absence is a large gap; the reclusive star—or is that the reluctant star?—could shed valuable light not only on the work process but also on how her persona influenced the changes in locale and character. As consolation, there are still plenty of fascinating commentaries from her coworkers on the television series, starting with some rather incisive analysis from James Hampton.

Hampton, who played genial goofball LeRoy B. Simpson, pinpoints Day's recognition of the wholesome image she was bringing into America's living rooms every week: "She was very aware of who she was and what she was doing all the time—she was aware of the impact that made." The most unexpected commentary comes from Larry Storch, who played Duke the boxer in the aforementioned two episodes from season two. He starts out by stating, "I had to bunk next to Al Jorden, Doris's first husband, in the service. When Doris and I first met on the show, I mentioned it to Doris who was not pleased to even hear his name." Of course in those days before Day published her revealing autobiography about the marriage, Storch had no way of knowing what a sore point he was raising. Clearly, and understandably, those wounds still festered. Yet Day and Storch overcame this first hurdle and he was invited back to guest-star on further episodes. Storch, who went on to television fame with *F Troop,* states, "She was a great vocalist and did wonderful dramatic work on screen. She was a very warm personality."

Clearly the atmosphere on the set was important to Day. This was not a star who engendered tension and confrontation—no Streisand she. Just as Day brought donuts and pastries to her recording sessions—this at the height of her recording stardom—she took pains to ensure a pleasant atmosphere on set for the television series. Speaking on the DVD reissue of the series in her gravelly New York–accented voice, series costar Rose Marie states simply, "When you walked on the set, it was such a warm feeling—like 'Hey, it's great to be here.' We never had an argument, no one was tempermental." This is not a case of canned encomiums at an awards dinner—Rose Marie clearly liked Doris Day very much. "It was just wonderful. She has a wonderful sense of humor and a great smile. She's a beautiful woman, a good actress, a clear woman who loves animals and enjoys her life. I love her very much. I think the world of her." Philip Brown, who played Billy, echoes: "Going to work every day with Doris Day was probably one of the greatest experiences of my life. . . . Denver and Doris taught us a lot—how to listen, how to behave. . . . Working with Doris Day—she was like my second mother. I really enjoyed going to the set every day just to see her and be around her. It felt so good just to talk to her. She was very present for Tod and I and gave us a lot of motherly advice."

So warm and sunshiny is Day's persona that when looking at the bloopers that complete the second-season DVD release of the show, it's almost a surprise to hear her exclaim, "Damn!" after every missed shot or take. Which makes it a near shock to read Doris's January 1976 *Ms.* Magazine interview with Molly Haskell, in which Doris states: "I don't go to movies very much. I don't want to see junk. . . . But to come out thinking it's a shitty world . . ." Other stars are more than casual with their use of profanity, but Doris Day?! That's how strong her good-girl image remains even today—well as Doris herself would say, there's that word again: "image." It's always about the image. Maybe "damn" was a strong exclamation for the sunny star, or it may simply have been a necessary release valve for her, because as genuinely fond of Day as her costars were, there was no question about who called the shots on the show; it was, after all, *The Doris Day Show*. The success rose and fell with her acting, persona, and reputation, and the pressure fell squarely on her shoulders. So it was that in the midst of the audio promos for the show, when she yells out, "Quiet, folks!" the ensuing silence is immediate and complete.

The DVD extras also contain an interesting audio clip that serves as a brief master class in comedic acting as Day attempts to fit her audio promo into five and a half seconds. Trying different inflections, deleting words, inserting pauses at various places in order to emphasize different beats, she repeats the same words again and again until she has nailed the promo to the precise half second and imparted the desired meaning. She may not have wanted to undertake this series, but there was a 1,000 percent commitment once the job had begun.

This intense commitment ensured that Day herself would sign off on all of the format and script changes that continued to flow at a dizzying pace. Just as the start of season two brought a change in locale from rural to urban, the beginning of season three brought about a marked shift in the characters deemed central to the series. Broadcast from 1970 to 1971, the third season jettisoned the ranch setting entirely (as well as father Buck). Instead, Doris and sons Billy and Toby moved into a San Francisco apartment located above Pallucci's Restaurant. Mr. and Mrs. Pallucci (Kaye Ballard and the remarkably nonethnic Bernie Kopell) were on hand to provide comic relief, as were Billy DeWolfe as Mr. Jarvis, Rose Marie as Myrna Gibbons, and McLean Stevenson as Mr. Nicholson. Airing at 9:30 P.M. on Monday nights, the show placed twentieth for the entire season, an indication that it was maintaining its footing.

In many ways, the opening credits, which were revamped yet again, prefigured those for the soon to air *Sonny and Cher Show,* where Cher paraded in one wild outfit after another. It is these third-season opening credits that viewers most strongly recall today: Doris briskly walks down the spiral staircase in her new city apartment as the camera explodes in six quick close-ups of her face, all set to the tune of the inevitable "Que Sera, Sera." It's a great opening, promising innovation and style. If the series didn't always deliver on those counts, it proved popular with viewers and provided a strong lead-in for *The Carol Burnett Show* that followed at 10 P.M.

The third season threw into bold relief exactly what was right and wrong with the series: The enormously appealing Doris Day went into battle each week with plots of extraordinary silliness, and in a good week wrestled the silliness to the ground, her star power overcoming every objection any rational adult would have to such balderdash. In a bad week, the viewer's reaction remained one of noncomprehension: How could Doris Day even attempt to act this nonsense? Couldn't anyone dream up a halfway realistic plotline? And how come one of the great singers of all time rarely sings?

The format change ostensibly held that father Buck was back on the ranch in Cotina, but in reality, Denver Pyle was on the set of the show as a frequent director. In fact, Pyle directed the first four episodes of season three and proved to be a smooth and professional, if rarely inspired, director. Then again, how could he be inspired when dealing with plots such as the third-season opener: Doris moves into the apartment over Pallucci's Restaurant but loses her lease when she throws a party to celebrate the move. How is the lease restored? Toby and Billy tell Mr. Pallucci that he makes the best pizza in town. Problem solved. Who knew that the hot real estate market in San Francisco could be negotiated with ease as long as the owner is complimented on his pizza-making abilities?

In episode three, "How Can I Ignore the Man Next Door," Billy DeWolfe joins the cast as a series regular, reprising his role as Mr. Jarvis and moving in next door to Doris. He visits Doris's apartment, throws out his back, and gets caught in the bed when Doris tries to fix it. These silly shenanigans are accompanied by much clowning from the talented and fussy DeWolfe. How could Pyle—or Doris—bring anything fresh to such stale proceedings? As it was, it appeared that while directing these episodes, Pyle yelled "Action!" and then stood out of the way, because DeWolfe was off and running on his own idiosyncratic path. This was not a performer given to understatement.

Yet even here there were instances of genuine wit, especially when centered on the series's running gag regarding Mr. Jarvis's dislike of Doris Day. When Doris Martin has Jarvis's television set fixed, Jarvis switches the set on, only to have Doris Day herself appear onscreen (the footage is from the season-one episode "The Fly Boy"). Upon seeing her onscreen, Mr. Jarvis snidely remarks, "Can't stand that woman!" whereupon the television set blows up. This is insider humor, but it is executed with great style—tongue-in-cheek, the star is poking fun at herself and in a much more humorous fashion than Tashlin's similar commentary in the motion picture *Caprice.*

Day's inclusion of Billy DeWolfe as a series regular, relatively close to the end of his life, provides an interesting sidelight into her persona. By all accounts Day is an enormously loyal friend, and she here went out of her way to include longtime friend DeWolfe in the show, just as she utilized Mary Wickes, Edward Andrews, and Lew Ayres. In the case of DeWolfe, it's also instructive of Day's relationship with gay men. Yes, Day has a substantial gay following, as do all larger-than-life female movie stars, especially those from the golden age of Hollywood. Just as proved to be the case with Rock Hudson, the affection between Day and DeWolfe is authentic. In those far-off days of the '40s through '70s when nearly all gay men stayed in the closet out of fear of rejection and ruined careers, Doris exuded a warmth and generosity of spirit that made gay men clearly feel very comfortable with her. She was totally nonjudgmental, indeed, almost maternal in her approach. These men were her friends—end of story. When Rock Hudson was near death from AIDS, he made his last public appearance on *Doris Day's Best Friends;* he may have wanted to prove that he could still appear in public, but he also appeared on the show because of his love for Day, a love that is apparent in their three films together and in that very poignant episode. After Hudson's death, Day stated simply, "People would ask me 'Is Rock Hudson really gay?' And I'd say 'It's something I will not discuss.' First of all, I know nothing about his private life, and if I did I wouldn't discuss it."

Billy DeWolfe's Mr. Jarvis was not the only character to return for further episodes. Fashion designer Montagne returned, which afforded another opportunity for Doris's fans to watch her change clothes at the seeming rate of one new outfit for each line of dialogue. The climax of this season's fashion episodes? The finale dress for Montagne's fashion show is stolen, but he turns this loss into a triumph by fashioning a replacement dress from a garment bag. . . . Needless to say, this all bore no relation to reality, but then again, neither did the very next episode, "Lost and Found," where Doris auditions as a go-go dancer (!) Why the audition? Suffice it to say that Myrna left a news article at the go-go club and together the women locate the article in a Dumpster. From there it's just a hop, skip, and a jump to Doris's go-go audition under the stage name "Peanut Brittle" . . . There is even another return of the singularly unfunny boxer Duke (Larry Storch), who this time around becomes a nightclub performer. Doris rehearses a song and dance routine with him—which affords the audience to see she's as great as ever—and then fakes laryngitis so that Duke can make a real success on his own. The problem is that, nice little message or not, what the audience wants is to see Doris Day singing songs in a nightclub, not Larry Storch.

There are, however, celebrity guest turns along the way that provide some viewer interest. Tony Bennett, playing himself, dines at Pallucci's Restaurant at Doris's suggestion but is besieged by fans. At episode's end Bennett delivers a sensational rendition of "I Left My Heart in San Francisco" with Doris providing beautiful harmony for the latter part of the song. There's even a witty coda when Angie (Kaye Ballard) gushes over Bennett's singing and in deadpan fashion ends the episode saying "And you're not so bad either Doris!" MGM golden age star Van Johnson drops by as Doris's drifter cousin Charlie, but the pros and cons of these "celebrity sweepstakes" episodes are really best summed up in the two-part episode "Doris Leaves Today's World," in which Lew Ayres returns as the Howard Hughes–like William Tyler.

These episodes find Tyler offering Doris a high-paying job as his personal secretary, an offer she accepts after Mr. Nicholson's proffered raise tops out at a mere $10 a week. Doris must now live at Mr. Tyler's globetrotting beck and call, a way of life that necessitates her constantly leaving sons Billy and Toby with father Buck. First stop for our globetrotting gal is Japan, where she appears in a kimono and geishalike hairdo, complete with flowers and crystals. Next stops on this jet-setting tour of the world? Switzerland and then Africa, where Doris sports a lavender safari suit and pith helmet. It's a very strange sight, as if Bob Mackie dropped in to dash off a little sportswear. Doris then misses a ball game with her boys—her sense of guilt is mounting. When Billy plaintively states, "I guess your job is more important than we are," the viewer knows where this one is heading, and it isn't to have Doris sign on for another three years with Mr. Tyler. Young Toby disappears after buying an airline ticket to visit his mother, and after he is found safe and sound, she decides to quit her new job. In order to see her boys more often, she will stay put in San Francisco and still work at *Today's World.* Order is restored to the universe. But . . .

It's not that this job versus family dilemma is irrelevant—far from it. It's as pertinent an issue today as it was in 1970. It's just that any inclination to take the episodes seriously is undercut by the cartoonlike nature of the proceedings. Since when does an executive secretary dress up as a geisha and then in the blink of an eye pop up in Africa sporting a designer safari outfit? When the heck does she ever get any work done? And yet. There's a qualifier to such disdain, because in the middle of all of these shenanigans, Doris Day reminds the viewer why she remained such a compelling figure. Learning that Toby is missing, she is simultaneously distraught but also wracked with guilt, and one actually feels her pain, her naked fear of losing her son. When given a real emotion to play, she remains a remarkably effective actress and one who puts the lie to *Variety*'s season-opening review that "Miss Day is still a one-note (poignancy) actress."

As the season progressed, Denver Pyle returned both as actor—"Buck Visits the Big City"—and again as director—"Doris vs. Pollution." In fact, with the broadcast of these episodes, it had become clear that all episodes of the series could now be fit into one of three categories of plot.

Plot Type Number One: Doris overcomes a seemingly insurmountable object—for instance, air pollution. What chance does pollution have when Doris is on the case? So it goes, in the aptly titled "Doris vs. Pollution," where Doris writes an article citing the air pollution emanating from a chemical plant that Colonel Fairburn owns. In quick order, the colonel's fish begin dying from the pollution, Doris's story runs, and changes are made at the plant. It's very easy: Doris writes an article, and an entire industry changes. Imagine the reaction if she sang about the problem.

Plot Type Number Two: Episodes revolve around nonsensical incidents that exist only in the minds of desperate sitcom writers. Take, for instance, "The Forward Pass," in which Doris pursues an interview with famous quarterback Joe Garrison (Dick Gautier). Doesn't matter what sport it is—boxing with Duke or football with Joe—Doris gets her interview. Joe Garrison chases Doris around his apartment and in the process breaks his leg. This is not exactly recognizable behavior—since when does a star quarterback run around his apartment chasing a somewhat older woman right before a big game? Of course this episode is positively Shakespearean compared to "Lassoin' LeRoy," where LeRoy B. Simpson returns and wins $20,000 at a rodeo. When LeRoy begins to spend his money carelessly, Doris simply takes the money and hides it in her broken toaster. Right. Toby and Billy of course give the toaster away to a library fund drive. This kind of silliness was tired even in the days of D. W. Griffith, and the only noteworthy aspect of the episode is that Winifred Coffin plays a character named Clara Bixby, one of the offscreen nicknames Doris Day's friends have given her.

Plot Type Number Three: A slapstick episode in which Doris displays her athleticism and clowning abilities. To wit: In a plot straight out of *I Love Lucy,* Doris Martin wins a Doris Day lookalike contest, the prize being a trip to a film studio. When she visits the studio, Doris Martin is mistaken for the real Doris Day, a mistake made by none other than guest star Henry Fonda. Doris Martin, a huge fan of Fonda's, tries to watch him at work but succeeds only in falling into a water tank. It is at this point, of course, that Doris Day comes by to meet the winner of the lookalike contest and is met by a very drenched Doris Martin. This is all very silly and highly reminiscent of Lucy Ricardo's relentless attempts to spend time with Hollywood stars (most notably an episode with William Holden, where she sets her false nose on fire), but it is also great fun. For one thing, Doris Day plays herself with much more humor than she did in the movie *Starlift.* For another, Doris Day is a great physical clown. She throws herself into the scenes requiring physicality with total abandon. She doesn't gingerly fall into the water, she dunks herself. It's great to see this impeccably attired star let herself look a mess and appear to have fun doing so. There is no pretense at reality or a real-life lesson here, just a silly farce executed with style by some very talented actors.

Even better is "Skiing Anyone?," an episode centering around Doris and Myrna's weekend skiing trip. Yes, there's silliness to sit through when Myrna sprains her ankle while still in the lodge, with Doris, of course, dating the handsome doctor (John Gavin) who takes care of Myrna. However, the set-up of the episode is terrific, featuring physical clowning by Doris and Rose Marie that rises to Lucy-Ethel levels of giddiness. Specifically, Myrna starts the ball rolling by insisting to Doris that they try on their skis while still in the office. Gamely playing along, Doris is, of course, at this point buzzed by Mr. Nicholson to instantly come into his office. Failing miserably at getting out of their ski boots, Doris and Myrna then try to walk in their very long skis, with

Myrna tangled up as she fails to unbuckle the boots, and Doris falling over as she tries to answer the phone. As Mr. Nicholson buzzes Doris frantically, she finally has to enter his office while still on skis, desperately trying to act as if nothing is out of the ordinary. It's a classic slapstick moment, and welcome proof that given a funny idea, Doris Day and Rose Marie could rise to heights of inspired lunacy.

This third type of plot incident also figured in the season's penultimate episode, "The Father-Son Weekend." Grandpa Buck can't bring Toby on a father-son camping trip, so Doris takes his place. It's a variation on the season-one episode where Doris replaced Buck as the umpire in Billy's Little League game. Here she takes over for Buck, and together mother and son win races, a fishing competition, and of course the overall father-son trophy. Day is so inherently athletic that winning the competitions actually makes sense; after all, as a little girl, Doris was so determined to win free lessons at Hessler's Dance Studio in Cincinnati that she won the contest to stand on her hands longer than anyone else by literally walking on her hands for weeks on end. Net result? Twenty-five free dance lessons. With a will like that, maybe she should have trained for the decathlon. Misplaced athletic career or not, it's a total kick for an audience to watch a middle-aged woman this athletic in action, a woman who is still never less than completely feminine. She is always Toby's mom, but if she occasionally has to be his dad as well, she can also manage that with total grace. Hell, in episodes like these, she's not just America's idealized mom—she's America's idealized parent.

All of these disparate strands come together in the season-three Christmas episode, "It's Christmas Time in the City," where Doris invites Mr. Jarvis to attend her Christmas party. Mr. Jarvis not only declines the invitation but also threatens to call the police if there is too much noise. The party starts, but when Mr. Jarvis hears Christmas carols emanating from the party, he asks Doris if he can in fact join the party. Yes, this is all predictable, and after exactly one minute of airtime, even recent non-English-speaking immigrants would know where this plot was heading. But somehow Doris Day makes it all work. She is such a welcoming, warm presence that her Christmas party in the city seems like the ideal place to spend the holiday, just as her second-season Christmas in the country made that seem like the best way to celebrate Christmas. *The Doris Day Show* Christmas episodes are like a small-screen version of *It's a Wonderful Life*—okay, minus all of the dark overtones, questions of mortality, and complex texture that make the Capra film one of the all-time great movies, in other words, minus all of the true substance . . . but nonetheless, Doris Day makes you root for her, just as

Jimmy Stewart did. This audience identification is what makes Stewart's and Day's occasional ventures into darker characters—very occasional ventures in Day's case—so fascinating. Day and Stewart are both Stars, actors who are far more complex than the casual viewer realizes, and they both possess "it." In spades. As Katharine Hepburn once said, "Whatever *it* is, I've got it." So does Doris Day.

In the midst of the five-season run of the television series, the first of Day's variety specials was aired on CBS. (The deal Marty Melcher signed with CBS for *The Doris Day Show* also called for her to make two television films. This contractual obligation was later changed to two variety specials, 1971's *The Doris Mary Anne Kappelhoff Special* and 1975's *Doris day toDay.*) In their own ways, both point up everything right and wrong with variety specials of the day, but they are invaluable for one simple reason: After Day's recording contract with Columbia Records expired, they remain the only extant example of Day's singing from 1967 onward. Yes, there are snippets of a few songs during the five years of the series, but these specials function as the only sustained filmed record of Doris Day's musical ability after the release of *Jumbo* in 1962. The quality of the specials varies all over the joint, but Day sounds, in a word, sensational.

Taped in 1970 and broadcast in 1971 between seasons three and four of *The Doris Day Show, The Doris Mary Anne Kappelhoff Special* is a pleasant television variety special of a type that no longer exists today; it's an innocuous hour but also proves frustrating in the extreme because it could have and should have been much better. If there are no major missteps in the hour, which was executive-produced by Don Genson and Terry Melcher—and fortunately there are no painful skits such as those that marred 1975's *Doris day toDay*—it is also true that the special proves to be truly inspired only in the closing solo concert sequence. Then again, that segment is so good that it makes the entire hour worthwhile. Genson himself sums it up best in the commentary he recorded for the DVD release of the special: "Doris was a honey—you had to love Doris. . . . She just had talent coming out of every pore of her body."

The special opens with an extended sequence of Doris riding a bicycle while she sings "Secret Love" in voice-over; it's a new recording of her all-time classic, featuring a slightly remodeled arrangement in what seems to be a lower key. Not having sung professionally in years, Day "chose to retrain her voice to ensure a professional delivery" and the result is utterly winning. "Secret Love" segues into "Who Will Buy," from the Broadway musical *Oliver,* followed by "Feelin' Groovy" and the Beatles' "Ob-la Di, Ob-la-da."

Third season Christmas show episode of *The Doris Day Show.* With her television children, Toby (Tod Starke, left) and Billy (Philip Brown). *Photofest*

It was son Terry who influenced Doris's selection of these new songs by Simon and Garfunkle and the Beatles, and Day actually sounds relaxed singing the songs. The problem with the segment is simply that it goes on for too long; it makes sense to see Doris Day riding a bicycle and leading a pack of school children on an expedition through suburban streets, but by the time that the vehicle motif morphs into silly speeded-up footage of Doris riding in Busby Berkeley formation with mororcycle cops, in an ugly barren parking lot (was CBS really stinting on the budget?), the viewer's interest starts to wane.

After this opening sequence, the rest of the special takes place on an enormous soundstage garden set, with Doris opening up the proceedings by singing "Hurry It's Lovely Up Here" to time-lapse close-ups of the flowers blooming. It's a nice touch (the song is from the Broadway musical *On a Clear Day You Can See Forever,* which employed the same plot device) and is followed by Doris's introduction of her first guests: her six dogs, to whom she sings "You Must Have Been a Beautiful Baby (Puppy)." It's actually a nice number, neither cloying nor overly sentimental, and serves to further establish the viewing audience's sense that they are seeing the real Doris Day. Fifteen minutes into the special, the viewer has seen Doris riding a bike, singing upbeat sunshiny songs, and playing with her dogs. In other words, viewers have seen the real Doris Day.

Doris's major guest for the special, Perry Como, next ambles onto the set, and sings the then very popular "Didn't We" in his typically understated manner. Como sounds great, and to call him relaxed is actually an understatement—by this stage of his career, he was murmuring more than singing, but with the camera and microphone close-ups, it all works nicely.

Next up is the obligatory fashion show sequence, with Doris offering a voice-over commentary about the outfits. It's always a kick to watch Doris parade around in these sometimes wacky fashions, but Day communicates a real sense of joy in modeling the clothes, and the segment is most noteworthy for the two production numbers that are interpolated into the runway proceedings: Doris performs a Fosse-like "Gypsy in My Soul" with two male dancers, and then a 1920s-style Charleston to "Them Was the Good Old Days." Forty-six years old at the time of filming, Doris Day looks great, with her still-sensational figure and an amazingly fluid dance style. It's downright remarkable to think that she hadn't undertaken any full-out production numbers in the eight preceding years since 1962's *Jumbo*.

The special then focuses on Day's interaction with guest star Como as they duet on "Everybody Loves a Lover" as part of a medley that flows into "Meditation" and "Quiet Nights," from Day's *Latin for Lovers* album. There is a funny moment of Perry beginning to sing a sweeping version of the Gershwins' "Summertime," which Doris interrupts with a raucous country-styled version of "In the Summertime." The two stars then sing a pensive medley of "If I Had to Live My Life Over" and "Let Me Call You Sweetheart," a song blend featured on Day's then yet to be released *Love Album*. These two great singers blend their silken voices very well together, but the medley is most interesting to view as a way to note the differences in the two on camera. Doris Day is such a winning personality that she naturally exudes warmth and sincerity; when she sings with Como, she fixes him with a gaze of such intensity, forging an extraordinary connection, that an audience member paying close attention can actually feel a slightly erotic charge. Conversely, Como takes a very different tactic, with a cool, slightly distanced style that finds him looking out to the camera and audience more than he does at Doris. They are two great stars, but this is a very clear illustration of why Doris Day became an enormous movie star and Perry Como didn't.

Day then begins to sing "You Oughta Be in Pictures" as an introduction to a solo segment in which she discusses her career-long habit of crying on film. And she's right—this woman did seem to cry in most of her films, whether it was over the nearly dead Frank Sinatra in *Young at Heart,* the villainous Rex Harrison in *Midnight Lace,* or the duplicitous Rock Hudson in *Pillow Talk*. (In fact, the only thing Doris seemed to do more often on film than cry was eat.) The real point of this humorous segment is that it affords a chance for special guest star, Rock Hudson, to drop by; even in this very brief interaction, it is clear that absolutely none of their rapport has been lost. These two movie icons just plain like each other. (As the outtakes on the DVD release of the special show, this segment originally contained what now registers as a true lost opportunity; unfortunately, the decision was made to cut a charming monologue wherein Day discussed the origin of her professional name, the star opining that the name Doris Day makes it sound as if she should be performing at the Pink Pussycat nightclub, complete with trained doves. In addition, this sequence also contained a fun anecdote about Doris's start in the movies with director/mentor Michael Curtiz, and his ongoing battle to have Doris stop eating! These segments are so much fun, giving the viewer a sense of the personable, fun, "real" Doris Day, that it's a shame they were cut from the finished hour.)

The hour then ends with what the entire special really should have been: Doris Day in concert. Singing solo, no gimmicks, just Doris alone on the soundstage set, she essays Joni Mitchell's "Both Sides Now" and follows up with new versions of "It's Magic" and "Sentimental Journey." Doris Day and Joni Mitchell may not seem like a natural pairing, but Day's vocal is first rate; she is here of an age that allows her to truly understand Mitchell's contemplative lyric chronicling life's complications and complexity (it also leads one to wonder how Mitchell understood that journey so well at such a young age). Good as that vocal is, however, it pales compared to the next two songs. The nearly fifty-year-old Day here sings "It's Magic" with a more wondering, grateful acknowledgment that she has found love than she ever could have managed as a twenty-four year old in *Romance on the High Seas*. The vocal is accompanied by a very nice mid-song jump cut for a change of outfits, with Day finishing the song in a white, silver-spangled pant suit, the only light color on the darkened set. This visual enhancement only adds to the song's effectiveness, and yet, great as the song is, it is topped by Day's special, closing rendition of her signature song "Sentimental Journey." Doris Day's singing of her anthem, of the World War II generation's anthem, is quite simply as good as anything she did in her entire career. She acts the hell out of the song, investing it with varying degrees of pathos, wistfulness, and eroticism. It's a brand-new arrangement with a near country flavor to the driving horns, and watching Day light into this song alone in the spotlight gives one a real sense of how sensational she would have been as a solo concert performer. This is acting and singing of the highest order, and the equal of anything ever delivered by Judy Garland or Barbra Streisand. If only the entire special had been of this caliber, the hour would have rated as an all-time television classic. But it's a pleasant hour, heightened by the electricity of the solo concert at the end, and serves as a very welcome reminder of why Doris Mary Anne Kappelhoff became one of the biggest stars in Hollywood history.

When *The Doris Day Show* returned to the air in September 1971 for its fourth season, it featured yet another format change, the most radical one of all. Doris Martin had now become associate editor at *Today's World,* and the viewer's reaction can only be, "Well, it's about time." Not only did she always project a total competence that should have already landed her higher on the corporate ladder, but additionally, a great many of the series's plots variously showed Doris the secretary landing the key interview, soothing royalty, saving the magazine, and generally winning the day. She was smarter than her bosses, so why the hell wasn't she an executive?

Summer break sure was busy around *Today's World* magazine, because in the blink of an eye, Mr. Nicholson and Myrna had disappeared, and Doris had a brand-new boss in the person of city editor Cy Bennett (John Dehner). Evidently Myrna had now joined Aggie, Juanita, LeRoy, Ron Harvey, and Mr. Nicholson in Witness Protection, because she vanished without a trace. The role of comic sidekick was now filled by Jackie Joseph as Jackie Parker, Mr. Bennett's secretary. Even so, the changes at *Today's World* weren't anywhere near as sweeping as those that had taken hold in Doris Martin's personal life. New boyfriend? New life living on a groovy hippie commune? Nope and nope. Faster than you can say "sitcom writers desperately in need of inspiration," Doris Martin had become a single working woman: Billy and Toby were nowhere to be seen, and neither was Buck. No children, no father—they seem never to have existed. This was asking a great deal of loyalty from the viewing audience; it's as if the producers are saying, "Hey, watch our show for three years but forget any interest you may develop in any of the characters—they're history. Doris is no longer anyone's daughter and she's no longer a mother. We've been watching *The Mary Tyler Moore Show*; that's really popular, and since she's a single working woman, Doris will be too."

Working mother or single working woman, one thing did remain constant in this, the world's fastest-changing sitcom: The opening credits continued to be the best part of every week's episode. The season-four credits began with the same twirl down the spiral staircase to the tune of "Que Sera, Sera," complete with jump-cut close-ups of the terrific-looking Day. Even *Variety,* in yet another dismissive season-opening review, admitted that "star Day—looks marvelous" but then went on to state that based on the premiere episode the show "has no place to go but up." Ouch. The opening visuals accompanying the credits had now been tweaked into what amounted to a Doris Day fashion show, featuring multiple outfits in the course of a mere thirty seconds. The credits actually made a curious kind of sense, because this was a sitcom that seemed to feature a different outfit and hairstyle in virtually every sequence of the show. Doris Day was presented as the mature, sexy woman that she was, and her look as a working woman was believable. It's just the plots that weren't.

The fourth season, even with a brand-new premise, seemed to operate at the same very mixed level of inspiration and success as the previous one. It's as if everyone involved were running as hard as they could just to stay in place, because once again, the series alternated genuinely funny episodes with plotlines of amazing stupidity. Even Doris couldn't render these plotlines coherent, leaving one to wonder why she and coproducer/son Terry Melcher didn't insist on some degree of believability in the proceedings. As it was, the plotlines tended once again to fit one of three molds: Doris exposes corruption and saves the day, Doris puts up with a nonsensical premise in order to engage in slapstick silliness, or, in a newly jerry-rigged category, Doris travels to exotic location and finds a new boyfriend.

How silly were these plotlines? Well, with Billy DeWolfe back on board as Mr. Jarvis, the season's second episode, "Mr. and Mrs. Raffles," found Doris and Mr. Jarvis returning stolen jewels to a store after the gems had been planted on Mr. Jarvis. Just so happens that when Doris and Mr. Jarvis are subsequently thrown in jail, they run into the real thieves, who ask them to help out in a robbery. Mr. Jarvis and Doris agree, and when the police arrive to arrest the genuine thieves, Mr. Jarvis and Doris are declared innocent. In a word, awful. It's not just the sight of the police actually believing that Billy DeWolfe is a jewel thief—although that could rate an entry in *Ripley's Believe It or Not.* It's that once again, there isn't one believable line in the entire episode. This was sitcom writing aimed at six-year-olds and as such proved very discouraging to the devoted Doris Day fan.

The next episode, which featured the first of two guest appearances by Cesare Danova as famed artist Carlo Benadetti, did at least possess a clever title, the best of the entire season: "When in Rome, Don't." This managed both to send Doris to Rome with Jackie and also try out a new boyfriend for Doris in the person of Danova. Danova in fact returned five months later in an episode that centered on his painting a cover for *Today's World.* The artistic angle may not have been particularly believable, but it did show that the producers were at least aware that a love interest for Doris was necessary in order to boost flagging audience interest.

To this end, other actors and characters were in effect "auditioned" on air. Robert Lansing made a one-time guest appearance as Sergeant Bill Winston, a police officer sent to expose Doris as the con woman the police believe is trying to bilk cash from unsuspecting computer-dating prospects. Sergeant Winston ends up dating Doris, but evidently Lansing didn't pass the test, because five weeks later Peter Lawford made his first guest appearance as Doris's new love interest, Dr. Peter Lawrence. In Lawford's first episode, Doris attempts to write a feature story on excessive doctor bills. Arguments ensue between Doris and Dr. Lawrence after he finds out her "angle," but so strong is their mutual attraction that they reconcile.

In many ways, this episode should have (but didn't) served as the template for the show's plotlines. Here is an adult romance, which is, within the boundaries of a sitcom, believable, and at the same time still quite funny: Doris, enthusiastic about watching Dr. Lawrence at work, faints dead away as soon as he begins operating. Dr. Lawrence takes Doris out to dinner but is constantly interrupted by work calls. Their relationship exists in a constant state of interruption, but for these two adults, their mutual attraction makes sense. They are roughly the same age, both look great, and their scenes together are nicely underplayed. It's obvious that things are going well when Day's favorite background music, "What Every Girl Should Know," is heard playing instrumentally in the background. It's a signal that this romance is heating up, which it does indeed on Lawford's second appearance of the season. For this return visit, Dr. Lawrence treats a famous Greek billionaire; turns out said billionaire has fallen for Doris, who, in order to obtain an interview with him, nurses him during his convalescence. Hmmmm, nursing skills and journalistic skills all employed at the same time. Is there anything this gal can't do? Evidently just one thing: make some sense out of this gibberish.

The plots don't make much sense, but Day and Lawford together do, and it's a good thing too, because by now it is evident that the character of Doris's boss, Cy Bennett, doesn't possess a shred of plausibility. He is a bumbling fool and immediately undercuts any pretense of believability as the magazine's top editor; if *The Doris Day Show* writers had really been paying attention to *The Mary Tyler Moore Show*, they would have noticed that Mary Richards's boss, Lou Grant (Ed Asner), was a smart television producer who deserved to be the boss of WJM television station. Cy Bennett, by way of contrast, should not have been in charge of the company cafeteria.

In other words, Mr. Bennett attains the same level of believability as do the plots. Falling under the Doris-saves-the-world type of plot is the early season-four episode "Charity Begins in the Office." In the space of a half-hour episode, Doris discovers that Mrs. Fairburn's charity ball is being bilked by the consultant, rolls up her sleeves to right the situation, exposes the thief, forces him to pay back the money he stole, and makes him pledge to abstain from any future fund-raising. Wow, pretty impressive. Of course, that's nothing compared to "Whodunit, Doris," where she does nothing less than solve a murder that of course has the police baffled.

It was in this same season that the type of episode best called "The Doris Day Travelogue" was perfected. Never mind the stock exterior footage that was then combined with sound stage interior sets to give the viewer a taste of the exotic on the cheap. No one really expected a sitcom film crew to fly all over the world capturing the real-life setting. What they did expect, however, were plots that made sense.

And what did they get? Besides the trip to Rome where Doris charmed an internationally known painter, Doris and Mr. Bennett were also good for a trip to the Mediterranean ("The Crapshooter Who Would Be King") and, wackiest of all, dealt with Middle Eastern revolutionaries in "The Sheik of Araby." How did the writer, Arthur Julian, come up with this doozy in which Doris is kidnapped by rebels who insist that they will kill her if the king does not give back the land that is rightfully theirs? When the rebels tell Doris to leave (too many choruses of "Que Sera, Sera" early in the morning?), there's only one possible solution for Doris. She stays. That's right—she sides with the rebels in their argument about the land, forcing the king to abdicate and thereby restoring democracy to the land. Now just which part of this did all parties involved think was best? That a middle-aged American woman who was kidnapped overseas would voluntarily stay with her kidnappers? That this very same middle-aged American carried such moral stature that a king would abdicate and restore democracy to his country? How were viewers supposed to take any of this nonsense seriously? Dick Gautier, who had guest-starred as football player Joe Garrison in the season-three episode "The

Forward Pass," returned here to play the extraordinarily unbelievable rebel Omar. About the only thing missing here is Omar having a cousin named Ali Baba.

This science fiction version of Middle Eastern diplomacy is unfortunately on a par with the season's penultimate episode, where the autocratic French designer Jacques Moreau (played by the very German Werner Klemperer) is persuaded by Doris to include the dresses of her designer, Louie Salkawitz (Joseph Mell), in a big international fashion show. And just who is this budding designer? A talented assistant at the house of Chanel? Nope. He's none other than Doris's dry cleaner. And what does the imperious Jacques Moreau do about this? The only thing he can do—he simply asks Louie to be his partner. Well, the show seems to tell us, never mind making connections and working your way up through the ranks in a major fashion houses. Just be a good tailor, design dresses on the side, and the Calvin Kleins of the world will make you an equal partner as soon as you ask. Yep, it's all that silly, but once again, there is the fun—and it really is fun—of being treated to another Doris Day fashion show. It's more than a little crazy, and some of the clothes are prime examples of the style-free 1970s fashions, but Doris looks great, and when she starts strutting her stuff on the runway, the energy level in the episode is ratcheted up 100 percent.

Things were better with the episode "Doris' House Guest"—but not because of the plot, which involved Colonel Fairburn's relative Thelma staying with Doris in order to get over her broken romance. (Good thing Doris is no longer a mother—now she has a spare bedroom where lonelyhearts can mend.) No, the attraction here is the funny sparring between Doris and Billy DeWolfe as Mr. Jarvis. The affection between Day and DeWolfe is palpable, and it is genuinely funny when Mr. Jarvis complains to Doris Martin about a neighbor watching *The Doris Day Show* on television. Sneers DeWolfe in his patented snippy fashion, "I can't stand Doris Day." Funny, self-referential, and self-mocking all at the same time, this is the wit the series could have used more of.

But the series sure didn't feature much of that wit. Instead, Van Johnson returns as cousin Charlie, in an episode of surpassing silliness centered on microfilm hidden in a toy elephant. Charlie hid the microfilm in the elephant, and then Doris gave the elephant away. As soon as Doris and Charlie retrieve the elephant, the spies who are after the film take the elephant. At this point, even a casual viewer can be forgiven for staring at the screen in disbelief. Microfilm in elephants? Van Johnson and Doris Day confronting international spies? What the hell is going on here? Ah, but there's nothing to worry about because everything ends happily after a wall hanging falls and snuffs out the robbery of the elephant. Faced with this utter waste of her talents—Laurence Olivier would look foolish stealing elephants and getting tangled up in a wall hanging—Doris Day does her best; she looks great and displays impeccable timing, but it is all for naught. In fact, this is worse than the idealized farm setting of the first season because at least there every show provided a glimpse of Day's terrific interaction with her two sons, thereby providing recognizable human moments no matter what the plotline. Compared to microfilm-carrying toy elephants, the apparently self-running farm of season one is as realistic as *The Grapes of Wrath*.

Doris Day is so compelling a personality that one continues to root for her, and *like* her, but even that loyalty falls by the wayside in the single worst episode of the show's five years: the fourth season's "A Weighty Problem." Spectacular in its own awful way, this episode finds Doris and Angie Pallucci (Kaye Ballard) registering at a spa in order to spy on the wife of a soon to be released felon, whose $2 million stash has never been found. Angie spies the mobster's wife, Mrs. Miggins (veteran character actress Iris Adrian), buying a pizza, which Mrs. Miggins then hides in a cornerstone of the spa, alongside the money. How does Angie find out all this? She sniffs out the pizza. That's right—she sniffs out the pizza. A $2 million, years-old robbery is solved because Angie Pallucci, Doris's trusty sidekick, can smell pizza through concrete. One can't even concentrate on how offensive this is to Italian women—evidently their biggest talents are making and smelling pizza. No, the plot point that lingers—no, throbs—in the brain is that this may well be the stupidest denouement in sitcom history. There's tough competition—after all, *My Mother the Car* found Jerry Van Dyke talking to his dead mother in her reincarnation as a car, but even that falls short when stacked up against Kaye Ballard's pizza-sniffing ability. This is the episode where *The Doris Day Show* "jumped the shark." Just as the hit sitcom *Happy Days* never recovered from the episode where Fonzie, wearing his black leather jacket and motorcycle boots, evaded danger in the ocean by jumping over a shark while on water skis, so too does one finally give up hope of a coherent sitcom series from *The Doris Day Show* writers. Doris could and still would be charming, but the viewing audience's expectations were now very low indeed.

This fourth season finished the year ranked a more than respectable number twenty-three, but the show was fast running out of steam and ideas, and while it slogged through one more season, with Doris functioning as executive producer, it never felt fully energized again. This lack of energy was reflected in the ratings for the fifth and final season: For the first time ever it did not place among the year's top twenty-five shows.

This lack of energy was even reflected in yet another new set of opening credits. In place of the fast-paced and great-looking series of jump-cut close-ups of Doris zipping down the spiral staircase, for the fifth season she walked down the staircase in a stylish black dress and opened the front door. Doris Day walking sedately? Never—she had enough energy to power the cable cars herself. This was not the woman her fans adored. The opening credits now also contained scenes from one of the fashion show episodes—a fine addition, but the characters have been changed yet again, much to the show's discredit and the audience's puzzlement.

All of a sudden the Palluccis have sold the apartment building in order to spend their time on the restaurant—evidently Angie needs more time to brush up on her pizza-smelling capabilities. Kaye Ballard and Bernie Kopell, not to mention Buck and the boys, are all gone. Mr. Jarvis has now bought the apartment building from the Palluccis, but the other big change is that much of the season is devoted to Doris choosing between two potential mates: Dr. Peter Lawrence (Peter Lawford) and potential congressman Jonathan Rusk (Patrick O'Neal). Which man will she choose? Doris gives her all to inject some interest into the proceedings, but even she seems distracted by it all. It's as if she's back in a Rock Hudson sex farce, but times have changed, and as *Variety* noted in its customary opening-of-the-season pan, "It is indicative of the febrile plotting that Miss Day's ambiguous virginity looms important at all in these times."

Peter Lawford makes his first appearance of the season right off the bat in the opener, and rival suitor Patrick O'Neal joins us up in the fourth episode, "The Press Secretary." How is Patrick O'Neal's presence explained? Doris temporarily leaves *Today's World* in order to work as his press secretary during his run for Congress. Turns out Jonathan was a former beau of Doris's.

Well, new beau or old beau, an odd strain entered these episodes regarding Doris's choice of boyfriend: Doris Day was repeatedly presented as being jealous of any woman who even seemed to cross the path of her boyfriends. In "Forgive and Forget," Doris is on assignment to write an article about forgiveness in marriages, yet when Dr. Lawrence makes a late-night house call at another (beautiful) woman's house, Doris instantly jumps to the conclusion that he has slept with her. Later in the season, in "Hospital Benefit," Doris offers to produce a fashion show as a fund-raiser for a new hospital wing. (Since Doris can easily serve as the sole model in any fashion show, why not produce the show as well. . . .) Doris meets attractive Lois Frazer (Lee Meriwether) and immediately assumes that she is having an affair with Dr. Lawrence. Turns out Lois is Peter's former wife and they are not carrying on an affair. To no one's surprise, the fashion show is a hit—c'mon, with Doris in charge it puts Ralph Lauren to shame—but what lingers in the mind is the unseemly sight of Doris Day in a jealous snit.

This jealous streak emerges once more in the third to last episode of the entire series, when Doris sees Jonathan with another woman. Before learning that the woman was being interviewed by Jonathan, Doris turns jealous yet again—this in the same episode in which Doris accepts Jonathan's proposal of marriage. Doris Day has too much on the ball to spend her time mooning over men and being jealous of each and every female on the scene. This theme of jealousy constitutes a very odd change being rung on the powerful Doris Day persona, and it is not a welcome one. What the viewer wants to see is Doris telling the man to get his act together and come back to see her when he has grown up. Doris Martin/Day should end up with a man who is worthy of her—honest, capable, and professional, not to mention being truly appreciative of her world-class skill at rapidly changing outfits. . . .

For such a relentlessly upbeat show, there were intimations of other sour-tasting plots. In "Debt of Honor," Doris finds out that she now owes $1,100 on a note she cosigned for a friend. In order to pay the note, she attempts to collect money owed to her by other friends, including a man who bought her car and never paid her for it. It all ends happily enough, but—Doris cosigning notes? Friends of Doris's welching on their loans? Next thing you know Doris will be getting involved with a young rock star. Whoops—she did in "The Music Man," an episode featuring Doris's romance with Johnny Reb. The times they were a-changin' but *The Doris Day Show* scriptwriters remained pretty clueless about just how much. Johnny Reb? Didn't a name like that go out with Marlon Brando and *The Wild One*?

On the one hand, Doris Day looks great for a forty-eight-year-old woman. On the other hand, while her screen charisma, impeccable comic timing, and natural empathy have never deserted her, for the first time in the series her heart doesn't appear to be in it, no matter how hard she tries. Maybe the cumulative weight of five seasons of middling plots has gotten to her. Who could look enthusiastic about suffering through yet more idiocy like "Jimmy the Gent" where Doris "goes undercover" in order to interview safecracker Jimmy the Gent in the hospital? Didn't Doris's proclivity for meeting gangsters just happen in season four's "The Wings of an Angel," where she tangled with mob boss Frankie Fury? Didn't this happen with Angie and Mrs. Miggins in the infamous pizza-smelling episode? And didn't this happen with season two's "Kidnapped," where Doris faces down mobster Barney Moore while simultaneously supplying his wife Flossie with marital counseling? Yes, yes, and yes. At this point, the only sensible response on the part of the viewer is to beg: Please, no more.

The only thing different about season five's gangster episode is that Dr. Lawrence tells—no, orders—Doris to stop this interaction with safecracker Jimmy the Gent, and Doris apologizes to the crook. Of course she does. And then she discovers that Jimmy and his brother have switched places so that Jimmy can continue his safecracking. Believe it or not, this wacky version of gangland only gets worse. "Follow That Dog" finds Doris embroiled in a plot that is best described as Lassie meets Scarface in Toyland. No other description can truly suffice for a plotline that features a gangster who hires dog lover Doris to take care of his pet for two weeks, in exchange for a $10,000 donation to a pet clinic. The only problem is that inside the dog's collar is the key to a locker that contains a list of other gangsters. Keys are switched, lookalike dogs are used—it's all so predictable and so unrealistic that the unthinkable happens for a Doris Day vehicle: One simply stops paying attention.

Maybe it was the exigencies of creating an entirely new script every week; weekly television is pressurized—twenty-six new episodes a season is the equivalent of multiple feature films, and quality is bound to vary. But why didn't Doris insist on better scripts that contained at least a shred of plausibility? In "The New Boss," when Colonel Fairburn replaces Mr. Bennett by making Doris editor in chief of *Today's World,* Doris turns down the offer of making this a permanent position, because in her mind Mr. Bennett is the right man for the job. Loyalty is nice, and yes we expect it of Doris, but c'mon, she broke every key story the magazine ever ran, consorted with kings, professional athletes, and many a mobster, overcame pollution, produced fashion shows, and even found spare time to solve murders, but she turns down the job and remains an associate editor who reports to a bumbling fool? This could occur only in the make-believe world of sitcom land; in real life, a Doris Martin would help Mr. Bennett pack his bags and give him a quick, "Don't let the door hit you on your way out." By 1972 the times had changed; feminism was on the rise, but Doris was acting like she was still "just a secretary." It's all wrong, not only because she is capable of so much more but also because audiences want to see Doris succeed at the very top—if they didn't, *Pillow Talk* and *Lover, Come Back* would never have garnered such popular acclaim.

Of course, some episodes show genuine flashes of wit or generate clever references to the Doris Day persona—they're just few and far between. In "The Hoax," Doris is screen-tested (shades of her own life) and lands a contract as a shampoo pitchwoman (shades of *The Thrill of It All*). This is what audiences wanted—Doris succeeding in show biz, Doris overcoming all obstacles. The talent scout offering her a job with his agency is a con artist, but good old Doris fulfills her contractual commitment for the commercial. Honoring her commitment—hmmm, must have sounded kind of familiar to Doris Day. Andy Griffith is on hand as guest star, and it's fun to have two such enormously likable television personalities together, but the real fun here is to see Doris landing back in show biz.

Even better, in "The Co-Op," Doris tries to organize the tenants of her building into a co-op. The plan doesn't work because Mr. Jarvis simply buys the building and raises the rent. How do the tenants strike back? By calling on Mr. Jarvis to make endless repairs, all at extremely inconvenient times. This is genuinely funny stuff because it's a solid idea; Doris can run with the ball as chief organizer—the can-do gal—and best of all, the mere idea of Billy DeWolfe as a landlord making repairs is funny. For once the humor actually arises out of character.

These episodes, however, proved the exception rather than the rule in season five, and the show was clearly nearing the end of its run. There was the obligatory animal lover episode in "It's a Dog's Life," where Mr. Jarvis allows Doris to keep a stray dog and even adopts one himself, and yet another romance with a titled, exotic foreigner, with Sir Robert Kingsley (Jon Cypher) returning to woo her. On the basis of season five, it's tough to decide which group was more attracted to Doris—mobsters or titled foreigners. Evidently Doris Martin was the poster girl for both groups. By the time Bernie Kopell guest-starred as Doris's Uncle August in "The Magnificent Fraud," the end was in sight. It was more nonsense about valuable stolen items (in this case a painting), but more to the point, how did the writers, or more accurately the casting directors, expect the audience to seriously consider Kopell as Doris's Uncle August when he had just spent the better part of two seasons as her landlord, the very Italian Mr. Pallucci? Did the writers/casting agents really think viewers had such a short memory that they would buy this bizarre casting? Then again, it was no odder than Kopell's season-two appearance as a Cuban military operative involved in the hijacking of Doris's plane.

And so it was that the series ended not with a bang but with a lethargy that resembled a hot-air balloon slowly losing altitude and desultorily drifting to earth. In the third to last episode Doris accepts Jonathan's proposal, in the penultimate episode they spend a romantic weekend at Big Sur (albeit with Jackie, her boyfriend Sid, and Mr. Bennett), and so Doris's loyal viewers tuned in to the final episode expecting a big wedding, or at the least a final send-off at *Today's World.* Right? Wrong. Instead, the series ends most strangely, with an episode centering around journalistic ethics: Doris helps out her fellow reporter Scott with two assignments and is chastised by Mr. Bennett for these actions. Five seasons and this is how it ends?

In her own words, Day felt that every possible situation and character had been explored. It's understandable that she did not want to continue the show, stating, "I'm tired . . . I feel that five years is enough. It's time to go on to something else. . . . I just don't think another season of *The Doris Day Show* in its present form is going to lead anybody anywhere except maybe to the bank." Yet it's hard to comprehend the fact that no one involved seems to have thought that the loose plot ends should be tied up. Maybe nobody cared at this point, but after 128 episodes running from September of 1968 through March of 1973, one would think a big send-off would have been planned. Maybe a wedding—with Doris singing at her own wedding (what the hell—Streisand did it at her own real-life wedding to James Brolin). Maybe Doris at long last would have become editor in chief of *Today's World.* Then again, maybe the finale would have featured a reunion with the hillbillies and mobsters the writers seemed to find so endearing and it was better to just let it all drift away.

When all was said and done, Doris Day had succeeded in carrying a five-year television sitcom series on her back, and most of the time it appeared that she was hefting the load completely on her own. Due to plot exigencies, she found herself in ridiculous situations that tested the patience of even the most die-hard Doris Day fans, but her talent never broke. It might have been stretched to the breaking point, not because she was exploring exhilarating new territory that challenged her as an actress but because she often had to play utter nonsense with a full commitment that must have proved exhausting, given the thinness of the material. To her everlasting credit, she did muster a full commitment, and in spades, without ever condescending to the audience or in effect winking at them to let them know she found the entire enterprise beneath her. Nope, this least cunning of actresses marched straight on and in the process became the first Hollywood star ever to successfully triumph in the wildly diverse worlds of motion pictures, recordings, radio, and weekly television.

This weekly television series proved to be the aspect of her career holding the least artistic merit; there was no *Love Me or Leave Me* here, no *Day by Night* concept recording, and as a sitcom, it certainly did not contain the succession of witty, perceptive plots found in *The Mary Tyler Moore Show*. But the show did present a successful one-woman battle to uphold an optimistic vision of everyday life in America, one without vulgarity, and with humor arising out of situations rather than increasingly cynical one liners. Over the course of five years, this was all presented with an often blinkered vision that refused to allow any ambiguity to enter the picture. The quality varied wildly and in fact was often subpar, but Doris Day herself was never less than compelling.

Once Day's contractual obligation to her weekly television series had been satisfied, she made a very few, but memorable, guest appearances on network television talk shows and specials. The first of these, a rare appearance at an A-list Hollywood awards ceremony, came straight from the heart: a nationally televised appearance at the American Film Institute Lifetime Achievement Award ceremony honoring beloved costar James Cagney. At a time (1974) when most golden age Hollywood stars were still alive, the star-studded audience turned out in droves to see Cagney feted. Day herself, in fact, was introduced by none other than Frank Sinatra, who stated simply, "Here's the lady Jimmy loved in that picture, the lady all of us love all of the time—Miss Doris Day." Looking sensational and elegant in a plain orange gown, Day, who was reported to be the only star who showed up for rehearsal on time—in fact, early—looked directly at her three-time costar and said, "Working with you was one of the happiest times of my life. . . . You're more than just an actor. You don't play the character—you live the character. . . . You make the rest of us really look good and tonight you make the whole world feel good just because you're here. What's really in my heart I think I said better a few years ago when we worked together"—and with that a clip of Day singing "You Made Me Love You" from *Love Me or Leave Me* unspooled. Ruth Etting may have had mixed feelings about Marty Snyder in that classic film, but it was obvious to even the most casual viewer that Doris Day flat-out loved Jimmy Cagney and the feeling was mutual. In fact Cagney had paid Day the ultimate compliment by stating, "Doris Day perfectly illustrates my idea of good acting. Just plant yourself, look the other actor in the eye, and tell him the truth."

It is worth noting that Day's appearance on the AFI salute to James Cagney was aired on March 3, 1974, exactly one day before five years of preparation paid off with Day's legal team finally bringing Jerome Rosenthal to trial in Superior Court of California (the trial continued until August 30, 1974). As

Day points out in her autobiography, this gargantuan trial employed twelve attorneys and cost $250,000 (at one point the legal bills were mounting at the rate of $40,000 per month). Rosenthal's mismanagement had cost Day her fortune, left her in debt, and forced her participation in her long-running television series. As a result, she exhausted herself with five years of hard work, and the effects on her professional career were enormous. No such enforced labor could produce a feeling of joy. Was the work satisfying at times? Sure. Fun on the set? Without a doubt. But the exhilarating sense of freedom that she experienced when recording? No way. It's no wonder, then, that when the verdict in the juryless trial was rendered by Judge Lester E. Olsen after nearly four months of court presentation, Day finally seemed to feel free to clean up her remaining professional obligations. The rendered verdict in effect registered as just as much a sign of professional closure as of personal vindication. Had the enforced labor on a television series truly sapped Day's remaining interest in performing, thereby hastening her complete retirement? Exactly how bad had Rosenthal's management of Day's finances really been? Answer: worse than anyone could have ever imagined.

In one of the many ironies involved in the Jerome Rosenthal saga, it was Melcher's ties with Rosenthal that had caused Day to stay married to Melcher after they had separated; after all, Melcher had told her that they had to stay married because all of their resources were jointly owned, tied up in a web of contracts that would ruin both of them if they divorced. Marty's explanation to his wife: "It's very complicated . . . if we split up we will lose everything." As a result, Day took Marty Melcher back for financial reasons but, as subsequent events revealed, she was already ruined financially. In fact, both Doris and Terry have stated that Marty's death saved her financially. In Terry's own words: "It's a brutal thing to say, but just about the best thing Marty did for my mother was to die when he did."

Three-plus months after the trial began, Judge Olson issued his ruling, an oral decision. Just how reprehensible did Judge Olson find Rosenthal's conduct? Consider the following: Reproducing Olson's verdict in Day's autobiography took up eight pages of dense type, and constituted a mind-numbing laundry list of dishonesty and chicanery. Some of the "highlights": "The oil and gas ventures in which Rosenthal placed his clients stand out as an incredible saga of attorney negligence. They resulted in a private community chest for drunken and dishonest operators . . . and worst of all, vast losses to the clients. . . . The conduct of Rosenthal with respect to the oil and gas ventures represents a breach of his fiduciary duty of full disclosure . . . other examples of negligence or worse: the use of outdated oil engineering reports, duplicative or dummy lists of equipment on oil leases . . . and the list could go on."

In fact, Olsen goes on to cite Rosenthal's "amateurish efforts" to build and operate two large hotels involving costly inefficient computer programs, management incompetence, disorganized accounting practices, and a lack of proper capitalization that "boggles the mind and created from the start an aura of financial crisis." Significantly, Olson states that such scare tactics allowed him to hold greater influence over Marty Melcher, thus permitting Rosenthal "to drain Doris Day of cash as fast as the money rolled in at the box office." In yet another of the endless ironies that pervaded the entire Rosenthal episode, this was, of course, money that stopped rolling in as soon as Day was forced into the unsuccessful third-rate "comedies" to which Melcher had obligated her in a desperate attempt to earn the cash needed to fund Rosenthal's ongoing ventures.

Citing evidence of a pattern of kickbacks and rebates disguised as attorney fees, as well as the resulting implication of clients Day and Melcher in tax fraud, Judge Olson admonished Rosenthal for taking advantage of his confidential relationship with Marty Melcher, for "grossly" failing to meet his obligations as Day and Melcher's attorney, and misleading his clients with inaccurate financial statements.

Interestingly, even Day herself was reprimanded by the judge for her naïveté. In chiding Rosenthal about his concern for personal gain at the expense of his clients, as well as for a history of ill-advised and illegal transactions, the judge also scolded the deceased Marty Melcher for being "apparently imbued with a false sense of his own intelligence and overly awed by his attorney," and chastised Day for being "too busy making movies to really pay attention to her own affairs." Such a mild criticism proved to be a mere bump in the road: The result was Judge Olson awarding Doris Day the sum of $22,835,646, the largest award ever given in a California civil suit up to that time. (When Rosenthal appealed, the judgments were affirmed in the Court of Appeals of California on August 8, 1985.)

It wasn't the money that really motivated Day—she eventually collected only a small percentage of the funds due her. It was a sense of justice that drove her, of wanting Rosenthal to be punished for his misdoings (which extended to his financial mismanagement of other well-known actors and actresses in Hollywood). And it was, she admitted, her hope that the trial might help to explain what really happened between Melcher and Rosenthal, and how much of Rosenthal's wheeling and dealing Marty Melcher actually participated in. Marty was dead; there never could be a definitive answer to that question. Instead, Doris Day would have to content herself with a conversation she had with Melcher when they reconciled after their brief separation; by her own admission, Day still loved him in many ways, and it was because of their reunion that Day was to utter words that brought both of them great comfort. At the time of their reconciliation, and even with new ground rules for their life together—no sex, the leading of separate lives—Day could still state, with total belief, " 'I just have a lovely feeling, Marty, that I would like to grow old with you.' He loved that."

Whatever the motivating factors behind the lawsuit, justice had been served. A chapter had been closed, and with this verdict, the completion of nearly all of Doris Day's entertainment obligations was near at hand. From 1974 onward, there were no new feature films, no further recordings, and only the one-season Christian Broadcast Network television series *Doris Day's Best Friends,* a series motivated by her love of animals, not by any desire to return to the spotlight. Doris Day's career was winding down—only one more CBS television special, *Doris day toDay,* lay in her future. There is, therefore, no discernible purpose behind her September 1974 visit to *The Tonight Show*. But in her conversation—absolutely no live singing involved—the many contradictions in Day's persona are writ large, and it's fascinating viewing all the way.

Right off the bat, any viewer, even a casual one, would notice that Doris looks pretty damn great—this fifty-year-old woman appears to be at least fifteen years younger, and wearing a seemingly sheer blue three-piece pants, top, and jacket outfit, accessorized with jewels, she walked onto the set to a prolonged standing ovation. Just as proved to be the case in *Teacher's Pet,* where Day's buttoned-down professor Erica Stone proved to be far sexier than blowsy Mamie Van Doren's Miss DeFore, a fifty-year-old Doris Day on *The Tonight Show* appeared to be far sexier than the favorite, and younger, "dumb blonde" television girl of the moment, Carol Wayne.

Reference is made to her previous *Tonight Show* appearance when television series costar McLean Stevenson served as the guest host, and Day states in an offhand, dismissive manner, "We seemed to spend a lot of time kissing so of course all of the fan magazines made it into a romance." There is filler chat about having had dinner with host Johnny Carson a few weeks previously and nonsense about Day's many nicknames: Clara Bixby, Suzy Creamcheese, and the like. More to the point, there is an on-air reunion with Jimmy Zito, a musician in Carson's band who was a member of Les Brown's Band of Renown (and the man who dubbed the trumpet playing of Juano Hernandez as Art Hazzard in *Young Man with a Horn*). When Carson asks Day about singing, she responds with a tantalizing hint of what might have been: "I'm rusty—but I'm going to start singing again. I really love it." Ah, if only. Unfortu-

September 18, 1974: $22 million judgment in favor of Day in her suit against attorney Jerome Rosenthal. *Photofest*

nately, this hoped-for event appeared to go the way of Day's statement on the same program that she was no longer afraid of flying: "I fly everywhere. I said to myself, 'I won't be scared anymore and now I love it.'" And yet, thirty-plus years later, Day's dislike of travel and of leaving home remain so pronounced that her refusal to travel has supposedly cost her the highly coveted Kennedy Center Honor for Lifetime Achievement, which requires the honoree to be present to receive the award. In fact, such fear of flying meant that Day did not even attend the 2004 ceremony when she received the Presidential Medal of Freedom—the United States' highest civilian honor—from President George W. Bush. In granting Day this honor, Bush's words came right to the point: "She captured the hearts of Americans while enriching our culture. . . . Doris Day is one of the greats, and America will always love its sweetheart."

The Tonight Show continued with the extremely odd juxtaposition of Day being followed onto the show by Rodney "I don't get no respect" Dangerfield. Although Day does not leave the show—no diva displays of I'm-too-big-to-stick-around for Doris—the contrast between the sunshiny Day and the perpetually dyspeptic Dangerfield is downright weird, and she does in fact look like she'd rather be anywhere else. Although she is cordial throughout, and warms up to Dangerfield by the end of the show, she appears to be more interested in the ninety-year-old "ordinary citizen" who followed Dangerfield as the show's final guest.

Finally, and most revealing of all, this appearance on *The Tonight Show* makes it publicly clear more than ever before that the early 1970s marked the real start of Day's concerted activism on behalf of animals; after Carol Wayne, in a somewhat overt display of wanting the focus back on herself, provocatively talks about not liking animals, animal lover Day responds with the most genuine passion she displays in the entire show: "People don't take care of their own children, and if they don't do that, they won't take care of their animals." There is intensity behind these words—children and pets are placed on equal footing—and Day is far more animated here than she was when discussing her own career.

With this burgeoning activism on behalf of animals pointing the way to Day's future, only one commitment remained before the writing of an autobiography would enable Doris Day to wrap up her professional career. No one realized it at the time, but it was as if with the writing of her autobiography Doris Day was seeking complete closure in regard to her movie, recording, and television careers. Her interests now lay elsewhere, and as soon as she fulfilled her CBS contract by filming the television special *Doris day toDay* she would be on her way right out of show business.

Filmed and broadcast in 1975, this one-hour special can be summed up with one sentence: Everything right with *Doris day toDay* stems from the charismatic, still beautiful star and her extraordinary singing voice, while everything wrong with the special comes from the hopeless "comedy" with which Doris and her guest stars were saddled.

Directed and choreographed by Tony Charmoli and produced and written by George Schlatter, things got off to a good start with the very sexy fifty-year-old star belting out a hot version of "Anything Goes," complete with the strange sight of Sammy Davis Jr. singing the lyric "And black's white today." After the trouble Davis had within the black community for hugging Richard Nixon, it's a very odd display indeed, and one can only hope that Davis was here indulging in a bit of postmodern irony and was not just clueless. Joined by guest stars Tim Conway, Rich Little, and John Denver for a reprise of "Anything Goes," Day segues into a beautiful version of "Day by Day" from the musical *Godspell.* With a smart, understated arrangement featuring bongos, guitars, and a (black-tie) string section, Day manages the neat trick of not only sounding great but conveying a sense of quiet and intimacy even with a large orchestra on hand.

This opening is followed by extended banter with John Denver. When Day had guest-starred on Denver's own network television special, the wholesome twosome had dueted on a medley of "By the Light of the Silvery Moon," "On Moonlight Bay," and "I'll See You in My Dreams." Here, the two Goody Two-shoes entertainers indulged in some fun at the expense of their sunshiny images and similar last names: Henry John Deutschendorf meets Doris Mary Anne Kappelhoff, and in specially crafted lyrics, each realizes that they are "exactly like" the other. Denver has a nice solo on "Follow Me," a silhouetted Doris harmonizing beautifully. This segment with Denver is tasteful, works musically, and raises hopes that the remainder of the special will adhere to such high standards. No such luck.

After the special treads water with a Day monologue regarding animal population control, things slide downhill precipitously with a dopey and endless skit featuring Tim Conway as a slob of a husband and Doris as his put-upon spouse. Nonsensical slapstick abounds, with Conway parading in a variety of costumes, all to be capped with a supposedly funny punch line showing the couple with an increasing number of offspring. Unfunny in the extreme, it's a waste of everyone's time, especially Doris's.

What follows is almost worse because it is so frustrating—a hint of what could have been. In this next segment, Doris duets with impressionist Rich Little; she looks great in a sexy black dress while singing "Everybody Loves a Lover" on a terrific sleek set, posters of her movies suspended in the air, but the movie setting serves only as an excuse for Little to impersonate Day costars Sinatra, Gable, Grant, and Cagney. These impersonations ruin the chance to hear Doris Day sing her greatest hits; the viewer receives exactly three lines of "Love Me or Leave Me" and three lines of "Secret Love." She sounds so good on these frustratingly brief interludes—modulating up on the "Secret Love" lyric "my heart's an open door" in a sexy, personal manner every bit as affecting

The second CBS variety special, *Doris day toDay,* aired February 19, 1975. *Photofest*

as the original recording from the song twenty years earlier—that it is with real irritation that the viewer has to settle for Rich Little's Kirk Douglas impression and his ruinous version of "Que Sera, Sera." It's not that Rich Little is untalented—he's very good at what he does—but this is supposed to be the Doris Day special, not the Rich Little comedy hour.

It is only after this botched opportunity that the viewer receives four minutes of grade-A television, so terrific that one can only wonder why on earth the entire special was not constructed in this manner. The four minutes in question: Doris Day in a black gown and sporting long diamond earrings, against a black background, singing a beautiful, understated version of "The Way We Were" as photos of her costars flash by: Rock Hudson, James Garner, Clark Gable, Frank Sinatra, and Ronald Reagan. It's a sweet nostalgia treat for the viewer, a reminder of Hollywood's heyday led by one of the all-time great singers delivering a beautiful version of the quintessential elegiac song. Doris Day still had it all—in spades.

As the hour neared its conclusion, there was a nice "sunshine" medley with optimistic "twin" Denver: "Sing a Little Sunshine Song," "You Are the Sunshine of My Life," "You Are My Sunshine," and "Sunshine Lollipops, Rainbows." Day and Denver sound great together, although the ending is marred by a terrible 1970s-style graphic showing Day and Denver dancing on a daisy. That's right, dancing on a daisy. . . . But these are small quibbles when compared to the horribly unfunny skit that takes up the last portion of the show, a skit that seems to last twice the length of *Gone With the Wind* all by itself. Teamed once again with Tim Conway, Day must galumph her way through a painfully moribund physical comedy skit centered on an unhappy couple waking up in a cramped motor home. The unfortunate conceit only gets worse, with John Denver showing up dressed as a sheikh, Rich Little as a 1940s-style gumshoe, and the Lockers dancing troupe improbably turning up for some high stepping. Who thought up this extraordinary waste of talent? Did someone sit around at a production meeting and say, "Let's not let one of the all-time great singers sing more than two solos. Instead, let's get Tim Conway to dress up as a slob and clown around in a motor home for ten minutes with Doris as his unhappy spouse. And, until the very end of the skit, we'll make them pantomime everything. We'll even cap it all off by dressing up John Denver as a Middle Eastern sheikh. That's the ticket"?

There is scant consolation at the end when Doris returns to reprise "Day by Day" in a lovely white dress; the star can show off her sensational figure and her even more sensational voice, but it's a capsule summary of the frustration any viewer has with the special—too little star, too late in the program. Barbra Streisand had it right when she insisted that her first two specials have no guest stars. When you've got stars as extraordinarily talented as Streisand and Day, no other guests are necessary. No other stars can sing as well as these two versatile actresses, and while Streisand's solo specials swept the Emmys, Day's frustratingly structured special—a textbook case of "if only"—serves as an abbreviated reminder of how truly splendid Day could be, if only given the right showcase.

At this point in time, Day still made the occasional television appearance, even making the full rounds of talk shows in 1976 in order to publicize her autobiography. It was, Day felt, time to reveal the real woman underneath the relentlessly cheerful image. Appearing on *The Mike Douglas Show,* she publicly discussed first husband Al Jorden, one of the very few times she ever did so: "We had a correspondence courtship and it was not good. . . . I do not recommend it. We got married and we really didn't know each other. . . . Had we been together more, I wouldn't have married him." The nightmarish experience with Jorden was a key reason why Day spoke publicly about her belief that couples should live together before marrying. It's not a comment that elicits much reaction in 2006, but in 1976, coming from the mouth of wholesome Doris Day, role model for the big-band generation, it was a source of surprise and some controversy.

These television appearances are noteworthy less for the occasion than for the insight they give into Day's persona and attitude toward public appearances. She had never appeared on such shows, not only because of her exceedingly busy film and recording schedule but also because she never felt the need to do so. Riding high on the movie and record charts, she did not have to appear on the shows to publicize her latest work—the films and records sold anyway. It's a strategy of tantalizing inaccessibility that Barbra Streisand perfected from the late 1960s until her comeback concerts in 1994—make the public desperate for what they can't have. Day and Streisand shared a perfectionist streak that thrived in the controlled settings of the recording studio and film sets, all the while shunning live concert or stage appearances. Of course, in Streisand's case there was an unmistakable air of the untouchable diva with hauteur to spare. Day was far too down to earth for any such displays. She just had no personal need to appear before an adoring live audience—and make no mistake, when she did appear on these shows, most notably to publicize her autobiography in 1976, the audiences were adoring. Whether appearing on *The Tonight Show* or *The Merv Griffin Show,* the adulation and cries of "We love you" resounded and resulted in prolonged standing ovations. In typical Day fashion, when a particularly fervent fan shouted out, "You're beautiful!" Day instantly responded, "No, you're beautiful!" The thing is, she's speaking from the heart here. She actually didn't think of herself as being beautiful or the once-in-a-generation talent she actually was. Watch the terrific 1991 PBS documentary *Doris Day: A Sentimental Journey.* Day actually means it when, speaking of her overwhelming success, she says, "If I can do it, you can do it. Anyone can do it."

1975 publication of the number-one bestseller *Doris Day: Her Own Story. Photofest*

This is utter nonsense, of course, but Day didn't see it that way, and that is another part of her enormous appeal. Audiences instinctively knew that she was sincere and it's why they wanted to protect her. She was self-sufficient, of course, but, audiences seemed to reason, she's far too nice for anyone to treat badly.

Day did consent to be interviewed for two of the documentaries made about her life and times: 1989's *I Don't Even Like Apple Pie* for BBC TV, and the aforementioned *Doris Day: A Sentimental Journey,* which is by far the best of all of the programs about her. There was a brief guest appearance in a documentary about Carmel, California, narrated by Day's neighbor, Clint Eastwood, titled *Don't Pave Main Street: Carmel's Heritage.* Such appearances, never plentiful to begin with, dwindled in number as the years passed: In October of 1993, Doris was interviewed by Joan Lunden on *Good Morning Amer-*

The first-rate PBS documentary *Doris Day: A Sentimental Journey,* 1991. *Photofest*

ica, as well as by Vicki Lawrence on her syndicated talk show *Vicki!,* appearances Day made solely in order to publicize her charity fund-raisers for animal welfare. One year later, there were two October 1994 appearances to promote the release of *The Love Album* in the UK: the *Pebble Mill Doris Day Special* for BBC and *Des O'Connor Tonight* for ITV.

However, Day declined participation in the 1998 A&E biography of her life, the very first of these hugely popular biographies to run a full two hours, nor did she agree to be interviewed for *Doris Day—Hollywood Greats* for the BBC. Both of these later documentaries featured interviews with costars such as Kaye Ballard, James Garner, and Howard Keel (as did the 2003 E! biography *Doris Day—E! True Hollywood Story*), but what did distinguish these two biographies was the participation of Terry Melcher and his candid, affectionate comments about his mother. In terms of Day's professional career, the most revealing comments were Terry's rather objective remarks about her acting and singing careers—this accomplished musician is a huge fan of his mother's singing, rating her on a par with Ella Fitzgerald. On a personal level, Melcher's few words confirm his written observation that often in their relationship it was he who assumed the parental role; using the nearly paternalistic tone of voice he adopted when speaking of his mother in personal terms, he refers to his mother as "Doris" more often than he calls her "mother." It's a fascinating insight into a relationship shaped by a mere seventeen-year age difference and one where mother and son became much closer after Terry reached adulthood.

By having Terry participate in the documentaries but declining to participate herself, Doris was sending a very clear signal: Her television career was over. The interest on the part of others definitely existed, but not on the part of Day herself. Let other stars play Norma Desmond, yearning for a return to the spotlight. Doris Day wasn't having any of it, no matter how big the role or offer. As is possible with only the very biggest stars, she had stayed true to her own vision through sheer force of talent and personality. Sixty years into her professional career, in a field where ten years of stardom is considered a good run, she remained internationally famous and a star of the first rank. And for all intents and purposes, none of that seemed to matter to Day. Television and its attendant fame didn't interest her a whit. Only animals did. Beginning and end of story.

Animals

I just love that I can make it better for the animals. I know I have—so far—with my pet foundation. That is thrilling for me.

—*Doris Day, 1991*

In her autobiography, Doris Day writes movingly about her childhood pet Tiny, a black and tan who stayed by her side during her convalescence from the auto accident that had wreaked havoc with her dancing career. This companionship proved to be a turning point in her life, because although she had owned other dogs previously, her relationship with Tiny started her "lifelong love affair with the dog." While Day was still on crutches from the car accident, she took Tiny, who was not on a leash, out for a walk; Tiny ran into the street and was killed by a car. In Day's own words, she was racked with "loneliness" and "guilt." It was the combination of the closeness with Tiny and the guilt she felt over not using a leash that seems to have marked the beginning of Day's interest in animal welfare.

A more practical, somewhat less flattering reason for Day's animal welfare activism was posited by journalist Richard Gehman, who wrote, "It may be that animals are the beneficiaries of her affection because she has worked so hard all her life that she simply hasn't had time enough to cultivate more complicated relationships." Whatever the reasons for Doris's love of animals, it's an interest that over the years deepened into outright activism, eventually morphing into the all-consuming focus of her life. This passionate activism, which dates from the end of *The Doris Day Show* in 1973, has now lasted for more than thirty years—nearly as long as her entire professional career. It's an activism that has drastically altered the very shape of her career because Doris Day is simply no longer interested in singing, dancing, or acting.

How much does Doris Day care about animals? Enough to write in her autobiography that her dogs are "just as much my family as are my mother and son." Certainly Doris's mother and son were well aware of this feeling, which began with Doris's 1971 confounding and active participation in Actors and Others for Animals, an organization devoted to issues both large and small, from the necessity of spaying in order to prevent pet overpopulation to locating the owners of wandering dogs. (Day did take a leave of absence from Actors and Others for Animals to care for her mother when Alma fell severely ill, nursing

With seven-year-old son, Terry, and French poodle Smudgie, 1949. *Photofest*

her until Alma's worsening condition necessitated moving her to a nursing home, where she lived until her death.) Actress Jackie Joseph, who costarred on the final seasons of *The Doris Day Show,* stated that cases of animal abuse were "the only time I saw Doris cry. Her personal life, she could put on the back shelf and handle it in her own internal way. But if an animal was abused, it was intolerable." What's most interesting about the early stage of Day's activism is that it was already based on a keen sense of pragmatism. Strong as her loving feelings toward animals were, her view was not based on dewy-eyed pictures of romping in the sunshine with a few telegenic dogs. Indeed, as early as 1972, Day stated, "Money is at the bottom of all the trouble with the pounds. Throw them in the decompression chamber. Make fertilizer out of them. Get the money for the fertilizer. Get the money, get the money, get the money." Not exactly a Pollyannaish worldview.

In fact, Day's own films cause her pain nowadays when she sees the lavish furs she wore in so many of them—particularly those from the sex farce comedies that began with 1959's *Pillow Talk*. Day not only posed for an ad in the early 1970s in which she wore a fake fur coat alongside other staunch advocates for animals such as Mary Tyler Moore, but also spoke out against her own film legacy: "It just breaks my heart that these films (most noticeably *That Touch of Mink*) are playing and I want everybody to know that I do not wear furs. . . . Killing an animal to make a coat is a sin. . . . I won't auction the furs. I won't do anything with them. They're in a big storage chest and that's where they're going to stay because I'm so against that." So strong is Day's connection to animals that she puts animals on the same level as human beings—actually, above human beings much of the time. "I don't separate cruelty to animals from cruelty to people at all. I think we really have to study animals as they are—and then learn from them. That's why they are here. I'm *convinced* that's why they are here."

In her autobiography, Day writes at some length about two books by J. Allen Boone, *Letters to Strongheart* and *Kinship with All Life,* in which Boone discusses direct communication between dog and owner. The key here, in Day's view, is the mental rather than the physical. Since Boone and Day feel that the owner must treat the dog as an intelligent fellow being who should not be limited in any manner, an owner must therefore try and help the dog make use of his thinking faculties. End result? Boone's dog Strongheart was able to share "precious dog wisdom," making it possible for Boone and Strongheart to exchange thoughts by means of a "mental two-way bridge." In fact, Day realizes that Boone's view can sound irrational, but she finds it logical. What it means to Doris Day is that she has been taught by dogs—taught to be patient, taught about love, taught about "fundamental love, such as Jesus taught." Day talks to her pets—tells them where she is going when she leaves the house and when she will return. It's a question of loyalty; Day simply finds dogs to be far more loyal than human beings.

As further evidence of her communication with dogs, in her autobiography she relates the story that in the middle of one particularly hot night, her dogs became very restless and woke her up. When she opened the door to let them out, they refused to run outside as was their custom. In fact, they remained completely quiet, looking up at Day and not moving. The dogs' unusual behavior, coupled with small noises from the giant sycamore tree in her yard, made Day shut the screen door and step back into the room. At that very second, the sycamore fell over with a thunderous crash—right into the open yard where Day and the dogs would normally have been walking. It is Day's fervent belief that the dogs, in refusing to budge from the screen door, were

1970s appearance with Mary Tyler Moore to dedicate the Fund for Animals booth at Lion Country Safari. *Photofest*

telling her not to leave her bedroom. It was, she felt, an act of God, and she thinks that "God had chosen to speak to me through my dogs . . ." If God is protecting Day through the animals, she seems to reason, then how can she not return the favor? Taken as a whole, these statements begin to provide an understanding of why Day has turned her back on her performing career; it's just not as important to her as are her animals, as are all animals. In effect, why waste time singing and dancing, when there are animals to be saved? After all, they saved Day's life. Faced with what she felt was a national crisis in terms of animal welfare, she found show business to be markedly diminished in importance. In the words of the notoriously reclusive Greta Garbo, whose behavior the increasingly private Day seems to emulate, Doris Day apparently has just "grown tired of making faces."

Actors and Others for Animals ran fund-raising bazaars, but the breadth and depth of its outreach were severely limited, not only by finances but also by staffing and personnel shortages. So it was that in 1977 Day started her own pet charity, the Doris Day Pet Foundation. This was a charity co-founded with her husband of the time, Barry Comden (Day and restaurateur Comden were married from 1976 until 1982). Day and Comden kick-started the organization with their own $100,000 contribution, and their mission grew beyond the parameters established by Actors and Others for Animals. Concentrating on the greater Los Angeles area, a kennel was opened in the San Fernando Valley, homes were found for dogs and cats, and urgent medical attention was provided for animals in need. In short, the Doris Day Pet Foundation enabled Day to pursue activism on a much larger scale. (An interesting side note is that when Day moved to the coast of California in 1981, she bought the Cypress Inn, in Carmel-by-the-Sea, along with son Terry and Dennis LeVett. This was not to be just any hotel, but rather a hotel with a difference: They hoped it would prove to be a profitable venture, but in reality, the purpose of the hotel was to allow tourists to travel with their dogs and cats. Indeed, the hotel established a pet-sitting service to accommodate such travelers. There was no word on the availability of babysitting services, but somehow one doubts it entered into the key plans for the hotel. For hotel owner Doris Day, the pets are the babies who need a sitting service.)

The Doris Day Pet Foundation may be the only nonprofit group in history whose founder could instantly access the president of the United States. When Day wanted to press the case for a particular piece of animal rights legislation, she called up the White House and told the operator: "Please tell the President that his costar from *The Winning Team* is on the phone, and she would like to speak with him." The call was put through to Ronald Reagan.

Presumably Day was more temperate on the phone with Reagan than she has been elsewhere. Since, in Day's view, dogs communicate with each other heart to heart, she finds it unfair for a pet owner to keep only one dog because it denies the animal "one of his own kind for companionship." A similarly strongly held opinion is that stores that sell dogs should actually "be outlawed." It's not just the outspoken nature of these remarks—it's that Day speaks in such absolute terms that there is no room for a dialogue on these issues.

Renamed the Doris Day Animal Foundation in 1997, the foundation now functions as a national nonprofit organization. Day herself is the president of the five-person Board of Directors, which includes actress Diane Keaton and baseball's Tony LaRussa as advisory members. According to the group's mission statement, the foundation is designed to mobilize individuals and communities, prevent violence against both animals and humans, and at the same time promote empathy and compassion in the treatment of these animals. Translated into nonbureaucraticspeak, the Doris Day Animal Foundation rents space in a kennel for lost pets, provides money for pet food, veterinary care, and vaccinations, and even attacks the issue of animal abuse through a program titled Beyond Violence: The Human-Animal Connection. The

Beyond Violence program engages trained personnel, namely, police and social workers, to travel around the country conducting seminars establishing the need to treat animal abuse as a serious crime.

More strikingly, another program, the Vicious Circle, explores the connection between violence against animals and violence against people. Aiming to eradicate any such behavior before it can take permanent root, the foundation creates programs for children, publishing the adult-level *Animal Guardian* magazine as well as the child-oriented *Comics for Compassion*, which utilize comic strips to teach children "heroism in standing up for empathy and compassion."

The foundation's most successful undertaking, and certainly the one with the highest national profile, has been the establishment of Spay Day USA, which tackles the growing problem of animal overpopulation and resulting euthanasia. Each February, one specific day is set aside to publicly galvanize national action in order to control the problem. The foundation's Web site states that since the inception of Spay Day, more than 1,225,000 spays and neuters have been carried out and, according to Gary McGee's *Doris Day Sentimental Journey,* in the year 2002 alone, the Animal Foundation spayed or neutered more than two hundred thousand cats and dogs. If, as has been posited, somewhere between ten and twelve million dogs and cats are put to sleep each year, a figure that Doris Day states represents "almost a quarter of all the pets in the country," then such action on the part of the Doris Day Animal Foundation represents a noticeable first step toward eradicating a problem that Day terms "a national shame."

How are such activities funded? How successful is the foundation? The most recent publicly released records of the foundation show 2004 revenues of $505,353; in order to raise additional funds, the foundation's online store sells T-shirts, wristbands, posters, and DVDs of Day's feature films. Want an autographed copy of the complete first season of *The Doris Day Show*? That little purchase will set you back $500.

So bedrock has been Day's activism on behalf of animal welfare that it proved to be the only issue that could prompt her return to show business twelve years after *The Doris Day Show* completed its five-year run. The Christian Broadcasting Network (CBN) came to Terry Melcher with the idea of a new weekly series starring Day, consisting of half-hour episodes all centered around animals. Broadcast on the Family Channel during the 1985–1986 season, the show's twenty-six episodes featured a blend of celebrity guests and serious segments on pet care and animal health issues. The series was not particularly inspired, but it was thoroughly professional, informative, and only occasionally as silly as much of *The Doris Day Show.* Doris Day's commitment to animals shone through every segment, and she appeared to take enormous pleasure in sharing her fervent beliefs with a national television audience.

Viewing the episodes today, even a casual viewer is struck by the fact that unlike almost all other actors, Doris does not seem to be particularly interested in appearing on camera. In fact she seems to regard it almost as a necessary evil, as if she'd be happier if the focus were solely on the animals. But the old professionalism still shines through, because even though the series's budget appears to be quite low, Day does care enough about her appearance to be carefully lit and shot at all times.

Clearly the power behind the series was Terry Melcher. He functioned as one of the show's two credited writers, as well as executive producer, music director, and writer of the theme song "Best Friend" (Day's first new recording in over a decade). The combination of son Terry's hands-on participation and Day's passionate belief in animal welfare transformed her. Gone was the somewhat distracted air evident during the last season of *The Doris Day Show.* This was a show to which she was totally committed.

Each episode was usually divided into three segments: Day and her celebrity guest would chat about animals, with a hint of show business thrown into the discussion, followed by a health-care segment focusing on topics such as animal diet and spaying, concluding with a serious issue story on topics that ranged from a ban on medical testing of animals to a depiction of how Seeing Eye dogs are trained.

Denver Pyle stopped by as one of the show's early guests, but even more noteworthy was the guest appearance of Les Brown and His Band of Renown. Brown, who was still touring the country into his seventies and eighties, spoke to Day about her Pet Foundation, a segment followed by veterinarian Dr. Tom Kendall explaining the necessity of spaying and neutering. Most winningly, the episode finished with Day lip-synching to "Sentimental Journey." Day did not want to sing live, feeling that she had passed her vocal prime, but it didn't matter one bit. To see Doris Day with a big band, *her* big band, was to see the years melt away, and forty years after she left the band, she appeared finally to be at home, both musically with her band, and literally inside her own home. Watching Day with the band, how she leaned into the piano while listening to the band play, her entire body language transformed, was to see how she remained, at heart, a singer. Music was and always would be in her soul.

There were change-of-pace episodes where noncelebrity experts spoke on animal-related topics—the most unusual when Dr. Kendall returned to speak about the then out-of-the-ordinary topic of pet health insurance. Some episodes were entirely educational, as in a show devoted to the California Rescue Dog Association and its work in locating missing earthquake victims. Seemingly most enjoyable of all to Day were the two segments in which her grandson Ryan Melcher guest-starred. The first time he appeared, he accompanied his grandmother to visit horses in the stable; his second appearance featured him introducing the family's new puppy.

Old pals Tony Bennett and Tony Randall filmed segments, as did the *Doris Day Show*'s wardrobe supervisor Connie Edney, the woman responsible for all of the wacky and fun fashion show sequences on the sitcom. It was on this episode with Connie Edney that the most extraordinary segment from the twenty-six-week run was broadcast: a feature on quadriplegic Sue Stron and the trained monkey whose help with specific everyday living tasks made Stron's daily routine possible. This segment registered as truly educational television, and it was to the show's credit that there were several such informative segments during the course of the run.

Only on three occasions did this series degenerate into the silliness that marred much of *The Doris Day Show.* The first was when America's first man in space, Alan Shepard, landed in Doris's backyard while inside a rocket (with a dog). Even with tongue firmly planted in cheek this seemed inane, although much of this foolishness was redeemed when Shepard spoke about space travel and the use of animals in space flights. The second nonsensical episode occurred when Howard Keel guest-starred, and the opening skit featured a goofy satire of *Calamity Jane.* The plotline of said skit? Doris's stagecoach is held up by an outlaw who then mistakes Doris for both Dinah Shore and Patti Page. All that was missing was a reference to Rosie Clooney, and the trip back to the 1950s would have been complete. . . . And who came to rescue Calamity/Doris? That's right—Wild Bill Hickok (Howard Keel). A little of such nonsense went a very long way.

Yet even with these missteps, only once did the show degenerate into low-grade skit writing left over from a bad episode of *The Doris Day Show*. When Angie Dickinson guest-starred, the segment started with the two women having lunch as they discussed Dickinson helping Day's pet foundation. Neither woman had money to pay for the lunch, so the restaurant manager called for the sheriff. The solution? The sheriff sees Doris and sings "Secret Love" to her; turns out he has always wanted to be in show business. The result was a waste of ten minutes of air time—all that's missing are the hillbillies from season one of *The Doris Day Show.*

Yet such flaccid sketches were the exception rather than the rule. For the most part the series was genial in tone, informative in content, and served to remind the public, albeit on a cable television station, that Doris Day was very much alive, kicking, and still looking great. An additional note of interest lies in the fact that during the run of the series, Doris recorded sixteen tracks that were used as background to accompany animal montages and footage of Doris romping with her pets. The tracks, which remain unreleased to this day, tended to be of the rock-lite variety: "You Are So Beautiful!" and "Crocodile Rock." Terry Melcher, who produced the recordings, also wrote several of the songs along with Bruce Johnston, mostly utilizing a heavy synthesizer backing due to the small budget. Day, who was sixty-one at the time of the recordings, sounds great throughout, but the overall effect inevitably suffers from the limitations of those early synthesizers. Of the sixteen recorded tracks, there is one unquestioned gem: "Everyone's Gone to the Moon," which was featured, naturally enough, in the opening sequence of astronaut Alan Shepard's guest appearance.

Doris Day's Best Friends also marked the turning point in the public's awareness of Day as an animal rights activist. After these twenty-six episodes, the public and press perception of Day was no longer Doris Day the movie star or Doris Day the singer. It had been decades since Day had functioned in either capacity. Instead, it became clear to everyone that the focus of Doris Day's life was on taking care of animals and utilizing her public profile to educate the public. Entertainment, in this case a television series, happened to be the vehicle through which she could accomplish her goals, but it was not entertainment or television that interested Day—animals did. Note her words when discussing her work with animals: "I just love that I can make it better for the animals. . . . That is thrilling for me." "Thrilling" is not a word Doris Day ever uses in connection with her films and recordings. She is "grateful" for the continued support of her fans, "amazed" at the continued popularity of her movies and music, and even enjoys hearing that her work has helped people through tough times in their lives. She is, however, never "thrilled" by the world of show business. That is a term she reserves for her work with animals, work that keeps her so busy that on more than one occasion she has joked that she "might make a movie just to take a rest!"

Airing opposite *60 Minutes,* a show that drew upon the same older demographic that *Doris Day's Best Friends* was courting, Day's series never found a large audience. Part of this may have simply been due to the fact that the public expected to see more of Day herself. Certainly many viewers tuned in to watch Doris Day but instead saw chunks of each half-hour episode with very little of her presence. Maybe viewers didn't quite realize in advance that the entire series was to be about animals, or it may just have been the fact that, to put it kindly, the show did not exactly possess a lush look. In the words of Leslie Halliwell, a program buyer for British television, "The quality of production did not warrant a purchase."

Whatever the reason, after twenty-six episodes the show quietly left the air. With the exception of Doris introducing and narrating the *Entertainment Tonight* three-part look at animals in films titled "Hollywood's Wildest Stars," it marked the end of Doris Day's nonretrospective career in television.

As her activism grew, in 1987 she founded a second animal rights group, the Doris Day Animal League, a nonprofit national lobbying group for animal rights located in Washington, D.C. The organization now claims close to three hundred thousand members and consists of eleven full-time staff members "working to reduce the pain and suffering of non-human animals through legislative initiatives." The Animal League attempts to influence both local and national legislation, spearheading efforts to ban greyhound racing and actually suing the United States Air Force over its transfer of chimpanzees. Over the years, the league's activities have run the gamut from aiding in the passing of a California law making counseling mandatory for people convicted of animal abuse (1998), to helping pave the way for the implementation of the Dog and Cat Protection Act, which bans the importation of products containing cat and dog fur (2000). Most recently, the Animal League, one of the original sponsors of 1998's Proposition Four in California, experienced success when the Ninth Circuit Court of Appeals upheld the ban on poison and "cruel animal traps" such as steel-jawed leghold traps and M-44 explosives.

The league has also joined with other animal rights organizations to file a lawsuit that aims to block the United States Department of Agriculture from implementing its plan to allow the slaughter of horses. Why the lawsuit? Because, the Doris Day Animal League contends, such slaughter is not for humane purposes but rather to provide for the sale of horse meat for human consumption overseas. No sweet animal images here; according to the league's Web site, some ninety thousand horses were slaughtered in the United States in 2005, at three slaughterhouses that were all foreign owned.

It was, however, Day's extraordinarily outspoken statements about testing on humans that caused the loudest public outcry. If, as has been written, she listens each day to talk radio, it is likely that the radio she listens to is conservative in nature, and her comments about product testing are not couched in terms to make her loved by the American Civil Liberties Union. Regarding product experimentation being tried on convicted killers instead of animals: "Why not? They owe society something. Don't stand aghast at that. They're sitting here having three meals a day and we're paying for it. What the hell are they going

President of the Doris Day Animal League. *Photofest*

to do for society to pay us back? . . . I think they'd want to do it to give back to society what they have taken from it. I should think it would make them feel better. I would volunteer if I'd done something so horrendous like those people on death row. Anyway, it's stupid to test on animals. They're not like us."

This is one black-and-white worldview—no ethical or moral shadings regarding personal responsibility or equal rights protection for Doris Day. She views these issues in absolutist terms and as a result it's no wonder she isn't interested in making movies. Instead, she appears in the news or grants interviews only when she wants to bring publicity to a major issue of animal welfare.

So it was that in October of 2005, the reclusive Day granted a telephone interview to nationally syndicated columnist Liz Smith. Was the interview about the continuing DVD release of Day's CBS variety specials and the entire five-season run of *The Doris Day Show*? Not a chance. Day didn't want to discuss her career, although she did laughingly admit that she can still tap dance. Instead, she wanted to speak with Smith about the latest efforts of the Doris Day Animal Foundation that had resulted in national publicity and landed Day back in the papers: In the October 2005 aftermath of Hurricane Katrina, the foundation had donated $20,000 to pay for the airlift of 130 dogs and cats—Operation Just Paws—from New Iberia, Louisiana, to the Santa Cruz SPCA. Day was elated with the success of the rescue and with the continuing efforts to place all of the animals in new homes. This was worth talking about. As for her storied entertainment career? Well, Liz Smith herself summed it up best at the close of the column: "Doris is shakin' the blues away. Just don't expect to see her doing it in public any time soon."

And no one does.

Which is what makes it all the more striking that the last time Day garnered national publicity for an entertainment venture was not for singing, dancing, or acting but rather for the very early episode of *Doris Day's Best Friends* on which Rock Hudson stopped by for a visit. Hudson's guest-starring role on the show marked his last public appearance, and sick as he was, he was determined to be on the show, such was the mutual respect and love between Hudson and Day. At this stage of his illness he was so gaunt that the viewer's reaction is one of shock and sadness; it is, in fact, hard to concentrate on the banter between the good friends as they discuss their favorite film together (both agree on *Pillow Talk*). The contrast between the frail Hudson and the beautiful and vibrant Day is poignant, as is the contrast between the dying Hudson and the pictures of his younger, strapping self. In a stirring finale, the episode ended with Doris singing "My Buddy" over a progression of stills from their three films together.

In reality, it was the opening of the entire episode that proved so memorable. Broadcast on October 2, 1985, after Hudson had died, Doris introduced the segment with a special filmed message: "All his friends, and there were many, could always count on Rock Hudson. Not only was he a very talented dramatic actor, as we all know, his favorite thing was comedy. And he always said to me, 'The best time I've ever had was making comedies with you.' And I felt the same way. We had a ball. . . . I can only tell you, my friends, that it was a heartbreaking time for me to see him. He didn't talk about his illness, not one time. . . . I said, 'You've come to the right place, my darling, because I'm going to put weight on you. I'm going to force-feed you.' And we laughed. . . . And of course, I felt that he wasn't feeling well enough to work. And I told him, 'You don't have to do this show and I don't want you to. I want you to forget it. I want you to just stay in Carmel for a while and relax and enjoy it.' And he said, 'Forget it. I came here to do your show and that's exactly what I'm going to do.' And he did. That's what he did, and he was wonderful." Choking back tears, Day concluded by stating simply, "And I feel that without my deep faith I would be a lot sadder than I am today. I know that life is eternal and that something good is going to come from this experience."

This was not acting—this was straight from the heart, a friend talking about the loss of a loved one; from any other actress, such a speech on television might have elicited whispers of grandstanding or attention seeking. With Doris Day, that most sincere of actresses, everyone instinctively knew it was the real thing. Originally shot as the series opener, this episode was broadcast as the second episode; suffice it to say that long after the final episode had been broadcast, this is the one moment from the series that lives on in people's memories. In a series devoted to Day's great passion in life, animal welfare, it is ironic—and totally fitting—that what lingers in the mind is her tender and entirely fitting tribute to her great friend Rock Hudson.

Rock Hudson's death proved to be a turning point in the American public's response to the AIDS epidemic: A beloved movie star's death from the disease had put a public and personal face on the illness that had heretofore largely been ignored because it affected only "them"—homosexuals and drug addicts. With Rock Hudson's death, which found most of the American public even unaware that Hudson was gay, the disease hit home. Loved by millions, heartthrob and genial all-around good guy, Rock Hudson forced the American public to confront the disease head-on. Hudson's death affected even the heretofore noticeably silent Reagan government in its response to AIDS. Rock Hudson was a friend of Ronald and Nancy Reagan's, and after Hudson's death, the Reagan government oh-so-slowly started to speak about AIDS, beginning, however tentatively, to formulate an official policy. It makes a curious kind of sense, then, that it was Doris Day's heartfelt tribute that resonated with the American public, a tribute that hit the front pages of many newspapers and was aired not only on her own television show but also in video clips broadcast around the world.

Forever happily entwined in the public's eye from their three increasingly iconic costarring films, Day and Hudson were now linked in an entirely different fashion by Hudson's untimely death. Far from dimming the luster of their three happy films, Hudson's death increased public affection for these glossy, cheerful, unrealistic yet often deeply funny films. In the world of Doris Day and Rock Hudson, all turns out happily—it's the way people wish life could be. These two stars seem made for each other, and forty-five years after their initial release, the films remain hugely popular through revival houses, videocassettes, and DVDs. The unique Day-Hudson chemistry could not ever be recaptured; 2004's *Down With Love,* a virtual remake of *Pillow Talk* with Renee Zellweger and Ewan McGregor playing, in effect, Doris Day and Rock Hudson, couldn't begin to rebottle that chemistry. America's innocence was long vanished: the pre-Vietnam, pre-Watergate, pre-ironic American worldview that had made the Day/Hudson films viable had disappeared. The gloriously vibrant and youthful Doris Day and Rock Hudson were no more, but the palpable affection that Doris Day displayed for her recently deceased friend did more than increase the affection the public held for the two superstars. It served as a reminder of the way we truly were and why Doris Day had become a star in the first place. Sincere, straightforward, enormously talented and, most crucially, always leading from the heart, Doris Day's tribute to Rock Hudson served as a fitting epitaph to the end of her own forty-five-year performing career.

Que Sera, Sera

With the passing of time Ms. Day, who turned 81 on April 3, looks less like a bluestocking and more like an important transitional figure in the history of pop-culture feminism.

—*Dave Kehr,* The New York Times, *April 26, 2005*

She's not just a survivor. She's a happy survivor.

—*A. E. Hotchner,* Doris Day: A Sentimental Journey

I always felt that making a living wasn't the easiest thing in the world, and I decided I was going straight ahead and try to be as uncomplicated as possible. The important thing in life is just living and loving.

—*Doris Day,* Ms. *magazine, January 1976*

And what of Doris Day today? Aside from singing on one track of son Terry's 1974 album and recording several tracks for *Doris Day's Best Friends,* she has not recorded for nearly forty years. Her last motion picture was made in 1968, her two television series have been off the air for thirty and twenty years, respectively, and she rarely makes public appearances. Yet interest in Day continues unabated, and it is a measure of the public's increasing affection for her that when rumors began to circulate in the 1990s that Doris would sing publicly at an AIDS benefit in Los Angeles, the explosion of public and press interest was so intense that she had to issue a statement that no such appearance was in the offing. Most interesting of all, on the few occasions when Doris Day can be induced to discuss her storied career, she refuses to use the term "retirement." In her own words, she "just became interested in other things."

She has spent the last thirty years of her life devoting her considerable energies and resources to the improvement of animal welfare. She seems to positively bask not in the adulation of the public but rather in the "normal" everyday life she now leads. In a statement that a few hundred million Americans might find ludicrous if Day were not so clearly sincere, the actress laughingly told a television interviewer, "I just love going to the market. I didn't have that chance I was working so hard." It's a sentiment backed up in typical laconic fashion by Day's Carmel neighbor Clint Eastwood: "Doris Day is my neighbor. I see her at her office—the Safeway Supermarket."

Doris Day's love affair with Safeway might seem nonsensical if it didn't happen to be true. Day didn't pursue stardom. She didn't have to be a star the way Bette Davis, Joan Crawford, and Barbra Streisand did—the very air of stardom fed those powerful women. But, when stardom came Day's way, she devoted herself 100 percent to the work itself. A perfectionist at heart, she would gladly deliver take after take on the set or in the recording studio in order to achieve her vision. But after her performing career ended—by her own choice—she never looked back. Just how great was her lack of interest in the past? Well, consider her chance meeting with a stranger twenty years after her divorce from George Weidler. In a story related by Day in her autobiography, she describes walking down Beverly Drive and being stopped by a man who greeted her with a simple hello. Day replied hello, at which point the man asked if she remembered him. When Day answered in the negative, he said, "Well, you didn't have *that* many husbands." It was George Weidler, and Day's totally blank response is laid out in even starker relief by her rueful self-analysis: "Can you imagine? Here was a man I was once deeply in love with . . . and married to." (One can only shake one's head in disbelief that Day's divorce attorney was Jerome Rosenthal, the same Jerome Rosenthal who wreaked such financial havoc in her life some twenty years later.)

No, the glories of a performing career no longer interested Doris. Not for her the descent into playing gargoyles as did Davis and Crawford. She remained true to herself and to her own vision of what she represented. In the words of Terry Melcher, "Doris felt a responsibility to her fans consistent with what they expected of her." As Melcher further pointed out, when this most brilliant of singers felt that the type of music she loved—Broadway show tunes and ballads from the golden age of the great American songbook—were no longer relevant, she simply stopped recording and walked away from it all. Presumably straight to the Safeway.

Hollywood still comes knocking, but all attempts to lure Day out of her "interest in other things" are met with polite refusal. Just as Day's feature film career was ending, shrewd director Mike Nichols offered her the lead role of Mrs. Robinson in *The Graduate,* a role that she turned down because of the sexual content in the film. Great as Anne Bancroft was, it's a shame Doris didn't take the role; it would have afforded her the chance finally to work once again with a truly great director, in the process providing her with the opportunity to fully explore her acting range in essaying the role of such a dark, sardonic, and ultimately sad woman. There is no doubt that Nichols would have guided Day to a great performance; it was Nichols, after all, who completely changed the course of Ann-Margret's career by directing her to an Oscar-nominated performance in *Carnal Knowledge,* a performance that awakened the eyes of the industry and public to her capabilities as an actress.

Similarly, Albert Brooks offered Day the juicy title role in his film *Mother* (supposedly after first discussing the role with Nancy Reagan!). In Brooks's own words, "I wanted to cast an actress whose participation would make the film a real event." Day went so far as to meet with Brooks, but she ultimately turned down a return to the world of filmmaking. The part went instead to the indefatigable Debbie Reynolds, who not only earned some of the best reviews of her career but a Golden Globe nomination as well.

The list of television proposals Day rejected is even longer: Day turned down "a new series that I liked—about a woman who ran a column like Ann Landers's" because at the time she was occupied with building her house in Carmel. She declined a chance to film the Broadway play *West Side Waltz* costarring Katharine Hepburn, and as recently as 2005, rumors abounded that Day would team up for a final film with Elizabeth Taylor. Nothing has come of any of the projects for one simple reason: Without saying so explicitly, Doris Day has had her fill of show business. She is grateful for the success, for the fans, and for the pleasure she has brought to millions, but it no longer interests her. She may, at age eighty-two, still be able to tap dance, but it appears very likely that Doris Day will never again set foot on a film set or recording studio.

For all the talk about a comeback for superstar Doris Day, there's one point that is consistently overlooked: One of the last stars from the golden age of Hollywood, Doris Day worked nonstop from 1939 through 1975. She made 39 motion pictures, well over 600 recordings, 2 television variety specials, 154 episodes of two television series, and wrote a best-selling autobiography. It's time for a rest.

A brilliant vocalist whose breadth and depth as a singer are rivaled and surpassed only by Ella Fitzgerald, she recorded a series of beautiful concept albums for Columbia Records, the best of which constitute a seamless and complex investigation of the great American songbook. In the process of creating these eighteen albums, Day delivered definitive interpretations of popular classics that served as the voice and spirit of mid-twentieth-century America. Before her feature film career dissolved in a series of abysmally scripted, tired sex farces, she had evolved from a lighthearted, lithe performer in pleasantly fluffy musical films into the finest musical actress in films (*Love Me or Leave Me, The Pajama Game,* and *Jumbo*). When given a first-rate script and the chance to work with a first-rate director, she could handle the heaviest dramatic roles with ease, as in *The Man Who Knew Too Much.* An expert comedian, she soared to great heights and became the single biggest movie star in the world, working with the best comedic actors in the business—Clark Gable in *Teacher's Pet,* James Garner in *The Thrill of It All,* and Rock Hudson in *Pillow Talk*.

In a time when feature films rarely featured working women as heroines, Doris Day proved to be nothing short of a pioneer. She personified the mid-twentieth-century American woman, free-willed and self-sufficient, a woman who, far from pegging her happiness to snagging a husband, reveled in her workplace success. At her best, just as Molly Haskell suggested, Day really did embody a "homegrown existential female lifted into the modern world."

During an era in which workplace opportunities for women were severely limited, she functioned as a role model through whom thousands of women worldwide lived vicariously. Aggressive, tomboyish, yet utterly feminine, she was the most self-sufficient, forward-looking woman in American movies. In short, Doris Day, the most American of film actresses, personified nothing less than an authentic American heroine of the twentieth century—"the American Century."

Hers is, it is safe to say, a hard-won perspective on life and priorities. After a tumultuous life—superstardom came at the cost of four failed marriages, personal bankruptcy, and the heartbreaking death of her son at age sixty-three—Doris has seemingly found peace of mind. Show business is over. In her own straightforward way, Day herself summed up the roller coaster journey, the desire to move on from the legendary career, no matter how storied: "I'm very grateful because I've had so many blessings. I've had a lot of trauma in my life—I've lost so many friends—two leggers and four leggers. Sometimes you think 'I can't go through it again'—but you do. I don't know if there's a heaven—I suppose this is heaven—when everything is going well this is heaven, isn't it, heaven right here.' "

Coda

Surely no other great American artist
and cultural icon was so willing to forgo
cleverness for the sake of truth.
—*Will Friedwald, music critic*

Writing in Day's 1976 autobiography, coauthor A. E. Hotchner relates the end of an exhausting day at a bazaar to benefit Actors and Others for Animals. After Doris Day had spent hours posing for pictures in the blazing sun, remaining until the very last person in line had successfully managed a photo with the star, Hotchner quietly spoke to Day about the adoration of her fans, the happiness she brought to so many: "I've never seen so much love." Day's poignant response: "If so many people love me, how come I'm alone?"

Perhaps the answer to Day's query lies in the words of close friend Don Genson, writing in the liner notes to the UK release of the long-lost *Love Album.* Musing about his close personal friend and professional colleague, Genson stated simply, "I think the whole world is in love with Doris Day. That's quite a legacy."

Career Scorecard

YEAR	WORK	GRADE	COMMENT
1948	*Romance on the High Seas*	C	First movie Already a star; not yet an actress
1949	*My Dream Is Yours*	B	Overly bright but improving
1949	*It's a Great Feeling*	C	Terrible script
1949	*You're My Thrill*—album	B	First album
1950	*Young Man with a Horn*—film Laurel Award (theater owners)—leading new personality in motion pictures	B	Growing as an actress
1950	*Young Man with a Horn*—album	A	Great singing; jazz inflected
1950	*Tea for Two*—film	C	Silly script; good music
1950	*Tea for Two*—album	B	Nice period tunes
1950	*The West Point Story*	D	Gibberish
1951	*Storm Warning*	B	Surprisingly effective; first dramatic role Only time Doris dies on film
1951	*Lullaby of Broadway* *Photoplay* Gold Medal Award—Best Actress	B	Nonsense, but worth it for the title number
1951	*Lullaby of Broadway*—album	B	Fun music
1951	*On Moonlight Bay* Quigley Poll of film exhibitors and distributors: #9 box office attraction	B	Better than the usual Warner Bros. fare

YEAR	WORK	GRADE	COMMENT
1951	*On Moonlight Bay*—album	B	Solid and smooth
1951	*Starlift*	D	Ridiculous; has to be seen to be believed
1951	*I'll See You in My Dreams*—album	A	Great songs; great singer
1952	*I'll See You in My Dreams* Quigley Ranking: #7 box office attraction	A	First-rate film
1952	*The Winning Team*	C	Nothing role—with Ronald Reagan, no less
1953	*April in Paris*	C	One great song and one bad script
1953	*April in Paris*—album	B	A lot better than the film
1953	*By the Light of the Silvery Moon*	B	Nostalgic fun
1953	*By the Light of the Silvery Moon*—album	B	Pleasant and somewhat disposable
1953	*Calamity Jane*	B	Rambunctious fun if somewhat exhausting
1953	*Calamity Jane*—album	B	Nice Fain/Webster score
1954	*Lucky Me*	D	Goes absolutely nowhere
1954	Golden Globe nominee—World Film Favorite		
1954	*Young at Heart*	C	Sweet nothing of a role; odd mix with Sinatra
1954	*Young at Heart*—album	B	Nice songs; better than the film
1955	*Love Me or Leave Me*	A	Great acting, great singing. Career peak
1955	*Love Me or Leave Me*—album	A	Brilliant
1956	*The Man Who Knew Too Much*	A	Terrific dramatic performance
1956	*Julie*	C	Ludicrous and overblown
1957	*Day by Day*—album	A	Nary a false step
1957	*Day by Night*—album	A	A near-perfect pop album
1957	*The Pajama Game*	A	A great Hollywood musical—great Day
1957	Golden Globe Award—World Film Favorite		
1957	*The Pajama Game*—album	A	Broadway baby with a great Broadway score

YEAR	WORK	GRADE	COMMENT
1958	*Teacher's Pet*	A	First-rate adult comedy
1958	*Hooray For Hollywood*—album	A	Terrific double album. Check out "That Old Black Magic"
1958	Grammy Award Nomination— Best Vocal Performance, Female: "Everybody Loves a Lover"		
1958	*Tunnel of Love* Laurel Award—Top Female Star Golden Globe Nominee— Best Actress in Musical or Comedy	F	Smarmy and offensive
1959	*It Happened to Jane*	A	Great teaming with Jack Lemmon
1959	*Cuttin' Capers*—album	A	Peak of her uptempo ventures; stands comparison with Sinatra's *Songs for Swingin' Lovers*
1959	*Pillow Talk* Quigley Ranking: #4 box office attraction Laurel Award—Top Female Star Photoplay Gold Medal Award— Best Actress/Most Popular Actress Academy Award Nomination—Best Actress	B	Iconic role
1960	Golden Globe Nominee—Best Actress in a Musical or Comedy Golden Globe—World Film Favorite		
1960	Grammy Award Nomination— Best Vocal Performance, Single Record or Track: "The Sound of Music"		
1960	*Please Don't Eat the Daisies*	A	Terrific comic performance
1960	*Listen to Day*—album	B	Not bad compilation
1960	*What Every Girl Should Know*—album	A	Top-drawer mood music
1960	*Midnight Lace* Quigley Ranking: #1 box office attraction Laurel Award—Top Female Star Golden Globe Nominee—Best Actress in a Drama	C	Hysterical and overwrought

YEAR	WORK	GRADE	COMMENT
1960	Laurel Award—Best Female Comedy Performance for *Pillow Talk*		
1960	*Show Time*—album	A	As good as Broadway gets
1961	*Bright and Shiny*—album	B	Jazzier effort
1961	*I Have Dreamed*—album	A	Another career peak
1961	Quigley Ranking: #3 box office attraction Laurel Award—Top Female Star		
1961	*Lover Come Back*	B	Best of the Day-Hudson films
1962	*Duet*—album with André Previn	B	Two great musicians
1962	*That Touch of Mink*	D	Dispiriting nonsense about DD's virginity
1962	Quigley Ranking: #1 box office attraction Laurel Award—Top Female Star Laurel Award—Best Female Comedy Performance for *Lover Come Back*		
1962	*Wonderful Day*	B	Compilation album
1962	*Doris Day's Greatest Hits*	A	Great sampling—brilliant "Lullaby of Broadway"
1962	*Billy Rose's Jumbo* Golden Globe Nominee—Best Actress in a Musical or Comedy	B	Terrific last musical
1962	Golden Globe Award—World Film Favorite		
1962	*Billy Rose's Jumbo*—album	B	First-rate score: first-rate singing
1962	*You'll Never Walk Alone*—album	B	Touching if overly solemn
1963	*The Thrill of It All*	A	Great comic acting—Oscar worthy
1963	*Move Over Darling* Golden Globe Nominee—Best Actress in a Comedy or Musical	C	Should have been better
1963	*Doris Day and Robert Goulet Sing* Annie Get Your Gun	A	Perfect match of singer and score

YEAR	WORK	GRADE	COMMENT
1963	Quigley Ranking: #1 box office attraction Laurel Award—Top Female Star Laurel Award—Best Female Comedy Performance for *That Touch of Mink*		
1964	*Send Me No Flowers*	C	One note; least of the Day-Hudson films
1964	Quigley Ranking: #1 box office attraction Laurel Award—Top Female Star Laurel Award—Best Female Comedy Performance for *Send Me No Flowers*		
1964	*Love Him!*—album	B	Interesting variation
1964	*With a Smile and a Song*—album	A	Excellent children's album
1964	*The Doris Day Christmas Album*	A	Beautiful and intimate
1965	*Do Not Disturb* Golden Globe Nominee—World Film Favorite	C	Second-rate "comedy"
1965	Quigley Ranking—#3 box office attraction		
1965	*Latin for Lovers*—album	A	Extraordinary genre album
1965	*Doris Day's Sentimental Journey*—album	B	Elegiac
1966	*Glass Bottom Boat*	B	Exhausting but fun
1966	Quigley Ranking: #8 box office attraction		
1967	*Caprice*	D	Overstuffed
1967	Laurel Award Nominee—Best Female Comedy Performance for *The Glass Bottom Boat*		
1967	*Ballad of Josie*	B	Surprisingly feminist
1968	*Where Were You When the Lights Went Out?*	F	From hunger. Awful
1968	*With Six You Get Egg Roll*	B	Great fun; should have been the start of a whole new film career
1968–1969	*The Doris Day Show*—television—Season One	C	Lifting nonsense all by herself

YEAR	WORK	GRADE	COMMENT
1969	Golden Globe Award Nomination—Best Actress in a Television Series		
1969–1970	*The Doris Day Show*—Season Two	B	Moving to the city—improvement
1970–1971	*The Doris Day Show*—Season Three	B	Hitting its stride
1971	*The Doris Mary Anne Kappelhoff Special*—CBS Special	B	Solid effort
1971–1972	*The Doris Day Show*—Season Four	C	Falling off
1972–1973	*The Doris Day Show*—Season Five	C	Time to end
1975	*Doris day toDay*—Special	C	Should have/could have been better
1975	*Doris Day: Her Own Story*—autobiography	A	Honest and compelling
1985–1986	*Doris Day's Best Friends*—CBN television series	B	Nice if one-note
1989	Golden Globe Award—Cecil B. De Mille Award—Lifetime Achievement		
1991	Comedy Awards—Lifetime Achievement—First-ever recipient		
1994	*The Love Album*—released in UK	A	Finally released—brilliant final album
1995	*The Complete Doris Day with Les Brown*	B	Great overview of DD's musical roots
2004	Awarded Presidential Medal of Freedom by President George W. Bush—Nation's highest civilian honor		
2006	*The Love Album*—released in the U.S.	A	Even better with three additional tracks

United States Top 40 Singles—Source: *Billboard Magazine* and *CashBox Magazine*

76 charting singles
21 singles in the Top 10
7 singles at number one
19 U.S. Top 40 songs charted for 12 weeks or more
7 gold singles

Filmography

Romance on the High Seas

Released July 1948
Warner Bros.
Producer: Alex Gottlieb
Director: Michael Curtiz
Screenplay: Julius J. Epstein, Philip G. Epstein; additional dialogue by I.A.L. Diamond
Cinematography: Elwood Bredell
Musical Numbers Staged by Busby Berkeley; Orchestrations: Ray Heindorf
Cast: Jack Carson (Peter Virgil); Janis Paige (Elvira Kent); Don DeFore (Michael Kent); Doris Day (Georgia Garrett); Oscar Levant (Oscar Ferrar); S. Z. Sakall (Uncle Laszlo)
Score by Jule Styne and Sammy Cahn: "I'm in Love," "It's You or No One," "Put 'Em in a Box, Tie It with a Ribbon," "Run, Run, Run," "It's Magic," "The Tourist Trade," "Two Lovers Met in the Night"

My Dream Is Yours

Released April 1949
Warner Bros.
Director/Producer: Michael Curtiz
Screenplay: Harry Kurnitz, Dane Lussier; Adaptation: Allen Rivkin, Laura Kerr; Story: Jerry Wald, Paul Moss
Photography: Ernest Haller, Wilfred M. Cline
Musical Numbers Staged by LeRoy Prinz; Musical Direction: Ray Heindorf
Cast: Jack Carson (Doug Blake); Doris Day (Martha Gibson); Lee Bowman (Gary Mitchell); Adolphe Menjou (Thomas Hutchins); Eve Arden (Vivian Martin); S. Z. Sakall (Felix Hofer)
Songs: "Love Finds a Way," "My Dream Is Yours," "Someone Like You," "Tic, Tic, Tic," "Canadian Capers," "Freddie Get Ready," "I'll String Along with You," "Wicky, Wacky Woo," "You Must Have Been a Beautiful Baby"

It's a Great Feeling

Released August 1949
Warner Bros.
Producer: Alex Gottlieb
Director: David Butler
Screenplay: Jack Rose, Mel Shavelson; Story: I.A.L. Diamond
Photography: Wilfred M. Cline
Choreography: LeRoy Prinz; Musical Direction: Ray Heindorf; Orchestrations: Sidney Cutner, Leo Shuken
Cast: Dennis Morgan (Himself); Doris Day (Judy Adams); Jack Carson (Himself); Bill Goodwin (Arthur Trent); Errol Flynn (Jeffrey Bushfinkle); appearing as themselves: Michael Curtiz, David Butler, Gary Cooper, Joan Crawford, Sydney Greenstreet, Ronald Reagan, Edward G. Robinson
Songs by Jule Styne and Sammy Cahn: "At the Café Rendezvous," "Fiddle Dee Dee," "Give Me a Song with a Beautiful Melody," "It's a Great Feeling," "There's Nothing Rougher Than Love," "That Was a Big Fat Lie," "Blame My Absent-Minded Heart"

Young Man with a Horn

Warner Bros.
Released March 1950
Producer: Jerry Wald
Director: Michael Curtiz
Screenplay: Carl Foreman, Edmund H. North, based on the novel *Young Man with a Horn* by Dorothy Baker
Photography: Ted McCord
Musical Direction: Ray Heindorf
Cast: Kirk Douglas (Rick Martin); Lauren Bacall (Amy North); Doris Day (Jo Jordan); Hoagy Carmichael (Smoke Willoughby); Juano Hernandez (Art Hazzard); Jerome Cowan (Phil Morrison); Mary Beth Hughes (Margo Martin); Orley Lindgren (Rick as a Child)
Songs: "Get Happy," "I May Be Wrong," "I Only Have Eyes for You," "Lullaby of Broadway," "Limehouse Blues," "The Man I Love," "Pretty Baby," "The Very Thought of You," "Too Marvelous for Words," "With a Song in My Heart," "Melancholy Rhapsody"

Tea for Two

Released September 1950
Warner Bros.
Producer: William Jacobs
Director: David Butler
Screenplay: Harry Clork, based on the Broadway musical *No, No, Nanette* by Frank Mandel, Otto Harbach, Vincent Youmans, Irving Caesar, Emil Nyitray
Photography: Wilfred M. Cline
Musical Direction: Ray Heindorf
Cast: Doris Day (Nanette Carter); Gordon MacRae (Jimmy Smith); Gene Nelson (Tommy Trainor); Patrice Wymore (Beatrice Darcy); Eve Arden (Pauline Hastings); Billy DeWolfe (Larry Blair); S. Z. Sakall (J. Maxwell Bloomhaus)
Songs: "Charleston," "Crazy Rhythm," "Do, Do, Do," "Here in My Arms," "I Only Have Eyes for You," "Oh Me, Oh My," "I Know That You Know," "I Want to Be Happy," "Tea for Two," "No, No, Nanette"

The West Point Story

Released November 1950
Warner Bros.
Producer: Lous F. Edelman
Director: Roy Del Ruth
Screenplay: John Monks Jr., Charles Hoffman, Irving Wallace, based on a story by Irving Wallace
Photography: Sid Hickox
Dance Direction: LeRoy Prinz
Musical Direction: Ray Heindorf; Orchestrations: Frank Perkins
Cast: James Cagney (Elwin Bixby); Virginia Mayo (Eve Dillon); Doris Day (Jan Wilson); Gordon MacRae (Tom Fletcher); Gene Nelson (Hal Courtland);
Songs by Jule Styne and Sammy Cahn: "Brooklyn," "By the Kissing Rock," "It Could Only Happen in Brooklyn," "Military Polka," "Long Before I Knew You," "Ten Thousand Four Hundred Thirty-Two Sheep," "You Love Me"

Storm Warning

Released February 1951
Warner Bros.
Producer: Jerry Wald
Director: Stuart Heisler
Screenplay: Daniel Fuchs, Richard Brooks
Photography: Carl Guthrie
Music: Daniele Amfitheatrof
Cast: Ginger Rogers (Marsha Mitchell); Ronald Reagan (Burt Rainey); Doris Day (Lucy Rice); Steve Cochran (Hank Rice)

Lullaby of Broadway

Released March 1951
Warner Bros.
Producer: William Jacobs
Director: David Butler
Screenplay: Earl Baldwin
Photography: Wilfred M. Cline
Musical Numbers Staged by Al White, Eddie Prinz
Musical Director: Ray Heindorf; Orchestrations: Frank Perkins
Cast: Doris Day (Melinda Howard); Gene Nelson (Tom Farnham); S. Z. Sakall (Adolph Hubbell); Billy DeWolfe (Lefty Mack); Gladys George (Jessica Howard); Florence Bates (Mrs. Hubbell)
Songs: "Fine and Dandy," "I Love the Way You Say Goodnight," "Just One of Those Things," "In a Shanty in Old Shanty Town," "Please Don't Talk About Me When I'm Gone," "Lullaby of Broadway," "We'd Like To Go on a Trip," "Somebody Loves Me," "Zing! Went the Strings of My Heart," "You're Getting to Be a Habit with Me"

On Moonlight Bay

Released July 1951
Warner Bros.
Producer: William Jacobs
Director: Roy Del Ruth

Screenplay: Jack Rose, Melville Shavelson, based on the *Penrod* stories by Booth Tarkington
Photography: Ernest Haller
Musical Numbers Staged by LeRoy Prinz
Musical Director: Ray Heindorf
Cast: Doris Day (Marjorie Winfield); Gordon MacRae (Bill Sherman); Jack Smith (Hubert Wakeley); Leon Ames (George Winfield); Rosemary DeCamp (Mrs. Winfield); Mary Wickes (Stella); Billy Gray (Wesley); Ellen Corby (Miss Stevens)
Songs: "Cuddle Up a Little Closer," "Christmas Story;" "I'm Forever Blowing Bubbles," "On Moonlight Bay," "Love Ya," "Pack Up Your Troubles in Your Old Kit Bag," "Tell Me (Why Nights Are Lonely)," "Till We Meet Again"

Starlift

Released December 1951
Warner Bros.
Producer: Robert Arthur
Director: Roy Del Ruth
Screenplay: John Klorer, Karl Kamb
Photography: Ted McCord
Choreography: LeRoy Prinz
Musical Director: Ray Heindorf
Cast: Janice Rule (Nell Wayne); Dick Wesson (Sgt. Mike Nolan); Ron Hagerthy (Cpl. Rick Williams); Richard Webb (Col. Callan); as themselves: Doris Day, Gordon MacRae, Virgina Mayo, Gene Nelson, Ruth Roman, James Cagney, Gary Cooper, Louella Parsons, Phil Harris, Jane Wyman
Songs: "Good Green Acres of Home," "I May Be Wrong (But I Think You're Wonderful)," "Lullaby of Broadway," 'S Wonderful," "Noche Carib," "What Is This Thing Called Love," "You Do Something to Me," "You're Gonna Lose Your Gal," "Look Out Stranger, I'm a Texas Ranger," "You Ought To Be in Pictures"

I'll See You in My Dreams

Released January 1952
Warner Bros.
Producer: Louis F. Edelman
Director: Michael Curtiz
Screenplay: Melville Shavelson, Jack Rose; Story: Grace Kahn, Louis F. Edelman
Photography: Ted McCord
Musical Numbers Staged by LeRoy Prinz
Musical Director: Ray Heindorf
Cast: Doris Day (Grace LeBoy Kahn); Danny Thomas (Gus Kahn); Frank Lovejoy (Walter Donaldson); Mary Wickes (Anna); Patrice Wymore (Gloria Knight); Jim Backus (Sam Harris)
Songs: "Ain't We Got Fun," "Ukelele Lady," "Carioca," "Carolina in the Morning," "Love Me or Leave Me," "Makin' Whoopee," "My Buddy," "Yes Sir, That's My Baby," "I Never Knew," "I Wish I Had a Girl," "I'll See You in My Dreams," "It Had to Be You," "The One I Love (Belongs to Somebody Else)" "Liza," "Memories," "My Island of Golden Dreams," "Your Eyes Have Told Me So," "No No Nora," "Nobody's Sweetheart," "Pretty Baby," "San Francisco," "Shine on Harvest Moon," "Toot Toot Tootsie Goodbye"

The Winning Team

Released June 1952
Warner Bros.
Producer: Bryan Foy
Director: Lewis Seiler
Screenplay by Ted Sherdeman, Seeleg Lester, Merwin Gerard
Photography: Sid Hickox
Cast: Doris Day (Aimee Alexander); Ronald Reagan (Grover Cleveland Alexander); Frank Lovejoy (Rogers Hornsby); Eve Miller (Margaret Killefer) James Millican (Bill Killefer)
Song: "Ol' St. Nicholas"

April in Paris

Released January 1953
Warner Bros.
Producer: William Jacobs
Director: David Butler
Screenplay: Jack Rose, Melville Shavelson
Photography: Wilfred M. Cline
Musical Numbers Staged by LeRoy Prinz
Orchestrations: Frank Comstock; Music Director: Ray Heindorf
Cast: Doris Day (Ethel "Dynamite" Jackson); Ray Bolger (S. Winthrop Putnam); Claude Dauphin (Philippe Fouquet); Eve Miller (Marcia); George Givot (Francois)
Songs: "April in Paris," "Give Me Your Lips," "I Know a Place," "I'm Gonna Ring the Bell Tonight," "Isn't Love Wonderful," "That's What Makes Paris Paree," "It Must Be Good," "The Place You Hold in My Heart"

By the Light of the Silvery Moon

Released May 1953
Warner Bros.
Producer: William Jacobs
Director: David Butler
Screenplay: Robert O'Brien, Irving Elinson, based on the *Penrod* stories by Booth Tarkington
Photography: Wilfred M. Cline
Musical Numbers Staged by Donald Saddler
Music Adaptation: Max Steiner
Vocal Arrangements: Norman Luboff
Cast: Doris Day (Marjorie Winfield); Gordon MacRae (Bill Sherman); Leon Ames (George Winfield); Rosemary DeCamp (Mrs. Winfield); Mary Wickes (Stella); Billy Gray (Wesley Winfield); Russell Arms (Chester Finley); Maria Palmer (Miss LaRue)
Songs: "Ain't We Got Fun," "Be My Little Baby Bumble Bee," "By the Light of the Silvery Moon," "I'll Forget You," "If You Were the Only Girl in the World," "Just One Girl," "King Chanticleer," "My Home Town Is a One-Horse Town," "Your Eyes Have Told Me So"

Calamity Jane

Released November 1953
Warner Bros.

Producer: William Jacobs
Director: David Butler
Screenplay: James O'Hanlon
Photography: Wilfred M. Cline
Musical Numbers Staged By Jack Donohue
Cast: Doris Day (Calamity Jane); Howard Keel (Wild Bill Hickok); Allyn McLerie (Katie Brown); Philip Carey (Lt. Gilmartin); Gale Robbins (Adelaide Adams)
Songs by Sammy Fain and Paul Webster: "The Deadwood Stage," "Higher than a Hawk," "Just Blew in from the Windy City," "The Black Hills of Dakota," "Tis Harry I'm Plannin' to Marry," "A Woman's Touch," "Secret Love"

Lucky Me

Released April 1954
Warner Bros.
Producer: Henry Blanke
Director: Jack Donohue
Screenplay: James O'Hanlon, Robert O'Brien, Irving Elinson; Story by James O'Hanlon
Photography: Wilfred M. Cline
Musical Direction: Ray Heindorf; Orchestrations: Frank Comstock
Cast: Doris Day (Candy Williams); Robert Cummings (Dick Carson); Phil Silvers (Hap Schneider); Eddie Foy Jr. (Duke McGee); Nancy Walker (Flo); Martha Hyer (Lorraine Thayer); Bill Goodwin (Otis Thayer)
Songs by Sammy Fain and Paul Francis Webster: "Bluebells of Broadway," "High Hopes," "I Speak to the Stars," "Love You Dearly," "Lucky Me," "Men," "Parisian Pretties," "Superstition Song," "Take a Memo to the Moon," "Wanna Sing Like An Angel"

Young at Heart

Released January 1954
Warner Bros./An Arwin Production
Producer: Henry Blanke
Director: Gordon Douglas
Screenplay: Liam O'Brien, adapted from the screenplay by Julius J. Epstein, Lenore Coffee, based on the story *Sister Act* by Fanny Hurst
Photography: Ted McCord
Musical Direction, Arrangements, and Conducted by Ray Heindorf
Piano Solos: Andre Previn
Cast: Doris Day (Laurie Tuttle); Frank Sinatra (Barney Sloan); Gig Young (Alex Burke); Ethel Barrymore (Aunt Jessie); Dorothy Malone (Fran Tuttle); Robert Keith (Gregory Tuttle); Elizabeth Fraser (Amy Tuttle); Alan Hale Jr. (Robert Neary)
Songs: "Hold Me in Your Arms," "Just One of Those Things," "One for My Baby," "Ready, Willing, and Able," "Someone to Watch Over Me," "There's a Rising Moon for Every Falling Star," "Till My Love Comes Back to Me," "You, My Love," "Young at Heart"

Love Me or Leave Me

Released June 1955
MGM
Producer: Joe Pasternak

Director: Charles Vidor
Screenplay: Daniel Fuchs, Isobel Lennart; Story by Daniel Fuchs
Photography: Arthur E. Arling
Musical Direction: George Stoll; Doris Day's Music: Percy Faith
Choreography: Alex Romero
Cast: Doris Day (Ruth Etting); James Cagney (Marty "The Gimp" Snyder); Cameron Mitchell (Johnny Alderman); Robert Keith (Bernard V. Loomis); Tom Tully (Frobisher); Harry Bellaver (Georgie)
Songs: "At Sundown," "Sam, the Old Accordion Man," "Everybody Loves My Baby," "I Cried for You," "I'll Never Stop Loving You," "It All Depends on You," "Love Me or Leave Me," "Mean to Me," "My Blue Heaven," "Shakin' the Blues Away," "Never Look Back," "Stay on the Right Side, Sister," "Ten Cents a Dance," "What Can I Say," "You Made Me Love You"

The Man Who Knew Too Much

Released June 1956
Paramount
Producer-Director: Alfred Hitchcock
Screenplay: John Michael Hayes, Angus MacPhail; Story: Charles Bennett, D. B. Wyndham-Lewis
Photography: Robert Burks
Costumes: Edith Head
Cast: James Stewart (Ben McKenna); Doris Day (Jo Conway McKenna); Brenda de Banzie (Mrs. Drayton); Bernard Miles (Mr. Drayton); Christopher Olsen (Hank McKenna); Ralph Truman (Buchanan); Daniel Gelin (Louis Bernard)
Songs: "Storm Cloud Cantata," "We'll Love Again," "Whatever Will Be, Will Be (Que Sera, Sera)"

Julie

Released November 1956
MGM/An Arwin Production
Producer: Martin Melcher
Director/Screenplay: Andrew L. Stone
Photography: Fred Jackman Jr.
Music: Leith Stevens
Cast: Doris Day (Julie Benton); Louis Jourdan (Lyle Benton); Barry Sullivan (Cliff Henderson); Frank Lovejoy (Detective Capt. Pringle); John Gallaudet (Detective Cole)
Song: "Julie"

The Pajama Game

Released August 1957
Warner Bros.
Producers-Directors: George Abbott, Stanley Donen
Screenplay: George Abbott, Richard Bissell, based on the Broadway musical based on the novel *7½ Cents* by Richard Bissell
Photography: Harry Stradling
Orchestrations: Nelson Riddle, Buddy Bregman
Choreography: Bob Fosse
Cast: Doris Day (Babe Williams); John Raitt (Sid Sorokin); Carol Haney (Gladys Hotchkiss); Eddie Foy Jr. (Vernon Hines); Reta Shaw (Mabel); Barbara Nichols (Poopsie)

Songs by Richard Adler and Jerry Ross: "Hernando's Hideaway," "Hey There," "I'll Never Be Jealous Again," "I'm Not at All in Love," "Once-a-Year Day," "The Pajama Game," "Racing with the Clock," "Seven-and-a-Half Cents," "Small Talk," "Steam Heat," "There Once Was a Man"

Teacher's Pet

Released April 1958
Paramount
Producer: William Perlberg
Director: George Seaton
Screenplay: Fay and Michael Kanin
Photography: Haskell Boggs
Costumes: Edith Head
Cast: Clark Gable (Jim Gannon); Doris Day (Professor Erica Stone); Gig Young (Dr. Hugo Pine); Mamie Van Doren (Peggy DeFore); Nick Adams (Barney Kovac);
Songs: "The Girl Who Invented Rock and Roll"

The Tunnel of Love

Released November 1958
MGM
Producers: Joseph Fields, Martin Melcher
Director: Gene Kelly
Screenplay: Joseph Fields, based on the play by Joseph Fields, Peter DeVries, based on the novel by Peter DeVries
Photography: Robert Bronner
Director: Doris Day (Isolde Poole); Richard Widmark (Augie Poole); Gig Young (Dick Pepper); Elisabeth Fraser (Alice Pepper); Gia Scala (Estelle Novick); Elizabeth Wilson (Miss MacCracken)
Songs: "Run Away, Skidaddle Skidoo," "The Tunnel of Love"

It Happened to Jane

Released June 1959
Columbia/An Arwin Production
Producer-Director: Richard Quine
Screenplay: Norman Katkor; Story: Max Wilk, Norman Katkor
Photography: Charles Lawton Jr.
Cast: Doris Day (Jane Osgood); Jack Lemmon (George Denham); Ernie Kovacs (Harry Foster Malone); Steve Forrest (Larry Hall); Mary Wickes (Matilda Runyon)
Songs: "Be Prepared," "That Jane from Maine"

Pillow Talk

Released October 1959
Universal/An Arwin-Universal Production
Producers: Ross Hunter, Martin Melcher
Director: Michael Gordon
Screenplay: Stanley Shapiro, Maurice Richlin; Story: Russell Rouse, Clarence Greene
Photography: Arthur E. Arling

Doris Day's Gowns: Jean Louis
Music: Frank DeVol
Cast: Rock Hudson (Brad Allen); Doris Day (Jan Morrow); Tony Randall (Jonathan Forbes); Thelma Ritter (Alma); Nick Adams (Tony Walters)
Songs: "I Need No Atmosphere," "Inspiration," "Possess Me," "You Lied," "Pillow Talk," "Roly Poly"

Please Don't Eat the Daisies

Released April 1960
MGM
Producers: Joe Pasternak
Director: Charles Walters
Screenplay: Isobel Lennart, based on the book by Jean Kerr
Photography: Robert Bonner
Cast: Doris Day (Kate MacKay); David Niven (Larry MacKay) Janis Paige (Deborah Vaughn); Spring Byington (Suzie Robinson); Richard Haydn (Alfred North); Patsy Kelly (Maggie); Jack Weston (Joe Positano)
Songs: "Anyway the Wind Blows," "Please Don't Eat the Daisies"

Midnight Lace

Released November 1960
Universal
Producers: Ross Hunter, Martin Melcher
Director: David Miller
Screenplay: Ivan Goff, Ben Roberts, based on the play *Matilda Shouted Fire* by Janet Green
Photography: Russell Metty
Costumes: Irene
Cast: Doris Day (Kit Preston); Rex Harrison (Tony Preston); John Gavin (Brian Younger); Myrna Loy (Aunt Bea); Roddy McDowall (Malcolm); Herbert Marshall (Charles Manning); Natasha Perry (Peggy Thompson)
Songs: "Midnight Lace," "What Does a Woman Do"

Lover Come Back

Released March 1961
Universal/A 7 Pictures-Arwin-Nob Hill Production
Producers: Stanley Shapiro, Martin Melcher
Director: Delbert Mann
Screenplay: Stanley Shapiro, Paul Henning
Photography: Arthur E. Arling
Costumes: Irene
Music: Frank DeVol
Cast: Rock Hudson (Jerry Webster); Doris Day (Carol Templeton); Tony Randall (Peter Ramsey); Edie Adams (Rebel Davis); Jack Oakie (J. Paxton Miller); Jack Kruschen (Dr. Linus Tyler)
Songs: "Lover Come Back," "Should I Surrender"

That Touch of Mink

Released July 1962
Universal/A Granley-Arwin-Nob Hill Production
Producers: Stanley Shapiro, Martin Melcher
Director: Delbert Mann
Screenplay: Stanley Shapiro, Nate Monaster
Photography: Russell Metty
Cast: Cary Grant (Philip Shayne); Doris Day (Cathy Timberlake); Gig Young (Roger); Audrey Meadows (Connie Emerson); Alan Hewitt (Dr. Gruber); John Astin (Everett Beasley)

Billy Rose's Jumbo

Released December 1962
MGM-Euterpe-Arwin Production
Producers: Joe Pasternak, Martin Melcher
Director: Charles Walters
Second Unit Director: Busby Berkeley
Screenplay: Sidney Sheldon, based on the musical play and book by Ben Hecht, Charles MacArthur
Photography: William H. Daniels
Musical Direction: George Stoll; Orchestrations: Conrad Salinger, Leon Arnaud, Robert Van Eps; Vocal Arrangements: Bobby Tucker
Cast: Doris Day (Kitty Wonder); Stephen Boyd (Sam Rawlins); Jimmy Durante (Pop Wonder); Martha Raye (Lulu); Dean Jagger (John Noble)
Songs by Richard Rodgers and Lorenz Hart: "The Circus Is on Parade," "Over and Over Again," "Little Girl Blue," "The Most Beautiful Girl in the World," "My Romance," "Sawdust, Spangles and Dreams," "This Can't Be Love," "Why Can't I"

The Thrill of It All

Released August 1963
Universal/A Ross Hunter-Arwin Production
Producers: Ross Hunter, Martin Melcher
Director: Norman Jewison
Screenplay: Carl Reiner; Story Carl Reiner, Larry Gelbart
Photography: Russell Metty
Costumes: Jean Louis
Music: Frank DeVol
Cast: Doris Day (Beverly Boyer); James Garner (Dr. Gerald Boyer); Arlene Francis (Mrs. Fraleigh); Edward Andrews (Mr. Fraleigh); Reginald Owen (Tom Fraleigh); Zasu Pitts (Olivia); Elliott Reid (Mike Palmer); Kym Kareth (Maggie Boyer); Brian Nash (Andy Boyer)
Songs: "The Thrill of It All"

Move Over, Darling

Released December 1963
Twentieth Century-Fox
Producers: Aaron Rosenberg, Martin Melcher
Director: Michael Gordon
Screenplay: Hal Kanter, Jack Sher; Story: Bella and Samuel Spewack, Leo McCarey

Photography: Daniel L. Fapp
Music: Lionel Newman
Cast: Doris Day (Ellen Wagstaff Arden); James Garner (Nick Arden); Polly Bergen (Bianca Steele Arden); Chuck Connors (Stephen Burkett); Thelma Ritter (Grace Arden); Don Knotts (Shoe Salesman)
Songs: "Move Over, Darling," "Twinkle Lullaby"

Send Me No Flowers

Released November 1964
Universal/A Martin Melcher Production
Producer: Harry Keller
Director: Norman Jewison
Screenplay: Julius Epstein, based on a play by Norman Barasch, Carroll Moore
Photography: Daniel Fapp
Cast: Rock Hudson (George Kimball); Doris Day (Judy Kimball); Tony Randall (Arnold Nash); Clint Walker (Bert Power); Paul Lynde (Mr. Akins)
Songs: "Send Me No Flowers"

Do Not Disturb

Released December 1965
Twentieth Century-Fox/An Arcola-Melcher Production
Producers: Aaron Rosenberg, Martin Melcher
Director: Ralph Levy
Screenplay: Milt Rosen, Richard Breen, based on a play by William Fairchild
Photography: Leon Shamroy
Cast: Doris Day (Janet Harper); Rod Taylor (Mike Harper); Hermione Baddeley (Vanessa Courtwright); Sergio Fantoni (Paul Bellasi); Reginald Gardiner (Simmons); Maura McGiveney (Claire Hackett); Leon Askin (Langsdorf)
Songs: "Au Revoir," "Do Not Disturb"

The Glass Bottom Boat

Released July 1966
MGM
Producers: Martin Melcher, Everett Freeman
Director: Frank Tashlin
Screenplay: Everett Freeman
Photography: Leon Shamroy
Cast: Doris Day (Jennifer Nelson); Rod Taylor (Bruce Templeton); Arthur Godfrey (Axel Nordstrom); John McGiver (Ralph Goodwin); Paul Lynde (Homer Cripps); Edward Andrews (Gen. Wallace Bleeker); Dom DeLuise (Julius Pritter); Dick Martin (Zach Malloy)
Songs: "The Glass Bottom Boat," "Soft as the Starlight," "Whatever Will Be, Will Be (Que Sera, Sera)"

Caprice

Released June 1967
Twentieth Century Fox
Producers: Aaron Rosenberg, Martin Melcher

Director: Frank Tashlin
Screenplay: Jay Johnson, Frank Tashlin; Story: Martin Hale, Jay Jayson
Photography: Leon Shamroy
Cast: Doris Day (Patricia Foster); Richard Harris (Christopher White); Ray Walston (Stuart Clancy); Jack Kruschen (Matthew Cutter); Edward Mulhare (Sir Jason Fox)
Songs: "Caprice"

The Ballad of Josie

Released November 1967
Universal
Producer: Norman Macdonnell
Director: Andrew V. McLaglen
Screenplay: Harold Swanton
Photography: Milton Krasner
Costumes: Jean Louis
Music: Frank DeVol
Cast: Doris Day: (Josie Minick); Peter Graves (Jason Meredith); George Kennedy (Arch Ogden); Andy Devine (Judge Tatum); William Talman (Charlie Lord); David Hartman (Fonse Pruitt)
Songs: "The Ballad of Josie," "Wait Till Tomorrow"

Where Were You When the Lights Went Out?

Released May 1968
MGM
Producers: Everett Freeman, Martin Melcher
Director: Hy Averback
Producers: Everett Freeman, Martin Melcher
Screenplay: Everett Freeman, Karl Tunberg, based on the play *Monsieur Masure* by Claude Magnier
Photography: Ellsworth Fredricks
Cast: Doris Day (Margaret Garrison); Robert Morse (Waldo Zane); Terry-Thomas (Ladislau Walichek); Patrick O'Neal (Peter Garrison); Lola Albright (Roberta Lane); Steve Allen (Radio Announcer)
Songs: "Show Time," "Where Were You When the Lights Went Out"

With Six You Get Eggroll

Released August 1968
Warner-Pathe/A National General Picture/A Cinema Center Film/An Arwin Production
Producer: Martin Melcher
Director: Howard Morris
Screenplay: Gwen Bagni, Paul Dubov, Harvey Bullock, R. S. Allen; Story: Gwen Bagni, Paul Dubov
Photography: Ellsworth Fredricks, Harry Stradling Jr.
Cast: Doris Day (Abby McClure); Brian Keith (Jake Iverson); Pat Carroll (Maxine Scott); Barbara Hershey (Stacy Iverson); George Carlin (Herbie Flack); Alice Ghostley (Housekeeper); John Findlater (Flip McClure)
Songs: "You Make Me Want You"

Selected Discography

Nearly all of Doris Day's studio recordings from 1947 to 1967 are collected in the beautifully assembled and very expensive Bear Family Records boxed sets. These boxed sets—particularly *It's Magic*—include all of the singles that Day recorded before the advent of the long-playing album (and as such were therefore never included on any of the Columbia Records albums). These boxed-set recordings are divided as follows:

It's Magic (1947–1950), 6 CD set
Secret Love (1951–1955), 5 CD set
Que Sera (1956–1959), 5 CD set
Move Over, Darling (1960–1967), 8 CD Set

A more specific chronological breakdown of the Day discography runs as follows:

Doris Day Complete Recordings with Les Brown

Released on Jazz Factory, 2001

"Dig It," "Let's Be Buddies," "While the Music Plays On," "Three at a Table for Two," "Between Friends," "Broomstreet," "Barbara Allen," "Celery Stalks at Midnight," "Amapola," "Easy as Pie," "Boogie Wooglie Piggy," "Beau Night in Hotchkiss Corners," "Alexander the Swoose (Half Swan-Half Goose)," "Made Up My Mind," "Keep Cool Fool," "Sentimental Journey," "My Dreams Are Getting Better All the Time," "He's Home for a Little While," "Taint Me," "I'll Always Be with You," "A Red Kiss on a Blue Letter," "Till the End of Time," "He'll Have to Cross the Atlantic," "I'd Rather Be With You," "Come To Baby, Do," "Aren't You Glad You're You," "The Last Time I Saw You," "We'll Be Together Again," "You Won't Be Satisfied Until You Break My Heart," "In the Moon Mist," "Day by Day," "There's Good Blues Tonight," "All Through the Day," "The Deevil, Devil, Divil," "I Got the Sun in the Morning," "My Number One Dream Came True," "The Whole World Is Singing My Song," "Are You Still in Love With Me" "Sooner or Later," "You Should Have Told Me," "The Christmas Song," "It Could Happen To You"

Soundtrack Recordings

(all released on Columbia Records)

Young Man with a Horn, 1950
Tea for Two, 1950
Lullaby of Broadway, 1951
On Moonlight Bay, 1951
I'll See You in My Dreams, 1951
April in Paris, 1953
By the Light of the Silvery Moon, 1953
Calamity Jane, 1953
Young at Heart, 1955
Love Me or Leave Me, 1955
The Pajama Game, 1957
Billy Rose's Jumbo, 1962

The heart of the Doris Day recording legacy lies in her eighteen original studio albums for Columbia Records.

You're My Thrill, 1949

Various Conductors

(Reissued with four additional songs as *Day Dreams*)
"You're My Thrill" (John Rarig conductor/arranger), "Bewitched, Bothered, and Bewildered" (John Rarig conductor/arranger), "Imagination" (George Siravo conductor), "I've Only Myself to Blame" (George Siravo conductor), "I'm Confessin'" (John Rarig conductor), "Sometimes I'm Happy" (John Rarig conductor), "You Go to My Head" (John Rarig conductor), "I Didn't Know What Time It Was" (John Rarig conductor), "If I Could Be with You" (George Siravo conductor), "Darn That Dream" (Axel Stordahl conductor), "When Your Lover Has Gone" (John Rarig conductor/arranger), "That Old Feeling" (John Rarig conductor)

Day By Day, 1956

Arranged and Conducted by Paul Weston

"The Song Is You," "Hello, My Lover, Goodbye," "But Not for Me," "I Remember You," "I Hadn't Anyone Till You," "But Beautiful," "Autumn Leaves," "Don't Take Your Love from Me," "There Will Never Be Another You," "Gone With the Wind," "The Gypsy in My Soul," "Day By Day"

Day by Night, 1957

Arranged and Conducted by Paul Weston

"I See Your Face Before Me," "Close Your Eyes," "The Night We Called It a Day," "Dream a Little Dream of Me," "Under a Blanket of Blue," "You Do Something to Me," "Stars Fell on Alabama," "Moon Song," "Wrap Your Troubles in Dreams," "Soft as the Starlight," "Moonglow," "The Lamp Is Low"

Hooray for Hollywood, 1958 (two-record set)

Arranged and Conducted by Frank DeVol

"Hooray for Hollywood," "Cheek to Cheek," "It's Easy to Remember," "The Way You Look Tonight," "I'll Remember April," "Blues in the Night," "Over the Rainbow," "Our Love Is Here to Stay," "In the

Still of the Night," "Night and Day," "Easy to Love," "I Had the Craziest Dream," "I've Got My Love to Keep Me Warm," "Soon," "That Old Black Magic," "You'll Never Know," "A Foggy Day," "It's Magic," "It Might as Well Be Spring," "Nice Work If You Can Get It," "Three Coins in the Fountain," "Let's Face the Music and Dance," "Pennies from Heaven," "Oh, But I Do"

Cuttin' Capers, 1959

Arranged and Conducted by Frank DeVol

"Cuttin' Capers," "Steppin' Out with My Baby," "Makin' Whoopee," "The Lady's in Love with You," "Why Don't We Do This More Often," "Let's Take a Walk Around the Block," "I'm Sitting on Top of the World," "Get Out and Get Under the Moon," "Fit as a Fiddle," "Me Too," "I Feel Like a Feather in the Breeze," "Let's Fly Away"

Listen to Day, 1960

(A compilation of various Day recordings, this album was released in 1960 to take advantage of Day's peak popularity. Mostly a collection of songs taken from her films, this is not one of the concept albums Day recorded throughout her tenure with Columbia.)

"Pillow Talk," "Heart Full of Love," "Any Way the Wind Blows," "Oh What a Lover You'll Be," "No," "Love Me in the Daytime," "I Enjoy Being a Girl," "Tunnel of Love," "He's So Married," "Roly Poly," "Possess Me," "Inspiration"

What Every Girl Should Know, 1960

Arranged and Conducted by Harry Zimmerman

"What Every Girl Should Know," "Mood Indigo," "When You're Smiling," "A Fellow Needs a Girl," "My Kinda Love," "What's the Use of Wond'rin," "Something Wonderful," "A Hundred Years from Today," "You Can't Have Everything," "Not Only Should You Love Him," "What Does a Woman Do," "The Everlasting Arms" (CD release includes "Falling" as a bonus track.)

Show Time, 1960

Arranged and Conducted by Axel Stordahl

"Show Time," "I Got the Sun in the Morning," "Ohio," "I Love Paris," "When I'm Not Near the Boy I Love," "People Will Say We're in Love," "I've Grown Accustomed to His Face," "The Surrey with the Fringe on Top," "They Say It's Wonderful," "A Wonderful Guy," "On the Street Where You Live," "The Sound of Music," "Show Time"

Bright and Shiny, 1961

Arranged and conducted by Neal Hefti

"Bright and Shiny," "I Want to Be Happy," "Keep Smilin', Keep Laughin', Be Happy," "Singin' in the Rain," "Gotta Feelin'," "Happy Talk," "Make Someone Happy," "Ridin' High," "On the Sunny Side of the Street," "Clap Yo' Hands," "Stay with the Happy People," "Twinkle and Shine"

I Have Dreamed, 1961

Arranged and conducted by Jim Harbert

"I Believe in Dreams," "I'll Buy That Dream," "My Ship," "All I Do Is Dream of You," "When I Grow Too Old to Dream," "We'll Love Again," "I Have Dreamed," "Periwinkle Blue," "Someday I'll Find You," "You Stepped Out of a Dream," "Oh What a Beautiful Dream," "Time to Say Goodnight"

Duet (Doris Day with André Previn and the André Previn Trio), 1962

Arranged and conducted by André Previn

"Falling in Love Again," "Give Me Time," "My One and Only Love," "Remind Me," "Wait 'Til You See Him," "Close Your Eyes," "Fools Rush In," "Control Yourself," "Who Are We To Say," "Yes," "Nobody's Heart," "Daydreaming"

Doris Day's Greatest Hits (compilation), 1962

"Everybody Loves a Lover," "It's Magic," "A Guy Is a Guy," "Secret Love," "Bewitched, Bothered, Bewildered," "Teacher's Pet," "Whatever Will be, Will Be (Que Sera, Sera)," "If I Give My Heart to You," "Why Did I Tell You I Was Going to Shanghai," "When I Fall in Love," "Lullaby of Broadway," "Love Me or Leave Me"

You'll Never Walk Alone, 1962

Arranged and conducted by Jim Harbert; Produced by Irv Townsend and Jim Harbert

"Nearer My God to Thee," "I Need Thee Every Hour," "You'll Never Walk Alone,"
"Abide with Me," "The Lord's Prayer," "Scarlet Ribbons (for Her Hair)," "Bless This House," "Walk with Him," "In the Garden," "The Prodigal Son," "If I Can Help Somebody," "Be Still and Know"

Wonderful Day, 1962

(Not an original studio recording, this was a limited edition of several songs from Day movies, released with two new songs from *Lover Come Back* to promote that film.)

"Lover Come Back," "Pillow Talk," "Be Prepared," "Whatever Will Be, Will Be (Que Sera, Sera)," "It's Magic," "Never Look Back," "Should I Surrender," "Teacher's Pet," "When You're Smiling," "Possess Me," "Julie," "Till My Love Comes to Me" (CD release adds "That Jane from Maine" and "A Perfect Understanding.")

Doris Day and Robert Goulet Sing Annie Get Your Gun, 1963

Arranged by Philip J. Lang; Conducted by Franz Allers

"Overture" "Colonel Buffalo Bill," "I'm a Bad, Bad Man," "Doin' What Comes Natur'lly," "The Girl That I Marry," "You Can't Get a Man with a Gun," "They Say It's Wonderful," "My Defenses Are Down," "Moonshine Lullaby," "I'm an Indian, Too," "I Got Lost in His Arms," "Who Do You Love I Hope," "I Got the Sun in the Mornin'," "Anything You Can Do," "There's No Business Like Show Business"

Love Him!, 1964

Arranged and conducted by Tommy Oliver; Produced by Terry Melcher

"More," "Can't Help Falling in Love," "Since I Fell for You," "Losing You," "A Fool Such As I," "As Long As He Needs Me," "Night Life," "Funny," "Softly, As I Leave You," "Lollipops and Roses," "Love Him," "Moonlight Lover," "A Whisper Away"

The Doris Day Christmas Album, 1964

Arranged and conducted by Pete King

"Have Yourself a Merry Little Christmas," "I'll Be Home for Christmas," "Be a Child at Christmas Time," "Toyland," "Christmas Present," "The Christmas Waltz," "Winter Wonderland," "Snowfall," "White Christmas," "Let It Snow! Let It Snow! Let It Snow" (CD release adds early Day recordings of "The Christmas Song," "Silver Bells," "Here Comes Santa Claus," "Ol' Saint Nicholas," and "Christmas Story.")

With a Smile and a Song, 1965

Arranged and conducted by Allyn Ferguson

"Give a Little Whistle," "The Children's Marching Song (Nick Nack Paddy Whack),"
"Getting to Know You," "Zip-a-Dee-Doo-Dah," "The Lilac Tree," "High Hopes," "Do Re Mi," "Whatever Will Be, Will Be (Que Sera, Sera)," "Inchworm," "Swinging on a Star," "Sleepy Baby," "With a Smile and a Song"

Latin for Lovers, 1965

Arranged and conducted by Mort Garson; Produced by Allen Stanton

"Quiet Nights of Quiet Stars (Corcovado)" "Dansero," "Fly Me to the Moon," "Meditation," "Summer Has Gone," "How Insensitive (Insensataez)," "Slightly Out of Tune (Desifinado)," "Our Day Will Come," "Be True to Me," "Perhaps, Perhaps, Perhaps (Quizas, Quizas, Quizas)," "Be Mine Tonight (Noche de Ronda)," "Por Favor"

Doris Day's Sentimental Journey, 1965

Arranged and conducted by Mort Garson; Produced by Allen Stanton

"The More I See You," "At Last," "Come to Baby, Do" "I Had the Craziest Dream/I Don't Want to Walk Without You," "I'll Never Smile Again," "I Remember You," "Serenade in Blue," "I'm Beginning to See the Light," "It Could Happen to You," "It's Been a Long, Long Time," "Sentimental Journey"
(CD release includes "There They Are" as a bonus track.)

The Love Album, 1967

Arranged and Conducted by Sidney H. Feller; Produced by Don Genson and Martin Melcher

"For All We Know," "Snuggled on Your Shoulder," "Are You Lonesome Tonight," "Street of Dreams," "Oh, How I Miss You Tonight," "Life Is Just a Bowl of Cherries," "All Alone," "A Faded Summer Love," "Sleepy Lagoon," "Wonderful One," "If I Had My Life to Live Over/Let Me Call You Sweetheart"

(This album was initially released in the UK in 1994. When it was finally released in the U.S. by Concord Records in 2006, it included three cuts taken from Day's 1971 television special, *The Doris Mary Anne*

Kappelhoff Special [renamed *The Doris Day Special* for its DVD release]: "Both Sides Now" [arranged and conducted by Jimmie Haskell; produced by Don Genson and Terry Melcher] and newly arranged reworkings of the Day classics "It's Magic" and "Sentimental Journey" [arranged and conducted by Jimmie Haskell; produced by Don Genson and Terry Melcher].)

Note: In 1985, Day recorded sixteen tracks for use during the run of her television series *Doris Day's Best Friends*. These tracks remain unreleased on any commercial recording: "Best Friends Theme," "Ryan's On His Way to the Roundup," "Disney Girls," "Rescue Me," "My Heart," "At the Zoo," "Heaven Tonight" (recorded but never used), "What a Day for a Daydream," "Make It Big," "Wildfire," "This Is the Way I Dreamed It" (recorded but never used), "Everyone's Gone to the Moon," "You Are So Beautiful," "Stuval Was a Racehorse," "Crocodile Rock," "Octopus's Garden."

Dozens of compilation Doris Day CDs have been issued throughout the years, grouped around themes such as *Doris Day: It's Magic—Her Early Years at Warner Bros.* and *Doris Day Sings Her Great Movie Hits*. Putting aside the all inclusive Bear Family Records boxed sets, probably the most representative compilation overview of Day's recording career is the three-CD Columbia release *Doris Day: Her Life in Music*. The three CDs include sixty cuts divided into "Movie Hits," "Golden Greats," and "Classic Collaborations." The three CDs also include interesting brief background on both the songs and Day's interpretations, as well as words of praise from Day admirers such as Sir Paul McCartney, Tony Bennett, and Burt Bacharach.

Selected Television Appearances

The Doris Day Show

(Half-hour sitcom, CBS Television)

Season 1 (1968–1969)
Tuesday, 9:30–10 P.M.
Cast: Doris Day (Doris Martin); Denver Pyle (Buck Webb); Fran Ryan (Aggie Thompson); James Hampton (LeRoy B. Simpson); Philip Brown (Billy Martin); Tod Starke (Toby Martin); Naomi Stevens (Juanita)
Twenty-eight episodes

Season 2 (1969–1970)
Monday, 9:30–10:00 P.M.
Cast: Doris Day (Doris Martin); Denver Pyle (Buck Webb); McLean Stevenson (Michael Nicholson); Rose Marie (Myrna Gibbons); Philip Brown (Billy Martin); Tod Starke (Toby Martin)
Twenty-five episodes

Season 3 (1970–1971)
Monday, 9:30–10:00 P.M.
Cast: Doris Day (Doris Martin); McLean Stevenson (Michael Nicholson); Rose Marie (Myrna Gibbons); Paul Smith (Ron Harvey); Philip Brown (Billy Martin); Tod Starke (Toby Martin)
Twenty-five episodes

Season 4 (1971–1972)
Monday, 9:30–10:00 P.M.
Cast: Doris Day (Doris Martin); John Dehner (Cy Bennett); Jackie Joseph (Jackie Parker)
Twenty-four episodes

Season 5 (1972–1973)
Monday, 9:30–10:00 P.M.
Cast: Doris Day (Doris Martin); John Dehner (Cy Bennett); Jackie Joseph (Jackie Parker)
Twenty-four episodes

Doris Day's Best Friends

Christian Broadcast Network
1985–1986
Executive Producer, Writer, Music Director, Composer of Theme Song "Best Friend":
Terry Melcher
Twenty-six half-hour episodes

CBS One-Hour Variety Specials

The Doris Mary Anne Kappelhoff Special
Sunday, March 14, 1971, 10:00 P.M.

Doris day toDay
Wednesday, February 19, 1975, 9:00 P.M.

Special Guest Appearance

The John Denver Show, ABC
December 1, 1974

Notable Documentaries

I Don't Even Like Apple Pie, March 1989, BBC
Doris Day: A Sentimental Journey, 1991, PBS

Notes

Introduction

1 *"I'm always looking for insights"* *Doris Day: A Sentimental Journey,* PBS documentary, 1991.
1 *"Doris Day's least-impressed fan"* Ibid.
1 *"I think that Doris Day is the most underrated"* Ibid.
3 *"I've never acted"* A. E. Hotchner, *Doris Day: Her Own Story* (New York: William Morrow and Company, 1976). p. 92.
4 *"How can I possibly be the lead?"* Ibid., p. 93.
4 *"It was not like actress reading"* Joe Hyams, *New York Mirror,* September 12, 1957.
4 *"felt a nice exhilaration"* *Hotchner, Doris Day,* p. 94.
6 *She spent ten years ranked* Gary McGee, *Doris Day: A Sentimental Journey* (Jefferson, NC: McFarland, 2005), p. 152. See also Jeanine Basinger, *A Woman's View* (New York: Alfred A. Knopf, 1993), p. 510.
6 *the Quigley Poll, which ranked her* McGee, *Doris Day,* p. 152.
7 *"Her music catalogue each year"* *A&E Biography: Doris Day*, A&E cable television network, 1998.
7 *"I think she's very surprised"* *Doris Day: A Sentimental Journey.*
7 *"She was both romantic and wild"* Ibid.
8 *"starriness has a challenging"* John Updike, *Hugging the Shore* (New York: Alfred A. Knopf, 1983), p. 798.
9 *"She exuded sex"* *Doris Day: A Sentimental Journey.*
9 *in order to compensate for* *A&E Biography: Doris Day.*
9 *"It was my pleasure to observe Miss Day"* Louis Berg, *New York Herald Tribune*, May 17, 1953.
11 *"For all her effervescence"* McGee, *Doris Day,* p. 26.
11 *"For what? I'm not being coy . . ."* Ibid., p. 2.

Beginnings

13 *"She lives in the belief that happiness has to be made"* Louella Parsons, *Cosmopolitan,* January 1954.
13 *"Nothing seems to daunt"* Hotchner, *Doris Day*, p. 18.
15 *"I'm still Doris Mary Anne Kappelhoff"* *Doris Day: A Sentimental Journey.*
15 *"When I mentioned this to her"* McGee, *Doris Day,* p. 8.
16 *In the mid-1950s Alma stated* Ibid., p. 9.
17 *"Sing each song as if directly to one person"* Hotchner, p. 39.

17 *"Grace Raine couldn't sing a note"* *Doris Day: A Sentimental Journey.*

18 *"I have never had any doubts"* Hotchner, *Doris Day,* p. 34.

18 *"What's your name?"* *Doris Day: A Sentimental Journey.*

18 *"It sounds phony"* Ken Bloom, *The American Songbook: The Singers, The Songwriters, and The Songs* (New York: Black Dog and Leventhal Publishers, 2005), p. 48.

19 *"It never occurred to me"* Hotchner, *Doris Day,* p. 52.

19 *"I really had no ambition about my singing"* Ibid., p. 51.

21 *"One beautiful thing came out of the marriage"* *Doris Day: A Sentimental Journey.*

21 *She herself relates that the psychiatrist* Updike, *Hugging the Shore,* p. 800.

21 *"denies herself luxuries and pleasures"* Hotchner, *Doris Day,* p. 283.

22 *"Les heard me and called"* *Doris Day: A Sentimental Journey.*

22 *"All the boys in the band were like brothers to me"* Ibid.

Film

25 *"She can sing, be sexy"* *Doris Day: A Sentimental Journey.*

25 *"Those eyes, the intelligence, the intensity"* Ibid.

25 *"Doris was everybody's darling"* Ibid.

28 *"Day has much to learn about acting"* *New York Herald Tribune,* July 1948.

29 "It's Magic" music by Jule Styne, lyrics by Sammy Cahn.

29 *"not think of a big audience out there"* McGee, *Doris Day,* p. 10.

31 *"with greater ease and naturalness"* Hotchner, *Doris Day,* p. 98.

31 *"There is one actress I know"* Marie Torre, "Lunch Bucket Gal is Doris," *New York World Telegraph and Sun,* May 2, 1953.

34 *"Great little personality isn't she?"* *My Dream Is Yours,* screenplay by Harry Kurnitz, Dane Lussier, adaptation by Allen Rivkin, Laura Ken, story by Jerry Wald, Paul Moss, Warner Bros., 1949.

35 *"We're on our way . . . Well, wherever we're going"* Ibid.

35 *"You wouldn't put soap . . ."* Ibid.

35 *not one to "gush" over children* McGee, *Doris Day,* p. 50.

36 *"Sometimes I think I should have studied"* *Doris Day: A Sentimental Journey.*

36 *"dazzling personality . . ."* Ibid.

37 *"I do that in all my pictures"* *It's a Great Feeling,* screenplay by Jack Rose, Mel Shavelson, story by I.A.L. Diamond, Warner Bros., 1949.

38 *"was the coolest and sexiest female singer"* Gary Giddins, "A Blond and Beaming Icon for a Blond and Beaming Age," *New York Sun,* May 3, 2005.

41 *"cheap mass-produced art . . . intellectual mountain goat leaping . . ."* *Young Man with a Horn,* screenplay by Carl Foreman and Edmund North, based on a novel by Dorothy Baker, Warner Bros., 1950.

41 *". . . so simple and uncomplicated . . ."* Ibid.

41 *"girl we would like to take a slow boat"* George Morris, *Doris Day: Pyramid Illustrated History of the Movies* (New York: Pyramid Communications, 1976), p. 37.

41 *"Call me sometime"* *Young Man with a Horn, Op. Cit.*

42 *". . . you're trying for something . . ."* Ibid.

43 *"about the remotest person I know"* Kirk Douglas as quoted in Hotchner, *Doris Day,* p. 273.

43 *"utterly joyless experience"* Ibid.

44 *"everything you have left over"* *Tea for Two,* screenplay by Harry Clork, based upon the musical *No, No, Nanette* by Frank Mandel, Otto Harback, Vincent Youmans, Irving Caesar, Emil Nyitray, Warner Bros., 1950.

48 *"Do you think I can swing it?"* *The West Point Story,* screenplay by John Monks Jr., Charles Hoffman, Irving Wallace, based on a story by Irving Wallace, Warner Bros., 1950.

49 *"We don't like the Klan but..."* *Storm Warning,* screenplay by Daniel Fuchs, Richard Brooks, Warner Bros., 1951.

50 *"Everything would be okay"* Ibid.

50 *"If you go on like this"* Ibid.

51 *"You are Doris Day, are you not?"* Alfred Hitchcock as quoted in Hotchner, *Doris Day,* p. 119.

52 *"... a stupid, vicious ape"* *Storm Warning, Op. Cit.*

55 *"kind of snuck up on me"* Hotchner, *Doris Day,* p. 123.

57 *"a girl who tried to grow up but"* Joe Hyams, *New York Mirror,* September 12, 1957.

57 *"misty water-colored memory"* "The Way We Were," music by Marvin Hamlisch, lyrics by Alan and Marilyn Bergman.

58 *"What's love when all of Europe..."* *On Moonlight Bay,* screenplay by Jack Rose, Melville Shavelson, based on the *Penrod* stories by Booth Tarkington. Warner Bros., 1951.

58 *"Papa, you're so old-fashioned"* Ibid.

60 *"I wonder what you get for manslaughter"* Ibid.

61 *her first appearance in the Quigley Top 10* Morris, *Doris Day,* p. 48.

64 *"When* Starlift *exploits a wardful"* *Time,* December 1951.

64 *"You've got to say 'I love you...'"* *I'll See You in My Dreams,* screenplay by Melville Shavelson, Jack Rose, story by Grace Kahn, Louis F. Edelman, Warner Bros., 1952.

65 *"Well, what did you come up for?"* Ibid.

66 *"My grandfather started every day"* Ibid.

67 *"There's such a thing as too much help"* Ibid.

68 *"... should just be a hobby"* *The Winning Team,* screenplay by Ted Sherdeman, Seeleg Lester, Merwin Gerard, Warner Bros., June 1952.

69 *"Miss Day gives her finest dramatic performance"* *Hollywood Reporter,* June 1952.

71 *"... an undertaker's convention"* *April in Paris,* screenplay by Jack Rose, Melville Shavelson, Warner Bros., 1953.

72 "April in Paris" music by Vernon Duke, lyrics by E. Y. Harburg.

73 *"Both films bring back such nostalgia for me"* *Doris Day: A Sentimental Journey.*

73 *"She's a symbol of female energy"* Ibid.

74 *"I have a hunch"* *By the Light of the Silvery Moon,* screenplay by Robert O'Brien, Irving Elinson, based on the *Penrod* stories by Booth Tarkington, Warner Bros., 1953.

76 *"Calamity Jane is the real me"* *Doris Day: A Sentimental Journey.*

76 *eager to film* Annie Get Your Gun McGee, *Doris Day,* p. 23.

77 *"As for Miss Day's performance"* *New York Times,* November 1953.

78 *"There's a kind of crisp androgynous something"* *Doris Day: A Sentimental Journey.*

78 *"You're the purtiest thing I've ever seen"* *Calamity Jane,* screenplay by James O'Hanlon, Warner Bros., November 1953.

79 *"Who are you to tell people who to love?"* Ibid.

79 "Secret Love" music by Sammy Fain, lyrics by Paul Francis Webster.

80 *"There were times when I didn't like scripts"* *Doris Day: A Sentimental Journey.*

80 *"To those leaning on the sustaining infinite"* *Science and Health with Key to the Scriptures,* Eddy, Mary Baker, Aequus Institute Publications, reprinted July 1986, copyright 1875.

80 *"... it brought spirituality into my life"* Hotchner, *Doris Day,* p. 102.

80 *"because I'd been thinking that I should be happier"* *Ms.* Magazine, January, 1976.

81 *"The cause of all disease"* Mary Baker Eddy, *Christian Science Prayerbook.*

81 *"pray to anything but just go inside yourself"* Hotchner, *Doris Day,* p. 140.

82 *"very personal, gratifying"* Ibid., p. 141.

86 *"When I actually slapped her"* James Cagney, as quoted in ibid., p. 157.

86 *"I hear an entire rhythm section"* *Doris Day: A Sentimental Journey.*

87 *"What kind of aunt are you?"* *Young at Heart*, screenplay by Liam O'Brien, adapted from the screenplay by Julius J. Epstein, Lenore Coffee, based on the story *Sister Act* by Fanny Hurst, Warner Bros., 1955.

88 *"The same thing applies to Doris's acting"* *Doris Day: A Sentimental Journey.*

89 *"with meditative intensity"* James Harvey, *Movie Love in the Fifties* p. 52 (New York: Alfred A. Knopf, 2001).

90 *"a cheap crook pushing people around"* *Love Me or Leave Me,* screenplay by Daniel Fuchs and Isobel Lennart, story by Daniel Fuchs, MGM, 1955.

91 *"You don't have to sell me"* Ibid.

92 *"It'll be a change, anyway"* Ibid.

92 *"What d'ya want"* Ibid.

93 *"Who are you, Marty?"* Ibid.

93 *"I'll make a deal with you, Johnny"* Ibid.

94 *"Miss Day comes through as a subtle and sure emotional actress . . ."* *The Hollywood Reporter,* June 1955.

95 *"When are we going to have another child"* *The Man Who Knew Too Much*, screenplay by John Michael Hayes, Angus MacPhail, story by Charles Bennett, D. B. Wyndham-Lewis, Paramount, 1956.

95 *"Are we about to have our monthly fight?"* Ibid.

96 *"You used to tell me I took too many pills"* Ibid.

96 *"in my head"* Hotchner, *Doris Day,* p. 168.

96 *"whatever I really need"* Ibid.

96 *" 'If I can do it' "* *Doris Day: A Sentimental Journey, Op. Cit.*

99 *" 'I wanted to be with other agencies' "* Ibid.

99 *"bizarre jealousy"* Eric Braun, *Doris Day* (London: Orion Books, 1994), p. 154.

100 *"Don't ever try to leave me"* *Julie,* screenplay by Andrew L. Stone, MGM, 1956.

101 *"I can't do it"* Ibid.

101 *"That's right, Julie!"* Ibid.

102 *"I wouldn't go through that again"* Ibid.

106 *"Don't treat me like a baby"* *The Pajama Game*, screenplay by George Abbott, Richard Bissell, based on their musical based on the novel *7½ Cents* by Richard Bissell, Warner Bros. 1957.

107 *"cockamamie university"* *Teacher's Pet,* screenplay by Fay & Michael Kanin, Paramount, 1958.

108 *"How do you feel about sex?"* Ibid.

109 *"The man on the street"* Ibid.

109 *"Where would I be if I just read books?"* Ibid.

110 *"I'm not angry—just hurt"* Ibid.

110 *"Experience is the jockey"* Ibid.

111 *"got theirs"* *The Tunnel of Love,* screenplay by Joseph Fields, based on the play by Joseph Fields, Peter De Vries, based on the novel by Peter De Vries, MGM 1958.

112 *"There's a tremendous demand"* Ibid.

112 *"Shut up, or I'll send you to reform school"* Ibid.

114 *"I'm sick of you, Westport, and everybody in it"* Ibid.

117 *". . . under that dirndl lurked"* Ross Hunter as quoted in Hotchner, *Doris Day,* p. 200.

118 *"peach of a hangover"* *Pillow Talk,* screenplay by Stanley Shapiro, Maurice Richlin, story by Russell Rouse, Clarence Greene, Universal, 1959.

119 *"Doris Day really in a sense led the way"* *Doris Day: A Sentimental Journey, Op. Cit.*

120 *"Some men are very devoted to their mothers . . ."* *Pillow Talk, Op. Cit.*

121 *"[Jan], you've gone out with a lot of men"* Ibid.

121 "Possess me" by Joe Lubin, I. J. Roth.

121 *"knowing many men"* *Pillow Talk, Op. Cit.*

121 *"The audience—* you *thought I was a virgin"* McGee, *Doris Day,* p. 38.

122 *"cringing"* Ibid. p. 66.
123 *"What with television" . . .* *Pillow Talk, Op. Cit.*
123 *"The guard is up"* *Doris Day: A Sentimental Journey.*
123 *"It never occurred to Doris"* Ibid.
123 *"What do stars mean to us, after all?"* Ibid.
124 *"I even lost five pounds"* *Please Don't Eat The Daisies,"* screenplay by Isobel Lennart, based on the book by Jean Kerr, MGM, 1960.
124 *"Just once I'd like to get dressed . . ."* Ibid.
124 *"Maybe you should have lost ten pounds . . ."* Ibid.
125 *"You were one of the dumbest children . . ."* Ibid.
125 *". . . stop jumping on those beds . . ."* Ibid.
126 *". . . keep Kate under your thumb . . ."* Ibid.
127 *"Are you a man or a woman?"* Ibid.
128 *"I wasn't* acting *hysterical"* Hotchner, *Doris Day,* p. 202.
130 *"Men must work and women must weep"* *Midnight Lace,* screenplay by Ivan Goff, Ben Roberts, based on the play *Matilda Shouted Fire* by Janet Green, Universal, 1960.
132 *"No, that's a woman's job!"* *Lover Come Back,* screenplay by Stanley Shapiro, Paul Henning, Universal, 1962.
133 *"Try to think, Linus"* Ibid.
134 *"Should I Surrender?"* by Adam Ross, William Landan.
135 *"Do you think you'd enjoy watching a girl undress?"* *Lover Come Back, Op.Cit.*
135 "You're *the real man*" Ibid.
135 *"What's this obsession with girls?"* Ibid.
138 *"I belted her"* *That Touch of Mink,* screenplay by Stanley Shapiro, Nate Monaster, Universal 1962.
138 *"We sold out for that touch of mink"* Ibid.
138 *"If only he got mad or hit me"* Ibid.
138 *"My raven hair wasn't too bad"* Ibid.
138 *"She's direct, sincere, uncomplicated . . ."* Ibid.
141 *"While other little girls were playing with dolls . . ."* *Billy Rose's Jumbo,* screenplay by Sidney Sheldon, based on the musical play and book by Ben Hecht, Charles MacArthur, MGM, 1962.
142 *"I'm not hunting him . . ."* Ibid.
143 *"Hand me that screwdriver"* Ibid.
143 *"My Romance"* music by Richard Rodgers, lyrics by Lorenz Hart.
145 *"Little Girl Blue"* music by Richard Rodgers, lyrics by Lorenz Hart.
145 *"Where are you going with that elephant?"* *Billy Rose's Jumbo, Op. Cit.*
148 *"Mommy, it smells like the cracks in the playground"* *The Thrill of It All,* screenplay by Carl Reiner, story by Carl Reiner, Larry Gelbart, Universal, 1963.
148 *"Did you know I'm a great doctor?"* Ibid.
148 *"this sexy whirlpool frothing around underneath"* James Garner as quoted in Hotchner, *Doris Day,* p. 196.
149 *"Hello. I'm Beverly Boyer"* *The Thrill of It All, Op. Cit.*
149 *"There is no reason for you to work"* Ibid.
150 *"Our money is what I've earned as a doctor"* Ibid.
151 *"I want to be a doctor's wife again"* Ibid.
152 *"It is interesting how a light romantic comedy"* Basinger, *A Woman's View,* p. 231.
152 *"The woman's film was successful"* Ibid., pp. 6–7.
157 *"What is the amortization of a mortgage?"* *Send Me No Flowers,* screenplay by Julius Epstein, based on a play by Norman Barasch, Carroll Moore, Universal, 1964.
157 *"Judy will never make it alone"* Ibid.

157 *"ebb tide . . ."* Ibid.
158 *"Bad news? Nothing that's going . . ."* Ibid.
158 *"It's okay, little lady"* Ibid.
158 *"I just figured she'd marry Cary Grant"* Ibid.
159 *"He's good looking . . ."* Ibid.
159 *"Do me"* Ibid.
166 *"This girl doesn't have the brains . . ."* *The Glass Bottom Boat,* screenplay by Everett Freeman, MGM, 1966.
167 *"Put me down!"* Ibid.
168 *"Clancy really didn't like women . . ."* *Caprice,* screenplay by Jay Johnson, Frank Tashlin, story by Martin Hale, Jay Jayson, Twentieth Century Fox, 1967.
168 *". . . sabotaging the national armpit"* Ibid.
170 *"Help me, help me!"* Ibid.
171 *"'Tis a consummation devoutly to be wished"* William Shakespeare as quoted in *Caprice, Op. Cit.*
171 *"Miss Day, of course, has been many things"* Judith Crist, *Today,* NBC, June 1967.
172 *"I have two hands . . ."* *The Ballad of Josie,* screenplay by Harold Swanton, Universal, 1967.
173 *"I don't want to be taken care of"* Ibid.
173 *"To you a woman is a species of idiot . . ."* Ibid.
173 *"Forget I'm a woman . . ."* Ibid.
173 *"What can I do, Jace."* Ibid.
174 *"I ain't tellin' you Josie . . ."* Ibid.
174 *"She'll take your position, Arch"* Ibid.
174 *"It's not good to get too independent"* Ibid.
175 *"he just couldn't bring himself to pay"* Hotchner, *Doris Day,* p. 187.
176 *"I liked* Love Me or Leave Me" *Newark Sunday News*, July 20, 1969.
176 *"Hello Peter, so you're here"* *Where Were You When the Lights Went Out,* screenplay by Everett Freeman, Karl Tunberg, based on the play *Monsieur Masure* by Claude Magnier, MGM, 1968.
177 *". . . freckle-faced American sweetheart"* Ibid.
177 *"I knew her before she was a virgin"* Ibid.
178 *"I don't need a man"* *With Six You Got Eggroll*" screenplay by Gwan Bagni, Paul Duboy, Harvey Bullock, and R. S. Allen, story by Gwen Bagni, Paul Dubov, Warner-Pathe/National General/Cenema Center, 1968.
178 *"I have to put a roast on broil . . ."* Ibid.
179 *"There's a man in Mommy's bed!"* Ibid.
179 *"I'm glad we're a family"* Ibid.
179 *"You know, you can grow to hate that word"* Ibid.
179 *"I was just walking down the street . . ."* Ibid.

Recordings

183 *"I dig Doris Day"* Sarah Vaughan, liner notes, "Classic Collaborations," *Doris Day: Her Life in Music 1940–1966,* Columbia Records, 2004.
183 *"Doris Day had the talent to be a great singer"* Ted Nash, quoted in Will Friedman, *Sinatra! The Song Is You: A Singer's Art* (New York: Scribner, 1995), p. 34.
183 *"I don't see my films"* *Doris Day: A Sentimental Journey.*
186 "Easy as Pie" by Les Brown, Ken Gannon.
186 "While the Music Plays On" by Irving Mills, Lupin Fien, Emery Heirn.
187 *"The song was released in January nineteen forty-five"* *Doris Day: A Sentimental Journey.*
188 "Till the End of Time" by Ted Mossman, Buddy Kaye.
188 "The Last Time I Saw You" by Marjorie Goetschius, Edna Osser.

188 "Day By Day" music by Axel Stordahl, Paul Weston, lyrics by Sammy Cahn.

189 "We'll Be Together Again" by Carl Fischer, Frankie Laine.

189 "The Whole World Is Singing My Song" by Mann Curtis, Victor Mizzy.

190 "Sooner or Later" by Charles Walcott, Ray Gilbert, from the Walt Disney film *Song of the South.*

190 "It Could Happen To You" music by James van Heusen, lyrics by Sammy Cahn.

192 "Pretty Baby" by Egbert Van Alstyne, Tony Jackson, Gus Kahn.

193 "Imagination" music by James van Heusen, lyrics by Johnny Burke.

193 "That Old Feeling" music by Lew Brown, lyrics by Sammy Fain.

193 "When Your Lover Has Gone" music and lyrics by Einar Aaron Swan.

194 *"Streisand is great with the big orchestra"* John Halliwell, "Will the Real Doris Day Sing Out," *New York Times*, October 27, 1968.

195 *"She can make a vocal sound like there's a smile"* *Doris Day: A Sentimental Journey.*

195 "You Can Have Him" music and lyrics by Irving Berlin, from the Broadway musical *Miss Liberty*

195 "Let's Take an Old Fashioned Walk" music and lyrics by Irving Berlin, from the Broadway musical *Miss Liberty.*

196 "With You Anywhere You Are" by Eddie Pola, George Wyle.

198 "Tea for Two" music by Vincent Youmans, lyrics by Irving Caesar, from the Broadway musical *No, No, Nanette.*

200 "The Best Thing for You" music and lyrics by Irving Berlin, from the Broadway musical *Call Me Madam.*

200 "Lullaby of Broadway" music by Harry Warren, lyrics by Al Dubin.

201 "It's So Laughable" music by Jimmy McDonald, lyrics by Jack Hoffman.

201 *"I always felt [Doris] was a better singer than she thought she was"* Paul Weston quoted in Joseph F. Laredo, liner notes to Bear Family Records boxed set *Secret Love—Doris Day 1951–1955.*

202 "(Why Did I Tell You I was Going to) Shanghai" by Milton deLagg, Bob Hillard.

202 "Baby Doll" music by Harry Warren, lyrics by Johnny Mercer.

204 "How Lovely Cooks the Meat" music and lyrics by Josef Marais.

205 "My Love and Devotion" music and lyrics by Milton Carson.

205 "A Full Time Job" music and lyrics by Gerry Teifer.

205 "A Guy Is a Guy" music and lyrics by Oscar Brand.

205 "It's Magic" music by Jule Styne, lyrics by Sammy Cahn.

206 "When I Fall in Love" music by Victor Young, lyrics by Edward Heyman, from the film *One Minute to Zero.*

206 *"I hated it"* Doris Day, quoted in Joseph F. Laredo, liner notes to Bear Family Records boxed set *Que Sera—Doris Day 1956–1959*, p. 19.

206 "A Purple Cow" music by Fred Sielmann, lyrics by Paul Francis Webster.

206 *"When I first heard Sammy Fain sing that song"* McGee, *Doris Day,* p. 23.

207 "The Deadwood Stage" music by Sammy Fain, lyrics by Paul Francis Webster, from the motion picture *Calamity Jane.*

207 "This Too Shall Pass Away" by Ervin Drake, Jimmy Shirl, and Irving Graham.

208 "If I Give My Heart to You" by Jimmie Crane, Al Jacobs, Jimmy Brewster.

210 "Que Sera, Sera" by Jay Livingston, Ray Evans.

211 "I Remember You" music by Victor Schertzinger, lyrics by Johnny Mercer.

212 *"a kind of instant, chemical reaction"* Will Friedwald, liner notes to Doris Day's *The Love Album,* Concord Records, 2006.

212 *"I liked to bring in donuts and coffee cakes"* Joseph F. Laredo, liner notes to Bear Family Records boxed set *Que Sera—Doris Day 1956–1959*, pp. 12–13.

212 *". . . she's hard to work with . . ."* Richard Gehman, *American Weekly,* June 9, 1963.

214 "Close Your Eyes" music and lyrics by Bernice Petkere.

214 "The Night We Called It a Day" by Tom Adair, Matt Dennis.

215 "Moonglow" by Will Hudson, Eddie deLange, Irving Mills.

215 *"I do think she's a terrific singer"* *Doris Day: A Sentimental Journey.*

215 "It Might as Well Be Spring" music by Richard Rodgers, lyrics by Oscar Hammerstein II.

216 "In the Still of the Night" music and lyrics by Cole Porter.

217 "Oh, But I Do" music by Arthur Schwartz, lyrics by Leo Robin.

217 "Night and Day" music and lyrics by Cole Porter.

217 "That Old Black Magic" music by Harold Arlen, lyrics by Johnny Mercer.

218 "Hooray for Hollywood" music by Richard Whiting, lyrics by Johnny Mercer.

219 "That Jane From Maine" by Joe Lubin, I. J. Roth.

219 "Cuttin' Capers" by Joe Lubin, Adam Ross.

220 *"gives me a sense of release"* Hotchner, *Doris Day*, p. 45.

220 "Let's Take a Walk Around the Block" music by Harold Arlen, lyrics by Ira Gershwin and Yip Harburg.

220 "Makin' Whoopee" music by Walter Donaldson, lyric by Gus Kahn.

222 "Let's Fly Away" music and lyrics by Cole Porter.

223 "Any Way the Wind Blows" by William Dunham, Joseph Hooven, and Marilyn Hooven.

223 "Pillow Talk" by Buddy Pepper, Inez James.

223 *"the most popular American singer in Russia"* "From Pinsk to Omsk They Love Doris Day," *World Telegraph*, April 4, 1959.

224 *by this time her record sales exceeded sixteen millions units* Joe Hyams, "Starring Doris Day," *This Week*, September 11, 1960.

224 "What Every Girl Should Know" by Robert Wells, David Holt.

225 "A Fellow Needs a Girl" music by Richard Rodgers, lyrics by Oscar Hammerstein II from the Broadway musical *Allegro.*

225 "What's the Use of Wond'rin'" music by Richard Rodgers, lyrics by Oscar Hammerstein II, from the Broadway musical *Carousel.*

226 "What Does a Woman Do?" music by Allie Wrubel, lyrics by Maxwell Anderson, from the motion picture *Midnight Lace.*

226 *"Who was Marty Melcher?"* Hotchner, *Doris Day,* pp. 234–35.

226 *"I do think that Marty loved Doris"* Ross Hunter as quoted in ibid., p. 238.

227 "I Love Paris" music and lyrics by Cole Porter, from the Broadway musical *Can-Can.*

228 "I Got the Sun in the Morning" music and lyrics by Irving Berlin, from the Broadway musical *Annie Get Your Gun.*

228 "A Wonderful Guy" music by Richard Rodgers, lyrics by Oscar Hammerstein II, from the Broadway musical *South Pacific.*

230 "Make Someone Happy" music by Jule Styne, lyrics by Betty Comden and Adolph Green, from the Broadway musical *Do Re Me.*

230 "I'll Buy That Dream" music by Allie Wrubel, lyrics by Herb Magidson.

232 "We'll Love Again" music by Ray Evans, lyrics by Jay Livingston, from the motion picture *The Man Who Knew Too Much.*

232 "All I Do Is Dream of You" music by Nacio Herb Brown, lyrics by Arthur Freed.

233 "You Stepped Out of a Dream" music by Nacio Herb Brown, lyrics by Gus Kahn.

233 "I Have Dreamed" music by Richard Rodgers, lyrics by Oscar Hammerstein II, from the Broadway musical *The King and I.*

233 *the most beautiful version* Richard Rodgers as quoted in Joseph F. Laredo, liner notes to Bear Family Records boxed set *Move Over Darling—1960–1967,* p. 20.

233 *"I knew that André admired Doris"* Jim Harbert, quoted ibid., p. 21.

233 "Nobody's Heart" music by Richard Rodgers, lyrics by Lorenz Hart.

234 "Walk with Him" music by Henry Vars, lyrics by By Dunham.

235 *"My favorite things are hymns"* Doris Day, quoted by Joseph Laredo, liner notes to *Move Over Darling—1960–1967,* p. 22.

235 "If I Can Help Sombody" music and lyrics by A. Bazel Androzzo.

236 *Day and Goulet recorded their vocal tracks* Joseph Laredo, liner notes to *Move Over Darling—1960–1967,* p. 21.

236 "Doin' What Comes Naturally" music and lyrics by Irving Berlin, from the Broadway musical *Annie Get Your Gun.*

236 "You Can't Get a Man With a Gun" music and lyrics by Irving Berlin, from the Broadway musical *Annie Get Your Gun.*

237 "Anything You Can Do" music and lyrics by Irving Berlin, from the Broadway musical *Annie Get Your Gun.*

237 "I Got Lost in His Arms" music and lyrics by Irving Berlin, from the Broadway musical *Annie Get Your Gun.*

237 "Moonshine Lullabye" music and lyrics by Irving Berlin, from the Broadway musical *Annie Get Your Gun.*

239 *"Jack Nitzche was the first guy"* Terry Melcher, quoted by Joseph Laredo, liner notes to *Move Over Darling—1960–1967,* p. 23.

239 *Doris Day was banned* McGee, *Doris Day,* p. 43.

239 *"I absolutely adored her"* Tommy Oliver, quoted by Joseph Laredo, liner notes to *Move Over Darling—1960–1967,* p. 25.

239 "Love Him" music by Barry Mann, lyrics by Cynthia Weill.

240 *"I'm not sure who else has ever done that"* Terry Melcher, quoted by Joseph Laredo, liner notes to *Move Over Darling—1960–1967,* p. 23.

240 *"I really think she and Ella Fitzgerald were all by themselves" A&E Biography: Doris Day.*

240 *"He and I are such good friends"* Doris Day, quoted by Joseph F. Laredo, liner notes to *Move Over Darling—1960–1967,* p. 23.

241 "Night Life" by Willie Nelson, Paul Buskirk, Walt Breeland.

241 *"Darkness comes and spreads its familiar sound"* Tommy Oliver, introduction to "Night Life" by Willie Nelson, Paul Buskirk, Walt Breeland, as quoted by Joseph F. Laredo, in liner notes to *Move Over Darling—1960–1967,* p. 25.

241 *"dark sweet places"* Updike, *Hugging the Shore,* p. 801.

242 "Toyland" by Victor Herbert, Glen MacDonough.

242 "Winter Wonderland" music by Felix Bernard, lyrics by Dick Smith.

242 "Snowfall" by Claude Thornhill, Ray Charles.

242 "With a Smile and a Song" by Felix Bernard, Dick Smith.

243 "Que Sera, Sera" by Jay Livingston, Ray Evans.

245 "Come to Baby Do" by Inez James, Sidney Miller.

245 *"It is simultaneously an exercise in wistful nostalgia"* Laredo, liner notes to *Move Over Darling—1960–1967,* p. 27.

246 *"When they first had a meeting and called me in"* Doris Day as quoted in ibid., p. 26.

246 "Meditation" by Norman Gimbel, Newton Mendonca, Antonio Carlos Jobim.

246 "Perhaps, Perhaps, Perhaps" by Joe Davis, Osvaldo Farres.

246 "Summer Has Gone" by Bill Comstock, Gene DiNovi.

247 "How Insensitive" by Norman Gimbel, Vinicius de Moraes, Antonio Carlos Jobim.

247 *"Her contract with Columbia expired in 1967"* Terry Melcher, as quoted by Joseph F. Laredo, liner notes to *Move Over Darling—1960–1967,* p. 27.

248 "Catch the Bouquet" music by Fred Spielman, lyrics by Hans Haller.

248 "The Glass Bottom Boat" music and lyrics by Joe Lubin.

248 *"She felt that what she loved to do"* McGee, *Doris Day,* p. 46.

249 *Feller smartly employs* Friedwald, liner notes to *The Love Album*.

249 *"I love these slow tempos"* Doris Day, quoted by Laredo, liner notes to *Move Over Darling—1960–1967*, pp. 27–28.

249 *"So she picked some of her favorites"* Ibid., p. 28.

250 "For All We Know" music by J. Fred Cootes, lyrics by Sam M. Lewis.

250 "Sleepy Lagoon" music by Eric Coates, lyrics by Jack Lawrence.

251 "Let Me Call You Sweetheart" music by Beth Slater Whitson, lyrics by Leo Friedman.

251 *"Someday over a drink I'll ask her"* Don Genson, liner notes to *The Love Album*, UK release, 1994.

Television

253 "The Doris Day Show *makes* Family Affair" *Los Angeles Times,* September 1968.

253 *"Acting with Doris Day was the most comfortable acting"* Larry Storch, interviewed for DVD release of the second season of *The Doris Day Show.*

257 *"he was my father"* Hotchner, *Doris Day,* p. 235.

257 *"I think Marty just trusted"* McGee, *Doris Day,* p. 56.

257 *"I had lost three things"* Hotchner, *Doris Day,* pp. 239–40.

257 *"never had a weight problem"* *A&E Biography: Doris Day*.

258 *"The situations [on the show] are real"* sponsors' greeting, DVD release of *The Doris Day Television Show, Season One, 1968–1969.*

258 *"The comedy we did was family comedy"* Rose Marie on DVD release of *The Doris Day Television Show, Season Two, 1969–1970.*

259 *still call her on Mother's Day* Phillip Brown, ibid.

260 *"Doris recognized that there were a lot of working moms"* James Hampton, ibid.

274 *"She was very aware of who she was"* James Hampton, ibid.

274 *"I had to bunk next to Al Jorden"* Larry Storch, ibid.

274 *"She was a great vocalist"* Ibid.

274 *"When you walked on the set"* Rose Marie, ibid.

275 *"It was just wonderful"* Ibid.

275 *"Going to work every day with Doris Day"* Phillip Brown, ibid.

275 *"I don't go to movies very much."* Molly Haskell, "An Interview with Doris Day," *Ms*. January 1976.

277 *"People would ask me"* McGee, *Doris Day,* p. 38.

287 *"star Day—looks marvelous"* *Variety*, September 22, 1971.

292 *"It is indicative of the febrile plotting"* *Variety,* September 20, 1972.

296 *"I'm tired"* McGee, *Doris Day,* p. 54.

297 *"Here's the lady Jimmy loved in that picture"* *The American Film Institute Salute to James Cagney,* CBS, March 18, 1974.

297 *"Working with you was one of the happiest times of my life"* Ibid.

297 *"Doris Day perfectly illustrates my idea of good acting"* James Cagney as quoted in Hotchner, *Doris Day,* p. 156.

298 *this gargantuan trial* McGee, *Doris Day,* p. 55.

298 *"It's very complicated"* . . . Marty Melcher as quoted in Hotchner, *Doris Day,* p. 210.

298 *"It's a brutal thing to say"* Terry Melcher as quoted in ibid., p. 232.

298 *"The oil and gas ventures"* Decision of Judge Lester E. Olson, Superior Court of California, September, 1974.

300 *"I just have a lovely feeling"* Hotchner, *Doris Day,* p. 226.

300 *"We seemed to spend a lot of time kissing"* *The Tonight Show,* NBC, September 2, 1974.

300 *"I'm rusty—but I'm going to start singing again"* Ibid.

301 *"I fly everywhere"* Ibid.

302 *"She captured the hearts of Americans while enriching our culture"* President George W. Bush awarding Doris Day the Presidential Medal of Freedom, 2004, quoted in McGee, *Doris Day,* p. 2.

302 *"People don't take care of their own children"* *The Tonight Show,* September 2, 1974.

306 *"We had a correspondence courtship and it was not good"* *The Mike Douglas Show,* 1976.

306 *"If I can do it, you can do it"* *Doris Day: A Sentimental Journey.*

Animals

311 *"I just love that I can make it better for the animals"* Ibid.

313 *"lifelong love affair with the dog"* Hotchner, *Doris Day,* p. 41.

313 *"It may be that animals are the beneficiaries of her affection"* Richard Gehman, "The Girl Next Door," *American Weekly,* June 9, 1963.

313 *"just as much my family"* Hotchner, *Doris Day,* p. 262.

314 *"the only time I saw Doris cry"* McGee, *Doris Day,* p. 65.

314 *"Money is the bottom of all the trouble"* Ibid.

315 *"It just breaks my heart"* Ibid., p. 66.

315 *"I don't separate cruelty to animals from cruelty to people"* Ibid.

315 *"precious dog wisdom"* Hotchner, *Doris Day,* p. 263.

316 *"God had chosen to speak to me through my dogs"* Ibid., p. 268.

316 *Day started her own pet charity* Doris Day Pet Foundation Web site.

317 *kick-started the organization with their own $100,000* McGee, *Doris Day,* p. 66.

317 *she bought the Cypress Inn* www.DorisDay.com, McGee, *Doris Day,* p. 64.

317 *"one of his own kind for companionship"* Hotchner, *Doris Day,* p. 265.

317 *the foundation is designed to mobilize individuals and communities* www.ddaf.com.

318 *"heroism in standing up for empathy and compassion"* Ibid.

318 *since the inception of Spay Day* Ibid.

318 *in the year 2002 alone* McGee, *Doris Day,* p. 67.

318 *"almost a quarter of all the pets in the country"* Ibid.

318 *revenues of $505,353* www.ddaf.com.

318 *$500* Ibid.

321 *"I just love that I can make it better for the animals."* *Doris Day: A Sentimental Journey.*

322 *"The quality of production did not warrant a purchase"* McGee, *Doris Day,* p. 64.

322 *"working to reduce the pain and suffering of non-human animals"* www.ddal.com.

322 *poison and "cruel animal traps"* Ibid.

322 *such slaughter is not for humane purposes* Ibid.

322 *"Why not? They owe society something"* McGee, *Doris Day,* p. 69.

324 *"Doris is shakin' the blues away"* Liz Smith, *New York Post,* October 17, 2005.

324 *"All his friends, and there were many"* *Doris Day's Best Friends,* October 1985.

Que Sera, Sera

329 *"I just love going to the market"* *Doris Day: A Sentimental Journey.*

329 *"Doris Day is my neighbor"* Ibid.

330 *"Well, you didn't have* that *many husbands"* George Weidler as quoted in Hotchner, *Doris Day,* p. 286.

330 *"Can you imagine?"* Ibid.

330 *"Doris felt a responsibility to her fans"* Terry Melcher, quoted by Joseph Laredo, liner notes to *Move Over Darling—1960–1967.*

331 *"a new series that I liked"* McGee, *Doris Day,* p. 276.

331 *"homegrown existential female"* *Doris Day: A Sentimental Journey.*

332 *"I'm very grateful because I've had so many blessings"* Ibid.

Coda

333 *"Surely no other great American artist."* Friedwald, liner notes to *The Love Album,* 2006.

335 *"I've never seen so much love"* Hotchner, *Doris Day,* p. 295.

335 *"I think the whole wide world"* Don Genson, liner notes to *The Love Album,* 1994.

Bibliography

Books

Basinger, Jeanine. *Gene Kelly: A Pyramid Illustrated History of the Movies*. New York: Pyramid Communications, 1976.

———. *A Woman's View*. New York: Alfred A. Knopf, 1993.

Bloom, Ken. *The American Songbook: The Singers, the Songwriters, and the Songs*. New York: Black Dog and Leventhal Publishers, 2005.

Braun, Eric. *Doris Day*. London: Orion Books, 1994.

Clarke, Jane, Diana Simmonds, and Mandy Merke. *Move Over Misconceptions*. London: BFI Dossier No. 4, December 1980.

Clooney, Rosemary with Joan Barthel. *Girl Singer*. New York: Doubleday, 1999.

Corliss, Richard. *Talking Pictures: Screenwriters in the American Cinema*. New York: Overlook Press, 1974.

Ehrenstein, David. *Open Secret: Gay Hollywood 1928–2000*. New York: HarperCollins, 2000.

Friedwald, Will. *Sinatra! The Song Is You: A Singer's Art*. New York: Scribner, 1995.

Harvey, James. *Movie Love in the Fifties*. New York: Alfred A. Knopf, 2001.

———. *Romantic Comedy in Hollywood, from Lubitsch to Sturges*. New York: Alfred A. Knopf, 1987.

Haskell, Molly. *From Reverence to Rape: The Treatment of Women in the Movies*. Second Edition. Chicago: The University of Chicago Press, 1987.

———, *Holding My Own in No Man's Land*. New York: Oxford University Press, 1997.

Hotchner, A. E., with Doris Day. *Doris Day: Her Own Story*. New York: William Morrow, 1975.

Hudson, Rock, with Sara Davidson. *His Story*. New York: William Morrow, 1986.

Katz, Ephraim. *The Film Encyclopedia*. 4th ed. New York: HarperCollins, 2001.

Laredo, Joseph F. *It's Magic: Doris Day 1947–1950*. Hamburg, Germany: Bear Family Records, 1993.

———. *Move Over Darling—Doris Day 1960–1967*. Hamburg, Germany: Bear Family Records, 1997.

———. *Que Sera—Doris Day 1956–1959*. Hamburg, Germany: Bear Family Records, 1996.

———. *Secret Love—Doris Day 1951–1955*. Hamburg, Germany: Bear Family Records, 1995.

McGee, Gary. *Doris Day: A Sentimental Journey*. Jefferson, NC: McFarland & Co., 2005.

Mann, William J. *Behind the Screen. How Gays and Lesbians Shaped Hollywood, 1910–1969*. New York: Viking, 2001.

Morris, George. *Doris Day: A Pyramid Illustrated History of the Movies*. New York: Pyramid Communications, 1976.

Peary, Danny, ed. *Close-Ups: The Movie Star Book*. New York: Workman Publishing Company, 1978.

Sennett, Ted. *Hollywood Musicals*. New York: Harry N. Abrams, 1981.
Shapiro, Nat. *An Encyclopedia of Quotations About Music*. New York: DaCapo Press, 1977.
Shipman, David. *The Great Movie Stars: The International Years*. London: Angus & Robertson, 1972.
Simon, George T. *The Big Bands*. New York: Schirmer Books, 1981.
Thomson, David. *A Biographical Dictionary of Film*. New York: William Morrow, 1976.
Updike, John. *Hugging the Shore*. New York: Alfred A. Knopf, 1983.
Young, Christopher. *The Films of Doris Day*. Secaucus, NJ: Citadel Press, 1977.

Archives

Billy Rose Theatre Collection, Lincoln Center Library for the Performing Arts, New York.
Museum of Television and Radio, New York City.

Magazines, Periodicals, and Newspapers

American Weekly: November 11, 1957; June 9, 1963, Richard Gehman, "The Girl Next Door."
BandLeader: March 1946, Cal Grayson, "All in a Day's Work."
Billboard: May 4, 1968, "Melcher Dies; Music Ties to Stay the Same."
Christian Science Monitor: July 21, 1959, Richard Dyer MacCann, "Hollywood Letter."
Collier's: January 7, 1950.
Cosmopolitan: January 1954.
Cue: May 12, 1956, "A New Day for Doris."
Forbes: October 15, 1974, "Day in Court."
Good Housekeeping: September 1979, Bob Thomas, "An Intimate Talk with Doris Day."
Ladies' Home Journal: January 1973, Ronnie Cowan, "My Most Costly Mistake as a Wife."
Life: October 10, 1960, cover story "Doris Day."
Look: December 5, 1951; June 20, 1961, Bill Davidson, "Doris Day—Her Fortunes, Her Fears, Her Failures, Her Faith."
Los Angeles Times: December 1, 1962, Art Ryon, "Rift Separates Doris Day and Marty Melcher."
Motion Picture Magazine: October, 1954, "This Is Doris."
Ms.: January, 1976, Molly Haskell, "An Interview With Doris Day."
Newark News: January 24, 1960, "Doris Day Season"; October 23, 1960, "Kappelhoff Is Day Now"; July 20, 1969.
New York Daily News: December 3, 1962, Florabel Mur, "Doris Quits Mate: Dodger Her Next"; April 25, 1971.
New York Herald Tribune: May 17, 1953, Louis Berg, "All This and 10% Too"; December 13, 1953; July 13, 1958; August 16, 1959, "Doris Day as Fashion Plate"; January 24, 1965, Judith Crist, "And Doris Led All the Rest."
New York Mirror: September 12, 1957; May 15, 1960, Frank Elmquist, "Oh What a Wonderful Day"; October 9, 1960.
New York Sun: May 3, 2005, Gary Giddins, "A Blond and Beaming Icon for a Blond and Beaming Age."
New York Times: October 27, 1968, John Hallowell, "Will the Real Doris Day Sing Out"; July 8, 1971, George Gent, "CBS Overhauls Its *Doris Day Show*"; April 26, 2005, Dave Kehr, "The Doris Day Collection."
New York World-Telegram and Sun: May 2, 1953, Marie Torre, "'Lunch Bucket' Gal Is Doris."
Pathfinder: July 12, 1950.
People: October 7, 1974, Lois Armstrong, "Doris Day Has Her Day in Court—And Wins $22.8 Million."
Photoplay: October 1955.
Pictoral TView: May 23, 1958, Louella O. Parsons, "Day Without End."
Saturday Review: November 17, 1956, Hollis Alpert, "*Saturday Review* Goes to the Movies."

Silver Screen: April 1952.
This Week: May 17, 1953; September 11, 1960, Joe Hyams, "Starring Doris Day."
TV Guide: May 13, 1967, Richard K. Doan, "Doris Day Takes the TV Plunge"; February 20, 1971, Bill Davidson, "The Change in Doris Day"; December 6, 1979, John L. Wasserman, "I Don't Even Like Apple Pie."
Variety: May 28, 1952.
Wall Street Journal: February 13, 2003, Mark Lewis, "And the Oscar for Perky Sexpot Should Go to . . . Doris Day."
World Telegraph: April 4, 1959, "From Pinsk to Omsk They Love Doris Day."

Web Sites

Doris Day Animal League: www.ddal.org
Doris Day Animal Foundation: www.ddaf.org

Index